Dystopian Fiction East and West
A Universe of Terror and Trial

Dystopian Fiction East and West suggests that the utopian pursuit of "the best of all possible worlds" is driven less by the search for happiness than by a determined faith in justice. Conversely, the world of dystopian fiction presents us with a society where the ruling elite deliberately subverts justice. In fact, twentieth-century dystopian fiction can be seen as a protest against the totalitarian superstate as the "worst of all possible worlds," a universe of terror and rigged trials.

After an original and comprehensive analysis of the tragic and satitical patterns underlying dystopian classics that warn against the possible emergence of a totalitarian state in the future (*We, Brave New World, Nineteen Eight-Four, Fahrenheit 451, Player Piano,* and *The Handmaid's Tale*), Erika Gottlieb explores a selection of about thirty works in the dystopian genre from East and Central Europe between 1920 and 1991 in the USSR and between 1948 and 1989 in Poland, Hungary, and Czechoslovakia. Written about and under totalitarian dictatorship, in these countries dystopian fiction does not take us into a hypothetical future; instead the writer assumes the role of witness protesting against the "worst of all possible worlds" of terror and trial in a world that *is* but should not be.

ERIKA GOTTLIEB is the author of *The Orwell Conundrum* (1992) and *Lost Angels of a Ruined Paradise: Themes of Cosmic Strife in Romantic Tragedy* (1982).

Dystopian Fiction
East and West

Universe of Terror and Trial

ERIKA GOTTLIEB

McGill-Queen's University Press
Montreal & Kingston · London · Ithaca

© McGill-Queen's University Press 2001

ISBN 0-7735-2179-8 (cloth)
ISBN 0-7735-2206-9 (paper)

Legal deposit third quarter 2001
Bibliothèque nationale du Québec

Printed in Canada on acid-free paper

This book has been published with the help of a grant from the Humanities and Social Sciences Federation of Canada, using funds provided by the Social Sciences and Humanities Research Council of Canada.

McGill-Queen's University Press acknowledges the financial support of the Government of Canada through the Book Publishing Industry Development Program (BPIDP) for its activities. It also acknowledges the support of the Canada Council for the Arts for its publishing program.

An earlier version of the concluding chapter, under the title of "Dystopia East and West: The Writer and the Protagonist," appeared in *Vite di Utopia*, ed. Vita Fortunati and Paola Spinozzi (Ravenna: Longo Editore 2000).

Pen and ink drawings are by the author.

Canadian Cataloguing in Publication Data

Gottlieb, Erika
Dystopian fiction east and west : universe of terror and trial
Includes bibliographical references and index.
ISBN 0-7735-2179-8 (bound) –
ISBN 0-7735-2206-9 (pbk.)
1. Fiction – 20th century – History and criticism. 2. Science fiction – History and criticism. 3. Dystopias in literature. 4. Totalitarianism and literature. I. Title.
PN56.D94G68 2001   809.3'9372   C00-901550-7

Typeset in Sabon 10/12
by Caractéra inc., Quebec City

To Paul, Peter, and Julie

Contents

Acknowledgments

I wish to thank Professors Dennis Rohatyn (University of San Diego), Gorman Beauchamp (University of Michigan), and Professor Emeritus Arthur O. Lewis (Pennsylvania State University) for their extremely helpful comments on earlier versions of the manuscript.

I am grateful to the Social Sciences and Humanities Research Council of Canada for the three-year research grant (1994–97) that made research and travel possible.

I am very grateful to Philip Cercone, executive director and editor of McGill-Queen's University Press, for his support and encouragement throughout the past years, to Denis Leclerc, program officer, Research Grants Division of the Social Sciences and Humanities Research Council of Canada, and to Nadine May, publication officer, Aid to Scholarly Publications Programme, the Humanities and Social Sciences Federation of Canada. I also wish to express my sincere thanks to my copy editor, Susan Kent Davidson, for her excellent contribution, and to Joan McGilvray, co-ordinating editor, for editorial guidance.

Dystopian Fiction East and West

Dystopia West, Dystopia East

Dystopian fiction is a post-Christian genre.

If the central drama of the age of faith was the conflict between salvation and damnation by deity, in our secular modern age this drama has been transposed to a conflict between humanity's salvation or damnation by society in the historical arena. In the modern scenario salvation is represented as a just society governed by worthy representatives chosen by an enlightened people; damnation, by an unjust society, a degraded mob ruled by a power-crazed elite. Works dealing with the former describe the heaven or earthly paradise of utopia; those dealing with the latter portray the dictatorship of a hell on earth, the "worst of all possible worlds" of dystopia.

Even a casual reading of such classics of dystopian fiction as Zamiatin's *We,* Huxley's *Brave New World,* or Orwell's *Nineteen Eighty-four* will make it obvious that underlying this secular genre the concepts of heaven and hell are still clearly discernible. In fact, the post-Enlightenment author's vision of a collective hell for society is not that far removed from Dante's medieval dream-vision of Dis, the city of hell. As for the function of hell in the overall framework of *The Divine Comedy,* we should remember that the purpose of the narrator-protagonist's entire journey in hell is to serve him – and his readers – as a warning to avoid the sin that condemns the sinner to eternal damnation, and to pursue instead the ways up to heaven: Beatrice, who watches over Dante from above, sends to him Virgil, the voice of reason, to lead him out of the Forest of Error – the pain and confusion caused by his sinful state. Under Virgil's guidance the narrator-protagonist has the unparallelled privilege of travelling through the nine circles of hell unscathed in order to witness the endless suffering of all those who died as sinners. Beatrice makes Dante confront these horrors in order to warn him about the possible consequences of his own erring ways and thereby to encourage him *not* to end up in hell.

ꞮThe strategies of Zamiatin, Huxley, and Orwell are also significantly the strategies of warning. As readers we are made to contemplate Zamiatin's One State, Huxley's World State, and Orwell's Oceania, each a hellscape from which the inhabitants can no longer return, so that we realize what the flaws of our own society may lead to for the next generations unless we try to eradicate these flaws today.Ɉ

The correspondence between religious and secular concepts in dystopian fiction is still so strongly felt that, if we examine *Nineteen Eighty-four* closely as the prototype of the genre, twentieth-century dystopian fiction reveals the underlying structure of a morality play. Orwell's protagonist, a modern Everyman, struggles for his soul against a Bad Angel; he struggles for the dignity of the Spirit of Man against the dehumanizing forces of totalitarian dictatorship.

The parallel could be carried further. While the medieval morality play implies that the fate of the human soul will be decided at the Last Judgment, the modern dystopian narrative puts the protagonist on an ultimate trial where his fate will be decided in confrontation with the Bad Angel in his secular incarnation as the Grand Inquisitor, high priest of the state religion and God-like ruler of totalitarian dictatorship. Given the injustice endemic to the "bad place," this decision will invariably be in the negative: in Zamiatin's *We*, D-503 is sentenced to lobotomy; John Savage in *Brave New World* to madness brought on by loneliness and ostracism; Winston Smith in *Nineteen Eighty-four* to a transformation of the individual personality until it embraces all it abhors, a state worse than the effects of lobotomy. The sinister and irrevocable transformation of the protagonist represents the irrevocable damnation of his society. It is one of the most conspicuous features of the warning in these classics of dsytopian fiction that once we allow the totalitarian state to come to power, there will be no way back.

As for the origin of the term "dystopia," we find it of comparatively recent coinage. In his 1946 preface to *Brave New World* Huxley still refers to the bad place as a utopia, using the term he felt stood for any speculative structure taking us to the future. It was only in 1952 that J.Max Patrick[1] recommended the distinction between the good place as "eutopia" and its opposite, the bad place, as "dystopia."

In discussing a selection of Russian novels written since Stalin's death and critical of the Soviet regime's allegedly utopian purpose, Edith Clowes borrows Gary Morson's term of "meta-utopia" – that is, a work that is "positioned on the borders of the utopian tradition and yet mediates between a variety of utopian modes." To distinguish these books from what she sees as the far more limited scope of dystopian fiction, she argues that meta-utopia represents a "much greater challenge to current readers ... than dystopian novels do" because it "refers to a social consciousness involving social and cultural pluralism." By contrast, according to Clowes, dystopian novels advocate a "nostalgic revision of the past age" and "deconstruct utopian schemes, only to abandon the notion of a beneficial social imagination," thereby embodying a "nihilistic attitude toward both the present and the future, closing both off to a new imaginative possibility."[2] But is her definition of dystopia valid if we examine it in the light of such classic examples of dystopian novels as Zamiatin's *We*, Huxley's *Brave New World*, and Orwell's *Nineteen Eighty-four*? And is the meta-utopia of Tertz's *The Trial Begins* or Daniel's *This is Moscow Speaking*, included among Clowes's examples, indeed all that different from the intentions, attitudes, and narrative strategies of these three classics of dystopian satire? This study will answer both questions in the negative.

As for a thematically more neutral definition of this "bad place,"[3] Lyman Sargent suggests that we look at dystopia as a social structure that is worse[4] than the present social system. If, however, we listen to postmodern criticism, relying on thinkers like Foucault, for example, any society functioning at the present time (or possibly at any other time as well) could be regarded as such a "bad place."[5] Although I believe that the postmodern critic's overly broad use of the notion of dystopia is counterproductive to a clear definition of what is unique about dystopian thought or dystopian fiction, I also believe that Professor Sargent's definition of dystopia as a system worse than our own probably does not cover all works with a dystopian impetus. In fact, if we take a look at works of political criticism produced in Eastern and Central Europe commenting on the injustice rampant in the writer's own society during periods of dictatorship and terror, these works are still clearly expressive of the dystopian impulse, although they deal with the writer's own society "as is." In other words, there are historical phenomena that create societies that should be described as dystopic, societies where the literary imagination refuses to envisage a world worse than the existing world of reality. Therefore, before we are to arrive at a comprehensive delineation of the salient characteristics of dystopian fiction as a genre, maybe we should also define the characteristics of a society that is dystopic.

It has been said by Hungarian essayist Béla Hamvas that the modern age has been spent "under the aegis of the tension between Messianism and dictatorship."[6] Throughout the nineteenth century the world awaited a secular Messiah to redress the ills created by the Industrial Revolution in a double incarnation: first as science, which was to create the means to end all poverty, and second as socialism, which was to end all injustice. By eagerly awaiting the fulfilment of these promises, the twentieth century allowed the rise of a false Messiah: state dictatorship.

It may not be unfair to speculate that the oscillation between the mask of the Messiah and the cruel face of an all-powerful Dictator behind the mask is what delineates the parameters of dystopian thought and creates the suspense in dystopian fiction of the protagonist's nightmare journey to "unmask" the secrets held by the "High Priest" of the political system. In Zamiatin's *We,* Huxley's *Brave New World,* and Orwell's *Nineteen Eighty-four* this nightmare journey ends invariably in the protagonist's trial, followed by retribution tantamount to his destruction or, even more horrifying, to his sinister transformation.

In the context of the Soviet experiment of building socialism, Koestler and Orwell were certainly not the first, although they were among the best-known thinkers in the 1940s who decided to show the real face of dictatorship behind the Messianic mask. This effort at "unmasking" was not well received by their confrères, the leftist intellectuals in the West, whose virtually religious infatuation with the Soviet Union as the only country in the world that was building socialism started at the time of the 1917 revolution. For some this infatuation was sustained through Stalin's show trials in the 1930s and into the early 1950s; for many, probably right up to the violent overthrow of the Hungarian Revolution in 1956, and for still others right up to the crushing of the Prague Spring by Soviet tanks in 1968.

At these various junctures in history the leftist intelligentsia in the West was confronted with the disheartening fact that the Messianic promise of the age-old utopian dream of socialism as a cure for the clearly obvious pathologies of capitalism had merely led to new pathologies in the form of the virulent psychoses of totalitarian dictatorship.

What should these new pathologies be attributed to? Stalin's pathological personality? To the fact that the young Soviet Union had to struggle with potentially overwhelming external enemies? Or to the historical irony that made the Bolsheviks successors of an autocratic regime that had created a tempting precedent? Perhaps to the fact that Stalin's revolution (or counterrevolution) in 1929 gave rise to a ruthlessly self-serving new bureaucracy – a new ruling class? These are not the questions to ponder at this point. Maybe one is left frustrated discussing the flaws of socialism because, as Chesterton said of Christianity, it is something that has never been tried yet. Thus, in the case of Stalin's regime, one could argue that the slogans ostensibly drawing on Marx's theories of socialism were nothing but a camouflage for Russian nationalism and imperialism, or simply for Stalin's and his self-serving elite's thirst for power.

Other historians and political analysts, of course, concentrate on elements in Marxist theory that they see as conducive to the development and legitimization of a totalitarian regime. Some ponder whether we should not relate the terror and coercion of Stalinism to the intellectual coercion implied by Marx's notion of historical determinism. Others raise the question whether the Party's oppression of all opponents and its disregard for the universal principles of human justice are not the consequences of Marx's failure to provide a sufficient model for a political process of persuasion and for a juridical system based on respect for human rights. Marx did make the assumption that once the proletariat came to power and established socialism, the very notion of political and legal mechanisms that had been necessary to resolve conflicts created by the economic injustice inherent in a class society would become superfluous.[7]

Be that as it may, in the field of history the shocking reversal between high utopian expectations and deep disillusionment with the Soviet attempt at socialism has been central to the nervous vacillation of the utopian-dystopian axis of our times, demonstrable not only in the more abstract realm of political thought but also in the internal and external politics of individual nations or entire power blocs.

In the realm of literature it has been a task worthy of the greatest of political satirists to comment on this reversal as having revealed the cruelty of dictatorship under the false Messiah's mask of hypocrisy, and to exhort the reader to see beyond the mask. At the same time it has also been a task awaiting the pen of the tragedian to express the emotional charge of the loss of faith and the disillusionment over what Camus called "the tragedy of our generation ... to have seen a false hope."[8]

Exploring this double impetus of satire and tragedy in the plethora of dystopian fiction in the twentieth century, this book asks three fundamental questions:

First, what are the most salient characteristics of dystopian fiction if we concentrate on such well-known representatives of this speculative genre as Huxley's *Brave New World*, Orwell's *Nineteen Eighty-four*, Bradbury's *Fahrenheit 451*, Vonnegut's *Player Piano*, and Atwood's *The Handmaid's Tale*? All these works are political satires, projections of the fear that their writers' own society in the West – a term confined here somewhat arbitrarily to Great Britain and North America – could be moving towards a type of totalitarian dictatorship already experienced as historical reality in the USSR and in Eastern and Central Europe. Although written in Russia, Zamiatin's *We* also belongs to this tradition by virtue of its undeniable influence on Orwell and the likelihood of its direct or indirect influence on Huxley. Written in 1920, only three years after the revolution and almost a decade before the Stalinist consolidation of terror, *We* also projects its writer's fear of a fully totalitarian rule almost ten years ahead of its realization;

undoubtedly, at the time of writing the novel Zamiatin still believed he could warn his contemporaries that such a system could take hold in the future.

But if fear of the emergence of a totalitarian regime is the major component of the dystopian impulse, can we still speak of dystopian fiction in the Soviet Union *after* Zamiatin and in the satellite countries *after* 1948? (The East is confined here, for the sake of space, to the USSR between the 1920s and 1991, and to Poland, Hungary, and Czechoslovakia between 1948 and 1989.) Can we speak of dystopian fiction in a society where the "greatest fear" so typical of this speculative, quasi-prophetic, exhortatory genre has already been fulfilled and become a fact of life, in the form of the State's "totalist" control through censorship, propaganda, intimidation, and indoctrination?

Finally, if we agree that works of dystopian fiction indeed emerged in the USSR and in the three satellite countries in the periods of dictatorship, how do these works differ from their Western counterparts, whose aim it was to warn against and *prevent* the coming of the nightmare state?

DYSTOPIA EAST AND WEST

The West

Let us begin, then, with our first question about some of the more general characteristics of dystopian fiction in our selection. Zamiatin's *We*, Huxley's *Brave New World*, Orwell's *Nineteen Eighty-four*, Bradbury's *Fahrenheit 451*, Vonnegut's *Player Piano*, and Atwood's *The Handmaid's Tale* constitute a clear counterpoint to utopian fiction; in addition, however, we must realize that the dystopian novel itself demonstrates the push and pull between utopian and dystopian perspectives. To a significant extent, each of these novels makes us ponder how an originally utopian promise was abused, betrayed, or, ironically, fulfilled so as to create tragic consequences for humanity.

THE PUSH AND PULL BETWEEN UTOPIAN AND DYSTOPIAN PERSPECTIVES   If we begin with *We*, *Brave New World*, and *Nineteen Eighty-four*, it becomes obvious that each dystopian society contains within it seeds of a utopian dream. These are articulated by the ruling elite's original promise when its new system was implemented, a promise that then miscarried (in *We*); was betrayed (in *Nineteen Eighty-four*); or was fulfilled in ways that show up the unexpected shortcomings of the dream (in *Brave New World*).

The inner contradiction between utopian dream and dystopian reality was, by the way, also a significant element of specifically anti-fascist dystopias, such as Jack London's *The Iron Heel*, Sinclair Lewis's *It Can't Happen Here*, and Katherine Burdekin's *Swastika Night*. However, the fascist utopia, even in its original promise, carried only limited appeal for humanity as a whole, since it was not only an elitist utopia designed exclusively for a master race but also a dream envisaging the elimination or domination of "inferior races" – the larger portion of humanity. The fear that such a "dream" might still have its followers in the West motivated Lewis and Burdekin, as it did Virginia Woolf's *Three Guineas*, which could also be read as some kind of non-fictional dystopian warning against fascism, exploring the potentially fascist elements of the patriarchal society of 1930s England.

In contrast to fascism, the age-old dream of socialism was a utopia incorporating the universal premises of humanism and therefore had an extremely wide appeal. Through the works of Marx, Engels, and the explication and analysis of their work, socialism became the foundation of one of the most comprehensive and compelling thought-systems ever created. The spectacle of this utopian aspiration buttressed by such a powerful theory turning into dystopian societies of terror and dictatorship produced a veritable onslaught of dystopian fiction in our century. The greatest fear of the authors of such fiction was that the totalitarian dictatorship operating in the Soviet Union and later in the Soviet bloc could too readily be condoned in the West precisely because the Western intelligentsia could not, or would not, recognize that it was terror that this allegedly socialist regime shared with its allegedly greatest opponent, fascism. Koestler's *Darkness at Noon* and Orwell's *Animal Farm* and *Nineteen Eighty-four* are among the most widely known works that articulate this fear.

In dystopias like *Fahrenheit 451*, *Player Piano*, and *The Handmaid's Tale* the new American ruling class does not start out with a consistent utopian ideology; it promises only to deal with an emergency situation, to find an allegedly efficient solution to a crisis. This "solution," then, becomes a modified system of a quasi-utopian ideology expressed through a limited number of slogans of the state religion. However, none of the High Priests – Bradbury's Fire Chief Beatty, Vonnegut's Papa Kroner, or Atwood's Commander – feels it necessary to justify his own role or to cover up for specific elements of totalitarianism such as denunciations, oppression, and the lies of propaganda, elements borrowed – without the coherent ideology – from both Stalinist and Hitlerian models of dictatorship. (I tend to think that the dystopias of Anthony Burgess's *Ripening Seed* or *1985* could probably also be classified as such "emergency" dystopias, where, except for unleashing the mass hysteria of violence against a specific group of scapegoats, the elite does not even pretend to offer the population a comprehensive faith or utopian ideology to believe in.)

Undoubtedly, *Brave New World, Nineteen Eighty-four, Fahrenheit 451, Player Piano*, and *The Handmaid's Tale* are addressed primarily to the Western reader; their most specific aim is to explore the social-political pathologies of capitalism in the context of Britain or North America. Nevertheless, the intensity of the "greatest fear" that drives the visionary aspect of Western dystopian fiction happens to be the fear that by falling for the seductively utopian promises of a dictatorship hiding behind the mask of the Messiah, Western democracy could also take a turn in the direction of totalitarianism, following the precedents of historical models already established by fascist and communist dictatorships in Eastern and Central Europe.

THE DELIBERATE MISCARRIAGE OF JUSTICE: THE PROTAGONIST'S TRIAL   The next common characteristic of the six works also follows from the conflict between the elite's original utopian promise to establish a just, lawful society and its subsequent deliberate miscarriage of justice, its conspiracy against its own people. The mystery of this conspiracy and of the elite's self-justification will be revealed to the protagonist at his own trial, followed by inevitably harsh punishment. The experience of the trial is imbued with the nightmare atmosphere typical of dystopia. We become aware of the duality of law and lawlessness, and the contradiction between advanced technology and a psychologically, spiritually regressive mentality at the heart of the regime. In this study I suggest that the protagonist's trial as an emblem of injustice is a thematically and symbolically central device of dystopian fiction. The structural and thematic importance of the trial is probably most conspicuous in *Nineteen Eighty-four*, where in the course of Winston's trial, which takes up one-third of the novel, in the very process that systematically deprives him of selfhood, consciousness, loyalty, and memory, the value we set on selfhood and consciousness are made fully apparent. The protagonist's trial plays a similarly significant role in *Brave New World, We, Fahrenheit 451*, and *Player Piano*, as the central scene that juxtaposes the protagonist's belief in individualism with the elite's ideology, aimed at the elimination of the individual. (In *The Handmaid's Tale* the ruling elite of Gilead no longer stages either public or secret trials: the recurring theatricals of "salvaging" combine the process of interrogation, trial, and execution within the same horrifying ritual.)

A BARBARIC STATE RELIGION – NIGHTMARE VISION   The next characteristic of these six works still follows from the experience of the trial, where the protagonist recognizes that instead of the rule of civilized law and justice, dystopian society functions as a primitive state religion that practises the ritual of human sacrifice. It is here that the reasoning that motivates the dystopian state's dualities of law and lawlessness, propaganda and truth, advanced technology and regression to barbarism is revealed to us, and this revelation further contributes to the nightmare atmosphere of the dystopian novel. Orwell's Oceania is ruled by hatred, fear, and treachery; Bradbury's world by firemen who do not extinguish fires but set fire to books, houses, and people; Vonnegut's Ilium by robots and computers that make human beings feel superfluous; Atwood's Gilead by men who use women as baby machines, eventually to discard them to die of the consequences of cleaning up nuclear waste. We are faced here with societies in the throes of a *collective nightmare*. As in a nightmare, the individual has become a victim, experiencing loss of control over his or her destiny in the face of a monstrous, suprahuman force that can no longer be overcome or, in many cases, even comprehended by reason. Beyond the sense of displacement typical of nightmares, we also become aware of the peculiar logic of a mythical, ritualistic way of thinking in dystopian societies, not unlike the logic inherent in obsessive-compulsive disorders and in what Freud observed as the coupling between megalomania and paranoia.[9]

THE DESTRUCTION OF THE INDIVIDUAL'S PRIVATE WORLD   What looms large in these six writers' greatest fear of totalitarian dictatorship is the particular horror of the monster state's propensity to combine the spirit of a barbaric state religion with advanced technologies capable of spreading propaganda and indoctrination by electronic means and through the use of mind-altering drugs. The power of the modern state not only to control action but also to enter what Orwell called "the few cubic centimetres" within the skull makes it capable of achieving total domination over the individual's private self, family feelings, sexuality, thoughts, and emotions.

In effect, the destruction of the demarcation line between the public and the private spheres is one of the most striking common characteristics of the societies depicted by the six novels in question.[10] In Zamiatin's One State the inhabitants live under a glass dome within ultramodern glass cages. In Orwell's Oceania, Big Brother's eyes follow Winston mysteriously in every situation, even in his dreams. In Huxley's World State people are never left alone. It follows from this emphasis on public exposure that even the most intimate personal relationships are prescribed and controlled by the state: in Oceania males and females are to deny their sexuality; in the World State and the One State they have to abide by the rules of state-enforced promiscuity. In *Fahrenheit 451* human relationships are so depersonalized that husband and wife simply do not remember any distinctive event from their private lives together; in *The Handmaid's Tale* sexual relationships are regimented and supervised by the ruling elite, ostensibly in the interest of producing the maximum number of children for the state but actually mainly to eliminate chances of forming personal relationships and private loyalties. The state's intent in all five novels is to deny the bonds of private loyalty and thereby to enforce not only uncritical obedience to the state but also a quasi-religious worship of the state ideology. In accordance with the same intent, the bond between parent and child is also radically broken: in Oceania children are trained to denounce their parents; in the One State and the World State there are no families. The overall effect is that actions and emotions that were previously associated with the individual's private world suddenly become public domain, fully under the punitive control of the state machine.

Even more important, by breaking down the private world of each inhabitant the monster state succeeds in breaking down the very core of the individual mind and personality – what remains is the pliable, numb consciouness of massman. Zamiatin, Huxley, and Orwell, as it were in unison, warn that once *we* accept such a process, it could become world-wide and irreversible. Ultimately, by being relentlessly bombarded by state propaganda while also being deprived of privacy and intimate relationships, we may be deprived of the core of our being, our personal memory of the past.

THE PROTAGONIST'S PURSUIT OF HISTORY: THE VITAL IMPORTANCE OF A RECORD OF THE PAST   Consequently, probably one of the most typical "messages" of dystopian fiction is that access to the records of the past is vital to the mental health of any society. Living in a nightmare world of mythical thought approaching the logic of a mental disorder that no longer differentiates between present and past, cause and effect, or lies and truth, each protagonist is eager to obtain and hold on to a genuine record of the past, a past the totalitarian regime would like to distort or deny completely. In order to create or obtain such a record, the protagonists in *We, Nineteen Eighty-four,* and *The Handmaid's Tale* decide to keep a diary. In *Brave New World, Fahrenheit 451,* and *Nineteen Eighty-four* the protagonists pursue what each considers the most important books from the past: Shakespeare and the Bible in *Brave New World*; the Bible and the classics of nineteenth-century fiction in *Fahrenheit 451*; and Goldstein's Book in *Nineteen Eighty-four.* It is through these diaries or these books that the protagonist wants to break the isolation the dictatorship has created by cutting off man from woman, parent from child, friend from friend, the present from the past, and the world within from the world outside the regime.

DYSTOPIA AS A NO-MAN'S LAND BETWEEN SATIRE AND TRAGEDY   The next two common characteristics of the Western model of dystopia relate more directly to the structural features of genre (although, naturally, the thematic and generic characteristics are closely related). Generically speaking, all six novels so far examined occupy some kind of no-man's land between tragedy and satire. The protagonist's experience and fate is tragic in the sense that it deals with irrevocable loss on the personal level: he or she loses his position, his beloved, his freedom, and in the first three examples faces a loss possibly even worse than the loss of life: the loss of his private, individual identity.

Yet the tragic elements of the protagonist's fate nothwithstanding, the overall strategies of the dystopian novel are those of political satire. The writer offers militant criticism of specific aberrations in our own, present social-political system by pointing out their potentially monstrous consequences in the future. The function of the message is that of a warning, an exhortation. "Should you not recognize these specific aberrations in your present, and should you allow them to go on unchecked," the writer can be heard to say to us, "you will no longer be able to prevent the development of the horrifying nightmare system of London 651 AF, Oceania, or Gilead, in which the protagonist's tragic fate will have become simply inevitable." Indeed, different as these six works may be from one another, they have this common generic denominator: each is a tragedy, but a somewhat unusual form of tragedy that also accommodates the didactic strategies of satire, a tragic story within the framework of an exhortation, a tragedy in the conditional mood only.

But let us take a closer look at the relationship between tragic and dystopian perspectives. Clearly, if we think of *Oedipus Rex* or *Hamlet*, it becomes evident that great tragedy touches upon the essential elements of the utopian-dystopian discourse. As long as that incestuous parricide, Oedipus, is basking in the false security of his kingship, the polis of Thebes turns into a dystopic nightmare society of illness, corruption, and paralysis. The plague-stricken society cannot purge itself or renew itself (babies are stillborn) until its ruler undertakes to administer justice by seeking out and punishing the criminal who upset the legitimacy of the social-political order by murdering Laius, king of Thebes.

The concept of utopia as a well-run model of an ideal state of justice, and its nightmarish reversal as a systematic miscarriage of justice in dystopia, play an equally important role in many other tragedies. In fact, utopia and dystopia could be defined as the mirror-images Hamlet holds up to his mother in the famous closet scene in order to make her recognize the right moral course she should be taking. Hamlet forces Gertrude to look at the images of two brothers: "Look here upon this picture and on this / The counterfeit presentment of two brothers" (III.iii.53–4). The first picture is the portrait of Hamlet's father, the model of the good king, the legitimate ruler who assures justice and harmony in society, a structure that (except for the pastoral retreat from politics in the Forest of Arden and the retreat into magic on Prospero's island) comes closest to Shakespeare's notion of utopia. The second picture is the portrait of Claudius, the ruler who came to the throne by breaking a law based on the universal concept of justice and who, if he wants to maintain his ill-gotten power, is obliged to keep on lying and committing one act of injustice after another until the entire state of Denmark comes to mirror its ruler's corruption and is led to its disintegration. (In his 1996 film version Kenneth Branagh directed *Hamlet* as such a political parable of dystopia. After Hamlet's death the troops of Fortinbras hurl themselves at the glass doors, meeting no resistance at the fortress of Elsinor, which has been left weak and defenceless by the corrupt king and his intrigues against his own people. Branagh adds a final touch of dystopian violence: as the troops take over, they knock down the statue of Hamlet's father, the reminder of the good king's rule of justice.[11]) How readily the characters of Claudius, Edmund, Macbeth, or Richard III lead us to smile in recognition as they prefigure the virtually unstoppable spiral of deceit and violence familiar from the workings of modern dystopian societies, where "what deceit wins, cruelty must keep" (Yeats), so that the original act of violent injustice is bound to breed further and further deceit and further and further violence.

Much as we acknowledge the utopian/dystopian propensities of tragedy, few of us can read such classics of political satire as *Gulliver's Travels* or *Candide* without experiencing occasionally something of the tragic shudder of Sophoclean irony, the ultimately tragic fate of man's ambition to reach perfection of self or society. Both tragedy and satire are capable of staking out the extremes of the human predicament: not only *Oedipus Rex* and *Hamlet* but also *Gulliver's Travels* and *Nineteen Eighty-four* make us ponder such ultimate questions as What does it mean to be human? Is there a point at which we could be made to lose our humanity?

Still, we should recognize the fundamental difference between tragedy and political satire. Unlike tragedy, dystopian satire is not satisfied with asking questions, and the questions it asks are not directly about our place in the universe and the limits of our free will in the face of suprahuman forces. Dystopian satire focuses on society, not on the cosmos, and it has a primarily social-political message, a didactic intent to address the Ideal Reader's moral sense and reason as it applies to the protagonist's – and our own – place in society and in history.

THE PROTAGONIST'S WINDOW ON THE PAST: TWO TIME-PLANES Ultimately, by recognizing the vital significance of a truthful approach to history in the protagonist's life, readers become increasingly aware of the important distinction between the two time-planes inherent in the structure of these dystopian novels. The protagonist's tragic fate is in the conditional mood only: how it plays out in reality depends on whether we come to understand the historical process that could destroy our society, so that we may break the impasse of the historical prediction. Here we come to another salient characteristic of dystopian satire. However compelling the protagonist's personal fate in the novel, as Ideal Readers we eventually have to recognize our distance from him or her: he lives on a time-plane different from our own; he exists in our hypothetical future. In fact it is crucial not only that we identify the difference between his time and ours but also that we recognize that these two time-planes are joined in a cause-effect relationship. Each of the six novels that we have chosen to represent the Western model of dystopia contains what I would call a "window on history," a strategic device through which the writer reveals the roots of the protagonist's dystopian present in the society's past. Of course, what the protagonist defines as the past happens to be the present of the Ideal Reader to whom the exhortation is addressed at the time the satire is written: "Beware: the protagonist's present could become your future." Consequently, it is in our world of the present that we should fight the specific trends that the satirist suggests could, but should not be allowed to, develop into the monstrous nightmare world of the future.

Each writer focuses on a different trend he finds threatening. In *Brave New World*, for example, we hear about the premoderns of the 1930s – "our" time, that is, the time of the writing of the novel – who were first faced with the challenge to distinguish between two alternatives: use the machine to serve humanity, or enslave humanity in the service of the machine. The world of 651 AF reveals the consequences of the premodern's failure (our potential failure) to rise to this challenge.[12]

In *Nineteen Eighty-four* the butt of the satire is probably more specifically focused. It is the satirist's Adversary, the Western intellectual of the late 1940s, who accepts and condones the totalitarian methods of Stalinism. Orwell's point is that the Adversary's condoning of Stalinism as a representative of true socialism is based on the Adversary's readiness to worship the God of Power. It is this totalitarian mentality in the West in the 1940s that could lead to the horrors of Oceania, a state consciously modelled on former totalitarian regimes such as Hitler's Germany and Stalin's Soviet Union. That the transformation of the West came from within and not from a foreign power is demonstrated by the perfect equilibrium that exists among Oceania, Eastasia, and Eurasia in 1984.

Since Winston is probably a far more psychologically compelling character than any of his fellow protagonists from the other novels, as readers we need a more complex distancing mechanism in order to be able to disassociate ourselves from the character's tragic fate while decoding the satirist's social-political message to us. Orwell achieves this distancing by introducing two "books within the book," Goldstein's Book, which describes how the past of the 1930s and 1940s led to the world of Oceania in 1984, and the Dictionary of Newspeak, which draws attention to the possible future of Oceania in 2035. Urged to contemplate the distance between these different time-planes, we are also expected to realize that Winston's fate is acted out not in our present but in our hypothetical future. The catastrophe responsible for his tragedy is still a catastrophe that we could help to prevent. (The conference of the historians after the fall of Gilead – the appendix to Atwood's novel – serves the same purpose of emotional distancing between the reader and the protagonist, and to the same effect.)

Bradbury's *Fahrenheit 451* (1951), Vonnegut's *Player Piano* (1952), and Atwood's *The Handmaid's Tale* (1985) are just as consistent in establishing the relationship between what the author sees as the flaws in his or her society in the present and the monstrous consequences of these flaws that could result in a nightmarish state in the future. In *Fahrenheit 451* the author lets the protagonist find out that the monstrous regime in his present could come about only because of the negative trends rampant in the early 1950s: the acceptance of political censorship in the McCarthy era, and the shift from the reading of the classics in favour of reading the *Reader's Digest* or watching television. In *Player Piano* we find out that it was the atrophy of the humanities and the worship of the machine, particularly the computer, in the early 1950s, together with the acceleration of technology after a Third World War, that prepared the monster world of the Ilium of the future. As for *The Handmaid's Tale*, the fundamentalist, anti-feminist military dictatorship of the Gilead of the future could come to power only as a result of our political sins of the 1980s: the effects of fallout following nuclear experiments; the rise of fundamentalism, with its anti-feminist backlash; and our inadequate resistance to these phenomena. The writer of dystopian fiction offers in each novel a warning against a future that could and should still be avoided by the Ideal Reader's generation.

It is only when we recognize the distinction between these two time-planes as well as their cause-effect relationship that we can proceed to decode the specific targets of the dystopian satire. This distinction between the two time-planes that forms an essential characteristic of the Western tradition of speculative fiction is conspicuously absent from the dystopian works written under the totalitarian dictatorships of Eastern and Central Europe.

The East: The USSR, Poland, Hungary, and Czechoslovakia

Having observed the interaction between some characteristic structural and thematic elements of the dystopian genre in six representatives of its classic Western model, I turn to my second and third questions. If the central impulse behind dystopian fiction is the writer's warning against the emergence of the monster state of totalitarian dictatorship in the future, can we speak of a genre of dystopian fiction in the Soviet Union between 1920 and 1991 and in what used to be the Soviet bloc between 1948 and 1989? If there are indeed expressions of the dystopian impetus in fiction here, do these works show a significant difference from their Western counterparts, and if so, what is the nature of their difference?

To narrow down the vast material relevant to this question, parts 2 and 3 of this study concentrate on a selection of works of fiction written under various phases of totalitarian dictatorship in the USSR, Poland, Hungary, and Czechoslovakia, dealing with the deliberate miscarriage of justice. After a brief examination of the Guidelines of Socialist Realism, which prescribed how writers should sing the praises of the "best of all possible worlds" of the state utopia, we look at a selection of political novels that demonstrate the reality of a dystopic nightmare beyond the facade of the state utopia, a genuinely dystopic society that complies in its essential features with most of the characteristics we have just delineated in the hypothetical societies of the Western classics of dystopian fiction.

The central thesis of this book, then, is based on the observation that in those works that the Western reader tends to regard as the classics of dystopian fiction, authors envisage a monster state in the future, a society that reflects the writers' fear of the possible development of totalitarian dictatorship in their own societies. By contrast with this body of literature, after Zamiatin the Eastern and Central European works of dystopia – written about, against, and under totalitarian dictatorship – present us with a nightmare world not as a phantasmagorical vision of the future but as an accurate reflection of the "worst of all possible worlds" experienced as a historical reality.

Because the political criticism behind the dystopian impulse in the East in this period deals with various phases of the nightmare of historical reality, the works to be explored will be arranged in chronological order according to the historical period they deal with. Part 2 concentrates on the period between 1919 and the 1950s. We begin with three accounts of the nightmarish phases of revolutionary terror in Russia between 1919 and 1921: Victor Serge's *Conquered City,* Vladimir Zazubrin's "The Chip," and Alexander Rodionov's *Chocolate.* We proceed to fiction dealing with the Stalinist revolution of forced collectivization, forced industrialization, and the Moscow show trials of the 1930s in Andrei Platonov's *Foundation Pit,* Anatolij Ribakov's *Children of the Arbat,* and Arthur Koestler's *Darkness at Noon.* We turn then to novels about the frightening rise of Russian chauvinism during the Second World War and a return to terror in the post-war years, in Vassily Grossman's *Life and Fate,* Abram Tertz Sinyavski's *The Trial Begins,* and Juliy Daniel's *Moscow Speaking.*

Part 3 deals with the experience of four countries in the Soviet bloc up to the late 1980s. The years of terror in Poland, Hungary, and Czechoslovakia between 1949 and 1953, and during the recurring crackdowns of the post-Stalin era, are represented by Jerzy Andzrejewski's *Inquisitors* and *Appeal,* Marek Hlasko's *Graveyard,* by the short fiction of Ladislav Fuks' *Mr Mundstock* and *The Cremator,* and by short stories and *feuilletons* of Istvan Örkény, Ludwik Vaculik, and Slavomir Mrozek. Three plays from Czechoslovakia represent the public theatricals of show trials and the satirical treatment of these trials on the stage, in Ivan Klima's *The Castle,* Petr Karvas's *The Big Wig,* and Vaclav Havel's *Memorandum.* The spiral of entropy that follows the spiral of terror is represented in Hungarian Tibor Déry's *Mr G.A. in X,* Polish Tadeusz Konwicki's *A Minor Apocalypse,* and Russian Alexander Zinoviev's *Radiant Future.* Finally, we look briefly at the reappearance of dystopia as speculative fiction with its futuristic structure of two time-planes in Vladimir Voinovich's *Moscow 2042* (1987), Vassily Aksyonov's *The Island of Crimea* (1983), György Dalos's *1985* (1990), and György Moldova's *Hitler in Hungary* (1972, 1992).

No doubt, all these are works of dystopian fiction because they display most of the thematic and generic elements we have observed in the six classics of the genre; they describe a hell on earth, an absurd, death-bound social-political system where the elite deliberately conspires against its own people, against the most universal principles of justice, with emphasis on nighmarish rigged trials, with make-believe accusations followed by all-too-real sentences to hard labour or death. There is also an interaction between utopian and dystopian perspectives within the same work, as the writer – up to the 1980s, a critic from within – struggles to maintain his faith in socialism against an allegedly socialist system. We also detect, in many cases, the interaction between satirical and tragic perspectives.

There are, however, four striking differences between the Western classics of dystopia as a speculative genre and the dystopian fiction of the East.

THE FATE OF THE WRITER AND THE MANUSCRIPT   The first difference relates to the fate of the writer and the manuscript. Many of these works revealing the shocking reality behind state propaganda were suppressed for decades; they could not be published unless the authors managed to publish them underground (samizdat) or abroad (tamizdat). Some of the authors were sent into exile; others were imprisoned, sent to labour camps, or even executed.

THE VANISHING OF SPECULATIVE FICTION WITH THE TWO TIME-PLANES   The second thing that strikes us immediately in this body of literature written under dictatorship is that for over sixty years – that is, between Zamiatin's *We*, written in 1920, and Aksyonov's and Voinovich's novels, written in the 1980s – the dystopian impulse did not seek its expression through works of speculative fiction. What are the reasons for this conspicuous absence of the Western model of the futuristic-speculative genre, with its distinction between two time-planes?

The first and most obvious reason is Stalin's "fantasectomy," his banning of works of speculative literature after 1929. As Zamiatin anticipated this in the "fantasectomy" of his protagonist at the end of *We*, as soon as "Stalin consolidated his power as the only legitimate source of utopian thought, he undertook his 'anti-fantasy project.'" His role as the Masterbuilder of the New Man was parallelled by that of the Masterdreamer, for "a crucial element of the cult of Stalin was his alleged ability to see far across the land and into the future. How could mere writers share his vision?" (It is interesting to note that at the emergence of another omniscient dictator, Hitler, speculative literature in Germany, including science fiction, "went through an almost identical transformation at the same time."[13])

But does such a political climate provide sufficient explanation to our question about the paucity of works with a futuristic structure in our period? We should first of all rule out the hypothesis that this paucity could have anything to do with national temperament or the literary traditions in these countries to which Philip Roth has referred as the "other Europe."[14] Prior to the introduction of Stalin's totalitarian rule, Poland, Hungary, and Czechoslovakia had a rich tradition of futuristic speculation or fantasy.[15] As for Russia, when Zamiatin wrote *We*, he had already completed another speculative novel with a futuristic structure and was also in a position to have read numerous other Russian novels of the previous generation that demonstrate this structure.[16] However, when a Russian translation of *We* appeared in Czechoslovakia in 1927, although without the author's consent, Zamiatin aroused Stalin's relentless anger against any kind of speculative literature as inherently subversive to what Stites calls Stalin's own "anti-utopian utopia." In 1931 Zamiatin was sent into exile: other writers of speculative fiction were punished more severely.

Yet Stalin's ban on the publication of speculative literature does not fully explain why writers stopped writing in this mode. After all, speculative literature was not the only type of literature suppressed by Stalin; any work that could be construed as directly or indirectly critical of the state utopia could come to the same fate. As we can see from the fate of the writers in our selection, works of the dystopian impetus *without* the futuristic time-frame were also repressed, their writers persecuted, and yet there was no dearth of works of this nature.

To find a second and probably equally important reason why no dystopias with a speculative, futuristic structure were written in the period in question we should probably assume that the imaginative process functions in a certain way when projecting the fear of catastrophe into the future, and in a different way when responding to catastrophe experienced as reality. After the 1920s the nightmare in the dystopian fiction in the East is no longer connected with a terrifying future that an author could warn readers about: it is simply a statement about the way things are, rendered most of the time through emotional understatement. In other words, at a time when an entire society seems to be labouring in the throes of an enormous fantasmagoria about the future, it may be quite natural that the writer's criticism of this society avoids the form of speculative fantasy, advocating instead the truthful examination of the flaws of the present and the past.

A DYSTOPIAN IMPETUS COMPATIBLE WITH SEVERAL GENRES   While the dystopian impulse in the Western tradition has been framed by the novelistic tradition of speculative fiction, the dystopian impulse in the Soviet bloc in this period was not bound by any particular genre. One finds significant presentations of dystopian themes in grotesques and allegories as well as in realistic fiction, and these may take the form of novels, short stories, *feuilletons*, cinema, and drama. In fact, in Czechoslovakia, Hungary, and Poland the dystopian impulse in drama seems as strong as if not even stonger than in the novel; see, for example, Mrozek's *Striptease* or *Tango*, Rozewicz's *The Old Woman Broods*, and Istvan Örkeny's *Family Toth*, or *Pisti in the Torrent of Blood* –

probably a subject rich enough for an independent study. This study, however, examines three representatives of the "Kafkaesque" theatre of the absurd in Czechoslovakia, one of the countries where "the absurdist playwright is the true realist, while it is the playwright of 'socialist realism' who deals in grotesque dreams."[17]

THE REPRESENTATION OF MALE-FEMALE RELATIONSHIPS IN DYS-TOPIAN FICTION Finally, another interesting difference between these two bodies of literature is in the different significance the writer attributes to romantic love in the protagonist's predicament. In the Western model Zamiatin, Huxley, Orwell, and Bradbury present the protagonist's awakening to the dystopic nature of his society through his awakening to a kind of love forbidden by the regime. Falling in love with a woman who offers affection, passion, or simply an intimate bond is essential to the protagonist's awakening to his private universe, an essential step in building resistance against the regime. That such a dystopian romance is doomed to failure by the regime is an essential feature of the plot in the classics of dystopian fiction. By contrast, sexual love or a search for greater intimacy does not seem to play a significant role in our selection of dystopian works from Eastern and Central Europe in this period. It seems here that the protagonist's (and the writer's) central, almost exclusive passion is political. Also, unlike the literary developments in the West, dystopian fiction in the Soviet bloc seems an almost exclusively male-centreed genre; female-centred or feminist dystopias appear only after our period.[18]

Further questions arising from the comparison between the dystopian perspectives in these two bodies of literature are explored in the detailed studies of individual works. As I assume that the dystopian works written under dictatorship are less well known to the Western reader, the six Western classics are discussed in two chapters in part 1, while the discussion of works from the East is considerably longer, taking up parts 2 and 3.

Before embarking upon the detailed juxtaposition of these two bodies of literature, let us turn to what I introduced as their first common characteristic: the notion that a dystopian novel reveals, within its own framework, the push and pull between utopian and dystopian perspectives. In the eloquent words of Krishan Kumar, anti-utopia or dystopia "is one side of a dialogue of the self within individuals who have been indelibly stamped with the utopian temperament."[19] Kumar does not go into detail about this temperament, and there is, most likely, a whole range of characteristics one could deduce by examining the works beginning with Zamiatin, Orwell, and Huxley and ending with Voinovich.

Within the framework of this study, however, the next two chapters concentrate on what I suggest are probably two of the most prominent characteristics of this utopian-dystopian temperament: a passionate, quasi-religious concern with the salvation of humanity through history, and an equally passionate preoccupation with the concept of the utopian pursuit of justice and the radical reversal of this pursuit in dystopia.

Part One

Dystopia West

Aldous Huxley

Yevgeny Zamiatin

George Orwell

Fodor Dostoevski

Margaret Atwood

Kurt Vonnegut

Ray Bradbury

CHAPTER ONE

What is Justice?
The Answers of Utopia,
Tragedy, and Dystopia

"What is truth?" asked Pilate, and did not stay for an answer. Had he wanted to pursue the mysteries of the truth of divine justice, he would have entered the grounds of tragedy. Had he had faith in Rome or Jerusalem as a perfectible society able to achieve earthly justice, he would have entered the groves of utopia. Had he not only washed his hands of searching for truth and justice but also deliberately set out to create the machinery of injustice, he would have qualified for the governorship of dystopia in the modern age.

"What is justice?" his pupils asked Socrates, and unlike Pilate he immediately settled down to give a lengthy lecture on the question – witness the "lecture notes" of his star pupil, Plato, in the ten books of *The Republic*. Early in book 2 Socrates comes to the conclusion that we cannot even approach the definition of a just man acting in a just fashion unless we try to picture something that has clearly never yet existed, a just society. It is worth noting that it is not in the pursuit of happiness but in the pursuit of justice that Socrates laid the foundation of a utopian society, the hypothetical city-state of the Republic.

"What is justice? How should we pursue it?" debates Raphael Hathloday, the narrator of Thomas More's *Utopia,* a book that claims "to match or beat" Plato's *Republic* "at its own game." Sitting at the table of Cardinal Morton in the England of the early 1500s, Raphael debates the connection between crime and punishment. England's legal system is clearly in a crisis; thieves are hanging from the gallows all over the country, yet the severity of the punishment does not act as a deterrent. Raphael points out that in a society where greedy landowners have forced thousands out of work so that the dispossessed are in turn forced to steal bread, it is society itself that first makes the thieves and then, in the name of justice, "very properly" turns them into corpses. This style of justice, Raphael argues passionately, is the "conspiracy of the rich to advance their own interests under the pretext of organizing society"; in other words, it is "injustice ... legally described as justice."[1]

To avoid the dilemma of such unjust punishment – indeed, to avoid the need for punishment whatsoever – Raphael offers to relate to More, his host, practices of a distant island that Raphael has encountered as a chance visitor. More invites him to do so after lunch, and thus we are invited along, to enter the Island of Utopia, again not in pursuit of happiness, but in pursuit of a just society.

In a sense the "good place" of *eutopia* cannot be fully understood without its counter-image, the "bad place" of the writer's own time and place, from whose flaws he would like to escape. In Plato's case, the Republic is a just society because it promises to construct a system in which only the true lover of wisdom can rise to the position of ruler, a society that offers a guarantee against Plato's most painful experience of blatant injustice, the sentencing of Athens' finest philosopher, Socrates, to exile or death.

As for More's Utopia, the image of the world "as it should be" cannot become compelling without our counter-image of the flawed world of reality around us. Although More completed the book of the ideal place in 1515, in 1516 he still felt the need to write another book dealing with the acute problems of the England of his time. It is the latter work he turned into book 1, so that the questions raised by the grave injustice in society "as is" could be answered by the institutions of a just society "as it should be" in book 2. (One wonders if the just society of Utopia would also have enshrined due process of law had More in 1516 been able to envisage the rigged trials and executions typical of an age of despotism to which he himself fell victim a mere two decades after writing his *Utopia*.) In a sense, then, the entire notion of a hypothetical society ruled by justice is predicated on the injustice in the "bad place," the real world the writer intends to condemn or criticize. Behind the well-groomed gardens of the hypothetical Utopia is the dark silhouette of the real gallows with thieves hanging "all over the place ... as many as twenty on a single gallows."[2] And behind More, engaged with Raphael in jovial talk about justice, emerges the dark shadow of his own future trial and execution. Just so, juxtaposed to the serene image of Socrates, surrounded by his admiring pupils deep in conversation about a just society, is the stark scene of the "Apologia," Socrates surrounded once more by his pupils, struggling with the injustice of the sentence meted out at his trial: the drinking of hemlock or exile from Athens.

These dystopian images of unfair trial and cruel retribution became central to the further development of the utopian-dystopian discourse in our time, but in its modern rendition the age-old concept of the "bad place" has turned into a genre of its own.[3] The new genre is still impelled by the criticism of satire directed at the writer's own society, just as utopian fiction is, but the strategies of the satire are different. While More's *Utopia* implies a reversal of our flawed, irrational, unjust society and the world of Utopia, classics of dystopian fiction, such as *We*, *Brave New World*, and *Nineteen Eighty-four* offer a definite sense of continuity between the flawed world of the present and the even more profoundly flawed, monstrous world of the hypothetical future, where our society's errors against justice and reason become a totalitarian dictatorship of organized injustice.

While the mirror of utopian fiction functions as an enthusiastic invitation to us as denizens of the flawed world of reality to enter the unflawed one, the dark mirror of dystopian fiction functions as a deterrent, a warning that we should not allow the still curable illness of our present world to turn into the abhorrent pathologies of the world of the future.

UTOPIA VERSUS TRAGEDY VERSUS DYSTOPIA

Having observed that utopian and dystopian fiction have a common ground in satire and that both criticize the injustice and irrationality of the existing social system, we should find a further distinction between the two genres. Utopia and dystopia reveal their significant difference from each other in their relationship to the tragic vision and to the sense of justice characteristic of the genre of tragedy.

"Why is there no justice? Why does the good man suffer?" we hear the tragic hero cry as he struggles with his fate. On a cosmic, metaphysical level, this has been a crucial question for the moral imagination ever since antiquity. Do we not hear Job's agonized cry challenging God's justice echoing from the Old Testament? "Doth it please thee to oppress, that thou shouldst despise the work of thy hands, and shine upon the counsel of the wicked?" (Job 9–11, 3). Why is suffering and humiliation visited upon the righteous? Why is it not the wicked whom God chooses to punish or reprimand?

In *Oedipus Rex* Sophocles raises the question of justice as something essential to the definition of being human. When examined from a cosmic perspective, the question of divine justice remains as mysterious here as in the Book of Job. Having appointed himself judge and detective, Oedipus is made to discover that he is the criminal he has been searching for; he is "the cursed polluter" of Thebes, his own kingdom. As he gets closer and closer to this shattering revelation, he cries out: "Oh gods, what have you plotted against me?" Still, as far as human justice goes, once he has established his own identity, Oedipus takes his punishment into his own hands. When he finally confirms that the prophecy he has feared all his life has been fulfilled and the man he killed was his father and the woman he married his mother, he blinds himself. When asked by the Chorus who is responsible for this horrible deed, he blurts out, "Apollo, my friends, Apollo – but my hands – I did it." It was the Sun god Apollo – that is, a superhuman force – that caused the chain of events that culminated in this deed, yet it is he, Oedipus, who takes personal responsibility for his action and takes the instrument of human justice into his own hands. In this scene we have a distinct sense that it is precisely the act of assuming individual responsibility that elevates the victim of Fate to the status of tragic hero, that by claiming responsibility for his actions, the pawn of Fate confers upon himself the dignity of the human being.

Still, what it takes to become or to stay human is not a criterion necessarily self-evident to every human being. In the resolution of *Oedipus Rex* there is a contradiction between the justice perceived by the Chorus and the justice perceived by the tragic hero. Unknown to the former, there is a new way of seeing that awaits the self-blinded Oedipus: at the very depth of his suffering he understands that it was not for nothing that the gods singled him out for his horrible fate: "And yet I know, not age, nor sickness, nor common accident can end my life; I was not snatched from death that once, unless to be preserved for some more awful [awesome] destiny" (1456–60). In contrast to Oedipus, the Chorus remain blind to the meaning of Oedipus's self-punishment to the very end, because they are of necessity blind to his new insight into a higher, a transcendent system of justice, albeit a postponed one.

There is a similar interaction between Job, when he challenges God before accepting his predicament unconditionally, and his three friends, who come allegedly to console him. Although surrounded by a chorus of "friends," Job and Oedipus must struggle alone with the mystery of divine justice, a justice not immediately apparent because it is transposed or "postponed" beyond the realm of human, social justice. Without this mystery we would probably have no sense of transcendence, that unique illumination of tragic knowledge that is mysterious because it emerges in spite of, or precisely through the darkness of tragic loss – a perception essential to the sense of tragic catharsis or purification.

Suffering from the cruelty of his two elder daughters as the consequence of his own act of injustice against his youngest, Cordelia, King Lear declares that he is "more sinned against than sinning" and becomes so obsessed with trials and imaginary seats of judgment that he goes out of his mind. He will find peace and the return of his sanity in his reunion with Cordelia, when he comes to experience the meaning of her true forgiveness and reclaims the natural bond of love between father and child. This bond restores the continuity of the disrupted Chain of Being that is for Shakespeare the demonstration of divine order and justice. Of course, it is after this reconciliation that Cordelia is murdered, and Lear dies of a broken heart because of it. The survivors are left with the poignant but unanswerable questions of tragedy: "Is this the promised end? Or image of that horror?" (v.iii.263–4) Even in this ostensibly pre-Christian play Shakespeare feels that the unpredictable mysteries of divine justice that allow the innocent to suffer can be addressed only by reference to the "promised end" of the Last Judgment.

The utopian vision is contrapuntal to the tragic vision. In utopia we are asked to disregard the cosmic dimensions of tragedy and the exceptional personality of a tragic hero and move on to the concerns of the chorus, the here and now of social and moral justice. Indeed, Plato expels the tragedian from his utopia. The education of the young guardians in the Republic has no room for the nourishing of the tragic emotions of pity and fear: "When we listen to a passage of Homer, or one of the tragedians, in which he represents some pitiful hero who is drawing out his sorrows in long oration, or weeping, or smiting his breast, [we] delight in giving way to sympathy, and are in raptures at the excellence of the poet who stirs our feelings most."[4]

Well aware of their power, the Republic exiles its best poets lest the feelings of "pleasure and pain [become] the rulers of the State" instead of "law and reason." Plato's guardian has no time for tragedy, where "the forces which shape or destroy our lives live outside the provenance of reason and justice." Therefore, it is not by accident that in the twentieth century's most potent utopian experiment, the Soviet Union, Education Commissar Lunacharsky announced that "one of the defining qualities of a communist society would be the absence of tragic drama."[5] When Gorky, one of the founding fathers of Socialist Realism, was asked about the possibility of tragic accidents in the Communist future, he expressed his invincible conviction that in the perfect world of Communism, tragic accidents would no longer occur.[6]

George Steiner points out that "the Marxist world view, even more explicitly than the Christian, admits of error, anguish, and temporary defeat, but not of ultimate tragedy. Despair is a mortal sin against Marxism no less than it is against Christ." It also follows from Marx's and Engels's pride in the scientific principles of their system that they deny the mystery connected with the blind necessity of tragedy: "Necessity is blind only when we don't understand it." In its denial of a tragic ending in the cosmic scheme of things, says Frye, "Christianity ... sees tragedy as an episode in the divine comedy, the larger scheme of redemption and resurrection. The sense of tragedy as a prelude to comedy seems almost inseparable from anything explicitly Christian."[7] Similarly, Steiner argues, "the Marxist conception of history is a secular commedia. Mankind is advancing toward the justice, equality and leisure of a classless society."[8] Steiner's parallel between Christianity and Marxism also draws attention to the religious, eschatological aura with which the inevitably paradisiac future in Communism is imbued, in spite of the allegedly secular, materialist approach Marx takes to history.

DYSTOPIA AS ORGANIZED INJUSTICE

We have noted that the utopian vision is diametrically opposed to the vision of tragedy. We should now also take into account that utopia, with its belief in the possibility of establishing justice in society, is also opposed to dystopian fiction, a genre that, I suggest, describes a society characterized by not only occasional errors in the execution of justice but by a machinery for the deliberate miscarriage of justice. What is then the relationship between dystopian fiction and tragedy, each of them a counterpoint to the vision of utopia?

To begin to answer this question it is necessary to examine the parallels between the tragic hero and the protagonist of dystopian fiction. If "any realistic notion of tragic drama must start with the fact of catastrophe," it would be useless to look for the principles of human justice in the interaction between the human being and the forces of the supernatural. "Oedipus does not get back his eyes or his spectre ... There is no use in asking for a rational explanation or mercy. Things are as they are; unrelenting and absurd. We are punished far in excess of our guilt."[9] By contrast, in his definition of tragedy Northrop Frye argues that we should "recognize in tragedy a mimesis of sacrifice," a definition that to me implies a justice different from social justice, where the "inscrutable tragic hero" becomes our pharmakos, who sacrifices himself for the community – or for the reader or the audience – so that "with his fall, a greater world beyond, which his gigantic spirit had blocked out, becomes for a moment visible, but there is also a sense of the mystery and remoteness of that world."[10]

Demonstrating the problematic relationship between human and divine justice, tragedy makes us examine anew the conventional notions of good and evil and the very concept of retribution. I suggest that there is a significant structural-thematic connection but also a difference between tragedy and modern dystopian fiction. The underlying situation in both is a trial and the threat of cruel retribution. At the beginning of Oedipus Rex Oedipus announces that he will act as detective and judge to find Laios's murderer. At the end he has to face his self-announced punishment. In *Antigone*, *King Lear*, *Hamlet*, *Macbeth*, even in *Romeo and Juliet*, the threat of trial and retribution are the central motivators of the plot and also lead to its climax.

Trial and retribution also take pride of place in dystopian fiction. In Zamiatin's *We*, Orwell's *Nineteen Eighty-four*, and Bradbury's *Fahrenheit 451* the narrative is "framed" by two trials: the trial and punishment of a subversive witnessed by the protagonist at the beginning, and the protagonist's own trial and punishment at the end. Yet there is a significant difference between the role of trial and punishment in tragedy and in dystopian fiction.

This difference is twofold: it relates first to the machinery of justice and second to the protagonist's response to retribution. We have suggested that neither Shakespeare's nor Sophocles' tragic view of earthly justice implies the denial of the very concept of justice. Even if Oedipus does not regain his sight and kingdom, the moment of his tragic fall, his *peripeteia*, also coincides with a new recognition, a new understanding of his fate, a new kind of spiritual insight (just as Gloucester in *King Lear* understands that he gained new understanding only after he was blinded, declaring: "I stumbled when I saw"). In this sense, in spite of the tragic loss that is fundamental to tragedy, we have also to note the double action in tragic drama, the material loss of light balanced by a spiritual or psychological illumination or the purification of sacrifice: "Man is ennobled by the vengeful spite of the gods. It does not make him innocent, but it hallows him as if he had passed through flame."[11]

In dystopian fiction the protagonist's trial results not in the postponement but in the denial of justice, its deliberate miscarriage. The central character with whom we tend to identify is an individual courageous enough to stand up against an elite ruling through a semi-divine leader, who is responsible for the enslavement of the population, for a deliberate conspiracy against the welfare of his own people. In this society trials can have only one result: no accused is ever acquitted.

But are we expected to have the sense of spiritual uplift characteristic of tragedy when we read of the tragic loss endured by Zamiatin's D-503, by Huxley's John the Savage, or by Orwell's Winston Smith? Given the nature of the punishment following their trial, none of these protagonists is in a position to reach a moment of recognition or new insight, and thus to undergo an experience of catharsis. D-503 is lobotomized; the Savage commits suicide; and Winston Smith is tortured physically and mentally until he undergoes a personality change comparable in its effects to lobotomy. Neither do they fulfil the fate of the tragic hero, who is able to sacrifice himself for the good of the community. The dystopian ruler makes sure that the protagonists' revolt is defeated and his name erased from the memory of the enslaved, benumbed population.

If there is a moment of catharsis implied in the protagonist's predicament, it is there only for the reader who has finished the narrative, and it is contained in an insight more in the nature of the cerebral recognition accompanying political satire than the emotional catharsis of tragedy. Dystopian satire has a primarily social message, a didactic intent to address the Ideal Reader's moral sense and reason as it applies to our place in society. Consequently, as a fundamentally cerebral genre, satire makes a more direct appeal to the rational thought-process than does tragedy, and the reader's catharsis must be appropriate to the cerebral nature of the genre. The catharsis peculiar to dystopian satire is probably best demonstrated in *Nineteen Eighty-four*:

"What happened had to happen" is the recognition reached by the end of *Oedipus Rex* or *Hamlet*. Only by confronting the darkness of evil and suffering can we liberate ourselves from it. Liberation comes in tragedy as a result, *after* the catastrophe. In satire the catharsis consists of another kind of recognition, and I suggest that it is the sense of relief that comes from a revelation accomplished by the force of reason; it consists of the recognition that we are still *before* the catastrophe, and hence in possession of the freedom to avert it. When reading Goldstein's Book and the Dictionary of Newspeak, dealing with the past and future of Oceania respectively, we are reminded that Winston's story, which we have just been reading, has not happened yet. Unlike Winston, we still have the freedom to shape the future according to our higher understanding and free choice."[12]

Such a distancing mechanism between the protagonist and the reader may take a variety of forms but is equally important in all the dystopian novels that follow the classical Western structure. However compelling the protagonist's personal fate in the novel, we are not expected to identify with him the way we are to identify with the hero of tragedy (an identification that would form the precondition of our tragic catharsis). Also, instead of concentrating exclusively on the protagonist's personal fate in the dramatic present, we are asked to scrutinize the historical forces that led from his society's past to the nightmare society in his present.

Since the dystopian fiction of Eastern and Central Europe deals with the nightmare society without the distancing mechanism of the hypothesis implied in speculative literature that projects the nightmare into our future, here our "speculation" is focused directly on the question: How did the utopian dream of socialism, shared by millions, turn into a nightmare of a dystopic, ultimately dysfunctional society? How did the utopian promise of universal justice implied in what Lenin called the "radiant future" of Communism turn into the organized injustice of totalitarian dictatorship?

TOTALITARIAN DICTATORSHIP: THE MISCARRIAGE OF JUSTICE

Directly or indirectly, both versions of dystopian literature to be examined in this study raise the question: Why does the elite that came to power with the utopian promise of universal justice end up establishing a system based on the deliberate miscarriage of justice? And how long can the elite justify this aberration to itself?

IDEOLOGICAL THINKING

As Karl Popper introduces this dilemma, undoubtedly "Marxism predicted and tried actively to further a development culminating in an ideal utopia that knows no political or economic coercion; the state has withered away, each person co- operates freely in accordance with his abilities, and all his needs are satisfied."[13] How could such a prediction lead to the totalitarian police state?

In the light of the totalitarian dictatorships of our century, Karl Popper, Milovan Djilas, J.L. Talmon, and Hannah Arendt (among many others) speculate about the surprising similarities between certain aspects of utopian thought and the ideology conducive to totalitarian rule. According to Milovan Djilas, "every tyranny begins with some absolute truths about man and society,"[14] and it has been often repeated that "whoever aspires to the articulation of final absolute truth about man and society has already planted the seed of tyranny."[15] In Karl Popper's definition, utopianism means that "rational political action must be based upon a more or less clear and detailed description or blueprint of our ideal state, and ... of the historical path that leads towards this goal."[16]

Inherent in such a "blueprint," according to Arendt, are the consequences of "ideological thinking" in Nazi Germany and Stalin's Russia. She names three specifically totalitarian elements that are peculiar to all ideological thinking:

First, in their claim to total explanation, ideologies have the tendency to explain not what is, but what becomes, what is born and passes away ... It promises the *total explanation of the past*, the total knowledge of *the present*, and the reliable prediction of *the future*. Secondly [it] becomes independent of all experience from which it cannot learn anything new even if it is a question of something that has just come to pass. Hence it becomes emancipated from the reality that we perceive with our five senses, and insists on a "truer" reality concealed behind all perceptible things, ... requiring a sixth sense that enables us to become aware of it ... Thirdly ... it orders facts into an absolutely logical procedure [that proceeds with *a consistency that exists nowhere in the realm of reality* (my italics).[17]

As if he wanted to illustrate these points, in *Nineteen Eighty-four* Orwell dedicates the last third of the novel to Winston's trial, where O'Brien demonstrates the Party's absolute, megalomaniacal certainty about its total knowledge of past, present, and future, that crazy "iron consistency" of logic that is, like a psychosis, entirely "emancipated from reality." O'Brien also insists on Winston's developing that "sixth sense" Orwell calls "doublethink," which would make him *see* how two plus two may make four or five, depending on the Party's latest position on the matter.

The entire narrative of *Darkness at Noon* deals with methods of interrogation as an exercise in an insane logic of iron consistency. Inter-rogating Rubashov, Gletkin demonstrates the same schizophrenic "sixth sense" by taking into account and denying Rubashov's innocence at the same time, a feat of ideological thinking that got Gletkin his job in the first place. Gletkin's absolute conviction that the Party's predic-tions about the future are irrefutable gives him the strength to denounce his boss and rival, Ivanov, and annihilate the defendant, a member of the Party opposition whose "heretical" views should be eradicated. Ultimately, it is O'Brien's and Gletkin's invincible faith in the historical predictions of their ideologies that justifies the most violent "suppres-sion of criticism and the annihilation of all opposition."[18]

What also follows from this faith is "the affirmation of the wisdom and foresight of utopian planners, of the Utopian engineers who design and execute the Utopian blueprint ... [They] must in this way become omniscient as well as omnipotent. They become gods."[19] The specula-tive fiction of *We, Brave New World,* and *Nineteen Eighty-four* describes the grotesque and sinister worship of the utopian planner as deity. This phenomenon, in a directly satirical form, is also central to the dystopian critiques of the worship of the "Big Man in the city" in Platonov's *Foundation Pit,* of the bloodthirsty Master in Tertz's *The Trial Begins,* and of No. I in Koestler's *Darkness at Noon.*

IN THE WAKE OF VIOLENCE –
PERPETRATING VIOLENCE

Almost all our examples of speculative dystopian fiction describe the origin of dictatorships in the violence and chaos of a cataclysmic war (long centuries of struggle in *We* and *Brave New World*; the war conducted with the help of the atom bomb in the fifties in *Nineteen Eighty-four*; a Third World War in *Player Piano*). The roots of total-itarianism, an unprecedented form of government that made its first appearance in our century, according to Arendt, should be located in protracted periods of violence (the First World War, revolutions, civil wars) that created a crisis for the masses who lost stability, traditions, their sense of personal connectedness with the world. They accepted, there-fore, the vague, holistic ideology articulated by a potentially semi-divine leader, who "must eradicate the existing institutions and traditions. He must purify, purge, expel, banish and kill."[20]

TOTALITARIANISM: THE DUALITY OF LAW AND LAWLESSNESS

Yet totalitarian regimes, in spite of being born of violence and aiming to perpetrate violence, are not essentially lawless, even if their "law-fulness" has little to do with any traditional concept of justice. The protagonists in *We, Brave New World*, or *Nineteen Eighty-four* are not simply killed or liquidated: they are brought to trial and sentenced by "due process." As Karl Dietrich Bracher observes, "the coincidence of radically arbitrary acts and apparent due process, manifested also in the façade of the legitimate constitutional state, is characteristic both of Hitlerism and Stalinism. Order and chaos, stability and revolution, are joined in the totalitarian 'dual state.'"[21]

In *Nineteen Eighty-four* Orwell emphasizes such a duality between strict, Party-enforced discipline and the unbridled ferocity of the Parsons children, who set fire to the skirt of a market woman for wrapping her wares in a newspaper with Big Brother's portrait printed on it. In fact, acts of ferocious violence against the "enemy" (and the dutiful and dogged pursuit of an ever-expanding circle of "enemies") become proof of the child's unfailing vigilance, an important part of Party discipline. In a sense, then, the trial and execution of the enemy, the outsider, becomes an essential part of the dystopian system. It is the strictest law that determines who is and who is not within the bound-aries of the law. This is the great leap backward to the pre-civilized state where the Other, the alien and the subversive, is beyond the pale, to be outlawed and demonized. In this sense, I suggest, societies can be characterized as dystopic when the prime function of the law is to define lawlessness and to segregate those inside the magic circle, who are to be placed under the law, from those who are thrust outside as enemies, demons, scapegoats. Such duality between law and lawless-ness was equally characteristic of Hitler's and Stalin's regimes. The one-party system of Germany justified its violence by its self-assigned function as the executor of the "higher" Law of Nature; in the USSR by its function as the executor of the "higher" Law of History. The leader of the party in both cases functioned as the head of the state religion, where "justice" was preserved for members of an inner circle, while those outside the circle were declared "outside the law," stripped of their rights and possessions, and deported and exterminated "justifiably," under due process of such laws.

Grossman's *Life and Fate* includes a particularly dramatic illustration of this process in the life of an old Jewish doctor, who as soon as the Germans occupy the Ukraine in 1941 finds out that from one day to another she has been stripped of her human rights. Suddenly she is treated by her neighbours and former patients in her own house as if she were no longer alive. The neighbours discuss in her presence how to divide up her furniture among themselves, and simply tell the elderly woman by way of explanation, "You are outside the law." As for "outlawing" the class enemy, Platonov's *Foundation Pit* presents memorable scenes of how all the peasants stigmatized as "kulaks" are stripped of their property and rights, and entire communities, young and old, men, women, and children, are sent without food and warm clothing to almost certain death in Siberia. Both victims and onlookers watch passively this process of "revolutionary justice" as if witnessing the enactment of the Law of History.

The ideology that introduced the notion of the racially inferior in Germany or of the class enemy in the USSR acted like a myth to justify depriving large groups of citizens of the protection of the law. In both cases people were designated victims by birth. Had one been born "racially inferior" in Hitler's dictatorship, or a child of the bourgeoisie, the kulaks, or cosmopolitan "class enemies" under Stalin's rule, there was simply nothing one could do to change that status. The continuous sacrifice of ever more scapegoats and the identifying of ever more categories of scapegoats as "enemies" were essential to the state machinery.

THE ROLE OF THE TRIAL IN THE STATE RELIGION

In fact, all six classic examples of dystopian speculative fiction – *We*, *Brave New World*, *Nineteen Eighty-four*, *Fahrenheit 451*, *Player Piano*, and *The Handmaid's Tale* – take us into a world that, we are shocked to realize, is ruled by a primitive religion based on human sacrifice, a clear regression to a pre-civilized, quasi-mythical state. The primal scene of each particular state religion is acted out as the theatre of a recurring ritual: an imaginary crime has been committed in the past by a variety of real or entirely fictitious "enemies," and the same crime fixed on an ever-widening circle of scapegoats calls for recurring acts of retribution by forces of the "Saviour" or "Messiah," the head of the dictatorship. In Oceania this primal scene is acted out in the annually scheduled Hateweeks, and on a daily basis in the ritual of the "Two-Minute Hate." The public trials, with their surreal air of phantasmagoric charges and even more phantasmagorical confessions, fulfil the same function.

Except for transplanting the surreal practices of totalitarianism from the USSR to England, Orwell here does not really take the liberty of exaggeration or distortion that often denotes the imaginative leap of satire. Like medieval morality plays or theological debates staged by the Inquisition, the trials in the USSR had indeed the combined function of religious theatre, political propaganda, and psychological safety valve, releasing the frustration of the masses, who, in the words of Koestler, were no longer allowed to "judge" events by their own individual assessment but were encouraged to "condemn" the enemy already sentenced to be executed. Historically, "the purge trials of the 1930s were not only devices to rid Stalin of real and suspected enemies, but also dramatized rituals familiar from revolutionary experience. In the Civil War, the authorities had staged trials in absentia of Karl Liebknecht and Rosa Luxemburg, of literacy, the louse, drunkenness, kulaks, landlords, Mensheviks, Christian and Jewish gods, and venereal disease. In the mock trial of the White leader Baron Wrangler, the actor was made to confess, tell conflicting stories, and help convict himself in the presence of 10,000 veterans of the Red Army."[22]

It is as if the sheer repetition of trials and executions was to convince the masses – all of them potential accused – of the legitimacy of the regime as an organized, and therefore also civilized, machine. At the same time, the chain-reaction of show trials in the thirties and early fifties also acted as a continuous warning that if even yesterday's leaders of the Party could be accused, tried, and executed, nobody could feel safe – a psychology of terror also well illustrated in the novels dealing with dystopic societies in Eastern and Central Europe. Ribakov's *The Children of the Arbat*, Koestler's *Darkness at Noon*, Tertz's *The Trial Begins*, Grossman's *Life and Fate*, and Andrzejewski's *The Inquisitors* render the nightmare atmosphere of purges, trials, and mass arrests with a compelling force that combines the power of documentary with the passion of imaginative fiction, bearing witness to a society "as is" and "as it should not be."

TOTALITARIANISM: ADVANCED SCIENCE
AND THE BARBARISM OF THE STONE AGE

Underlying this duality of law and lawlessness in totalitarian dictatorship is the duality of modern methods of technology and the regressive acts of a pre-civilized, prehistoric mentality. It has been observed, for example, that at the beginning of his regime Hitler delighted in evoking in the population a shocking sense of regression: while boasting of the most advanced war technology, he reverted to having his opponents beheaded with an axe – a conspicuously medieval form of punishment, no doubt to create the shock effect of the barbaric, the archetypal power of the state as a cruel father. In his *Repentance*, an incisive film satire rendering the dictator's personality as a composite figure of Stalin, Mussolini, and Hitler, Georgian director Abuladze emphasizes the contrast between the sophisticated intelligentsia in Grusia and the Stone Age appearance of the helmeted, club-wielding state police who come to drag victims away from their homes.

The propensity of Nazism to combine the most advanced technology with regression to a prehistoric, barbaric past was observed by Orwell in 1941, when he pointed out that H.G. Wells's "equation of science with common sense does not really hold good. The areoplane, which was looked forward to as a civilizing influence but in practice has hardly been used except for dropping bombs, is the symbol of that fact. Modern Germany is far more scientific than England, and far more barbarous." Orwell makes it clear that there is no point in looking for a "rational" or "common sense" explanation of political behaviour in an age of fascism. No doubt, "much of what Wells has imagined and worked for is physically there in Nazi Germany. The order, the planning, the State encouragement of science, the steel, the concrete, the aeroplanes, are all there, but all in the service of ideas appropriate to the Stone Age."[23]

But Wells's prophecy about a sensible, hedonistic utopia, Orwell asserts, is contradicted not only by the Nazis but also by the Bolsheviks, who did not introduce "a Wellsian Utopia but a Rule of the Saints, which, like the English Rule of the Saints, was a military despotism enlivened by witchcraft trials."[24]

The regression to the barbarism of the Stone Age or to the medieval spirit of "witchcraft trials," purges, deportations, and executions draws upon psychic forces in our "enlightened" twentieth century, where, Orwell finds, "creatures of the Dark Ages have come marching into the present, and if they are ghosts they are at any rate ghosts which need a strong magic to lay them."[25] Although none of the six classics of speculative dystopias deal with this directly, historically the essential nature of totalitarian dictatorship expresses itself in the con-centration camps, where the scientific methods of our modern age are combined with the most regressive psychic forces of barbarism.

In *On Revolution* and *Totalitarianism* Hannah Arendt suggests that series of wars, revolutions, and civil wars create a spiral of violence and coercion, giving birth to totalitarian dictatorship. Born from violence and determined to perpetrate it by law, totalitarianism fulfils its essential nature in its glorification and justification of the ultimate violence, the concentration camp.

Orwell's anatomy of totalitarianism certainly agrees with Arendt's; still, in spite of showing that the torture chamber in Room 101, a place "as deep as it was possible to go," constitutes the very essence of the totalitarian regime, *Nineteen Eighty-four* does not deal with the camps behind the Ministry of Love. Among the six works here examined it is probably Margaret Atwood's *The Handmaid's Tale* that comes closest to alluding to a particularly harrowing aspect of the psychological degradation of concentration camp inmates. In the theocracy of Gilead – a regression to the barbarism of a theocracy from the Middle Ages – the depersonalized women of the community are allowed, at regular intervals, to become executioners, tearing apart a randomly selected scapegoat thrown in their way by the military elite, at the periodically recurring rituals of "salvaging." Clearly, acts of terror are no longer a means to an end; they have become the very language in which the elite in power addresses the population. But the full cycle of totalitarianism, which finds its essential expression in the camps as a prototype for the rest of the population, who are made to feel that resistance is impossible, is illustrated most fully not in speculative fiction but in works offering the historical veracity of realism, such as Vassily Grossman's description of both Soviet and German camps in *Life and Fate*.

WHY DO THE MASSES SUPPORT DICTATORSHIP?

How can we explain the precondition of this regression, the mass support of both Hitler and Stalin, without which they could not have stayed in power?

Orwell considered it one of the greatest traumas of our civilization that the modern individual has lost faith in personal immortality.[26] As a result, we are left with a vacuum, a psychological need that may easily be filled by the totalitarian ideology's promise of collective immortality. People are drawn to the security offered by belonging to the community, to the implicit promise of sharing in a collective immortality.

It is this yearning for belonging, suggests J.L. Talmon, that explains the motivation of the multitudes to accept totalitarian dictatorships. However, he argues, we should realize that "the yearning for salvation and the love of freedom" cannot be satisfied at the same time. In order to reject the seductive power of ideology, with its promise of a "final resolution of all contradictions and conflicts," we have to keep in mind the "incompatibility of the idea of an all-embracing creed with liberty."[27] In their dystopian novels Zamiatin, Huxley, and Orwell present the totalitarian state as a primitive state religion that can exert its power over the true believers because of their initial need to find a framework for human continuity in the face of death.

As Lifton points out, in a totalitarian system "there is an overall assumption that there is just one valid mode of being – just one authentic avenue of immortality – so that an arbitrary line is drawn between those who do and those who do not possess such rights."[28] O'Brien's explanation of the slogan FREEDOM IS SLAVERY confirms Lifton's observation that "collective relationship to immortality depends upon its collective denial to others." O'Brien explains to Winston that only those who give up their individuality to "enslave" themselves to the collective body of the Party can hope to achieve this privilege, the "freedom" of partaking of the Party's immortality. By contrast, for proles and other outsiders, their seeming "freedom" from Party surveillance – "Proles and animals are free" – is simply a sign of their true slavery.

That the entire concept of immortality is related to exclusion, the branding, the eventual scapegoating of the outsider, is also noted by Mircea Eliade, who points out that early cultures made a sharp distinction between "sacred space" and "unknown and undetermined space," which they saw inhabited by "demons, ghosts, and foreigners."[29] Totalitarianism goes back to this fundamentally atavistic distinction between the in-group and the outsider. In Zamiatin's *We* the outsider held in contempt is the half-savage inhabitant of the free world outside the glass dome of the cities of the One State. In Huxley's *Brave New World* these outsiders are the people of the Reservation outside the World State. However, it is in *Nineteen Eighty-four* where the pattern of totalitarian scapegoating and its function in the mass rituals of state religion is worked out in greatest detail. It is by scapegoating Goldstein and his alleged cohorts that the Inner Party succeeds in whipping up hatred for "Satan," and then converting this hate into adulation of Big Brother as "Saviour."

In the dystopic societies of *Fahrenheit 451*, *Player Piano*, and *The Handmaid's Tale* the ruling elite no longer desire to evoke in citizens a belief in a party's immortality, or in a quasi-eschatological system of a particular ideology; they confine their activities to evoking fear in the population that anyone could be pushed into the circle of the outsiders.

WHAT DYSTOPIAN FICTION DEFINES AS A GENUINELY DYSTOPIC SOCIETY

In searching for a definition of a dystopic society, dystopian fiction looks at totalitarian dictatorship as its prototype, a society that puts its whole population continuously on trial, a society that finds its essence in concentration camps, that is, in disenfranchising and enslaving entire classes of its own citizens, a society that, by glorifying and justifying violence by law, preys upon itself. Like a dysfunctional family that maintains its framework but is unable to fulfil its function to advance the good of each member of the family, who would, in unison, form a community, dystopian society is what we would today call dysfunctional; it reveals the lack of the very qualities that traditionally justify or set the *raison d'être* for a community. As a result, dystopian society is ultimately a moribund, death-bound society that is incapable of renewal, where the ruling elite cling to their existence as parasites on their own people, whom they devour in the process.

Of course, what has been asked about Orwell's literary treatment of totalitarianism in *Nineteen Eighty-four* could also be asked about Arendt's political analysis: How could a system like totalitarianism survive if it is based on a continuous need for an inexhaustible supply of scapegoats until it literally devours itself? Arendt anticipates this question in pointing out that after the First World War, totalitarian mass movements emerged in several countries, but fully totalitarian regimes could develop only when the supply of victims appeared to be inexhaustible: millions within the Soviet Union, and millions combined from Germany and the occupied countries: "Only where great masses are superfluous or can be spared without disastrous results of depopulation is totalitarian rule, as distinguished from a totalitarian movement, at all possible." Consequently, Arendt points out, the "danger is not that they might establish a permanent world. Totalitarian domination, like tyranny, bears the germs of its own destruction. Its danger is that it threatens to ravage the world as we know it – a world which everywhere seems to have come to an end – before a new beginning rising from this end has had time to assert itself."[30]

All six dystopian novels of speculative literature make an attempt at a more or less comprehensive understanding of ideological thinking that shapes and lends legitimacy to total state control so that they can warn against such developments in their own society. In each novel the essential goal of the state is to control not only the political behaviour of human beings and every aspect of their political actions but also to enter what Orwell called the "few cubic centimetres" within the skull: the total domination of thoughts and feelings. Although none of these six novels includes direct reference to concentration camps, ultimately each regime aims at reducing human beings to inmates, deprived of free will, of a private consciousness and conscience, of any sense of justice.

The dystopian works we have selected from the USSR, Poland, Czechoslovakia, and Hungary, written under dictatorship, seem less

bent on providing a comprehensive analysis of the dynamism of totalitarianism and more interested in the dramatic rendering of a particular
aspect of their authors' lived experience in a society "as is" and as it
"should not be."

Nevertheless, whether we look at the six novels that warn against the
nightmare state of the future or at the fiction from Eastern and Central
Europe written during the nightmare of totalitarian dictatorship, it
becomes clear that all these novels deal with the prototype of the totalitarian state, whether in its full force or in a period of its decline. And
all these novels reveal that at the heart of this dystopic society is the
radical and deliberate reversal of the utopian pursuit for justice.

Questions about the deliberate miscarriage of justice take centre-
stage in the dystopian fiction of Eastern and Central Europe; they
emerge as more vital issues than love between man and woman, parent
and child, the personal relationships between human beings. To find
justification in the Law of History for the regime's organized injustice
is a crucial issue for Rubashov in *Darkness at Noon*, where he goes
through a serious soul-searching while waiting for his trial and execution. A prominent member of the Party, he was willing to denounce
and sacrifice others in the interest of the Party; now it is his turn to be
sacrificed. Where did he go wrong? By following what he believed to
be the Law of History, did he offend against a concept of justice that
is at once universal and deeply personal to all human beings? Krymon
in Grossman's *Life and Fate* and Zugyin in Rodionov's *Chocolate* are
faced with a similar dilemma, and we could find many more examples.

Characters in Zinoviev's *The Radiant Future* argue endlessly whether
the deliberate miscarriage of Soviet justice over long decades can be
explained mainly by the harshness or vagaries of historical circumstances or as an essential, organic feature of the Soviet regime from
the beginning. Central to all these discussions, all this soul-searching,
is a passionate commitment to the utopian ideal of justice, as if the
chances of socialism in the sweep of historical forces were a matter of
humanity's salvation or damnation.

To shed more light on what is at stake in contemplating these secular
concepts with that quasi-religious intensity that is so typical of the
dystopian fiction of the twentieth century, let us go back to some of
the nineteenth-century precursors of utopian-dystopian thought.

CHAPTER TWO

Nineteenth-Century Precursors
of the Dystopian Vision

We have suggested that in the secular modern age beginning with the Enlightenment, the Christian drama of salvation and damnation by deity was transposed to the conflict between a utopian "salvation" and a dystopian "damnation" by means of history. This transposition was already visible in the intensity of utopian hopes awakened by the French Revolution and the 1848 democratic revolutions, and in the reversal of these hopes into disillusionment and cosmic despair upon the revolutions' failure or defeat. This reversal formed the psycho-historical background to Romanticism in England and on the Continent. (The twentieth-century parallel to this process is manifest in the intensity of a world-wide hope in socialism inspired by the Russian Revolution, and in the reversal of this hope into disillusionment and despair following the failure – noticed by many only step by step – of that utopian experiment). Ironically, it is precisely the Enlightenment's transposition of the originally cosmic, spiritual drama of salvation to the secular, historical arena that now lends a quasi-religious intensity to the contemporary contemplation of history. It is this push and pull between secular and religious notions when contemplating history that marks the nineteeth-century precursors of twentieth-century dystopian fiction. Imre Madách's *The Tragedy of Man* is a case in point.

ADAM AND EVE'S JOURNEY THROUGH HISTORY:
THE TRAGEDY OF MAN

Written in 1860 in Hungary, *The Tragedy of Man* is one of those curious late Romantic verse dramas where theology, biblical studies, and the scientific, and consequently secular, philosophy of the modern mind are almost seamlessly intertwined. The play commences with a scene in Heaven, where the Creator debates the fate of Man with the

great naysayer, Lucifer. In the next scene Lucifer appears to Adam and
Eve and causes their expulsion from Eden. As if to display to fallen
man the fruits of the Tree of Knowledge, in the next twelve scenes
Lucifer takes Adam on a dream-journey through history. At the end,
to complete the biblical framework, Adam awakes from the nightmare
of history and returns to Eve outside the gates of Paradise.

Although often staged (according to prominent director Sándor
Hevesi's suggestion)[1] as a medieval mystery play, I suggest that *The
Tragedy of Man* is essentially a Romantic precursor of the dystopian
fiction of the twentieth century: it is speculative fiction, including a
trip into the future (it even includes space travel); it demonstrates the
continuous interaction between utopian and dystopian perspectives in
the numerous political dreams of Messianism that inevitably turn into
the nightmares of dictatorship; and it introduces a consistently compelling parallel between the eschatology of salvation and damnation
and the secular, political images of utopia and dystopia.

The play reflects political disillusionment during a period of conservative oppression that followed the defeat of the 1848 Hungarian War
of Independence, one of the many defeated or betrayed democratic
revolutions of the period. Just as significantly, it reflects the wider
philosophical-theological issues of the Romantic cosmic revolution.
Whether Blake was right in assuming that, in writing *Paradise Lost,*
Milton subconsciously must have been "of the devil's party," what
Milton most explicitly had set out to do was "to justify the ways of
God to Man." By contrast, Goethe's Faust, and Byron's Manfred and
Cain refuse to justify God's authority to forbid Man the Tree of
Knowledge; in the company of these romantic rebels, Adam, the hero
of *The Tragedy of Man,* expresses no sense of guilt for having succumbed to naysayer Lucifer's temptation and partaken of the forbidden
fruit. Going even further, by making Lucifer accompany Adam on his
trip through history, Madách embraces Lucifer's very "spirit of negation," appointing him an essential player not in the struggle between
good and evil but in the dialectic between affirmation and negation in
the enfolding process of history. In fact, when Madách's Lord announces
that Lucifer's "cold knowledge and negation will / Become the yeast
to make man's spirit still / Ferment and deviate," Adam absorbs the
energies of the naysayer with impunity.

Although Madách struggles valiantly to reconcile Man's historical
destiny with the biblical framework, I would suggest that the Scriptures
are used here in an essentially figurative way, as if to justify, or even
raise to the power of mythology, the relatively new "religion of humanity" as formulated by the Enlightenment and carried on by the Romantic

movement. From the beginning of the play we see the Lord as a distant, Newtonian creator, who, once he produced the clocklike machine of the world, is ready to withdraw: the first lines of *The Tragedy of Man* announce this distance emphatically: "The giant structure is completed, yes! / The engine turns, while the Creator rests." Also, Adam is unlike Goethe's Faust or Byron's Manfred in being engaged neither in personal battle with, nor in passionate search of, God. He is engaged exclusively in exploring the dilemma of human nature in the arena of history.

The questions Madách raises about the goal of existence in the interaction among the Lord, Adam, Eve, and Lucifer clearly create a religious framework. But does this framework alone guarantee a religious solution to a religious dilemma?

Both Northrop Frye and George Steiner have observed that in an age of faith there is no room for tragedy: Creation, Original Sin, Redemption, and Paradise Regained form a compelling proof that what God has planned for humanity is ultimately a Divine Comedy, with an assuredly happy ending. By contrast, Adam's journey in *The Tragedy of Man* is genuinely tragic. Adam feels no sense of sin and no fear of hell. Most significantly, except for one fleeting remark made by Eve, the play does not hold out faith in a Messiah or Redeemer, or in an afterlife, for that matter. (It is a serious misconception when in certain performances of the play some directors have felt it necessary to introduce the Virgin Mary[2] into the last scene.) Adam does battle without the reassurance of eschatology. His ambition to go through the historical struggle and advance the cause of humanity is juxtaposed to the possibility that the sun might be cooling off and humanity might regress to a primitive, bestial state, engaged in a ruthless battle for survival (a notion anticipating Darwin's concept of the survival of the fittest as the most ruthless members of the species). It is in its juxtaposition of the individual's high aspirations and overwhelming, inevitable disaster that *The Tragedy of Man* anticipates the catastrophism of Capek, Kafka, and Witkiewicz, the dark historical diagnosticians of Eastern Central Europe in the first half of the twentieth century. Unlike these, however, Madách's vision is not absurd; it is genuinely tragic in asserting the value and nobility of Adam's striving, even in the midst of his suffering and frustration.

The staging of such a complex play as effective theatre has posed several obvious dilemmas. Mystery play or tragedy? Religious drama or a secular contemplation of history? What should be the interaction between the biblical framework (in scenes 1, 2, and 15) and the more concrete historical texture of the scenes between? These questions find their answer if we follow the consistent dialectical pattern of high aspirations alternating with disillusionment suggested by Madách in the historical scenes.

In Egypt, Adam is Pharaoh, who makes millions of slaves toil and die building the pyramid for his eternal glory. Eve appears as the beautiful wife of a slave tormented to death; it is she who draws Pharaoh's attention to the injustice of millions dying for one. By contrast, in the next scene in Athens, Adam appears as Miltiades, the heroic general ready to sacrifice his life for the multitudes. But the multitudes are fickle: they denounce him as a traitor and take his life.

The next scene takes us to Rome during its decline: the disillusioned Adam is Sergiolus, a Roman playboy, and Eve is his companion in pleasure, a prostitute. But hedonism is not a satisfactory answer to the questions of existence; faced with the plague and the appearance of St Peter as a Christian preacher, the hero expresses his desire to pursue higher spiritual aspirations by becoming a Christian.

According to the consistent dialectic between aspirations and disillusionment, the next scene takes us to Constantinople, where Adam appears as Tancred, the triumphant Christian hero returning from the Crusades. But now the character of the Apostle Peter, representative of the spirit of Christ in the previous scene, appears as a fanatical preacher expressive of the cruelty and pettiness of the Church as an institution; he is ready to burn those whose form of belief the Church declares a heresy.

Disillusioned by the abuses of the religious ideal, Adam now appears in Renaissance Prague as Kepler, the scientist. But in the corrupt and callous court of the Habsburgs, the great scientist is an object of ridicule. In his despair he wishes himself into an epoch with higher aspirations; consequently, in the next scene of Kepler's dream, Adam appears in Paris as Danton, inspired leader of the French Revolution. He is idolized by the crowd as long as they know him as an orator urging them to the execution of more and more traitors. But when he reveals sympathy for Eve, now one of his aristocratic victims, the angry mob turns against him. Danton himself is led to the guillotine as a traitor.

Undoubtedly, the scene of the French Revolution is a precursor of the dystopian impulse. When Danton announces "Liberty, Equality, Fraternity!" the crowd echoes: "And death on those who fail to recognize them" (Scene 9.1–2). Here, and not in original sin, is the crux of the dilemma of human nature: high ideals are diametrically reversed by the mob's willingness to bring hatred, injustice, and cruelty into the methods of fulfilling these ideals.[3]

Still, Adam draws a conclusion from this episode that is unique among his commentaries on each stage of his journey through history. In spite of the bloodshed and mass hysteria of the Reign of Terror,

Adam upholds the ideals of the French Revolution: "What mighty visions were before my eyes, / All but the blind could see and realize / The godly spark, covered by blood and mire: / How great they were in virtue, sin and ire!"

It is this nostalgia for the ideals of a democratic utopia, and not the religious hope for Paradise Regained, that forms the emotional centre of the play. It is probably by emphasizing the emotional intensity of this scene, which so well supports its philosophical content, that the play has been staged most effectively: in fact, in a Prague production in 1892, this was the scene that sparked a revolutionary demonstration that ended in the authorities' banning of the play.

Still searching for the ideals of Equality, Fraternity, and Liberty, in the next scene Adam appears in the London of the Industrial Revolution, the Vanity Fair of capitalism, where the owners of the factory exploit the worker, the worker turns to drink and crime, and where everything, even love, is for sale. Madách here foreshadows Marx's metaphor of the self-destructiveness of capitalism: at the frenzied ending of the scene, the entire crazed Vanity Fair jump into a huge grave, dug by themselves.

To find a society that assures not only scientific progress but also the just distribution of the goods produced, Madách now takes a look at socialism – a version of Charles Fourier's utopian socialism, centred on the phalanstery. In this scene Madách also takes Plato to task for suggesting in *The Republic* that the young guardian should be separated from his mother, or that the child of guardians should be demoted to the "iron" of the lower classes if his mental powers are not sufficiently promising for the "silver" upper class. In its parody of the cruelty of "pure reason," this scene is a direct precursor of that classic of the dystopian genre, Huxley's *Brave New World*. What promises to be the fulfilment of man's utopian hopes and expectations turns out to be the dictatorship of the mass mind: Michelangelo is forced to spend his talent carving chair legs, and Plato himself is punished when caught thinking or daydreaming. Madách's phalanstery scene emphasizes the indignities implied by the rule of pure reason, the scientist engaged in measuring the child's brain capacity to determine his caste, a nightmarish society very much like those in Huxley's or Zamiatin's dystopian fiction.

In the next scene, set in the frozen Arctic, Madách takes us even further along the road of disillusionment: Adam finds that even science has proved impotent in saving humanity from the cosmic disaster, the cooling off of the sun. Food is scarce, and only the ruthless have a chance of surviving. (The scene foreshadows the bleak vision of the distant future in H.G. Wells's *The Time Machine*.) Seeing that Adam

despairs of the inevitable pattern of high utopian aspirations followed
by dark valleys of dystopian despair throughout history, Lucifer takes
him on a journey in space, to tempt him to leave the Earth's orbit: at
the last minute Adam resists this temptation. Still, he contemplates
suicide. But when he returns to Eve at the gates of Paradise, he learns
that she is expecting a child. For the sake of the unborn child Adam
is ready to enter that unending struggle for the future that is the stream
of history. However, he finally turns to the Lord for counsel. The words
he hears offer neither the historical hope of achieving utopia nor the
theological promise of Heaven and Redemption. No wonder. The
words of the Lord are simply an echo of Adam's own words uttered
earlier in the depth of despair: Man must keep on striving; our destiny
is fulfilled in the endless process of striving, not in the reaching of any
particular goal.

An evocative commentary on the loss of Paradise, the play offers no
hope for regaining Paradise in any of its dimensions except, temporarily, through romantic love, through the cultivation of memory, and
through poetry. In her role as the Eternal Feminine, Eve is the guardian
of the memory of Paradise: "And I shall build a bower like the one /
We had before; and so I shall bring back / Our lost Garden of Eden"
(scene 3.5–6). To Adam, in her various incarnations throughout the
play Eve is not only the reminder of but also the personification of
Paradise, almost as if he has dreamed her – the personification of the
"lost Eden" as well. (Madách's own marriage collapsed, probably
under the tremendous weight of expectations the Romantic mythos
imposes upon woman.)

Even in this respect Madách is a precursor of twentieth-century
dystopian fiction: many readers of *Nineteen Eighty-four* have felt that
Julia is primarily a phenomenon of Winston's mind; only after he
dreams about meeting her in the Golden Country do they actually meet
and visit the Golden Country. The same could be said about Lenina's
portrayal in Huxley's *Brave New World*; she is as much a beautiful
object of the Savage's Romantic dream of love as a full-fledged character. Does Madách anticipate the twentieth-century world of dystopia,
or do, for some reason, Huxley and Orwell return to the Eternal
Feminine of the Romantic cosmos as a counterpoint to the protagonist's
dehumanized world of dystopia?

Be that as it may, Adam's feelings for Eve contribute to the continuous interaction between religious and secular motives in *The Tragedy
of Man,* which turns this late Romantic throwback to the medieval
mystery play into the precursor of twentieth-century dystopian fiction.
In spite of the biblical framework, the aspirations of the work are

secular and historical. Both the voices of the Lord and of Lucifer are voices within Adam: advocating man's task as the process of endless striving, the play focuses on the moral and psychological aspects of the religious question about the purpose of existence. It offers a primarily secular answer to the religious dilemma.[4]

The play remains a powerful reminder of the surprisingly close relationship between the heaven and hell of the religious biblical framework and its secularized version, the messianic political aspirations of utopia, and the infernal nightmare of the dystopic societies of our times. It is also a reminder that it was the Romantic movement that registered this transition most vividly, and hence created precursors to dystopian fiction.

THE GRAND INQUISITOR

In his exploration of utopian-dystopian discourse in the historical process, Madách creates a dialectical relationship between the Roman scene, where the Apostle Peter appears to introduce the new faith, and the following scene in Constantinople, in which Peter reappears as a fanatical preacher. He no longer represents the live spirit but the dead letter of Christianity; the Church becomes a tyrannical institution that burns the heretic at the stake. In this reversal Madách foreshadows another, far better-known nineteenth-century precursor of twentieth-century dystopian fiction, and the most memorable metamorphosis of the Messiah into the Dictator, in Dostoevski's "Legend of the Grand Inquisitor" in *The Brothers Karamazov*, written in 1880.

Memorably, Dostoevski's tale is built on a shocking reversal: if Christ returned to Earth, he would be killed or turned away again, and this time by the very Church that was founded to preserve his spirit on Earth. The tale is set in sixteenth-century Seville. When Christ appears, he is thrown into the dungeon of the Inquisition, and the Grand Inquisitor passes judgment on Christ's teachings, although it is allegedly in the name of these teachings that the Church rules over the multitudes.

The horrible secret Dostoevski's Grand Inquisitor reveals here is that it is Satan and not Christ who is embraced by the Church. Christ failed to obtain power over the world because he rejected all three of Satan's temptations: "You would have accomplished all that man seeks on earth, that is to say, whom to worship, to whom to entrust his conscience and how at last to unite them all in a common, harmonious and incontestable ant-hill, for the need of universal unity is the third and last torment of men. Mankind as a whole has always striven to organize itself into a world state." As an institution in the world, the

Church had to choose the emblems of worldly power, "And so we have taken the sword of Caesar and, having taken it, we of course rejected you and followed *him*."[5]

The Grand Inquisitor argues that he is ruling over men in their own interest, because "men do not really want to be free; they want to be happy. They can only be happy by giving up their freedom." According to Krishna Kumar, "what made the 'legend' so seductive was its capacity for general deployment against a much wider range of modern thought and practice ... modern hedonism, utilitarianism, liberalism, positivism, socialism and practically any other social philosophy which drew on Enlightenment rationalism and modern science."[6] Although Kumar is fully justified in drawing such a wide circumference of targets, on the whole I tend to agree with E.H. Carr that, more specifically, "the Legend of the Grand Inquisitor enables Dostoevski to air his hatred, the time-honoured Russian hatred, of the Roman Catholic Church by putting the condemnation of Christ into the mouth of one of its principal agents. In more than one passage of his earlier works he had compared Catholicism with Socialism: both strive to make a man happy by relieving him of his personal responsibility ... The degradation of mankind to the level of 'cattle,' the defence of free will not as a metaphysical but as a moral proposition, is one of the cornerstones of Dostoevski's thought."[7]

But no matter how wide or narrow we set the political resonance of the parable and its target, it must be obvious that its vast influence on literature is due to its illumination of the inevitable contrast between spirit and institution; the contrast between the Messiah and the Church forces the institution to corrupt the spirit if it wants to survive in the world. This paradigm would later express the same kind of contrast between the spirit of the socialist revolution and the Party or the state, turning this spirit inside out and twisting its concept of universal justice into the terror of dictatorship. As a result, Dostoevski's parable served as an "encouragement and ammunition to all those who sought to resist the encroachment of the modern totalitarian state – the central concern of the anti-utopians."[8]

Hannah Arendt draws attention to Christ's silence throughout the scene and to the fact that the confrontation ends "by a gesture, the gesture of a kiss, not by words." In exploring the inevitable defeat of the spirit in the hands of the institution, Arendt suggests that "the tragedy is that the law is made for men, and neither for angels or for devils," or, to put it another way, "that absolute goodness is hardly less dangerous than absolute evil" when it comes to the political realm where people should be able to use "the language of persuasion, negotiation and compromise." The defeat of Christ in this scene, then, is not due to the weakness of the good in the world, since "goodness is strong, stronger perhaps even than wickedness, but that it shares with 'elemental evil' the elementary violence inherent in all strength and detrimental to all forms of political organization."[9]

Picking up on this same detail, George Steiner also feels that "the Dostoyevskijan position is gathered into the silence of Christ; it is realized not in language, but in a single gesture." Steiner considers this gesture a tragic admission of powerlessness in the world: "the kiss which Christ bestows on the inquisitor [is] something of an evasion."[10]

Three of our dystopian satires, *We*, *Brave New World*, and *Nineteen Eighty-four*, allude to this tragic confrontation in the climactic scene of the protagonist's trial, where he confronts the "Grand Inquisitor" of the state religion.

It is probably typical of Huxley, as a practitioner of Menippean satire, primarily a satire of ideas, that in his rendering of the scene in the confrontation between the Controller and the Savage, the Savage happens to be brilliantly eloquent, and at least as verbal as his opponent.

Zamiatin, by contrast, renders Dostoevski's scene in its original cast: D-503, the protagonist, is almost entirely silent at his trial, while his Grand Inquisitor, the Benefactor, explains the mystery of his worldly power in short, staccato phrases in an impressionistically rendered sketch of the Crucifixion. The Benefactor here admits he acted in this scene as an executioner, and offers a twofold justification for the role he assumed then and has been practising ever since. He is convinced of the necessity of fulfilling the executioner's role to allow the majestic tragedy designed by God to reach its fulfilment. He also argues that God himself is at least as cruel as the executioner of Christ, in making men suffer in hell for eternity. Here Zamiatin touches upon another Romantic precursor of the dystopian vision, Percy Bysshe Shelley. Articulating the essential "sympathy with the devil" of the Satanic school of English Romanticism, Shelley argues: "If the devil takes but half the pleasure in tormenting a sinner which God does, who took the trouble to create him, and then to invent a system of casuistry by which he might excuse himself for devoting him to eternal torment, this reward must be considerable." Shelley concludes by declaring that it is "God's government" that is responsible for "the exertion of the Devil, to tempt, betray, and accuse unfortunate man,"[11] and in the hero of his *Prometheus Unbound* he creates a complex image of the Romantic poet, who acts both as the satanic rebel against the sky god as well as the "gentle youth upon the cross" who will redeem humanity without violence.

Interestingly, Zamiatin reveals here the same Shelleyan contrast between the tragic goodness of Christ and the tyrannical authority of

God the Father, as if carrying on the notions of the Romantic cosmic revolution, reinforced further by the imagery of Bakunin's anarchism (based on the condemnation of any form of political authority.) In Zamiatin's interpretation, the Christ archetype in the heretic, the poet, the tragic hero, the protagonist-narrator becomes the counter-image not of Satan but of God the Father: D-503 forms an alliance with the "Mefi" rebels who proudly assume a Satanic stance in the Mephistophelian rebellion against God the tyrant. Undoubtedly, the archetype of Christ as the heretic, the revolutionary, the Promethean rebel against the sky god is also alluded to in several images related to the protagonist's lover, I-330, whose face "is marked with a cross"(53) and who becomes the martyr of the Mefi revolution against the Benefactor, "crucified" for her faith in freedom, poetry, music, individualism, and for her attack on the entropy inherent in any kind of dogmatism that stands in the way of the energies of change. This archetype also comes to the surface in the protagonist's own persona. When, after the defeat of the revolution, he is awaiting his trial, he envisages the scene of the Piéta, with the old woman with the wrinkled mouth he had met at the Ancient House in the role of his grieving mother: "And let me nail, or let me be nailed – perhaps it is all the same – but so that she would hear what no one else heard, so that her old woman's mouth, drawn together, wrinkled." (216).

As for Orwell's interpretation of The Legend of the Grand Inquisitor, Winston's trial takes place in the Ministry of Love, in the torture chamber. Winston argues for the power of the "Spirit of Man" that will break the eternal rule of the Party's tyranny; O'Brien reveals the mystery behind the Party's infinite strength as a self-renewing spiral; it is precisely the inevitable and incessant interaction between tyrant and heretic that is the principle of total domination. O'Brien's Grand Inquisitor no longer justifies himself, as the Controller or the Benefactor does: he is not saying that he also offers a self-sacrifice when he makes a sacrifice of the heretic; he no longer claims that he wants to make the multitude happy (albeit at the price of depriving them of consciousness, individuality, and the chance of exercising free will). O'Brien reveals to Winston that the naked truth is that "the object of persecution is persecution. The object of torture is torture. The object of power is power" (227). In other words, he is entirely without shame or pretensions, having no sense of morality any more. What Orwell suggests here is that modern totalitarian rule, in this instance Stalinism, no longer even pretends, even to itself, to maintain any ties with the original spirit of the Messiah in whose name it came to power.

It is interesting that all three of these classics of dystopian fiction reflect upon Dostoevski's parable by concentrating on the impasse between Christ and the Grand Inquisitor at Christ's second trial. Allusions to this parable are still present in Bradbury's Fahrenheit 451, when Fire Chief Beatty renders a cynical self-justification of his role as the burner of books, houses, and subversives, by presenting himself as the upholder of the people's peace and happiness; in the same speech he warns Guy Montag, the protagonist, about the price the subversive must pay for non-conformity. In a more skeletal form the confrontation is also acted out in *Player Piano,* in the scene of Paul Proteus's confrontation with Kroner, when the latter justifies the role of the managers and technocrats who deprive the population of their right to work, their right to human dignity. Occasional hints at the scene are also traceable in *The Handmaid's Tale,* in Offred's conversation with the Commander, who considers his own role justifiable.

Yet there is also another angle worth exploring in Dostoevski's influential parable: the responsibility of the masses who not only tolerate the dictator without resistance but also celebrate and deify him. The passage George Steiner singles out from Dostoevski's "Legend" is the Grand Inquisitor's description of the masses, their childlike need for belonging and their deep-seated fear of freedom:

Then we shall give them the quiet humble happiness of weak creatures such as they are by nature ... We shall show them that they are weak, that they are only pitiful children ... They will marvel at us and will be awe-stricken before us, and will be proud of our being so powerful and clever, that we have been able to subdue such a turbulent flock of thousands of millions ... And they will have no secrets from us. We shall allow them or forbid them to live with their wives and mistresses, to have or not to have children – according to whether they have been obedient or disobedient – and they will submit to us gladly and cheerfully ... And they will be glad to believe our answer, for it will save them from the great anxiety and the terrible agony they endure at present in making a free decision for themselves. And all will be happy, all the millions of creatures except the hundred thousands who rule over them."[12]

According to Steiner, here Dostoevski foresees the irrational frenzy of the millions who deified Hitler and Stalin: "recent history has made it difficult to read this passage ... with detachment. It testifies to a gift of foresight bordering on the daemonic ... It does foreshadow, with uncanny prescience, the totalitarian regimes of the twentieth century – thought control, the annihilating and redemptive powers of the elite, the brutish delight of the masses in the ... rituals of Nuremberg and the Moscow Sports Palace, the instinct of confession, and the total subordination of private to public life."[13]

Hungarian Frigyes Karinthy's short dystopian parable of 1935, "Barabbas," examines the same dilemma, the irrational bond between the dictator and the masses. For three days after the Crucifixion, the parable tells us, the people of Jerusalem had to suffer the consequences of having asked Pilate to spare the life of Barabbas and not that of the Nazarene. Barabbas is a robber and a murderer, and once set free, creates a reign of terror among the people of Jerusalem. When "at sunset on the third day" the Nazarene returns and the same people complain to him about Barabbas, they bitterly regret their mistake. When they are led back to the house of Pilate, Pilate asks once again:

"Whom, then, will ye that I release unto you? Barabbas or the Nazarene? And now he made a sign.
And then there arose an uproar, and the cry went forth from the multitude like thunder.
And the multitude shouted, "Barabbas!"
And they looked upon each other in great fear because each of them, separately had shouted "The Nazarene!"[14]

Karinthy returns here to Dostoevski's "Legend" with a significant variation, to point out the responsibility of the masses in allowing the fascist dictator to come to power in Italy and Germany; he also suggests that mysterious difference between the political attitudes of human beings as individuals and the political attitudes of mass man in the crowd. "And the Master became pale, and turning, looked upon the multitude. And he did recognize of each and everyone his countenance; but in the twilight of the eve, these many faces became a single one, an enormous head, which was grinning stupidly and malignantly and with impudence at his face."[15]

Here is the Savage's nightmare, in *Brave New World*, of the "interminable stream" of people with one face, as the crowd of Deltas turn against him when he attempts to liberate them. It is the same enormous head, the same stupid grin, the same impudence and malignance. It appears again in Koestler's *Darkness at Noon*, where Rubashov looks at the gloating, malignant crowd at his trial.

It is significant how often allusions to Dostoevski's parable exploring the responsibility of the masses appear in the dystopian fiction written in Eastern and Central Europe in our period. In Abram Tertz's *The Trial Begins*, at the dictator's funeral a young girl is crushed to death, together with hundreds of others, in the mad rush of the vast crowd eager to have a last glimpse of their idol. In the midst of this turmoil, hysterical voices start screaming that they should "unmask" the enemy agents hiding among them and responsible for these accidents.

In his *Makepeace Experiment* (also translated as *Lyubimov*) Tertz gives many more palpable illustrations of how easily the masses succumb to the deceptions of dictatorship. As usual on the Day of Solidarity, the population of Lyubimov waits patiently at the town square for the leader's address, because "after Comrade Tishchenko's speech, there was nothing to stop us from drinking for the rest of the day." Tertz introduces the conceit that Leonard Makepeace has hypnotic powers and can make Tishchenko ask the crowd "unanimously to elect" Leonard as their new leader. Used to this method of "election," the people immediately comply. The satirist's point is that, forced into the anonymity of the crowd, the people are so used to expressing enthusiasm by decree that they don't know or care which leader they are cheering: "Within half a minute ... isolated voices rang out in the crowd and very soon the whole multitude was stirring, rumbling and shouting its approval of the proposed resolution: 'Long live Makepeace! Long live our glorious Leonard!' – Only one villager asked who Leonard Makepeace was and how he deserved the highest of honours, but he was immediately shouted down."[16]

At this point, to dramatize the childishness of the people's traditional worship of any authority, the satirist interjects a grotesque image of the crowd as a two-month-old infant who now "bared its toothless gums from ear to ear and squealed: 'I want Lenny to be our Tsar! I want Lenny Makepeace to be our Tsar!'"[17]

In Voinovich's *Moscow 2042* – another eccentric but powerful rendering of the triangle of protagonist, Grand Inquisitor, and thoughtlessly cheering masses – the dying Genialissimo explains to Vitalij, the narrator-protagonist in the novel, why a one-man rule is still preferable to the rule of the people: "'My friend,' said the former Genialissimo sadly, 'what people are you talking about? And who are the people anyway? Is there any difference between the people, the populace, society, the mob, the nation, the masses? What do you call those millions of people who run enthusiastically after their leaders, carrying their portraits and chanting their senseless slogans?'"[18] Genialissimo concludes, just as sadly, that "it's much more difficult to convince an individual of an idiotic idea than an entire people," and thereby he justifies his own role as dictator.

What becomes apparent from most of the works of dystopian fiction examined in this study is the extraordinary resonance of Dostoevski's parable. A dramatization of a religious mystery, the parable has nevertheless inspired an essentially secular political-philosophical discourse that debates the form of government and the dilemma of social justice in the course of history.

If it is true that "the Russian novel did come out of [Gogol's] *Cloak*,"[19] it could be said with equal justice that the central dramatic situation for twentieth-century dystopian fiction in both East and West came out of Dostoevski's "Legend of the Grand Inquisitor": it is the dramatic emblem of the protagonist's trial, followed by inevitably harsh retribution, presided over by the Grand Inquisitor of the state religion, with a crowd of faceless, cheering mass men in the background.

CHAPTER THREE

The Dictator behind the Mask:
Zamiatin's *We*,
Huxley's *Brave New World*, and
Orwell's *Nineteen Eighty-four*

YEVGENY ZAMIATIN: *WE*

At first glance Zamiatin's *We* (1920) seems to be a direct continuation of the phalanstery scene in Madách's *The Tragedy of Man*, parodying the stifling of creativity in Fourier's phalanstery and pointing at the ultimate cruelty of pure reason in Plato's *Republic*. Zamiatin refers to the Dictator as a "bald, Socratically bald, man" (215), a double-edged thrust at Lenin and at the central voice in *The Republic*. The novel also continues the nineteenth century's secularized meditation about the fate of Adam and Eve in "that ancient legend of Paradise," and acts out once more that central debate between freedom and happiness introduced in Dostoevski's "Legend of the Grand Inquisitor": "Those two in paradise," explains the protagonist's friend R-13, "were given a choice: happiness without freedom, or freedom without happiness. There was no third alternative. Those idiots chose freedom [... and] for ages afterward they longed for the chains" (61). The One State, one thousand years after "our time" in 1920, is run on the conviction that the leader, "the Benefactor ... protects our unfreedom – that is our happiness" (62). But the glittering city under a glass dome, a structure reminiscent of Chernishevki's utopia with its allusions to the Crystal Palace, and even further back, of the New Jerusalem as "the city [of] pure gold, as it were transparent glass,"[1] gradually reveals that what was to shelter and protect this glittering paradise also happens to choke its vitality. By cutting off the city from the green wilderness that accommodates the world of instinct, the glass dome also stands for the airlessness of pure reason; its stifling effect is repeated in its most lethal version in the Gas Bell that happens to be the miniature replica of the glass dome both in its shape and substance, combining a "glass jar [and] the air pump" (80), a contraption deliberately designed to asphyxiate the subversive.

While the novel continues the nineteenth-century theme of the reversal between utopia and dystopia, it is also an exceptionally "timely" representation of the 1920s. In this decade the fear of the machine that turns human beings into machines is demonstrated in many dystopian works in the West – for example, in the films of Fritz Lang (*Metropolis*) and Charlie Chaplin (*Modern Times*). Zamiatin wrote *We* in 1920, the same year in which Capek wrote RUR: The idea of robots as "human beings who worked without thinking"[2] was very much present in the public mind, and was also connected with the atavistic fear of the eventual annihilation of the humanity of our species, the collective loss of our individual soul, of being reduced to mere cyphers. The people of Zamiatin's One State have no names, only numbers. The protagonist, D-503, is a mathematician and the designer of a spaceship, a true disciple of pure reason. When he is told that ten of his men died while working on the spaceship, he reacts by congratulating himself on not being "prone to arithmetically illiterate pity." He regards their loss as negligible, "less than a hundred millionth part of the population" (108). Reduced to numbers, people lose their identity and are no longer unique or irreplacable: in the world created by and for the machine, human beings become redundant. (Henry Foster, in Huxley's World State, expresses the same attitude when he casually announces that the number of people who died in a Japanese earthquake will easily be replaced in the laboratory by the same number of the same type and caste. In Orwell's rendering of a similar concept, Winston Smith, a propaganda writer, creates the imaginary figure of a hero he names Comrade Ogilvy, who from then on will assume the existence of a citizen of Oceania while at the same time thousands of victims are daily vapourized by the state; they disappear in the memory hole without a trace of having ever existed.)

At its widest Zamiatin's satirical target is universal; from a closer range the satirist targets machine worship in Russia under Lenin, who declared that the introduction of electricity would accomplish half of the task of building Communism. However, Zamiatin's most immediate target among the machine worshippers is Alexei Gastev, a mechanic and a "factory poet, who was given the task by Lenin to set up an experimental laboratory of human robotry known as the Central Institute of Labor," which functioned between 1920 and 1938. In his factory poems Gastev's "wildest visions of 1918–19 are pre-visions of Capek and Zamiatin and celebrations of a coming event often warned about in science fiction: the takeover by machines." Horrified by this takeover, Zamiatin satirizes Gastev, who "publicly praised Taylor and Ford as his models, and apparently recognized the Ford plant ... as a model for cultural transformation."[3]

Machine worship and idolization of Ford and Taylor were also expressive of the political climate. In effect, it could have been the

Soviet Union as much as America that Huxley had in mind when he made the World State in *Brave New World* substitute the name of OUR FORD for OUR LORD: "Lenin was explicit about the need to adopt Taylor-like methods of labor organization, piecework, progressive wages, scientific management and one-man control," while Stalin in the first five-year plan struck "one of the largest technical import deals" with Ford." With the parts, the tractors, and the engineers came also the ideas and values that had made Ford the auto king and the symbol of colossal productivity ... To some Ford's conveyor belt was not only the model for the factory but for society as well."[4]

Like a factory, the society of the One State runs according to Taylor's Table of Hours, and it is the spirit of Taylor, that mania for mathematical order and logic that insists on translating the immeasurable into the measurable, that comes to control Eros (by dedicating exactly one "Personal Hour" to sexual pleasure), as well as to rein in Pegasus by declaring that poetry is to be "used" for propaganda tasks. In the entire cultural heritage of mankind, the narrator finds the twentieth-century Railway Guide "the greatest literary monument to have come down to us from ancient days" because it anticipates the beauty of Taylor's Table of Hours, and he compares R-13, the state poet, to Columbus, for versifying the multiplication table.

Zamiatin's focus on the role of poetry is clearly meant as a satire of Lenin's insistence that the energies of poetry and literature must be harnessed into the service of the state, a narrow utilitarian approach that is paralelled by Lenin's intolerance of any opposition. In the One State the poet, the representative of the creative spontaneity of our mind in society, always in search of new ways of thinking and seeing, is reduced to a mindless civil servant, designated to sing the praises of the dictator in "Daily Odes to the Benefactor," to legitimize the execution of subversives, and to versify court sentences and such mundane pieces of propaganda as "He Who Was Late to Work" or "Stanzas of Sexual Hygiene."

Had Zamiatin intended to parody Lenin's "On The Function of Art,"[5] he could not have come any closer. He also shows the symmetry between the dictator's insistence on "extracting electricity from the amorous whisper of the waves" and on subjecting the "once wild energy of poetry" to the strictest state censorship. Of course, Zamiatin's parody here is particularly powerful because he puts these words of severe accusation into the mouth of the narrator, who at this stage of the novel is still a "true believer" and lavishes praise on the dictator for having organized the poets into the Institute of State Poets and Writers, for turning poetry into "civic service," and for practising strict censorhip, whereas in the past "it's simply ridiculous – everyone wrote anything he pleased."

In fact, throughout the novel the satirist keeps returning to the poet as the incarnation of the spirit of our creative freedom, whose very existence is regarded as a threat to dictatorship. As we can see from the more and more metaphorically foregrounded language in the protagonist's diary, the narrative device of the story, gradually D-503 himself becomes a poet, under the influence of another powerful energy the dictatorship would like to but cannot totally harness to its own purposes: Eros.

Like many other dystopian works of fiction, Zamiatin's novel reveals a process in which the protagonist, originally in a fairly prestigious position and reasonably well adjusted to an oppressive society, experiences a quasi-mystical awakening to his true self through a woman who makes him challenge the dictatorship's strict rules about sexuality. The protagonist's awakening to a new consciousness has sexual, spiritual, and political dimensions, resulting in a subversive act: in *We* he participates in a revolution; in *Brave New World* he instigates a riot; in *Nineteen Eighty-four* he joins the underground organization of the Brotherhood to overthrow Big Brother; and in *Fahrenheit 451* he starts to read and get in touch with other readers, a most subversive act in a society where books are to be burnt. As a result, each protagonist is put on trial and punished severely until he no longer poses a threat to the system.

In *We* D-503's awakening is a complex process, since the person by whom he is awakened to unprecedented sexual passion is I-330, not only the prototype of the sexually liberated *femme fatale* of the beginning of the twentieth century but also a gifted concert pianist, the centre of a circle of friends and former lovers consisting of a poet, a doctor, and a highly placed member of the secret police – all this, and she also happens to be the mastermind, the leader, and finally the martyr of a revolution against the dictator. Inevitably, falling in love with her activates all the repressed or dormant powers of the mathematician's psyche, and he undergoes a transformation instigated by the liberating power of true music, true poetry, true sexual passion for her, and political passion for the revolution against tyranny. To him this transformation feels many times like a sickness, and indeed he is told by a doctor: "You are in a bad way! Apparently you have developed a soul" (89). At the end his soul will be destroyed by the "Operation," a surgical removal of the imagination, the core of the subversive instinct for freedom.

The narrative is framed by two trials, followed in both cases by execution – a pattern I have suggested directly relevant to the dystopian society's reversal of the utopian pursuit of justice. The first trial, held on the "Day of Justice," focuses on the plight of a heretic poet who would not sing the praises of the dictator and who, it is whispered, insisted that he was a genius and called the Benefactor an executioner. A mathematician with no more than a perfunctory interest in poetry, the narrator at this point finds it perfectly natural that the subversive will be put on trial, which means first the denunciation of his crime, then his torture and "liquidation" by the Benefactor's Machine, which becomes emblematic of the murderous consequences of combining the worship of machinery with the worship of the dictator.

Of course, at a satirical level the "Day of Justice" is shown to be the celebration of Injustice, the Benefactor's tyranny. The poet, in Zamiatin's eyes, represents the natural freedom of the imagination that simply cannot function unless it breaks the "iron chains of the law" forbidding freedom. Zamiatin also condemns poets who yield up their creativity to tyranny – for example, the state poet whose function it is to denounce the subversive and praise the tyrant's Machine, and at whose voice "the fresh, green trees withered, shriveled ... sap dripping out – nothing remaining but the black crosses of their skeletons," until every living thing "was new, everything was steel – a steel sun, steel trees, steel men "(47). The character of the state poet is an allusion to Gastev, who in fact praised the "New Messiah" of the machine as "the iron demon of the age with the soul of man, nerves of steel and rails for muscles."[6] That these images relating to the new Communist Man must have appealed to Bolsheviks even before the revolution seems quite probable; in 1913 one Joseph Vissarionovich Dzugashvili, for example, decided to take the *nom de guerre* of Stalin, the man of steel.

It is in this scene of the first trial that the Benefactor makes his first appearance, "a motionless figure, as if cast in metal," with "heavy hands" and with a "slow cast-iron movement." Zamiatin is consistent in relating political tyranny to the images of iron, steel, and machinery, and relating poetry, passion, the subconscious, dreams, and revolution to the free, indomitable green world of nature outside the glass dome. The gigantic iron fist of the Benefactor, most readers would assume, must be an allusion to Stalin; ironically, however, in 1920 Stalin had not yet come to power. Rather, the image personifies dictatorship in general, whose actions follow from the ruthless "iron logic" of an ideology based on the "animation of machinery and the mechanization of man."[7]

Of course, Zamiatin was not the only one to recognize "the despotic character of Taylorism" underlying its neurotic "frenzy for order," as well as its anti intellectualism and hatred of any form of individualism. The insurgent sailors and workers of the Kronstadt commune, observing that the Bolsheviks planned to introduce the sweated-labour system of Taylor, included it in their bill of indictment of the Soviet regime in 1921.[8] To associate Taylorism and machine worship with one-man dictatorship was not that unusual at the time. What makes Zamiatin's vision unique, however, is the revelation of a profound paradox: in the guise of worshipping the enlightened and civilized world of science and the powers of reason that had cast aside the "superstitions" of Christianity, the citizens of the One State actually regressed to the worship of the Benefactor, a barbaric primitive deity whose power is based on the ritual of human sacrifice. Thus the "guardians" who function as a sophisticated secret police encourage people to denounce anyone suspect – that is, "to surrender upon the altar of the One State their loved ones, their friends, themselves" (40). But the ultimate moment of human sacrifice takes place at the altar on Justice Day, when the Benefactor's Machine "liquidates" the subversive after he has been tortured under the gas bell. Watching this ritual, the narrator feels nothing but awe for the Benefactor-executioner and for the legalized injustice of the monster state, where "I can have rights to the State; a gram to the ton." He also approves of the purgative role of the state religion, which, he admits, has retained certain beneficial elements of ancient religions. "Yes, there was something of the old religions, something purifying like a storm, in that solemnn ceremony" (49).

Of course, the politically naïve narrator's approval reveals the satirist's savage condemnation of the inversion of Christ's offering himself as sacrifice into the sacrifice of human beings at the altar of "our God, the One State" and the semi-divine Benefactor.

In the scene of the first trial Zamiatin exposes to us the recurring conflict between the One State, which reduces human beings to numbers, and the individual, who cannot or will not accept this. By this act he also establishes the framework for the second trial, which is a repetition of the same scene at an emotionally more intense level.

The second trial is the climax of the novel. The narrator has undergone a transformation; he has admitted to himself his love for I-330. At the revolutionary outburst on Election Day he carried her away in his arms, and to aid the revolution he was preparing to pass over his spaceship to her. After the revolution is overthrown and it is D-503's turn to face his own trial, he comes to recognize the Benefactor as his own cruel executioner. In this confrontation with the Benefactor the narrator is asked to denounce his accomplices, first of all his lover, the revolutionary I-330. Their dialogue is followed by his punishment: the "Operation" of fantasectomy, the lobotomy of the imagination, the destruction of his soul. Once he receives his punishment, he becomes once more a compliant assistant to the Benefactor: he is ready to participate in the interrogation, torture, and execution of I-330, not even remembering that they had been lovers. Just like Winston Smith, who is forced to betray Julia, D-503 is made to betray his lover. He also resists, but once he has his "Operation" it seems to him most natural to denounce her and take his seat next to the Benefactor. This betrayal, in both cases, is equivalent to the protagonist's losing his soul, as well as a complete loss of memory of the old self.

In the course of their confrontation the Benefactor also reveals the secret of the machinery of injustice and justifies his own role in this machinery. Like the Grand Inquisitor, the Benefactor does not deny that he has indeed taken on the role of the executioner, the one who crucifies the best, the most honest, the most gifted in society. Nor does he deny that, given the opportunity, he would assist at the Crucifixion again and again. However, he explains that as an executioner he also offers a self-sacrifice: "An executioner? ... a blue hill, a cross, a crowd. Some – above, splashed with blood, are nailing a body to a cross; others – below, splashed with tears, are lookng on ... Does it not seem to you that the role of these above is the most difficult, the most important? If not for them, would this entire majestic tragedy have taken place?" (213).

The Benefactor's role is to execute the law of historical necessity, to bring to its fulfilment the "majestic tragedy" God has designed for humanity. And the Benefactor is willing to fulfil his role in this recurring drama in the interest of the "happiness" of the multitude. Of course, he admits that his role requires that he be cruel, but he justifies himself by arguing that the God of Christianity is equally cruel: "And what about the most merciful Christian God, slowly roasting in the fires of hell all who would not submit. Was he not an executioner? And was the number of those burned by the Christians on bonfires less than the number of burned Christians?" (213).

In effect, the Benefactor simply performs an *imitatio dei*, or imitates the role of God the Father. Moreover, he also believes that his own love of humanity is actually more benevolent since he, a utilitarian philosopher, is well versed in mathematics and aims for the greatest happiness for the greatest number. It is in order to keep this majority "happy" – that is, willing to accept their slavery uncritically – that he must eliminate the poet, the subversive, the rebel – the representative of the heretic spirit of the Messiah. He does this out of an "algebraic love for humanity," and Zamiatin makes him admit that "algebraic love of humanity is inevitably inhuman; and the inevitable mark of truth is – its cruelty" (213).

According to Mirra Ginsburg, who translated the novel into English, Zamiatin's *We* is one of the great tragic novels of our time.[9] At the same time, I suggest, it is also a dystopian satire with a clear political message based on the distinction between two time-planes: the One State a thousand years after our time, and the extraterrestrial reader whose intellectual level, the narrator assumes, must be at the stage of the society that existed a thousand years before – that is, precisely at the time the novel is written.

The narrative is presented in the form of entries in D-503's diary, which originated as a piece of state propaganda: he was asked to gather inspiring pamphlets about the One State for the benefit of the inhabitants on the various planets that his spaceship, the Integral, was expected to contact and prepare for colonization by the utopian One State. Pointing at this satirical conceit, Zamiatin could ostensibly suggest to the censor that the narrative is sheer fantasy, where D-503 addresses his words to the inhabitants on "the moon, on Venus, Mars, Mercury" (20) one thousand years into our future. Of course, when D-503 speculates that the inhabitants of these planets must be functioning at the intellectual level of the narrator's ancestors a thousand years before, the reader cannot fail to realize that D-503 is speaking to "us," Zamiatin's contemporaries and Ideal Readers, in 1920.

At one point Zamiatin has D-503, ostensibly writing about his own life experience in his diary, slip into the role of the satirist, when D-503 admits that he uses the camouflage of the suspenseful dramatic adventure only to capture his contemporaries' attention and thereby communicate his bitter message safely: "like children you will swallow ... everything bitter I shall give you only when it is coated with the thick syrup of adventure" (103). This admission leads us to Zamiatin's core concept of the cure for the deadly "dogmatization in Science, religion, social life or art [that] is the entropy of thought." Poets, free thinkers, the heretics of any orthodox dogma "are the only (bitter) remedy to the entropy of human thought."[10]

In *We* this "bitter remedy" undoubtedly implies a warning: the worship of the machine, Taylorism, utilitarianism, the cold, emotionless worship of reason in the 1920s could easily lead to a totalitarian One State where the original promise of the Messiah of science and socialism would be subverted by the Deceiver, the totalitarian dictator posing as the Benefactor of his people.

Gorman Beauchamp is right in reminding us that "the satire in *We* is inclusive of much more than a specific regime or a particular revolution; it comprehends modes of thought, millennial expectations, chiliastic dogma, a mechanistic *Weltanschauung* that have come increasingly to characterize Western culture and of which Soviet Marxism is only one manifestation."[11] Nevertheless, the "red, fiery, deadly" centre of Zamiatin's satirical passion is undeniably in the lived historical experience, in the fear of seeing the live spirit of the revolution turn into the dead dogma of dictatorship, an anticipation born from the historical moment at the time of writing in 1920.

Here, in spite of the existence of two time-planes and the projection of the dystopian society into a very distant future, the contemporary "guardians" of Russia were not fooled by what the immediate target was. On the basis of a few public readings *We* was recognized to be a powerful satire of the regime and promptly denied publication. It first appeared in Russian in 1927 in an émigré journal published in Czechoslovakia, without the writer's consent. In 1929, at the consolidation of Stalin's power, when the Benefactor and his death machine "became too readily recognizable as living, immediate realities ... the hounding of Zamiatin rose to a fever pitch."[12] With the intervention of Gorky, Zamiatin received Stalin's permission to leave Russia for France in 1931. The novel, first published in English in 1924, had a greater effect on Western readers – although this, too, restricted to a small circle – than on those extraterrestrial readers on "Venus, Mars, Mercury" in the Russia of the 1920s, to whom its warnings were most specifically addressed.

ALDOUS HUXLEY: *BRAVE NEW WORLD*

Like Zamiatin's *We*, Huxley's dystopia is a warning against adulation of the machine. Nevertheless, a close study of Huxley's 1946 foreword to his 1930 novel should dispel critical notions that *Brave New World* is "the most powerful denunciation of the scientific world-view that has ever been written"[13] and that, by rejecting the potential of a technological future, Huxley urges us to a nostalgic, pastoral return to utopia in the Reservation.[14]

There is no doubt that *Brave New World* – like the majority of dystopian fiction – evokes our sympathy with the protagonist who indeed finally arrives at a "denunciation of the scientific world-view." But to what extent does the fate of the protagonist express the satirist's intellectual position? Does the Savage at any point suggest that he would prefer the Reservation to the Brave New World of London 651 AF? And to what extent is the Savage the mouthpiece of Huxley's norm of sanity and good reason in the satire?

To answer these questions we begin by noting that Huxley carefully imposes a point-counterpoint structure over the entire line of the narrative, a structure delineating an extended debate conducive to a Menippean satire of ideas. The entire novel is structured so as to prepare us for the final clash between the Controller and the Savage, his opponent, at the climactic scene of the subversive's trial, as if to flex our intellectual muscles for the argument between the pros and cons, the utopian and the dystopian aspects of the scentific-tehnological world of the World State in 651 AF, a debate whose outcome is essential for setting our own directions for the future.

In this context, the narrative structure is predicated on the juxtaposition of two oppposing mindsets, those of the Reservation and the Brave New World of London six centuries after our time, in the following pattern:

Chapters 1–6: Brave New World is introduced from a bird's-eye view.
Chapters 7–10: The Reservation
Chapters 11–15: Brave New World is revisited from the Savage's point of view.
Chapters 16–17: The Trial
Chapter 18: Resolution and Retribution

The first six chapters introduce the Brave New World of London 651 AF, as it were from a bird's-eye view, without establishing the emotional or a perceptual focus that usually comes with the reader's identifying with the central character. Having no such focus, we are on our own, left to ponder the strange society in which we have landed. The first two paragraphs take us to the "CENTRAL LONDON HATCH-ERY AND CONDITIONING CENTRE," carrying the World State's motto, "COMMUNITY, IDENTITY, STABILITY." (15) Is there anything wrong with these slogans, with their unmistakable hint of a latter-day version of the triple slogan of the French Revolution and of democratic socialism: Fraternity, Equality, and Liberty? Only if Community comes to refer to the community of the anthill, Identity to being identical to one another, and Stability to eternal stagnation.

Within the Huxleyan laboratory we immediately recognize the hard metallic sheen, glassy glitter, and antiseptic whiteness familiar from the Wellsian utopia in images such as "a harsh thin light [that] glared through the windows." But is the white here a symbol of purity, as in hygiene and comfort, or is it associated with the whiteness of a blood-less, soulless sterility, with the ghostly image of Coleridge's pale "death in life"? We see further that in the laboratory "wintriness responded to wintriness" and that "the overalls of the workers were white, their hands gloved with a pale, corpse coloured rubber, [and that] the light was frozen, dead, a ghost" (15). Still, although we are somewhat shocked when we gradually find out that the "hatchery" refers to the birth process of human beings, we are not quite sure yet whether we have landed in the "good place" of utopia or in its opposite.

In fact, up to the end of this section in the first six chapters, the reader is tempted to anticipate that eventually Bernard Marx, the brilliant critic of the system, a brainy but physically flawed Alpha-plus, may emerge as our central consciousness in the novel. It is only as we see that he is an opportunist who gives up his critical stance as soon as he becomes popular in the system that we tend to change our mind about the reliability of his point of view. By not having a central guide up to the end of part 1, we are deliberately made to feel uncertain about charting the direction of the writer's course between utopia and dystopia.

In these first six chapters the reader is faced with a "cognitive estrangement," hit by the strangeness of a society of test-tube babies divided into castes according to the first five letters of the Greek alphabet, of state-enforced promiscuity and state-directed addiction to the drug soma, and of the most unabashedly hedonistic applications of advanced technology. Still, to this point it has not become clear whether the "strangeness" of this society has overwhelmingly negative or positive connotations.

The second structural unit (chapters 7–10) takes us to the Reservation to create the counterpoint: it juxtaposes the ultramodern world of London 651 AF (hypothetically the world of our distant future) and the dirty, backward, unhygienic world of the Reservation (the repellent world of our distant past). It is here that Lenina, the attractive Beta heroine, spends a short, soma-protected holiday in the company of that subversive intellectual Bernard Marx, and they meet young John, himself born on the Reservation but from a mother who is an unwilling exile from civilized London. When the couple decide to take these two back to London, both mother and son are delighted: Linda's sexual habits engendered in her birthplace scandalized the backward, violent inhabitants of the Reservation, and John spent his young life alone as an outcast, dreaming about distant London as Paradise.

There seems nothing to detain any of the characters – or us – in this backward, primitive, and violent world of the Reservation or to assume, at this point or later, that it is a pastoral world of utopia.

The third structural unit (chapters 11 to 15) takes us to London once again, but now we see it from the point of view of John, the outsider, whom the people in London choose to call the Savage. He is a sensitive, poetic young man, brought up on a stray volume of Shakespeare that had somehow fallen into his hands in childhood. Full of happy anticipation, he now greets London, the delightful home of beautiful Lenina, as the miraculous "brave new world" that the inno-cent Miranda greets in *The Tempest* after setting eyes on dashing young Ferdinand. Within a short time, however, John grows more and more disillusioned with all those aspects of this society we originally regarded as strange but neutral. With him as our emotional guide, we also recognize Brave New World for what it is, a nightmare of soulless uniformity. In his growing disgust with this society the Savage decides to "liberate" the Delta semi-morons, whom he sees as slaves to soma, by starting to throw the drug out of the window and causing a riot.

As a result of his insubordination the Savage and his friends, Bernard and Helmholtz, who participitated in the riot, have to face trial, described in great detail in chapters 17 and 18. Although at first glance the trial seems more like "a caffeine solution party than a trial" (171), and we see nothing of the fear of cruel physical punishment usually associated with such scenes in dystopian fiction, these two chapters still represent the thematic and structural climax of the novel: the subversive's trial and the dictator's revelation of the machinery of injustice at the heart of the dictatorship. In fact, at times it seems as if Huxley must have written the rest of the novel – the fictional plot often barely disguises his passion for ideas – for this opportunity to dramatize an expository debate between two philosophical voices: the voice in favour of this phantasmagorical world of live but soulless robots produced on a biological assembly line, and the voice against it. These two chapters of the trial clearly establish the thematic and structural centre of the novel as Menippean satire.

Science is not denounced per se. Instead, Huxley denounces the society where even the research scientist is prevented from pursuing his research, where only "applied science" – that is, science applied to serve the totalitarian state machine – is allowed to flourish. The story the World Controller delivers at the trial is a clear illustration of this point. To the amazement of Helmholtz, who aspires to the creativity of Shakespeare but is allowed to write only propaganda jingles, the Controller reveals that "it's not only art that's incompatible with happiness; it's also science; we have to keep it most carefully chained and muzzled [because] every change is a menace to stability ... Every discovery is potentially subversive; even science must sometimes be treated as a possible enemy. Yes, even science" (176).

As a young scientist the Controller himself wanted to follow a line of experiments different from the guidelines in the "orthodox cookery book" prescribed by the state. As a result he was tried and "given the choice: to be sent to an island, where [he] could have got on with pure science, or to be taken on to the Controller's Council with the prospect of succeeding in due course to an actual Controllership. I chose this and let science go" (178).

This is a point parallel to the Benefactor's revelation of his painful task to Zamiatin's protagonist in *We*, when the High Priest reveals the innermost secret of the dystopian state religion. Both scenes allude to Dostoevski's allegory about the Grand Inquisitor. Should the Messiah reappear, he would be a most dangerous threat to the institution of the Church originally established in his name. Just as the Grand Inquisitor justified his act of imprisoning Christ in the dungeons of the Inquisition in the interest of the "happiness" of the masses, the Controller justifies the silencing of the pursuit of truth in pure science, since "truth's a menace, science is a public danger. As dangerous as it's been beneficial" (178). Just like the Grand Inquisitor, Huxley's

Controller had also been forced to make an act of self-sacrifice; he gave up his creative ambition and chose to enslave his talent to the state because "happiness is a hard master – particularly other people's happiness" (178).

At this point the Controller gives us one of the many clues to the decoding of the satire: which trends that develop in the society of the Ideal Reader in Huxley's time (which also happens to be Our Ford's time on Earth) will prepare the world for what Huxley calls the "horror" of Brave New World? In the Controller's words, "Our Ford did a great deal to shift the emphasis from truth and beauty to comfort and happiness. Mass production demanded the shift. Universal happiness keeps the wheels steadily turning; truth and beauty can't." It is the lack of spirituality that we, Huxley's contemporaries, have come to accept uncritically: we have given up truth and beauty in exchange for the comforts and illusory "happiness" of hedonism.

At this stage of the subversives' trial the Controller's account of his own sacrifice justifies his right to sentence Helmholtz Watson, the would-be writer of Shakespearean tragedy, to lifelong exile: "Happiness has got to be paid for. You're paying for it, Mr Watson – paying because you happen to be too much interested in beauty. I was too much interested in truth: I paid too." The Controller fully understands Helmholtz's desire to choose conflict and hardship to be able to "write better" (just like Plato's Philosopher King, who was full of admiration for the tragic poet when sentencing him to exile for reasons of state). When Helmholtz asks for an island with a "thoroughly bad climate," the Controller expresses his approbation: "I like your spirit, Mr Watson. I like it very much indeed. As much as I officially disapprove of it" (179).

Had we doubts about the era in which Huxley wrote the trial scene, we could easily confuse it with an example of postmodern literature, rich in irony, parody, playfulness, and ending with the "deconstruction" of its own premises. (Of course, such a sense of confusion should by itself indicate that the ambiguities, complexities, and surprises inherent in dimensional writing probably did not originate in postmodern literature.)

The Controller, just like Zamiatin's Benefactor, justifies his role, believing that he works for the benefit of humanity and is performing a difficult task when, in the interest of Stability, he eliminates the subversive. Both Zamiatin's Benefactor and Huxley's Controller represent the predicament of the Grand Inquisitor, the only person who carries the burden of freedom in a society of happy slaves conditioned "to love their servitude." Both stifle opportunities for change and chance: their aim is to create a fully predictable, static, stagnant, ultimately moribund society. Zamiatin's Benefactor undertakes the painful task of acting as executioner to the subversive; Huxley's Controller-Inquisitor executes the subversive within himself first.

It is in chapter 17, the second stage of the trial, that the Savage and the Controller lock horns on the issues of pure versus applied science; art versus propaganda; Shakespearean tragedy versus the inane mass entertainment of jingles and "feelies"; romantic love versus state-endorsed promiscuity; and true spirituality versus the soma-induced, orgiastic state religion of "orgy-porgy." Of course, in the debate the Savage has all the lines, and we simply cannot help but watch his heroic struggle against overwhelming odds with a great deal of sympathy. He concludes his debate with the all-powerful Controller by announcing that he is ready to take all the pain and suffering of the past in order to maintain what most of us would identify as the central concept of being human, the choice of freedom over the state's deceptive concept of happiness.

"But I don't want comfort. I want God, I want poetry, I want real danger, I want freedom, I want goodness, I want sin."
"In fact," said Mustapha Mond, "you're claiming the right to be unhappy."
"All right, then," said the Savage defiantly, "I'm claiming the right to be unhappy."
"Not to mention the right to grow old and ugly and impotent; the right ... to be tortured by unspeakable pains of every kind."
There was a long silence.
"I claim them all," said the Savage at last.   (187)

Had the novel ended at this point, Huxley would have left us with the proposition that the world of the past is superior to the scientism of the world of 651 AF, and the Savage would have left the stage as the tragic hero. Equally important, Huxley would have settled the debate between Technology and Nature clearly in favour of the latter.

But the novel does not end at this point.

In the last structural unit, chapter 18, we see the aftermath of the Savage's trial, the consequences of his self-chosen sentence. Faced with a choice between two equally maddening alternatives, to stay in Brave New World or return to the Reservation, the Savage chooses solitude. He hated the Reservation and was delighted to enter the Brave New World of London, his mother's birthplace, about which he had dreamt throughout his childhood as a secular heaven or paradise. But by the end of his stay in London he has come to reject this world also. Consequently, he is in what we would call a time-warp between our distant past and our distant future; he has no place to go. Huxley makes it quite clear that by rejecting the primitive horrors of the

Reservation and the sophisticated ones in the London of 651 AF, the Savage is left in a limbo; in fact, he has no choices. Enacting his unresolvable philosophical dilemma, the Savage goes insane and finally commits sucide: "Slowly, very slowly, like two unhurried compass needles, the feet turned towards the right: north, north-east, south-east, south, south-south-west ..." (200). He is still unable, even in his death, to find a resting place between his two equally horrible options.

Contrary to Eric Rabkin's or Edith Clowes' suggestion,[15] Huxley does not end on a note of nostalgia, urging us to return to our distant past as a utopian pastoral, a Rousseauean "return to Nature." In Huxley's own words from the foreword, the Savage "is made to retreat from sanity; his native Penitente-ism reasserts its authority and he ends in maniacal self-torture and despairing suicide" (8) – not exactly a note of nostalgia or an invitation for us to follow his example.

Huxley makes it clear that even if the young man may be in many ways closer to us than are the denizens of London 651 AF, he is also a flawed human being who suffers from many of our typical psychopathologies that Huxley cannot – and does not want to – present as exemplary. Steeped in the concepts of Freudian depth psychology, the intellectual currency of his time, Huxley shows the Savage to be suffering from an Oedipal fixation; consequently, he is suffering from guilt and chronic remorse, and for Huxley "chronic remorse ... is a most undesirable sentiment. If you have behaved badly, repent, make what amends you can and address yourself to the task of behaving better next time. On no account brood over your wrongdoing. Rolling in the muck is not the best way of getting clean" (7).

At the end the Savage resorts to "maniacal self-torture"; he whips himself, and finally commits suicide. Of course, he is locked into the nightmare situation created by the monstrous future that we, the writer's generation, have allowed to come about; ultimately we can blame only ourselves for his insoluble dilemma. Nevertheless, in the light of Huxley's last novel, *Island*, which, among other things, is a utopia because it heals the protagonist of the most serious signs of the psychopathology of our age – guilt, remorse and self torture – it becomes clear that the Savage is a representative of this pathology and the reader is not invited to identify with him entirely.

Having been born on the Reservation and ostracized for Linda's unorthodox sexual behaviour, understandably the lonely young boy develops a strong Oedipal hatred for his mother's numerous lovers, as well as a passionate need for her affection. When as a young man he has a chance to make love to Lenina, the attractive young Beta woman who also falls in love with him, the Savage rejects her, ostensibly because he is full of the romantic notions he learned from Shakespeare's poetry and therefore feels repelled by the impersonality implied in Lenina's conditioning to be promiscuous because "everyone belongs to everyone else." We should remember, however, that Lenina is not following her conditioning in this instance. Although she cannot put this into words, her feelings also turn her into a subversive: she finds her feelings for the Savage quite different from those she had for others earlier, and she is also willing to take unusual risks for him. She takes the initiative by visiting the young man and risking his rejection. (As we see in the last chapter of the novel, she returns to him after his trial as if drawn to him irresistibly, even after being violently rejected.) In this scene Huxley makes us look further to shed light on something in the Savage's behaviour that may not be fully explained by the unbridgable difference between the Savage's words of love, inspired by Shakespeare, and Lenina's jingles, inspired by the likes of Helmholtz Watson.

It is at the end of this tragicomic scene, so confusing and frustrating for both young people, that the Savage receives a call from the hospital that his mother is dying. In his behaviour at his mother's deathbed Huxley reveals the psychological reason for the young man's earlier rejection of Lenina. John the Savage is locked into the childhood Oedipal relationship with his mother, a neurotic condition that keeps him unable to engage in a relationship with a woman of his own age and also makes him suffer from neurotic guilt.

Still upset by the scene with Lenina, and anguished about his mother's condition in the hospital, the Savage is hit by the "interminable stream" of identical twins with the "nightmare ... of their faces, their repeated face" (159), as they are brought to the ward of the dying for their "death conditioning," encouraged to observe the dying Linda with impudent indifference. Now, as the young man's confusion, anguish, and anger come to a boiling point, in her soma-induced stupour Linda mistakes her son for her former lover, Popé. In a jealous rage that is aggravated by his emotional turmoil, his son begins to shake her, angry to get her attention. Linda dies in his arms, and the former turmoil of the young man's emotions is transformed into violent grief and remorse. This guilt becomes intermingled with feelings for Lenina and with his childhood hatred of his mother's lover, his rival. To relieve his guilt, he suddenly transfers his attention to the Deltas by making a mental connection. In his mind the slavery imposed on Linda's mind and soul by soma is forcibly connected with the enslavement of a group of Delta adults before him, who are awaiting their weekly soma distribution. It is to "atone" for Linda's death that he sets out to "liberate" the Delta semi-morons by throwing their soma portions out of the window – that is, it is the Savage's psychological misery that makes him turn to political action, and Huxley shows that such action is, not surprisingly, doomed to miscarry.

John the Savage is clearly an allusion to Rousseau's concept of the Noble Savage, and in referring to the Deltas, the young man also echoes Rousseau's words to "force them to be free." But does this mean that Huxley advocates a Rousseauean "return to nature," or simply that he shows that the old-fashioned nobility of the Savage, uncorrupted by this society, is bound to come to a sad end here? In the context of the novel John Savage has no ties left with the Reservation: he never regarded it as his utopian destination or his spiritual home to return to.

In contrast to the political options opened up by meta-utopia, Edith Clowes argues, classics of the dystopian genre arrive at an "either/or" solution that of necessity urges the reader to return to the past and be willing to give up hope of social change.[16] I suggest, however, that if we juxtapose the Controller's intellectual argument in favour of science and advanced technology to the Savage's counter-argument, the Savage does not necessarily emerge as the winner. By giving us a convincing picture of the Savage's psychological disease, which results in neurotic guilt and remorse, Huxley also tends to undermine the validity of the Savage's political-intellectual position. By setting up a debate between two opposite poles and showing that there can be no winners, Huxley leaves the reader with a position not of "either/or" but of "neither/ nor," and ultimately with a desire to search for a third alternative. I also suggest that the urgent invitation that *we search for the third alternative* is typical of the strategies of great satire in general, and of dystopian satire in particular.

In his 1946 foreword to the novel Huxley sheds light on the responses expected from the Ideal Reader by pointing out that "the Savage is offered only two alternatives, an insane life in Utopia, or the life of a primitive in an Indian village, a life more human in some respects, but in others hardly less queer and abnormal" (7). For the Huxley of 1930, a young writer with a strong philosophical and satirical bent, the idea "that human beings are given free will in order to choose between insanity on the one hand and lunacy on the other, was one that I found amusing and regarded as quite possibly true"(4). However, when returning to the same questions in his 1946 foreword, he writes:

If I were now to rewrite the book, I would offer the Savage a third alternative. Between the utopian and the primitive horns of his dilemma would lie the possibility of sanity – a possibility already actualized, to some extent, in a

community of exiles and refugees from the Brave New World, living within
the borders of the Reservation. In this community economics would be decen-
tralist and Henry-Georgian, politics Kropotkinesque and cooperative. Science
and technology would be used as though, like the Sabbath, they had been
made for man, not (as at present and still more so in the Brave New World)
as though man were to be adapted and enslaved to them.   (8)

Clearly, for Huxley this "third alternative" would be the only sane
alternative, in contrast to both forms of insanity outlined in the distant
past of the Reservation and in the distant hypothetical future in the
London of 651 AF. And the essential feature of this sane alternative,
Huxley writes, would be the spiritual awareness that "the Greatest
Happiness principle would be secondary to the Final End principle –
the first question to be asked and answered in every contingency of life
being: 'How will this thought or action contribute to, or interfere with,
the achievement ... of man's Final End?'" (9). On this point, Orwell's
essay on "Pleasure Spots" arrives at a remarkably similar definition of
the "happiness" provided by science and industrialism: "Man needs
warmth, society, leisure, comfort and security: he also needs solitude,
creative work and a sense of wonder ... If he recognizes this, he could
use the products of science and industrialism eclectically, applying
always the same test: Does this make me more or less human?"[17]

Brave New World is not necessarily a "denunciation of the scientific
world-view," as Kumar would have us believe. As Huxley (and Orwell)
would say, humanity should partake of the advantages of science, but
since science can be used not only to enslave nature but also to enslave
human beings by turning them into machines, it should not be used
indiscriminately; science can be beneficial only if it is used in harmony
with a human being's "Final End," if it meets the test each time Orwell's
question is applied: "Does this make me more or less human?" If used
to uphold the fundamental principles of humanism, Huxley suggests,
science could be instrumental in building a real utopia, "to use applied
science not as the end to which human beings are to be made the
means, but as the means to producing a race of free individuals" (14).

As Huxley explains further, the theme of the book "is not the
advancement of science as such; it is the advancement of science as it
affects human individuals" (9). This is to say, what he objects to in the
World State of *Brave New World* is not the phenomenon of scientific
or technological progress but the dehumanization of the individual
that could – but does not necessarily have to – follow.

Of course, Huxley's and Orwell's standard of sanity is that of humanism, based on the assumption that there could be a consensus on what
the human being's Final End is, that there is universal agreement on the

question of what makes one human – concepts many a postmodern critic, sadly, I think, would have difficulty recognizing, let alone endorsing.

Yet such a humanistic norm, based on a consensus of reason, is the foundation of Huxley's dystopian satire, implying also the norm for sanity – ultimately the modern equivalent of the goal of the "good place." As he wrote in 1946, just after the Second World War had ended: "Today I feel no wish to demonstrate that sanity is impossible. On the contrary, though I remain no less sadly convinced than in the past that sanity is a rather rare phenomenon, I am convinced that it can be achieved and would like to see more of it" (8).

He is particularly careful here in describing the mental state of the rulers of Brave New World, who "may not be sane ... but they are not madmen and their aim is not anarchy but social stability. It is in order to achieve stability that they carry out, by scientific means, the ultimate, personal, really revolutionary revolution." This revolution, Huxley explains, goes beyond the political and economic revolutions to that "in the souls and flesh of human beings" (10).

This is the revolution that the "bad places" of Zamiatin's We and Huxley's Brave New World explore. Both deal with what Huxley calls "'the problem of happiness' – in other words, the problem of making people love their servitude, ... the result of a deep, personal revolution in human minds and bodies" (13). This is also Orwell's ultimate fear of the unprecedented scientific power at the disposal of modern dictatorships, their ability to alter human nature, as readily "to produce a breed of men who do not wish for liberty as to produce a breed of hornless cows."[18]

Comparing his own vision with that of Nineteen Eighty-four in a 1949 letter to Orwell, Huxley argues that his own scenario of the painless, seductive, hedonistic nature of future dictatorships is more probable. Already in his 1946 foreword he points out that in the novel of 1930 he "projected [the horror of the future] six hundred years into the future. Today it seems quite possible that the horror may be upon us within a single century" (14).

But within the universal target of the warning inspired by a tragic humanism, what is Huxley's more specific satirical target?

In his Dystopian Impulse Keith Booker suggests that Brave New World "is the classic bourgeois dystopia ... which depicts a future society so devoted to capitalist ideals that its central hero is Henry Ford." Although Booker also admits that Huxley's novel "incorporates numerous elements of Communism into his dystopian vision,"[19] he leaves the innate contradiction – a classically bourgeois dystopia, with capitalist ideals that incorporate elements of Communism – unresolved.

A closer look at the text indicates that Marxists or neo-Marxists should have trouble justifying the use of the word "capitalist" for Huxley's novel. In Brave New World there is no private property; the workers have reached a comfortable living standard and a sense of eternal well-being; no one is exploited economically (in fact, if the state wanted to, it could eliminate human labour altogether). The means of production and the goods produced are not in the hands of the capitalist: although the World State has not introduced a classless society, it has definitely eliminated class distinctions based on money or property, and has fulfilled Marx's central criterion of Communism, "from everyone according to his ability, to everyone according to his needs." (Of course, the World State is fully capable of creating a perfect equilibrium between needs and abilities in the human specimen within each caste that it chooses to manufacture on the biological assembly line, an equilibrium also enforced by early childhood conditioning. By having the World State embrace Marx's criteria and incorporate these into its nightmarish state machinery of injustice, Huxley makes the point that Marx's universal reign of justice is not at all guaranteed by the simple elimination of economic injustice, as Marx believed. Its critique of Marxism, of course, does not yet make the novel a bourgeois dystopia advocating capitalist ideals, as suggested by Booker.)

As for Henry Ford, he incidentally plays a role quite different from "a central hero"; he is the deity chosen by the World State, referred to as OUR FORD, not for living up to the "capitalist ideal" of making a great deal of money but for being the first to introduce the assembly line. This is the Fordian invention that the World State has taken over and developed to the point where human beings can be manufactured according to the state's "engineering" specifications in test tubes, that is, on a biological assembly line. As we noted in the discussion of Zamiatin's We, in the twenties and thirties Ford was also worshipped in the Soviet Union, together with Taylor, the inventor of time-and-motion studies and the Table of Hours, which created the perfect ideology for turning human beings into robots. In this sense the worship of Our Ford in the London of 651 AF is not in itself an indication either of capitalism or of Communism; rather, the World State is presented to us as a society that has fulfilled the nineteenth century's utopian dream of a marriage between science and socialism, and we are to see how sadly this dream is wanting.

In fact, Huxley's strategies borrow a great deal from the Soviet experience of Taylorism and Fordism. As he points out elsewhere, "interestingly, it is the new Soviet state, rather than America, which has shown the Fordian impulse in its clearest form ... The Bolsheviks here are only indicating the tendencies apparent in all mass democracies, to organize the whole of society according to the dictates and the image of the machine." As one reads Huxley's description of the Soviet attitude to the machine, his comments sound like a summary of *We*, including Zamiatin's satirical point about his protagonist who became "encumbered" with a soul, a serious disease in the "factory" of the One State. But Huxley's comments also shed light on his satirical allusions to the Messiah of science and socialism: "To the Bolshevik idealist, Utopia is undistinguishable from one of Mr Ford's factories. It is not enough, in their eyes, that men should spend only eight hours a day under the workshop discipline. Life outside the factory must be exactly like life inside. Leisure must be as highly organized as toil ... The condition of their entry into the Bolsheviks' Earthly Paradise is that they shall have become like machines."[20]

As for the enforced promiscuity in Brave New World, Huxley "carries out to its logical end the Bolshevik precept that 'sex should be taken as a drink of water.'"[21] Indeed, Huxley establishes a grotesque association between the leaders of the Russian Revolution and the unhampered sexuality in London 651 AF by having the Director, in the course of a lecture to his students about the benefits of "erotic play" among young children, point at a little girl called Polly Trotsky (36), and by naming the woman embodying the state-enforced promiscuity of this dictatorship Lenina.

It is also worth pointing out that having overthrown traditional religion, for OUR LORD the World State has substituted not only OUR FORD but also OUR FREUD; in fact, Huxley tells us, these two names are used "interchangeably." To appropriate the insights of depth psychology – the workings of the subconscious and the role of sexual repression in causing neurosis – is as important to the World State for its enslavement of human beings through conditioning and sleep teaching as is the application of the biological assembly line with the test-tube babies for genetic control.

I would suggest that to see *Brave New World* from its proper perspective, we should probably concentrate on its strategies as a Menippean satire, that is, as a satire of ideas. First of all, it is a satire of the two great dreams by which the nineteenth century defined humanity's utopian hope of finding redemption from the problems created by the Industrial Revolution. These dreams were science and socialism, as most clearly defined in the Wellsian utopia, a "complex mechanized society of the future run by a scientific elite."[22] In the ideology followed by Huxley's World State, the twofold dream is allowed to run its full course and turn into a nightmare by being carried to its absolute conclusion.

Huxley indicates that it was a dream that concentrated only on material progress, was narrowly utilitarian, and was hence lacking in spiritual dimension. Indeed, in the London of 651 AF we come across Marx, Lenin, Trotsky, all the great names associated with the socialist revolution (or even with revolution in general, as indicated by the name of Bonaparte). We also come across the great names in science, the physicist Helmholtz, the psychologist Watson, as well as Darwin and Freud. It seems, then, that the World State of 651 AF has fulfilled the two-pronged utopian dream of the nineteenth century. But what has happened to this pantheon of "heroic materialism" in the process? It is a society that can no longer produce, or tolerate, genius; it is a world of mediocrities at best. One has only to look at the whining, cowardly Bernard Marx, the almost totally mindless Lenina, the insignificant little Polly Trotsky, not to mention the unsavoury journalist Darwin Bonaparte and the emotional engineer Helmholtz Watson, whose creativity is thwarted by the system, to see that they are all mediocrities. Just as we have seen in the phalanstery scene of Madách's *The Tragedy of Man*, where Plato is punished for daydreaming, once the great designs for utopia have been translated into practice, the inventor-genius himself falls victim to the uniformity imposed on people by his own design. All that this "brave new world" can produce are mediocrities: there is no tolerance for the spontaneity of the creative mind once the dream of the earlier geniuses has been realized.

Plato's idea of justice also returns in Huxley's "horror" world in its cruel parody. As we may remember, Plato's definition of justice depended on the concept of harmony between gold, silver, and iron – that is, a harmony within the hierarchy of lower and higher attributes in the personality and of the lower and higher classes in society. In Huxley's world the scientist guarantees this harmony by making sure that human beings are produced genetically and conditioned through their early years to "fit" their pre-established status as Alphas, Betas, Deltas, Gammas, and Epsilons. Paradoxically, by the very act of predetermining each human being's physiological, mental, and psychological makeup, the scientist commits the gravest act of injustice: the elimination of free will and individuality, the essential components of being human.

At the same time, by deliberately applying the principle of more and more severely arrested development to produce human beings for the lower and lower social echelons, the scientist also makes use of the insight that, during its gestation, the human foetus re-enacts the evolution of the species. Once more the scientist deliberately reverses the principle of evolution into a principle of enforced retardation for the majority, in order to achieve the unchanging stability of the World State.

Still, I would suggest that what Huxley denounces here is not the tradition of utopian socialism or the scientific world-view: neither the dream of socialism nor that of science is demonstrated here as evil in itself. The society created in 651 AF is dystopic because it functions as the fulfilment of an exclusively materialistic dream, where the original goals of liberating mankind and establishing universal justice – a precondition of individual freedom – are deliberately reversed.

There is no doubt that *Brave New World*, just like Zamiatin's *We* and Orwell's *Nineteen Eighty-four*, expresses the writer's fear about the survival of our species in terms of what the humanist defines as the essential qualities of being human. All three novels present us with the paradigm of a totalitarian state as an enormous laboratory for the transformation of human nature, the birthing process of creatures no longer human. In *We* the centre of this transformation is the Great Operation of fantasectomy and the fear of the Benefactor's Machine that can literally "liquidate" – that is, turn into water – the heretic with a live imagination. In *Brave New World* the essence of the state machine is represented by the Hatchery, in which human beings are decanted at various stages of arrested development. In *Nineteen Eighty-four* the essence of the state machine is revealed, appropriately, in the torture chamber, at the last stage in Winston's seven-year trial, where he finally receives O'Brien's answer to his gnawing question: "I understand how; I don't understand why."

GEORGE ORWELL: *NINETEEN EIGHTY-FOUR*

In Zamiatin's One State and Huxley's World State, the twofold dream about the new Messiah as the incarnation of science and socialism is allowed to run its full course and turn into a nightmare by being carried to its absurd conclusion. By contrast, *Nineteen Eighty-four* shows us that the same twofold dream was deliberately betrayed by those who assumed power in its name. Although science in 1984 is sufficiently advanced to improve the lot of people all over the world, and the three totalitarian superpowers have achieved a peaceful equilibrium among themselves, the three dictators deliberately create the fiction of unceasing war between two of the three partners so that they can "use up the products of the machine without raising the general standard of living" (166). They know that dictatorships can exist only when the masses are held in poverty and ignorance. Science is used here only for perpetrating terror – that is, for designing weapons against a fictitious enemy and for perfecting psychological methods to break down the individual's private conscience and consciousness. As for the alleged goal of the socialist paradise, O'Brien, this most cynical of Grand Inquisitors, admits his contempt for those "cowards and hypocrites who pretended, perhaps ... even believed, that they had seized power unwillingly and for a limited time, and that just around the corner there lay a paradise where human beings would be free and equal." O'Brien is convinced that "no one seizes power with the intention of relinquishing it ... One does not establish a dictatorship in order to safeguard a revolution: one makes the revolution in order to establish the dictatorship" (211).

The Wellsian dream of "a future society unbelievably rich, leisured, orderly and efficient [that had been] part of the consciousness of every literate person" (166) was betrayed by the new rulers who emerged at the world crisis of the 1950s. But Orwell makes it clear that the people who allowed the totalitarian dictatorship to come to power were also responsible for accepting, even justifying, the betrayal of the dream. The power-hungry new elite was able to come to power only because "by the fourth decade of the twentieth century all the main currents of political thought were authoritarian. The earthly paradise had been discredited at exactly the moment when it became realizable. Every new political theory, whatever name it called itself, led back to hierarchy and regimentation" (177). Consequently, with the help of the new electronic technology, the Inner Party met with little resistance in enforcing "not only complete obedience to the will of the state but complete uniformity of opinion" (177). To understand Orwell's satirical target, we should recognize that throughout the novel the satirist is engaged in argument with an Adversary, the self-deceived leftist intellectual in the West, who refuses to admit that socialism has been betrayed in the USSR, and who refuses to acknowledge, or finds excuses for, Stalin's terror.

If for Huxley totalitarian dictatorship is defined by the terror of science, for Orwell it is defined by the science of terror, the systematic and sophisticated perpetration of violence directed by the Inner Party against its own people in the name of socialist ideals. Yet Orwell emphasizes that *Nineteen Eighty-four* was not intended "as an attack on Socialism or the British Labour Party (of which I am a supporter)."[23] Orwell's bitter satire of Stalin's system does not signify disillusionment with the socialist ideal, rather concern about the betrayal of this ideal. In fact, Orwell claims, "nothing has contributed so much to the corruption of the original idea of Socialism as the belief that Russia is a socialist country and that every act of its rule must be *excused if not imitated*. And so for the past ten years I have been convinced that the destruction of the Soviet myth was essential if we wanted the revival of the Socialist movement" (my italics).[24]

While Huxley gives the world over six hundred years to reach the horrors of the World State, in *Nineteen Eighty-four*, written in 1948,

Orwell's warning about the future has an urgency that relates to imminent danger. Huxley wrote his novel in 1930, before Hitler had come to power and before the Moscow trials – that is, before the full disclosure of the extent of the political terror that we now associate with totalitarianism. Also, with the emergence of the "spheres of influence" after the Second World War, Orwell had good reason to fear the threat posed by the superpowers to the autonomy of smaller countries, and to the autonomy of the individual within the giant state. At the beginning of the Cold War, Orwell anticipated a crisis among the superpowers some time in the 1950s, after which the atom bomb might act as a deterrent to further wars, so that the *status quo* of three totalitarian giants in perfect equilibrium would have to remain unchallenged. Another thing Huxley could not have been concerned about in 1930 was the curious paradox in Western public opinion in the late 1940s, known as the "Stalingrad syndrome"; many a Westerner's sympathy for the Soviet people, who sacrificed millions of lives to save the world from fascism, was uncritically transferred to the Soviet leaders, as if these were not the same leaders who were responsible for the terror within the USSR, which sent further and further millions of the Soviet people to forced-labour camps and their ultimate destruction. Orwell felt that such an uncritical transference of sympathy was tantamount to accepting, justifying, and even desiring to emulate totalitarian methods – a way of thinking he parodies in the mental disease of "blackwhite," a deliberate "falsification" of the thought process he also calls "crimestop," or "protective stupidity," all of them symptoms of the "organized schizophrenia" of Doublethink. With his increasing concern about a potential crisis, to Orwell the Western intellectuals' adulation of Stalin indicated their willingness to internalize the totalitarian mentality and betray the chances of establishing democratic socialism in the West. In such a political climate, when "the British public are wholly unaware of the true state of Russia and imagine that it is some [kind of a] workers' Utopia,"[25] Orwell believed that "the willingness to criticize Russia and Stalin is the test of intellectual honesty."[26]

If we read, with Winston, the children's history book he picks up in his neighbour's apartment, it becomes obvious that when Big Brother came to power in the 1950s, he borrowed his slogans from Stalin; as for his methods of terror and persecution, these have been clearly borrowed from both Hitler and Stalin. "Fascism," Orwell points out in argument with his self-deceived intellectual Adversary, "is often loosely equated with sadism, but nearly always by people who see nothing wrong in the most slavish worship of Stalin ... All of them are worshipping power and successful cruelty."[27]

Through Winston's fate we become fully aware of the gratuitous cruelty implied by the state religion that worships God as Power. By the end of Winston's trial through the various torture chambers enwombed within the Ministry of Love, O'Brien declares himself the Priest of Power and reveals that "the object of persecution is persecution. The object of torture is torture. The object of power is power" (227). Here Orwell's brilliant insight into the dynamics of totalitarian dictatorship that is centred in the torture chamber essentially coincides with the diagnosis of Hannah Arendt, that the "real secret, the concentration camps, fulfill the function of laboratories in the experiment of total domination." Arendt's conclusion that totalitarian dictatorship relies on the deliberate perpetration of terror as the style, "the very essence of government,"[28] is also echoed by Albert Camus, who defines the universe Stalin created under the camouflage of building socialism as "a universe of terror – terror and trial."[29]

In fact, Winston's personal predicament could be said to be acted out between two trials: the show-trials of three of the former leaders of the Party, Rutherford, Aaronson, and Jones, which Winston remembers from the 1970s, and Winston's own trial in 1984. The novel introduces Winston as a somewhat sickly, middle-aged man deeply afraid of the inevitable trial and punishment awaiting the "thought criminal." Yet, since his work in the Ministry of Truth consists of doctoring the documents of the past in order to make them agree with the ever-changing pronouncements of Big Brother in the present, he is obsessed with the need to find out the truth in a society where "everything faded into mist. The past was erased, the erasure was forgotten, the lie became truth." This is why he feels compelled to explore simultaneously the political history of Oceania and his own personal history, while he keeps dreaming about an escape into the political and sexual freedom of the Golden Country (part 1).

In spite of his fear, he goes further and further in resisting the regime that denies the individual's right to know the truth about the past, just as it denies the right to think, to feel, to write down ideas, or to create a private bond of loyalty and love. Given his fear of his inevitably cruel trial, when Winston forges a forbidden relationship with Julia and subsequently joins the Underground with her, the character of this unexceptional Everyman assumes tragic-heroic dimensions. (When, during his interrogation, he stands up for the Spirit of Man against the God of Power, he reveals the same tragic-heroic courage.)

Winston knows, the moment he opens his diary, that he is committing "thought crime" and his act cannot remain undetected by the Thought Police. Having seen in his twenties the victims of the public trials, "outlaws, enemies, untouchables, doomed with absolute certainty to extinction," Winston knows full well that "no one who had once fallen into the hands of the Thought Police ever escaped in the end" (69). Still, part 1 ends on a note of mystery: "When once you have succumbed to thoughtcrime it was certain that by a given date you would be dead. Why then did that horror, which altered nothing, have to lie embedded in future time?" Speculating about the nature of that mysterious horror, his attention wanders to the three Party slogans that are phrased like riddles asking for a solution:" WAR IS PEACE. FREEDOM IS SLAVERY. IGNORANCE IS STRENGTH." He knows all his questions relate to his desire to understand not only the methods but also the motivation for the Party's actions – "I understand how – I don't understand why" – and intuitively he turns to the omnipresent portrait of Big Brother for an answer. He is, however, confronted only with yet another aspect of the same puzzle: "The face gazed up at him, heavy, calm, protecting: but what kind of smile was hidden beneath the dark moustache?" (92).

By the end of the novel Winston will find out the answer to all three riddles, and will also find out that they are interconnected, each revealing a different aspect of the central mystery: by facing the "horror [that had been] embedded in future times" all along, in Room 101 he also finds out that the horror of the real face behind Big Brother's benevolent mask is that of the insatiable God of Power who demands the recurring ritual of human sacrifice.

Reading Goldstein's Book, Winston learns that WAR IS PEACE means that war is a pretence, a "fiction," "an imposture." After the war in the 1950s, with the help of the atom bomb that only superpowers could afford to manufacture, the modern world was divided among three totalitarian dictatorships. The perfect, unchangeable equilibrium among the three has created the precondition for world peace. However, each dictator has been pretending to be at war all the time because only continual war gives him the excuse to keep his own population enslaved, undernourished, overworked, as well as in a permanent state of fear of the "satanic" enemy and traitor, and consequently ready to worship the dictator as the Saviour. In effect, it is Big Brother – or the Inner Party that rules in his name – that acts as the only real enemy or traitor, conspiring against the welfare of his own people. To cover up for this, Big Brother wears the mask of the benevolent protector and saviour, and the Ministry of Truth fabricates the most sophisticated lies of propaganda to prove that he is benevolent and infallible. To prevent people from testing these blatant lies, the Thought Police intimidate "thought criminals" with the threat of trial and interrogation in the Ministry of Love.

FREEDOM IS SLAVERY, as O'Brien explains to Winston at his trial, means that only by enslaving his mind and soul to the Party can the individual become part of the Party's collective immortality and therefore free from modern man's anguish about personal mortality. But the last slogan, IGNORANCE IS STRENGTH, will become clear to Winston only after his final ordeal in Room 101, located in the Ministry of Love "as deep as it was possible to go" in human degradation. It is here that each individual victim is faced with the particular version of psychological pressure that his or her psyche can no longer sustain, until the personality breaks down and the victim betrays others, including his nearest and dearest. Those betrayed will, in turn, also be broken until they betray others – hence the chain reaction of betrayals and denunciations that fuels the state machinery with newer and newer victims.

To appreciate Orwell's unique achievement in combining depth psychology with political satire in his analysis of totalitarianism, we should examine the following questions: Why in Room 101 does the Party require from Winston that he offer up Julia as a human sacrifice to be devoured by the starved rats in their cage? And why are the rats the inevitable choice for Winston's final humiliation and annihilitation?[30]

Answers to these questions spring from the fact that the scene in Room 101 is, in effect, the re-enactment of a previous crisis. It relates to that significant childhood "memory that [Winston] must have deliberately pushed out of his consciousness over many years" (142), a repression that made him suffer from recurring guilt dreams and a number of psychosomatic symptoms for almost thirty years. After his "breakthrough dream," he remembers and relives this painful, shameful scene in detail, when, as a starving child, he "snatched" the last piece of chocolate out of his starving sister's hand "and was fleeing for the door ... His mother drew her arm round the child and pressed its face against her breast. Something in the gesture told him that his sister was dying" (144-5). It is the mother's protective gesture around her dying child that Winston has seen on the screen of a "flick" that triggers the first vague memory that compels him to start writing in the diary. Once he starts the process of writing, Winston also has several dreams, until the repressed memory gradually surfaces and he understands its significance. As he discusses this memory with Julia, he realizes that, although he could not have caused his mother's death – it was the Party that vapourized her – he was none the less guilty. When, in his uncontrollable hunger, the child Winston snatched away the last piece of food from his starving mother and sister, he betrayed his love for them by willing their death, as if ready to devour them to appease his own hunger. Just as important, he realizes that with Julia he has another chance to forge an emotional and spiritual bond based on private loyalty and devotion. To liberate himself from the past and expiate the guilt, this is his second chance. The lost Paradise of childhood can be regained by re-entering Paradise with Julia in the Golden Country.

Betrayal, guilt, striving for redemption, and inevitable damnation at the trial form the spiritual-psychological *leitmotiv* of Winston's story. Winston's phobia of the rats – creatures who attack sick and dying people and, when driven to madness by being starved, are willing to devour their own species – is connected with that part of Winston's own psyche that awaits behind that horrifying "wall of darkness" after the walls of the personality – the basis of our humanity – are broken down. When in Room 101 O'Brien presents him with the masklike cage of the starved rats, in his uncontrollable fear and horror Winston is forced to break through the walls of darkness, until he faces another, by now final breakdown and re-enacts his childhood act of betrayal. When he screams "Do it to Julia! Not me, Julia!" symbolically, once more, he offers up the body of the only person he loves as a surrogate for his own. By allowing himself to be degraded to the level of the starving rats, he has become what he most abhorred; O'Brien's laboratory experiment in the science of domination has been successful: Winston is turned into a will-less, obedient instrument in the hands of the Party.

Politically, Winston's capitulation was preordained by the totalitarian regime. Room 101 is at the heart of the novel because it is the centre of the psychosis of betrayal; it is here that any victim can be broken down and turned into the victimizer of others by being forced to give up his private bond of loyalty, his private conscience, his private self. Having gone through this process, Winston is ready to join in the collective insanity imposed upon the population by Big Brother, as if joining all the other starved rats in their cage. Ultimately the real face behind the masklike cage is the face of Big Brother, the God of Power. It is Big Brother himself who turns his subjects into hate-filled brutes like himself, forcing them to act out his prime betrayal as the further and further repetition of ritual human sacrifice. Winston's own final, crucial act of betrayal is some kind of horrible *imitatio dei*; in the moment he betrays his loved one, he becomes one with the godhead, acting out the inevitable yet horrible mystery, the loving union between victim and victimizer.[31] This is the horror that had to lie embedded in the future, the secret of Big Brother's horrible smile hiding behind the dark moustache. It is the smile of that cruel deity, the God of Power, who transforms his victims into his own image.

The psychological dimension of the novel does not contradict but gives vital support to the political analysis, and is indispensable to the humanistic warning: since totalitarianism is built on the self-perpetuating lies of false charges and false confessions and on the unstoppable chain reaction of betrayals in the political arena, it also leads to the irreversible disintegration of the individual's "inner heart," the core of private love, conscience, and loyalty.

The central instrument through which the Inner Party can reassert its grip over the population is the ritual of the trial. Private trials like Winston's are largely the re-enactment of the scenario established by the public show-trials of such former leaders of the Party as Aaronson, Rutherford, and Jones. Like Stalin's Moscow trials in the 1930s, these public theatricals are staged by the Party to create hatred against ever newer categories of scapegoats and, at the same time, to discourage anyone from opposing Big Brother. Working in the Ministry of Truth in the 1970s, Winston had held in his hand a document that proved that Aaronson, Rutherford, and Jones had been innnocent; they were forced to make public confessions to the most phantasmagorical charges. It is widely known in Oceania that the trial consists of being coerced into confession, but the population practise Doublethink: they know and do not accept the facts of knowing. After the defendants are broken by torture and make their public confessions, they are released, given a sinecure, and then rearrested and executed by a bullet in the back of the head. For Orwell's contemporaries these details are unmistakably allusions to the phantasmagorical fabrications of the Moscow trials of the 1930s, through which Stalin wiped out the former leaders of the Party and the army whom he considered his potential rivals for power. Orwell's point is that his Adversary engages in a potentially disastrous practice of Doublethink when refusing to acknowledge the deliberate miscarriage of justice behind Stalin's conceptual show-trials, which were followed by mass arrests and the deportation of millions to Siberia.

But the satirist also transplants the Moscow show-trials to British soil, moving them from the 1930s to the 1970s, just as he transplants Stalin's persecution of Trotsky to Big Brother's persecution of Goldstein. He also transfers "the period of the great purges in which the original leaders of the Revolution were wiped out once and for all" from the 1930s in the USSR to the 1960s in England. "By 1970 none of them was left, except Big Brother himself. All the rest had by that time been exposed as traitors and counter-revolutionaries, Goldstein had fled and was hiding no one knew where, and of the others, a few had simply disappeared, while the majority had been executed after spectacular public trials at which they made confession of their crimes." Orwell suggests here, in 1948, that the power-hungry Inner Party that came to power in Oceania in the 1950s is willing not only to condone but also to imitate the Soviet historical example, step by step, as it were, and on an even larger scale.

Symbolically, the rituals of Hate Week and the daily rituals of the Two-Minute Hate are also trials, where the Party gives the population a chance to publicly condemn those already singled out to be sacrificed by the Party, providing thereby intermittent catharsis for the under-nourished, overworked, frustrated population. The Party provides such a catharsis on a recurring basis to accomplish the emotional conversion of the people's fear and repressed hatred of Big Brother into hatred of the enemey and the traitor, and then, by the "fiat" of Doublethink, the conversion of the hysterical hatred for the Party-appointed "Satan" into hysterical "love" for Big Brother, the Saviour. The best illustration of this process is the Hate Week demonstration at Victory Square, when the Party decides to switch the enemy in the middle of the expressions of orgiastic hatred; the hate goes on, as if the population did not even notice the switch – as if, indeed, they were not interested in whom they are asked to hate, condemn, destroy.

The ritual arousal of hate at these various trials assumes the barbaric connotations of the medieval witches' trials and the mass hysteria of witch-hunts. The forced confessions of the "traitors" and "heretics" in Oceania reveal the same clichés, the same blatant disregard for the physical rules of the natural world, the same sense of "sur-realité revealed by an imaginary universe"[32] as the confessions obtained by medieval witches' trials. At the trial of Rutherford, Aaronson, and Jones, Winston observes, "very likely the confessions had been rewrit-ten until the original facts and dates no longer had the smallest significance" (71). When Winston wants to terminate his own torture at the Ministry of Love, he repeats all the same grotesque clichés, admits to all the "crimes" impossible for anyone to have committed, that he knows to be associated with the vocabulary of deviation: "He confessed to the assassination of eminent Party members, the distribu-tion of seditious pamphlets, embezzlement of public funds, sale of military secrets, sabotage of every kind. He confessed that he was a religious believer, an admirer of capitalism, a sexual pervert" (209).

Like Aaronson, Rutherford, and Jones, Winston is also released after his "trial" and given a sinecure, allowed to spend his time in the notorious Chestnut Café, the haunt of those broken men who have been made to betray themselves by betraying those closest to them. After his release from Room 101 Winston is no longer able to feel, to remember, to dream. When, uncalled for, a happy memory emerges from his childhood, he dismisses it as a "false memory."

Sitting in the Chestnut Café, Winston knows that, like other "thought criminals," he will be rearrested and shot with the inevitable bullet in the back. But he is so completely transformed by now that he can no longer even dream about getting away from Oceania into the Golden Country: instead, he celebrates the light-flooded corridor leading to the torture chamber as if this were now the fulfilment of his wishdream of the Golden Country. Finally, while listening to the announcements of the Party's latest victory, not only is Winston willing to obey the state religion; he also has become a true believer. Wiping out every memory of his rebellious past, of his outrage over Big Brother's atrocious miscarriage of justice, of his love for Julia and his mother, Winston reaches the ultimate stage expressed by the last slogan: IGNORANCE IS STRENGTH. He no longer abhors, he worships the tyrant. He has learned to practice Doublethink; he genuinely "loves" Big Brother. This also means that he chooses to remain ignorant of what he has experienced, and draws strength from his hysterical faith in the Party.

Gifted pupils of Stalin, Hitler, and the Inquisition, the Inner Party of Oceania have superseded them all by applying their principles but on a larger scale. The deeper the Ignorance – the abnegation of reason and common sense that the Party demands – the stronger the faith this abnegation generates in the true believer. Ultimately, beyond the practical, political reasons for enslaving the population, this is the most important reason for the Party's insistence on the "imposture" of war and its fabrication of show-trials based on false charges and false confessions that will be received by the masses' hysterical condemnation of "criminals." Orwell's consistent analogy of the Adversary's faith in the Party and the medieval true believer's faith in the Church, including the institution of the Inquisition, has a significant satirical function. The memorable image of Oceania as a demonic world brought to life by a fervent "secular religion" is predicated on this analogy.[33]

To decode the satirist's target, we should recognize that Goldstein's Book holds up the mirror to Orwell's contemporaries, demonstrating the potentially disastrous results of their self-deception. The central purpose of his satire, as Orwell explains it, was "to indicate, by parodying them, the intellectual implications of totalitarianism,"[34] a pathology no longer explicable by Marx's "direct economic explanation" of political behaviour because "the world is suffering from some kind of a mental disease which must be diagnosed before it can be cured."[35] Accepting and practising the mental disease of Doublethink in 1948 could, by 1984, lead to the triumph of the diseased totalitarian mentality all over the world. However, when warning his Adversary against making the wrong choice by condoning and trying to emulate Stalin's dystopic society as if it were a socialist regime, Orwell implies that there is a right choice available as well, that of creating a society that provides "economic security without concentration camps" – that is, the choice to return to the original utopian aspiration and "to make democratic Socialism work."[36]

CHAPTER FOUR

Dictatorship without a Mask:
Bradbury's *Fahrenheit 451*, Vonnegut's *Player Piano*, and Atwood's *The Handmaid's Tale*

Ray Bradbury's *Fahrenheit 451* (1951), Kurt Vonnegut's *Player Piano* (1952), and Margaret Atwood's *The Handmaid's Tale* (1986) are dystopias different from *We*, *Brave New World*, and *Nineteen Eighty-four* on several counts. They are not dealing with a world-wide dystopia but narrow their scope to the United States. The three dystopic societies described in them borrow liberally from the methods of totalitarian regimes, mostly from fascism, but they no longer offer a quasi-Messianistic ideology to cover up for the organized injustice of those in power.

RAY BRADBURY: *FAHRENHEIT 451*

In Bradbury's *Fahrenheit 451* the terms of injustice are dictated by a government that rules through firemen who do not put out fires but burn books, set houses on fire, and, like Zamiatin's "guardians" or Orwell's Thought Police, spy upon people and urge them to report on subversive elements. The story takes place in the United States some time in the future. In order to have a stable society, the government uses the anti-intellectual argument that reading is conducive to critical thinking, and thinking creates unrest and disorder – in other words, psychological and social instability.

Bradbury's plot-line is strongly reminiscent of Orwell's in *Nineteen Eighty-four*: fireman Guy Montag, a man in a privileged position, is suddenly awakened, by the love of a young woman, to dissatisfaction with his life in the oppressive system. It is the young woman's contrast to Montag's wife, Mildred, a complacent product of the system who spends her days watching the three wall-size television screens in her living room, that makes Montag awaken to a light buried within him. The young girl's name is Clarisse, and appropriately she clarifies

Montag's subconscious thoughts for him: "How like a mirror, too, her face. Impossible; for how many people did you know that refracted your own light to you?" (10).

Awakened to a sense of his unhappiness and the oppressive nature of the political system, Guy Montag gradually also finds himself in conflict with the firemen's perceptions of justice. In the course of his work he is in a position to hide away some books; he starts to read them with increasing fascination, and for this offence he eventually faces the gravest punishment. Even if he is not expected formally to stand public trial, his trial is nevertheless extremely important for the structure of the book: he is "tried" in a series of seemingly casual interrogations by the Firechief, Captain Beatty, who also happens to open for him the traditional "window on history" by explaining how the firemen came to power as a result of the decline of book-learning, the public acceptance of censorship, and the seductive power of the media in the United States of the early 1950s.

After his "trial in installments," Montag is not even told that he has been found guilty and condemned. Beatty simply orders his subordinate to join him on the fire truck on its way to the daily task of setting a subversive's house on fire. It is only when they arrive that Montag recognizes whose house he is expected to burn down: "Why," said Montag slowly, "we've stopped in front of my house" (99).

Without laying charges or providing evidence, Beatty lets the trial take its final stage: the meting out of justice. As a fireman Montag is to carry out his own sentence, just as he has been carrying out the sentence on others who have been found guilty. At this point, however, Montag takes justice into his own hands: instead of setting his house on fire, he turns the flame-thrower against Firechief Beatty, kills him, and then runs for his life. Unlike the protagonists in *We, Brave New World*, and *Nineteen Eighty-four,* Montag gets away with his rebellion against the system; he escapes and takes shelter among the Book People, a subversive group whose members have memorized entire books to save the heritage of humanity.

Like Zamiatin's, Huxley's, and Orwell's dystopias, *Fahrenheit 451* is a society that denies its past; it has no records of past events, no books, no documents, and as a result, no framework for personal memory. However, unlike Huxley and Orwell, Bradbury does not represent the burning of books and the persecution of writers and readers as an *effect* of political dictatorship; rather, he creates a society that became a dictatorship *as a result of* burning books and discarding the classics of our civilization, all records of the past, indeed anything conducive to the development of personal memory and the working of the

imagination. No doubt, Bradbury borrows elements from Hitler's and
Stalin's dictatorships. For example, it is Montag's wife who denounces
him to Firechief Beatty; according to the laws established by both
Hitler's and Stalin's dictatorships, a citizen's loyalty to the government
should take precedence over loyalty to a spouse. Signs of dictatorial
terror and violence are clearly discernible: subversives suspected of
being critical of the system are quietly eliminated; children are taught
to be obedient to the state but are encouraged to commit violence and
risk their own lives and those of others by reckless driving and fighting.
Bradbury's point is that this behaviour is natural in a society where
people are bored and dislocated by the mental poverty that follows
from lack of reading. Most significantly, and Bradbury suggests this to
be the source of all its evils, this society burns books, just as Hitler
did. Often what begins as the burning of a few books and the house
where these have been found turns into a real *auto-da-fé*, a religious
ritual of human sacrifice, as in the case of the old woman who decides
to remain in her house and die with her books. She dies like a martyr,
reciting the parting words of Hugh Latimer, burnt at the stake and
martyred for his faith in 1555.

The old woman's trial and execution has a profound effect on
Montag, completing the process begun by his meeting with Clarisse,
the wish for radical change in himself and in society. While the
Mechanical Hound, a deadly machine capable of detecting books and
readers, is already sniffing at the Montags' door, Guy Montag is trying
to explain his transformation to his wife: "That woman the other night
... You didn't see her face. And Clarisse. You never talked to her ...
But I kept putting her alongside the firemen in the House last night,
and I suddenly realized I didn't like them at all, and I didn't like myself
at all any more" (61).

The burning of books is not just the central but the only phenomenon Bradbury is interested in when describing how the entire political
process of the United States could be moving towards a police state. In
his 1966 introduction, written fifteen years after the novel, Bradbury states
that he feared that the McCarthy era, with its anti-intellectualism,
censorship, and its encouragement of citizens' denunciations of one
another, could introduce in the United States a society very much like
Hitler's Germany or Stalin's Soviet Union. In commenting on the movie
version that François Truffaut made of the novel, Bradbury sheds
further light on the love of books as his central theme, and maybe
also on the rather two-dimensional characterization that is more
appropriate to an allegory than to a novel aiming for psychological
verisimilitude. He congratulates Truffaut for capturing "the soul and
the essence of the book," which is "the love story of, not a man and

a woman, but a man and a library, a man and a book. An incredible love story indeed in this day when libraries, once more, are burning across the world."[1]

By the end of the novel the burning of books can be recognized as the prefiguration of the approaching Apocalypse, the final war that may destroy our civilization. What Bradbury focuses on is one particular aspect of a police state, namely the repression of free speech, free thought, free press, the freedom of the imagination. He also draws attention to the power of the media not only to lie but also to fake events as a means of state propaganda. When Montag escapes without a trace, the crew of the television newscast improvises a scene where a man, chosen at random and photographed from a distance, is shot on the spot in order to convince viewers that "justice" has been served; the subversive has been instantly eliminated.

Ultimately Bradbury regards the suppression of truth as virtually the only, the core crime of totalitarian dictatorships, from which all other crimes follow. He tells us that "when Hitler burned a book, I felt it as keenly, please forgive me, as killing a human, for in the long sum of history, they are one and the same flesh."[2] And he completes the thought: "Mind or body, put to the oven, is a sinful practice, and I carried this with me as I passed countless firehouses."[3]

The narrower scope of his criticism notwithstanding, Bradbury follows the traditional strategies of dystopian satire, which asks the reader to examine the social pathologies of the present that could lead to the nightmare world in the future. In fact, Bradbury makes a concentrated effort to open for Montag "a window on history" that will clarify for the reader the satirist's targets by having both Firechief Beatty and Faber describe the past, the fifties – the time when the novel was written. Faber, a former English professor and a friend of Montag, points at the past, regretting that in the 1950s the humanities started to atrophy, began slowly to be destroyed in the name of the machine civilization. Students at universities abandoned courses in literature; *Readers' Digest* reduced classics to a quick, superficial one-page read; and it became such a sensitive political issue to write about minorities or various ethnic groups that publishers gave up on publishing literature, and cheap works on sex and violence pushed out the classics to please the masses. Faber calls this process "the tyranny of the majority," a false egalitarianism that reduces everyone to the lowest common denominator, making Americans willing to give up what Matthew Arnold would have called the best and most beautiful voices of humanity in the name of efficiency and saving time. Bradbury suggests that the American public of the fifties is responsible for the new regime. "Remember, the firemen are rarely necessary. The public itself stopped reading of its own accord" (78). The political change, then, was not violent; it was simply the aftermath of cultural decline: "And then the Government, seeing how advantageous it was to have people reading only about passionate lips and the fist in the stomach, circled the situation with your fireeaters" (79).

While Faber's description of the sins of the fifties becomes a lament over the decline of book-learning, Montag's boss, Firechief Beatty, describes the same process as the rise of the media, and with it, the triumphant rise of the police state. A representative of dictatorial power, Beatty celebrates the firemen's reign, although he fails to explain how and why the firemen came to power and what motivates them to stay in power. In most general terms, of course, the Firechief reproduces the Grand Inquisitor's explanation of the happiness and stability the masses would enjoy at the price of accepting limitations on their freedom. Instead of turning directly on the heretic, the Grand Inquisitor here admits his anti-intellectualism: "the word 'intellectual,' of course, became the swear word it deserved to be. You always dread the unfamiliar" (53).

What for the Grand Inquisitor was the happiness of the masses is for Beatty the economic well-being of the market. But the conclusion is the same: the masses should be protected from the burden of thinking for themselves: "the bigger your market, Montag, the less you handle controversy ... Authors, full of evil thoughts, lock up your typewriters. They did. Magazines became a nice blend of vanilla tapioca ... No wonder books stopped selling ... comic books ... three-dimensional sex magazines ... It didn't come from the Government down. There was no dictum, no declaration, no censorship, to start with, no! Technology, mass exploitation, and minority pressure carried the trick, thank God! Today, thanks to them, you can stay happy all the time" (53–4).

Beatty's speech recalls the self-justification of the Grand Inquisitor, who is convinced that by subverting the original spirit of Christ he can make the people "happy." However, Beatty's agenda does not explain exactly what that original spirit was that became subverted by the "Happiness boys" who forbade reading. Is it the original spirit of democracy? Then why did this spirit weaken in the fifties? "If you don't want a man unhappy politically, don't give him two sides to a question to worry him; give him one. Better yet, give him none. Let him forget there is such a thing as war. If the government is inefficient, top-heavy, and tax-mad, better it be all those than that people worry over it. Peace, Montag. Give the people contest ... cram them full of noncombustible data. Then they'll feel they're thinking, they'll get a sense of motion without moving. And they'll be happy, because facts of that sort don't change" (55).

Justifying the power of the firemen, Captain Beatty is like the high priest of the state religion, the only person who still knows the forbidden lore of the past. He is able to quote from the books he has burnt in his long years of service, and there is also an indication that, by giving up his love for reading in order to serve the anti-intellectual government, he made a sacrifice, just like Zamiatin's Benefactor or Huxley's Controller. Yet Beatty cannot fully justify this sacrifice to himself and is consequently an unhappy man. Montag recognizes this suddenly when he is already on the run and recalls the circumstances of his trial and punishment. He cries out, "Beatty wanted to die!" He must have been tired of life when he exposed himself to the flame-thrower in Montag's hands.

Beatty is an ambiguous character: in the course of Montag's gradual conversion to book-reading, Beatty gives several signs that he is fully aware of Montag's thoughts and feelings, including his fear of the Mechanical Hound. Beatty's personal visit to Montag's house when the latter stays home from work is also an ambiguous episode: it combines the possibilities that Beatty has come to spy on his subordinate, to carry on a pre-trial investigation, or to offer a friendly warning in his parting words to Montag: "Be well and stay well" (68). Still, Beatty's consistent analysis of the world of the 1950s that led to the world of *Fahrenheit 451* indicates that as Ideal Readers we should be careful about censorship, the atrophy of book-reading, and the media's unchecked rise to power if we wish to stop a decline that may lead to a destructive total war in which "our civilization is flinging itself to pieces" (78).

Unlike Zamiatin's D-503 or Orwell's Winston Smith, Guy Montag manages to kill the "high priest" or Grand Inquisitor of the system and escape. Behind him the city is being destroyed by the war, but Guy Montag finds a chance for survival in the country among a group of bibliophiles who memorize entire books to make sure their words will not be forgotten. It is from these words, Bradbury suggests, that our civilization may be reborn, like the phoenix who "everytime he burnt himself up ... sprang out of the ashes ... born all over again" (146).

Although Jack Zipes has reason to say that "throughout the novel, war lurks in the background until it finally erupts," there is little evidence that "the obvious reference here is to the Cold War and the Korean War which might lead to such an atomic explosion as that which occurs at the end of the book."[4] In fact, when Beatty opens the "window on history" for Montag, describing to him the problems in the fifties that precipitated the reign of the book-burning firemen, he does not refer to any specific war. The story suggests that when "our civilization is flinging itself to pieces" (78) and when it is "born all over again" as a phoenix, both the destruction and the rebirth of the world are connected exclusively with the elimination or the survival of books. The reader may well find that the equation of the decline of book-reading with the increased chances of the world's destruction by nuclear war is not sufficiently convincing. The novel reads more like a parable about the importance of book-learning and of assuring the survival of our cultural heritage than a convincing political analysis of a society on its way to the dystopia of dictatorship and destruction.

One of Bradbury's critics objects to the naïveté of Bradbury's political analysis, claiming that "Bradbury does not locate the source of destruction in the state, class society, or technology, but in humankind himself."[5] In itself, I do not believe that drawing attention to the complicity of the masses in allowing the emergence of the dictator is a sign of political naïveté. If we recall Frigyes Karinthy's "Barabbas," or Hannah Arendt's political analysis of this phenomenon, the question of why the people would opt for the dictator is a question well worth asking. The problem in Bradbury's analysis of dictatorship is rather that we do not see the clear connection between the people's desire for "happiness" and the ways the government seduces them to follow its own agenda. Except for trying to stay in power, the government in this dystopic society has no agenda, no program, not even a program to fabricate its own self-justification.

In concentrating on book-burning, Bradbury chooses one element he finds most frightening in totalitarian systems and works on that theme, as it were in isolation, to show how the United States could also turn into a dictatorship like societies in Eastern and Central Europe. As a political critique of a society on its way to totalitarianism the book is not quite convincing. But *Fahrenheit 451* is probably less a full-fledged political dystopia than the diagnosis of a new cultural phenomenon that Marshall McLuhan explored in *The Gutenberg Galaxy* (1962), foreshadowed by *The Mechanical Bride* (1951). With open fascination McLuhan follows the passing away of a civilization based on the printed word, on reading and writing. Reading McLuhan, it seems that the old world is stepping aside and saluting the rise to power of a new world created by the electronic media, in the character of a rather absent-minded new dictator not yet entirely set on either a benign or a malignant course. Yet it is a dictator when it dictates new terms to our perceptions, modes of thinking, political discourse, until "the medium [becomes our] message." Unlike McLuhan, Bradbury responds to this phenomenon by expressing the moral apprehension of the humanist. Not quite a convincing dystopian critique of the dangers of a totalitarian political system or a police state, the novel is a memorable and passionate outcry against the cultural losses implied

by the passing away of book culture in the media-controlled consumer
society of the 1950s.

KURT VONNEGUT: *PLAYER PIANO*

Kurt Vonnegut's *Player Piano* (1954) is a technological dystopia, significantly indebted to Huxley's *Brave New World* for its subject-matter
and to Orwell's *Nineteen Eighty-four* for its structure, although it does
not aspire to match either the scope or the philosophical breadth of
these two novels. In contrast to the settings of the other dystopian novels
discussed so far, the atmosphere of *Player Piano* does not strike one as
nightmarish. The reader is not hit by cognitive estrangement;[6] Ilium
seems to be a society with which we are familiar, within the range of
our normal, everyday experience. The more immediate, therefore, Vonnegut's warning becomes about a particular kind of technological development in North America that may drastically undermine the rights of
the majority and wreak havoc with the democratic system of justice.

Written in 1952, *Player Piano* focuses on the effects of a Second
Industrial Revolution in the United States, instigated by a new stage in
the computer-driven robotization of production, whereby the vast
majority, including skilled workers, technicians, and professionals lose
their right to work, although not their right to prosperity. Permanently
unemployed, this vast majority are still granted their own washing
machines, television sets, and glass and steel houses in Homestead, a
new version of the Wellsian utopia as a combination of a high-tech
slum and the welfare state. To give the people an illusion of being
useful, the elite presses them into lengthy service in a weaponless army
and into an equally useless industrial army, the Reeks and Recks
engaged in make-work road repairs. This social transformation, which
is tantamount to making the population feel superfluous, is sanctioned
by a state religion based on machine worship, ministered to by a very
small elite of technocrats and managers under the aegis of the "national
holy trinity, Efficiency, Economy, and Quality" (261). Vonnegut's trinity recalls Huxley's slogans of the World State, "Community, Identity,
and Stability," which were in turn to draw attention to the political
degradation of the World State that had come to power in the name
of "Fraternity, Liberty, and Equality," the original inspiration for
democracy and democratic socialism.

Vonnegut's protagonist, Paul Proteus, perceives that just as medieval
government was based on the divine right of kings, the American ruling
class claims its legitimacy according to the "divine right of machines"
(260). This ruling class of managers and engineers celebrates "the
annual passion plays at the Meadows" (268), where people act out,

with machinelike precision, the ritual competition of who will best serve the big Corporation, which represents the essence of the American state machine. The novel is set in Ilium, in the indefinite yet not too distant future in the United States after a Third World War, fought with nuclear weapons, in which Americans came to "owe their lives to superior machines, techniques, organization, and managers and engineers" (261). It is the Americans' technological advantage over other countries that allowed them to win the war and create great prosperity for the masses, at the same time transferring all political power to the ruling elite.

Like Orwell, Vonnegut is less interested in the devastations of such a future war than in the long-term threat it might pose to political institutions based on democratic freedom. The machine that was originally expected to redeem humanity from the suffering of poverty and back-breaking labour paradoxically turns into an ominous weapon against human dignity: "During the war, in hundreds of Iliums over America, managers and engineers learned to get along without their men and women, who went to fight. It was the miracle that won the war – production with almost no manpower" (1). The unforeseen result of the advanced technology in this Second Industrial Revolution makes not only muscle work and routine mental work but also human thinking dispensable: the big master computer, called EPICAC, has come to "devaluate human thinking" (13) itself.

In these two American dystopias of Bradbury and Vonnegut, the object of worship is not a half-deified dictator but a quasi-superhuman machine: in *Fahrenheit 451* it is the Mechanical Hound, which can sniff out books and subversives; in *Player Piano* it is EPICAC, the master computer, which has changed society and the workings of the human mind to such an extent that it now gives commands to the whole population, even to those few who believe they are privileged to give it their own commands.

Paul Proteus, a brilliant thirty-five-year-old technocrat-manager running Ilium Works, has all the advantages of belonging to this very small and very privileged ruling elite, both for his own merits and because his father was the head of the National Industrial Planning Board, one of the founding fathers of the new regime. Consequently, Paul can look forward to further promotion to the even more prestigious Pittsburgh Works. However, like Winston, D-503, and Guy Montag, Paul also grows dissatisfied with his position in society as he becomes aware that his privileged status is based on injustice.

He understands that it was the miraculous formula of "technology without people" that won the war, yet he believes that once the war is over, to replace men "without regard for the effects on life patterns is lawlessness." The narrative formula familiar from *We* and *Nineteen Eighty-four* reveals Proteus growing more and more alienated from his wife, Anita, who represents the code of values of this society, including its ruthless ambition to get ahead, to conform, and to flatter those above. Through his friend, the subversive Ed Finnerty, Paul Proteus gradually becomes aware of the loss of dignity suffered by the masses. He considers joining the rebellious Ghostshirt Society, which, like the Luddites in the First Industrial Revolution, wants to break the machine and is "prepared to use force to end the lawlessness" (261).

Undoubtedly, Proteus's heart is in the right place because he recognizes the injustice implied in the elite's reversal of the age-old utopian dream that the masses had a right to expect to see fulfilled after the war. He sees that "Man has survived the Armageddon in order to enter the Eden of eternal peace, only to discover that everything he had looked forward to enjoying there, pride, dignity, self-respect, work worth doing, has been condemned as unfit for human consumption" (260).

His sympathy for the underdog turns him against his paternal benefactor, Dr Kroner, one of the leaders of the corporate world in the country, as well as against his own wife, Anita. After his first visit to Homestead with his friend Finnerty, Paul senses that he is going through a transformation – just like Zamiatin's D-503, who diagnoses his own "sickness" of developing a soul: "Along with [Paul's] feeling of dizziness was a feeling of newness – the feeling of fresh, strong identity growing within him. It was a generalized love – particularly for the little people, the common people, God bless them ... This was real, this side of the river, and Paul loved these common people, and wanted to help, and let them know they were loved and understood, and he wanted them to love him too" (88).

Vonnegut's tone in this passage introduces his own ambivalence towards a revolution coming from above. Although Paul Proteus is full of sympathy and good will, his attitude is a combination of sentimentality and condescension "for the little people, the common people, God bless them." He has no clear notion how to help them; neither does he know how far he is willing to go against his own class. All he knows is that he would be willing to sacrifice himself for them: "If his attempt to become the new Messiah had become successful, if the inhabitants of the north and south banks had met in the middle of the bridge with Paul between them, he wouldn't have the slightest idea what to do next" (99).

It is only when Paul finds himself more and more alienated from his own circle that he makes a more definite attempt to join the rebels, by now including several subversives from his own class. These subversives are indeed looking for a "Messiah with a good, solid, startling

message" (252) and would like Paul to become their leader, but when
Paul realizes that they would like to "give America back to the people"
by wrecking all the automatic factories, he turns down the offer. He
also finds that the rebels are just as ruthless and ruthlessly "business-
like" as Anita, Kroner, and the other successful members of the ruling
class. When the rebels decide they could use a man from the ruling
class with Paul's pedigree as their leader, Ed Finnerty, Paul's best friend,
is ready to blackmail or even kill Paul if he refuses. Of a Protean nature
and disposition, Paul Proteus is once more caught in the middle: "The
managers and engineers still believed he was their man; the Ghost Shirt
Society was just as convinced that he belonged to them, and both
demonstrated that there was no middle ground for him" (265).

While still in a state of indecision, Proteus is approached by Kroner
and Anita, who offer him a chance to regain and enhance his privileged
position by denouncing Finnerty, who is known to be one of the leaders
of the underground Ghostshirt Society. Proteus refuses to inform on
him, not on ideological nor on political, not even on moral grounds,
but simply because "Bad guys turned informer. Good guys didn't – no
matter when, no matter what" (269). To taunt Kroner and Anita
further, he declares that he himself is the leader of the Ghostshirts; he
is put on trial as a subversive, a traitor to his own class.

As in the other dystopian novels, the scene at the trial marks the
climactic point in the narrative and in the symbolic action. Paul stands
up here for the rights of the people, the whole of humanity, announcing
that "the main business of humanity is to do a good job of being human
beings ... and not to serve as appendages to machines, institutions or
systems" (73). Still, his specific goal remains undefined: he knows what
he objects to in a society based on the worship of machines, but he has
no political agenda to tell him how far to go with their destruction.
When asked, he vaguely says that "some of the machines" should be
destroyed but details "would have to be worked out" (270).

Here the author also reveals a further irony: although it is Paul's
ambition to become the "Messiah" of the people of Illium – and of
humanity – his opposition to the system is also driven by a personal
grudge emanating from a well-known neurosis (he is here not unlike
John Savage in *Brave New World*). When at the trial Paul is forced to
take a lie detector test, the audience comes to realize that his revolutionary ideas may be genuine and heartfelt, but he is also driven by
an Oedipal rebellion against his deceased father, who represented to
him all that he disliked in society. At this embarrassing point of his
own "confession," the trial is interrupted by the outbreak of the
Ghostshirt revolution; Paul is called upon to become one of its leaders,
together with the violent Lasher and the ruthless Finnerty.

After a period of a violent and large-scale destruction, the rebels are threatened by a blockade unless they give up their leaders: the leaders decide to give themselves up. Vonnegut reveals further ambiguities in the situation: none of the leaders has a positive goal; although they hate the system based on machine worship, they have no new ideas about resolving the social injustice created by the computer revolution. As Paul also realizes, the leaders of the machine breakers are themselves enamored with beautifully made machines: "a good part of their lives and skills had gone into making what they helped to destroy in a few hours" (287). Even those workers and technicians who have been forced to yield up their jobs to the machine cannot help worshipping the machine's ability to replace human beings: it is a mentality that is typical of the whole country. Their complaint "wasn't that it was unjust to take jobs from men and give them to machines, but that machines didn't do nearly as many human things as good designers could have made them do" (218). Even while preparing to break the machines, one of the rebel commanders is engaged in designing yet another beautiful machine, "an armored car to which he was adding antennae, a radar dome, spikes, flails, and other instruments of terrible slaughter" (255).

To the end the leaders of the revolution remain unsure about the extent to which they would like to destroy the machine civilization; neither do they know what should be put in its place after the destruction. Consequently, when they attempt to restrain the angry mob on a rampage to destroy the Ilium Works, they are indecisive and end up being beaten up by their own people. Vonnegut makes it clear that such a revolution had to be defeated, and Proteus is not really surprised that the system of managers and technocrats will be restored and the damaged state machine rebuilt. At the end of the novel he is left undecided, with a drink in his hand: "'To a better world,' he started to say, but cut the toast short, thinking of the people of Illium, already eager to recreate the same nightmare" (295).

Vonnegut leaves us with a sense of ambivalence: was it worthwhile to stage the revolution? What else could have been done? There is no doubt that the world of the machine is inhuman, as also suggested by Zamiatin and Huxley. In an amusing episode Vonnegut makes it clear that this society no longer exists for the benefit of human beings; they have become superfluous, fully dispensable. There is a Shah visiting the United States who is examining advanced American technology with an eye to introducing some of its benefits to his own country. The American elite is eager and willing to send experts to his backward country "to test and classify his people, arrange credit, set up the machinery." However, having seen the inhumanity implied by the

"machinery" of the American state apparatus, the Shah rejects the
whole offer by asking a very simple question: "Before we take the first
step, would you ask EPICAC what people are for?" (277) Also, seeing
that the majority of the citizens of this prosperous country are in effect
fully enslaved by the machine, the Shah keeps referring to them as
"Takaru," which means slaves in his own language, and he will not
be corrected.

There is no doubt, then, that the dilemma created by the worship
of the machine and by the superior capacity of the thinking machine
is not being resolved. Paul Proteus expresses the Protean position of
unresolvable ambivalence about the future. According to Howard
Segal, "*Player Piano* treats technology and human nature similarly.
Much of the ambivalence toward mankind's future at the conclusion
of the novel stems exactly from Vonnegut's view of human nature as
permanently, inherently flawed."[7] Just as important, I believe, like
Huxley before him, Vonnegut sees the paradox of technological
advance and warns against its potentially dehumanizing effect. Unlike
Huxley, however, he is satisfied to diagnose the problem without
feeling compelled to find a cure at the political level.

According to Hillegas, *Player Piano* offers the same nightmare vision
as other technological dystopias, but it "seems closer to coming reality
as we may come to know it."[8] From our vantage-point in the twenty-
first century, this novel, written in 1952, is indeed remarkable for its
vision of the tremendous changes introduced by the computer, in effect
a Second Industrial Revolution, capable of causing the same kind of
dislocation and upheaval as the first.

Probably just as importantly, this novel, like *Fahrenheit 451*, also
reveals many of the sexual attitudes and biases typical of the 1950s.
It is interesting, for example, to see the relatively insignificant role that
women play in these two American dystopias from the early fifties. It
is true that Clarisse signals Montag's awakening to a new self, and he
has to tear himself away from his wife, Mildred, who represents the
code of the dystopian society. However, Guy Montag's relationship to
both women is almost entirely asexual and impersonal: playing a much
smaller role than women in Huxley's or Orwell's novels, both Clarisse
and Mildred remain two-dimensional abstractions.

As for the women in *Player Piano*, Paul Proteus's wife Anita is a
parody of the ambitious corporate wife who dedicates herself whole-
heartedly to her husband's career. She is less of a character than a cruel
caricature, the incarnation of conformism and social climbing in society, with no individual features – an abstract emblem of the evil ways
of the ruling class, without any personal touches. Her obsessive interest

in her husband's career and her determination to keep him under her influence are presented with harsh contempt by the writer, who paints her as a mercenary, a cold and calculating woman using her feminine wiles – that is, her sexual powers – as the only means to get what she wants from a man in a man's world. Describing the way she rehearses with her husband for his important business appointments, Vonnegut uses the strategies of fairly crude satire, with hints at some latent misogyny in Paul's – or, perhaps, Vonnegut's – perception: "This was the game she never tired of – one that took every bit of Paul's patience to play. She was forever casting herself as a person of influence and making Paul play dialogues with her. There would then be a critique, in which his responses were analyzed, edited, and polished by her ... *how primitive a notion she had of men's affairs and of how business was done*" (68; my italics).

It is, therefore, entirely predictable that the moment Paul is no longer a worthy investment, Anita turns away from him coldly. (Of course, Mildred also turns away from Montag, but she lives in fear of the regime; in effect it is Mildred who denounces Montag to the Firechief.)

The other woman character in *Player Piano* is Dr Kroner's wife, who is called "Mom" by all who know her, a rather sinister caricature of the American mother as domineering, hypocritical, enforcer of the worst attributes of a conformist, mindless, competitive society – as if she had stepped out of the pages of Philip Wylie's *Generation of Vipers* to illustrate the phenomenon Wylie christened "momism." Significantly, the only women presented with a measure of sympathy are the two young prostitutes Paul meets at his first drinking excursion in Homestead.[9]

It is probably also worth noting that, although Vonnegut's novel follows the dystopian formula, beginning with the protagonist's awakening, followed by alienation, resistance, trial, and punishment, in *Player Piano* this traditional structure receives a slight variation: Paul Proteus's awakening is not introduced by an inspiring woman character but by his experience of male bonding with his friend, Ed Finnerty.

By contrast with the two American dystopias of *Fahrenheit 451* and *Player Piano*, women characters play a far more significant and positive role in *We, Brave New World*, and *Nineteen Eighty-four*, even if their characterizations do not go much beyond psychological archetypes. In *We* Zamiatin presents both O-90 and I-330 with a certain degree of sympathy. In his relationship with O-90 the protagonist follows the "rational" sexual attitude prescribed by the One State. Abandoning placid O-90 for the audacious I-330, the protagonist becomes both sexually and politically subversive. However, in Zamiatin's presentation, O-90 is not altogether a conformist either: she is determined to have the protagonist's child, even if she does not qualify for the "maternity norm" established with mathematical rigidity by the regime. O-90 knows that by getting pregnant without the state's permission she may face execution by the Benefactor's Machine; nevertheless, she risks her life to have a child from the man she loves. The course of the protagonist's political and spiritual development against the social machine is inextricably interlinked with his psychological relationship to these two women; he is deeply attached to both.

Also, somewhat against the straight polarization of women characters familiar from the dystopian cast, Zamiatin has I-330 be of assistance to her rival: she helps O-90, pregnant with the protagonist's child, to escape to the world behind the green wall. Although the two women are temperamentally opposites, in their own way they share in the protagonist's rebellion against the state machine.

As for Lenina in *Brave New World*, at first glance she fully represents the code of sexual behaviour and the mindlessness of the orthodox Beta she was "hatched" and conditioned to be in London 651 AF. Both Bernard Marx and John Savage find her physically enticing, but they also look at her as the embodiment of the mentality they find most oppressive in this dystopic society. Nevertheless, even though intellectually she is a perfect product of her society – precisely because as a Beta she has no intellect, no mind of her own – Huxley also reveals her significant emotional and sexual rebellion against her world's inhumanity. She has a tendency to form relationships that last longer than those prescribed and are less casual than they should be in a state where "everyone belongs to everyone else." When she falls passionately in love with John Savage, emotionally she rebels against her entire conditioning, including years of sleepteaching, which should make her reject personal, romantic attachments as absurd. In one of the most memorable scenes Huxley explores the grotesque comedy of errors between John and Lenina when she appears at his apartment, ready to take the initiative. Although they learned the language of love from a different dictionary, the Savage is not the only one with a heroic notion about romantic love. No doubt the words the Savage borrows from Shakespeare genuinely confuse and irritate her, yet Lenina also takes in this instance an unusual risk to express her feelings for the Savage: the risk of making herself ridiculous or being rejected. At the end of the novel she reappears, rushing towards the self-flagellating Savage with open arms, as he is trying to purify himself from the corruption of society – and from what he sees as his "sinful" desire for her.

In *Nineteen Eighty-four* Winston's relationships to Katherine, his wife, and to Julia, his lover, follow the traditional pattern of dystopian fiction: he is awakened to his new self by Julia, who also takes the initiative by handing him a note confessing her love for him. Both risk their lives; they live in a society that denies sexuality and channels all feelings into a fanatical love for Big Brother. Sexual activity is strictly confined to producing children for the Party, and genuine attachment between man and woman is regarded as a politically subversive act. Winston's awakening to his sexuality also means his total rejection of his former wife, Katherine, a political bigot who refers to making love as "doing one's duty to the Party." Julia has a central role in the course of Winston's life and in his psychological and political development; we cannot even begin to understand Winston's greatest fears and strongest desires without recognizing that Julia is the centre of his Golden Country; it is when the Party forces him to betray Julia that we realize it has been successful in finally breaking down Winston's personality.

There is no doubt, then, that sexual or romantic love plays a more significant role in *We, Brave New World,* and *Nineteen Eighty-four* than in *Fahrenheit 451* or *Player Piano,* although all five of these novels concentrate on the thoughts, feelings, and actions of a male protagonist. Yet, whether we look at the first three or the last two of these five novels, it is clear that they all represent dystopian fiction as a male-centred genre, dealing with society primarily from a male point of view. This tradition is radically changed with the appearance of feminist utopias and dystopias in the seventies; Margaret Atwood's *The Handmaid's Tale* (1986) is one of the most powerful examples of this newer development.

MARGARET ATWOOD: *THE HANDMAID'S TALE*

In Margaret Atwood's *The Handmaid's Tale* the regressive, primitive state religon characteristic of dystopian societies no longer wears the mask of a secular ideology. Unlike Big Brother, the rulers of Gilead have never held out the dazzling promise of a secular, utopian future; their excuse for taking control was to redress the crisis in a failed industrial society, endangered by its inability to reproduce itself – by turning back directly to a medieval, even Old Testament theocracy, based on a fundamentalist reading of the Bible.

The "window on history" we found essential in all the five dystopias discussed so far is particularly prominent in this novel, because the central character, Offred, is also the narrator of the story, and she is trying to deal with her entrapment by a series of juxtapositions between her deprived, degraded self in Gilead and her former emancipated self in the United States in the 1980s. Nevertheless, the narrative never enlightens us about the nature of the political change that was responsible for turning the United States of the eighties into the

Gilead of the millennium. Neither does the narrative clarify what is usually at the heart of the suspense in the dystopian plot: what is it that the governing elite believes in? How does it justify to itself the legitimization of blatant injustice, the scapegoating of a terror-stricken population, with a particular emphasis on the enslavement of women?

How did the takeover start? The intense suspense Atwood creates so effectively in the novel is probably due to the necessary limitations of subjectivity and partial information inherent in a first-person-singular point of view, as Offred is trying to recall the details of her past before she was forcibly separated from her daughter and husband. In making Offred recapture memory as the only means to return to truth and a basis for human dignity, we can detect the influence of Orwell: the act of memory is an act of resistance against the totalitarian state with its insistence on changing history, on eradicating the very concept of historical records, because knowledge of history would form the basis for a fair comparison between the past and the new regime – a comparison dictatorships cannot afford. This emphasis on the protagonist's pursuit of the private self, of free expression and criticism, through the pursuit of individual memory is a fundamental theme in Orwell's, Bradbury's, and Atwood's dystopias, and it connects with the theme of censorship and the freedom of public opinion in the dystopias descriptive of political reality in the Eastern bloc as well.

Like Winston Smith, Offred bewails the fact that private memory has severe limitations as a public record. Since she is shut into her inner world – she is not allowed to talk unless talked to, and she has no access to written records – Offred has to rely entirely on her memory to conjure up the past, to explain to herself how she got imprisoned, with the rest of her sex, in Gilead. Her memory of sweeping political changes is of necessity vague and fragmented. This blurry quality, incidentally, adds to the psychological versimilitude, but also imposes a limitation on Atwood's political analysis of the new system and its connection with the old one. A somewhat more detailed answer to some of the questions about the old system of which the narrator has no full recollection will be delivered in the epilogue to the novel, the "Historical Notes on the Handmaid's Tale" (a satirical device that fulfils a function similar to that of Orwell's epilogue, "The Principles of Newspeak"): "Stillbirths, miscarriages and genetic deformities were widespread and on the increase, and this trend has been linked to the various nuclear-plant accidents, shutdowns, and incidents of sabotage that characterized the period, as well as to leak-waste disposal sites ... and to the uncontrolled use of chemical insecticides, herbicides, and other sprays" (286).

Atwood presents the United States of the 1980s as a society in social and physiological decline, devastated by the AIDS epidemic and the appearance of genetic deformities resulting from the use of certain birth-control pills. On the excuse of this decline, the new military government chooses to have the American Constitution suspended and return society to the grim justice of the distant past of antiquity, the ancient days of the Bible. Or, to be more precise, the government chooses the letter but not the spirit of the Bible to cover up for its own self-serving, power-hungry actions.

As Offred remembers it, the takeover of the theocracy came about gradually, as a response to the breakdown of consumerist capitalist democracy, to the infertility caused by the ecological imbalance of nuclear experiments, fallout, and toxic waste, a crisis responded to or precipitated by (one does not quite know which) the right-wing fundamentalist backlash of a large segment of the population, who regarded the signs of consumerism and the social changes introduced by Women's Liberation and the sexual revolution of the 1970s as excesses to be eliminated, and who were eager to endorse a puritanical, openly patriarchal and fundamentalist government.

Whether it was a mass movement or an elitist coup that turned the United States of the 1980s into the theocracy of Gilead, middle-class professionals like Offred and her husband Luke had their share in bringing it about. Intimidated by the obvious signs of terror, they showed little resistance to the process through which women were first deprived of their right to hold a bank account and then to hold a job."I didn't go on any of the marches. Luke said it would be futile and I had to think about them, my family, him and her. I didn't think about my family. I started doing more housework, more baking. I tried not to cry at mealtimes. By this time I started to cry, without warning, and to sit beside the bedroom window, staring out. I didn't know many of the neighbours, and when we met, outside on the street, we were careful to exchange nothing more than the ordinary greetings. Nobody wanted to be reported for disloyalty" (169).

In this sense, the misogynist legislation of Gilead is simply the end result of the timid attitude of an entire generation in the 1980s, of the women themselves who gave their consent by not having the courage to protest or even to discuss their situation with others. Of course, one should be careful not to blame the victim of violence too readily. The ruling elite of Gilead is a military junta able to have objectors or those suspected of being subversives not only exterminated but also tortured. Like Iran, Gilead returns to a medieval theocracy in the middle of the twentieth century, at the same time modelling its advanced methods

of intimidation on the terror of Hitler's and Stalin's dictatorships. It
borrows a great deal from the one-party system of the USSR; it has
periodic purges of leaders supected of liberal tendencies, first with
public, later with secret trials, and it works to create fear and intimidate the masses through the ritualized, that is periodically recurring,
secret trials and public execution of "culprits." Thus Gilead demonstrates that peculiar duality of law and lawlessness we have observed
in totalitarian dictatorships, where the exclusion of an entire class –
here an entire sex – becomes a legally acceptable measure to assure
the cohesion of the system.

In its disenfranchisement of women the elite of Gilead followed the
methods of Hitler in Germany, who managed to isolate, encircle, and
disenfranchise an entire class of scapegoats, former citizens, by depriving them of their human rights gradually, through a step-by-step
"legal" process. The elite of Gilead do not justify their legitimization
of blatant injustice by racist theories but use a latent gender hatred or
misogyny within the general mechanism of scapegoating. The process
leads to the regression of a modern state with its civilized legal system
based on inalienable human rights to a barbaric state where the entire
female sex is enslaved by the state through law.

Ostensibly, it is to solve the crisis of infertility that the women are
enslaved, their identity, even their names taken away. But on closer
inspection the crisis of infertility is merely an excuse for a government
that has no other interest than to establish the elite's privileged position
in the hierarchy. Even within the enslaved population of women there
are still class differences: the Commanders' wives are of higher standing
than the "Marthas," or domestic servants. The "handmaids," whose
function it is to bear children by the Commanders, become "surrogate
mothers," giving up their child to the Commander's wife – ultimately
to the state authorities. The handmaid unable to conceive is sent to the
colonies to join the millions of "useless" women who are forced to
perform the deadly task of cleaning up nuclear and toxic waste, Gilead's
own version of the "final solution." Clearly, Gilead here borrows its
methods of terror and intimidation from fascism: the entire female population is reduced to life in an enormous system of concentration camps,
with inmates at various levels of degradation. Subversives and infertile
and aging women are forced to live and work in the colonies that are
death camps; every woman is afraid of being sent there and is therefore
more compliant in fulfilling the role assigned to her by the authorities.

The women in the Rachel and Leah Re-education Centre are being
trained and coerced to be fit for their new roles. The "Aunts" who
are in charge of their re-education follow the methods of the SS, but
they are inmates themselves because the most "cost-effective way to

control women for reproductive and other purposes was through women themselves" (290). Here Gilead follows the ways of colonizers all over the world who "control the indigenous by members of their own group." The Aunts are women who originally believed in "traditional values" or wanted the benefits that go with their position: "When power is scarce, a little of it is tempting" (290).

As well as living in fear of the extermination or punishment camps, the women are also isolated from their children, their men, and even from one another, another reason why they accept their various roles in a fairly docile manner. Except for the Commanders and their wives, men and women are segregated, each imprisoned in his or her respective role, forbidden to talk to each other.

Of course the men, whose position resembles that of the guards, the state police, and the military, are also deprived and degraded: the majority of the men are isolated from women, except for the high-ranking Commanders, who have their wives and a series of concubines, although these men tend to be middle-aged or aging, and less likely than young males to engender children.

So in Gilead the original generic "emergency" designed to compensate for the ecological disaster and the resulting infertility is not handled effectively at all. Which males are and are not entitled to handmaids is determined by the individual's rank; it becomes a matter of political power. After a while it becomes clear that whatever excuse the government had to attain power, by now its sole purpose is to sustain the dictatorship. This becomes obvious when Offred finds out that, although the Commanders parade in public as puritanical, patriarchal upholders of family values, it is tacitly understood that they have the right to partake of the sexual services of the Jezebels, women sentenced to work as prostitutes in the state brothels maintained for the elite's entertainment.

The dictatorship, like the totalitarian dictatorships of Stalin and Hitler, follows the principles of keeping the entire population in fear and trembling and of reducing victims to a subhuman state. To this end victims who spend their lives in fear of the victimizer are on occasion given the privilege of acting as victimizers. "The architects of Gilead knew, to institute an effective totalitarian system ... you must offer some benefits and freedoms, at least to a privileged few, in return for those you remove" (290). To begin with, the entire population is repeatedly exposed to the bodies of those executed by the authorities following an allegedly "secret trial" – in fact, no trial at all: "The three bodies hang there, even with the white sacks over their heads looking curiously stretched, like chickens strung up by the neck in a meatshop window" (260).

But there is an even more effective ritual in which the "criminal" –
in effect, a victim selected at random by the authorities – is torn to
pieces by the handmaids themselves: "Scapegoats have been notori-
ously useful throughout history, and it must have been most gratifying
for these Handmaids, so rigidly controlled at other times, to be able
to tear a man apart with their bare hands every once in a while" (289).
At this ritual, we hear from Offred, she feels "an energy building here,
a murmur, a tremor of readiness and anger. The bodies tense, the eyes
are brighter, as if aiming" (261). It is after witnesssing this ritual that
Offred feels "for the first time, their power" (268).

Offred's fear for her own safety is enhanced by her understanding
that anyone could be singled out at random as a victim, that in fact
the religion practised in the theocracy of Gilead is a religion based on
human sacrifice. Offred looks at the victim: "He says something. It
comes out thick, as if his throat is bruised, his tongue huge in his
mouth, but I hear it anyway. He says: 'I didn't …'" (262).

Allowing the victims to act as executioners of other victims is probably the single most important ritual expressing the essential mechanism of dictatorship. One could say that the entire population is
enslaved, but the males still feel more privileged than the females, the
wives and Aunts more than the other females, and the general mass of
female slaves are still given the privilege of looking down on the victim
singled out to be torn apart as less privileged (even if only temporarily).

In spite of the constant reminders of terror, in Gilead just as in
Oceania, people occasionally find the courage to explore means of
resistance or escape through the Mayday Underground movement. Of
course, one's contact from the movement could turn out to be an *agent
provocateur*. When Offred fails to get pregnant by the Commander,
Selina, the Commander's wife, arranges a clandestine meeting between
Offred and Nick, the young chauffeur, to enhance Offred's chances of
being impregnated and thereby adding to Selina's family prestige. This
has, of course, to be kept secret from the Commander and the authorities. But Nick and Offred fall in love and begin to see each other more
frequently, and this further secret has also to be kept from Selina: by
offending against any of the strict sexual rules, the offenders play with
their lives. In addition to this risk, Offred cannot know whether Nick
is truly a member of the resistance or an *agent provocateur* working
for the state police. Still, when she gets pregnant and Nick sends a van
for her to take her into hiding and then, ostensibly, to arrange her escape
to Canada, she decides to go; neither she nor the reader can tell
whether she is to be taken to freedom or to her death: "The van waits
in the driveway, its double doors stand open. The two men, one on
either side now, take me by the elbows to help me in. Whether this is

my end or a new beginning I have no way of knowing: I have given myself into the hands of strangers, because it can't be helped. And so I step up, into the darkness within: or else into the light" (276–7).

Since these are the last words of the narrative, the novel ends on a note of ambiguity. This ambiguity is not dissolved in the epilogue either. In the form of the "Historical Note" Atwood uses the framework of an academic conference held two hundred years after the demise of Gilead, where learned and pretentious history professors agree that Offred must have had a chance to transfer her story to tape while in hiding, before her trip to Canada. They also agree that her fate after the period of hiding simply cannot be known. We are left, then, with the fact that Offred took a tremendous risk by entrusting herself to Nick, who may have been her saviour or her betrayer. For a chance of winning her freedom, she took the risk of being captured or tortured if intercepted.

Stillman and Johnson argue that, in contrast to the more heroic stance of resistance taken by Offred's friend, the spirited and rebellious Moira, (condemned to the fate of a Jezebel), or to Offred's mother, who was politically active in the transition period of the 1980s, Offred is complacent, in many ways complicit with the political disaster that turned the United States into Gilead. They state that "in a sense, Offred has betrayed both her mother and her best friend through her complicity, her ignoring that is no ignorance. Ultimately, of course, Offred betrayed herself ... She has given herself 'over into the hands of strangers.'"[10]

I believe this is somewhat unfair as a character description. It would be equally unfair to blame Zamiatin's D-503, Huxley's Savage, or Orwell's Winston Smith for the failure of their struggle for freedom in the totalitarian system. In fact, the entire point of dystopian satire is to emphasize that once we, the Ideal Reader's generation, allow the establishment of a totalitarian dictatorship, it becomes overwhelming, and no effort on the part of an individual within that system is capable of ending it. Our collective failure today dooms the individual in the future. Since the dystopian regime denies its subjects' free will, the central character cannot be made responsible for his or her ultimate failure or defeat in the repressive system that overpowers individuals by isolating them from one another and by transforming them into nameless, faceless numbers. It is inherent in the genre as we have seen it in the six examples so far that, unless *we prevent* the repressive system from coming into being by standing up against harmful trends around us today, we ruin the chances for the protagonist's generation in the future. (In general, one of the threats implied in the author's warning is the longevity of the dystopian system: O'Brien warns Winston that the Inner Party is eternal; in Gilead the words of the

Bible also conjure up, indirectly, an image connected with Eternity, or at least longevity.)

Offred cannot be blamed for trying to appear compliant, since the semblance of compliance is the condition of survival in dictatorship. Also, she is in the biological bind of the parent who has been forcibly separated from her child; she is willing to take any risk to her personal safety so that she can find out about her daughter, hear about her. In the meantime she can survive in this nightmarish society only by becoming pregnant once more. She must comply with the system to assure her life and maintain her hope of seeing her lost child once more. (In fact Offred is persuaded to escape only after she finds out from Selina that her daughter is alive in Gilead, but she has no way ever to make contact with her.)

There is no doubt, as Stillman and Johnson suggest, that Offred's behaviour in the 1980s should be open to scrutiny. They suggest that Offred is the American Everywoman who could "exemplify what not to do before Gilead consolidated its power [because] she was complacent about her own status and rights, [and because] her small resistances were ineffective or counterproductive."[11] Once again, however, I believe it would be unfair to single out Offred for blame more than we individually blame ourselves for being "ineffective" in stopping nuclear experiments, being "counterproductive" when trying to stop fundamentalist hysteria all over the world, or "complacent" about every possible manifestation of sexism.

In fact, it is at times quite difficult for the Ideal Reader to translate the manifold warning implied in the narrative if we read it as a political satire of the American 1980s. It seems clear that the fundamentalists who came to power must have considered the trends introduced by feminism, the sexual revolution, and of a hedonistic consumerism excessive and therefore repellent; the society of Gilead represents a *deliberate reversal* of all these trends by taking away women's freedom, introducing extreme sexual puritanism, and denying people consumer goods that used to provide comfort and entertainment. Yet it is difficult to see how and why these trends could have developed in the context of nuclear accidents, the ecological disaster caused by toxic waste, and the somewhat mysterious phenomenon of infertility. In this case, one assumes, the extreme right wing simply used its latent misogyny to declare women the scapegoats for unsolvable biological and ecological problems. But there is something haphazard in Offred's political analysis here that is not truly clarified by the epilogue either; consequently, the dystopian novel's "message" which usually emerges from our decoding of the satirical target from the interaction between the two time-planes, is not entirely clear.

Booker admits that "Atwood's book is a little vague about the mechanism by which the theocracy of Gilead actually managed to supplant the United States government," but he praises the power of Atwood's dystopian vision, claiming that "the seeds of her dystopia clearly do exist in the contemporary efforts of the American religious right to enforce its beliefs through political power."[12] Here, however, I believe that we should also notice that the attitude to women in Gilead is not simply a continuation of the American attitude to women in the 1980s: it is a reversal, a grotesque backlash to what reactionary forces must have seen as the extremes of feminism. By the same token, the extreme sexual puritanism of Gilead, where both male and female are forced to deny or repress their sexuality, is not a continuation of the mores introduced by the sexual revolution of the 1970s (following upon the Freudian revolution several decades earlier) but its reversal. And here I come to what I see as the general problem of postmodern readings of *The Handmaid's Tale,* which pay no attention to the structural strategies of dystopian satire.

In discussing how the women of Gilead are "stripped of their original names," Booker calls upon Althusser's argument that "the interpellation of the subject begins even before birth in the complex of expectations that the family and society develop concerning the infant to be."[13] Booker's point here implies a seamless continuity, even an identity between attitudes to language in the United States of the 1980s and the dystopic Gilead of the future. But if the subversive or dehumanizing qualities of the practices of Gilead are simply an unchangeable part of the way language operates in any society at any time, we overlook the distorting, aggrandizing mirror of dystopian satire, whose function it is to warn us how to prevent the monstrosity envisaged in a totalitarian dictatorship of the future from becoming a reality. If we insist that the horrors of Gilead are already in full force today in our society, we miss the specific target of the satire as well as the direction of the writer's warning, which is based on the assumption that a democratic society, in spite of its flaws, is still essentially different from a totalitarian dictatorship and, most importantly, that it is therefore still possible to prevent the transformation of democracy into dictatorship.

On the whole, when we compare Bradbury's, Vonnegut's, and Atwood's novels, the three North American dystopian satires, and *We, Brave New World,* and *Nineteen Eighty-four,* we find that all six make an important distinction between the two different time-planes, the time of the writing of the novel and the vision of a hypothetically nightmarish future. The society described in each case demonstrates the legitimization of blatant injustice by a ruling elite, a nightmarish society with the recurring ritual of trials and cruel punishments as occasions to demonstrate the power of the state religion. With the exception of Zamiatin's *We*, which warns of the further development in Russia of the tyranny of 1920, all five Western dsytopian classics borrow elements of foreign totalitarian dictatorships in Eastern and Central Europe to develop their warnings to their own society in the West.

All six novels show an interaction of elements of satire and tragedy, with the tragic elements less prominent in the three North American novels. This is probably because these three works happen to find a solution to the central character's predicament in a situation where hope for the future is still a possibility: Guy Montag escapes and finds shelter among a group of Book People; at the end of a defeated revolution, Vonnegut's Paul Proteus is disillusioned, somewhat cynical, but not entirely incapacitated to fight further; and Atwood's Offred is willing to risk her life to find freedom outside of Gilead.

It is probably also worth noting that the structural principle of the protagonist's awakening, rebellion, and punishment can be observed in all six works; however, in Bradbury's, Vonnegut's, and Atwood's novels the love relationship in the protagonist's awakening seems a great deal less important psychologically, or, to put this another way, here the political involvement of the central character does not coincide with a need for psychological and personal intimacy to the same extent it does in *We*, *Brave New World*, and *Nineteen Eighty-four*.

Another point worth noting is that Bradbury, Vonnegut, and Atwood seem unconcerned with the phenomenon of a Big Brother – that is, the worship of a mythologized, semi-divine leader. The only flirtation with superhuman power is shown in the extraordinary power of a man-made machine: the Mechanical Hound in *Fahrenheit 451*, and the master computer, EPICAC, in *Player Piano*. Finally, it might also be pointed out that Bradbury, Vonnegut, and Atwood do not go beyond the United States in mapping out the borders of their dystopia, while *We*, *Brave New World*, and *Nineteen Eighty-four* project the nightmarish future on to a world-wide screen.

In conclusion, not only do these six dystopian novels show common themes and structures; they also reveal a strong sense of interconnectedness – that is, the earlier "classic" examples put their stamp upon the rest of the genre. Thus, regardless of the different satirical targets in each novel, both *We* and *Brave New World* had an undeniable influence on Orwell, and all three North American dystopias fall into the tradition established by Zamiatin, Huxley, and Orwell.

Part Two

Dystopia East: The Soviet Union 1920s–1950s

Anatolij Ribakov

Vassily Grossman

Abram Tertz Sinyavski

Arthur Koestler

Victor Serge

Andrei Platonov

CHAPTER FIVE

The Writer on Trial:
Socialist Realism and the Exile
of Speculative Fiction

While the Western writers of dystopian fiction have projected their fears of a monster state into a hypothetical future, warning against something that could, but should not be allowed, to come to pass, during the long decades of totalitarian dictatorship the writers of Eastern and Central Europe offered an indignant, often bitter criticism of a dystopic society "as is," a *fait accompli* of historical fact. The reader is also faced with another striking difference between these two bodies of literature: unlike the relatively narrow rivulets formed by the utopian-dystopian genre in the West, in the Soviet Union and the Soviet bloc the utopian-dystopian discourse swelled to become the mainstream of literature in the period under discussion.

With the victory of the revolution, Russia (from 1920 the Soviet Union) became the land of an unprecedented utopian experiment, and the entire body of official Soviet literature written during this experiment became "utopian" by necessity, in that it became the writers' state-assigned duty to reflect, celebrate, and inspire optimism for the building of the state utopia. Lenin and Stalin expended a great deal of energy articulating the "task," the "function," the "duties" to be assigned to literature because they saw the tremendous political importance of the literary work in imbuing the dark, violent, hungry world of the present with the light reflected from the "radiant sun" of Communism fixed safely at the end of the historical process. This function of official literature, to sing the praises of the Communist future by also covering up the flaws of the present, became established right after the revolution; after all, to a regime that rests its legitimacy on a fiction about the future, it must seem natural to buttress this legitimacy with a fiction about the present.

Nevertheless, the codification of this function in "the doctrine of Socialist Realism was launched out of the blue [only] in 1932. During the following years it took shape in several pronouncements at the highest level (by Zhdanov in his speech to the first Writers' Congress in 1934, and then again in 1947 in his "report" on the journals *Zvezda* and *Leningrad*) and, more importantly, through the gradual establishment of an illustrative canon which started with Maxim Gorkij's *The Mother* (1906)."[1]

Of course, one should by no means imagine a climate of freedom for any work of fiction expressing doubt or criticism about the state utopia, whether before or after the 1934 Guidelines. The year 1929 marks Stalin's "fantasectomy" of the literary imagination, the banning of works on future societies (including science fiction). What both Hitler's and Stalin's bans on such works indicate is that, when the state engages the whole of organized society in testing a speculation about the future, there is no longer room for genuinely speculative literature. The imagination is itself nationalized, taken under state control. Written in 1920, Zamiatin's *We*, which follows the Western tradition of speculative futuristic structure, was rejected for publication; but so was Zazubrin's "The Chip: A Story about a Chip and Her," written in 1923, though it does not follow that structure. Another work of a dystopian impulse, Victor Serge's critique of the revolution, *Conquered City*, was written between 1929 and 1930, smuggled abroad in instalments, and published abroad: Serge knew the work had no chance of publication in the Soviet Union, where by 1929 "full power in the literary field was placed in the hands of the Russian Association of Proletarian Writers which, at the 'Stalinist Revolution' plunged into the role of executioner with gusto. Many journals and publishing houses were closed. There was a wave of suicides among writers and poets. Recantations became an epidemic."[2] Platonov wrote *The Foundation Pit* in 1930, but in this atmosphere received nothing but repeated rejections; he solicited the help of Gorky, who saw merit in the work but was also convinced that it was unpublishable for both aesthetic and ideological reasons.

If the official mainstream of literature became utopian literature, it followed that those who held back from their state-appointed task to praise the Party according to the political-aesthetic Guidelines to Socialist Realism would become, in our definition, anti-utopian or dystopian writers. From the point of view of the state utopia they were simply subversives, to be censored or banned.

The Guidelines and the establishment of the Writer's Union in 1934 played an important role in codifying both the ideological and the aesthetic principles of state policy on literature. As for "the Union of Soviet Writers, [it] has been a paradoxical institution. It was structured at the outset in such a way as to enable writers to police literature on behalf of the party."[3] It worked often in co-operation with the KGB, and ultimately under the close control of the Party's Central Committee itself. As Boris Groys has pointed out in *The Total Art of Stalin*, "it is of course irrelevant to object here that Voroshilov or Kaganovich or Stalin himself were not experts on literature or art, for they in reality were creating the only permitted work of art – socialism – and they were moreover the only critics of their own work."[4] But one should probably add here another point as well. Stalin needed the sanction of literature and the arts to offer justification to the ever-changing policies of the Party line dictated by his interpretation of the *realpolitik* of the day, in the name of an ideology based on a fixed image about the future.

The close interaction between the Party's Central Committee, the KGB, and the Writer's Union also provided the regime with a consistent method of singling out and destroying many a loyal and well-established writer by turning him into a *cause célebre* in demonstration of the newest "heresy" the Party decided to introduce to the public. A case in point would be Vassily Grossman, author of *For a Just Cause*, who "enjoyed the full support of the General Secretary of the Writer's Union" until, in February 1953, a new series of purges, directed particularly at Jews, gathered momentum. Suddenly, Grossman's fiction was attacked, "possibly at the instigation of Stalin himself. During the following months he was repeatedly and hysterically denounced as a Jewish nationalist, a reactionary idealist alienated from Soviet society ... and saved from almost certain arrest not by his own 'letter of repentance' but by the change in the political climate following Stalin's death in March 1953."[5]

The interaction between the cultural bureaucracy of the Writer's Union, the Central Committee, and the KGB was still important in the post-Stalin years. Having completed *Life and Fate* in 1960, Grossman submitted the manuscript to the journal *Znamya*: "Even at the height of Khruschov's 'thaw' the editors wasted no time in handing over the manuscript to the Cultural Section of the Central Committee ... In February 1961 two KGB officers came to his home with orders to confiscate the manuscript ... Grossman died of cancer in 1964, deeply depressed ... that his masterpiece would [never] see the light of day."[6]

Another logical consequence of this comprehensive politicization of art and literature is that any writer caught deviating from the aesthetic or philosophical model set by Socialist Realism was pronounced ideologically deviant. Being declared a "formalist," or in Grossman's case an "idealist," implied that the writer had offended against the canon of Socialist Realism; the plethora of such "deviants" demonstrates that "it is impossible to impose a single approach on literature, an act which by its very nature invites dialogue, discussion and disagreement."[7] Yet it seems that the greater Stalin's intolerance of the very principles of literature and freedom of expression, the greater also became his need to hear writers sing his praises. There is a grotesque irony in Stalin's insistence on having poets, including Akhmatova, Mandelstam, and Pasternak, compose odes to him during the darkest terror of the Moscow show-trials in the 1930s – as if he wanted to provide a live performance in illustration of the fictional trial scene in Zamiatin's *We*, where the true poet is executed while the official state poets sing hymns to the executioner as their "Benefactor."

"HYMNS TO THE GODS AND PRAISES OF FAMOUS MEN": PLATO'S PHILOSOPHER KING AND THE STRAITJACKET OF SOCIALIST REALISM

What are the origins of the Guidelines to Socialist Realism? When we speak of the Guidelines, the government decree introduced at the 1934 meeting of the Soviet Writers' Congress and then restated in Zhdanov's decree of 1946, we should recall the inextricable connection between the state's encouragement of the arts and concomitant severe censorship throughout the history of utopian thought.

When Plato's Philosopher King expels the tragedian and the lyric poet from the Republic for encouraging the richness and range of the emotions, he explains that "poetry feeds and waters the passions instead of drying them up; she lets them rule, although they ought to be controlled." Clearly, the Republic does not declare the poet redundant as long as his work is confined to writing hymns and praises of the state, thereby demonstrating his function as the gardener of young souls whose emotions must be pruned and guided in the interest of the community, to be ruled in every aspect of life by "law and reason." Preoccupied by the splendours of technology, Stalin no doubt believed he was paying the supreme compliment to literature by designating the writer "the engineer of the human soul." The unique power of the gardener – or the engineer – to mould the new man who will fit the new model of society is the reason why the Philosopher King acts as a circumspect censor, legislating on every aspect of literature and mythology, beginning with Homer, and determining which stories about gods and goddesses would have to be banned so as not to interfere with the creation of the model state: "We are ready to acknowledge that Homer is the greatest of poets and first of tragedy writers; but we must remain firm in our conviction that *hymns to the gods and praise of famous men* are the only poetry which ought to be admitted into our republic."[8] Does it not seem, then, that in demanding "hymns" to socialism and odes of "praise" to the Master, Stalin and Zhdanov took dictation directly from the Philosopher King?

It was precisely Plato's tremendous respect for the artist's creative power, for the power of language to persuade, mould, evoke, and inspire, that made the Philosopher King wish to exercise absolute control over literature and the writer. In reality, in the Republic it is the Philosopher King who is the Master of all artists, ultimately the prototype of the only "real" artist. All professional artists employed by the state are mere replicas, partial mirror-images or shadows of his creative prerogative, sharing only conditionally in his power to mould the perfect specimen for the perfect society.

The role of the state and the head of the state are very similar in this respect in the greatest utopian experiment of the twentieth century, with its fiat of human engineering, its "casting" or "building" or "forging" the "new Socialist man" of tomorrow. In his famous speech Zhdanov points out the function of literature "to select the best feelings and qualities of the Soviet person" and "to reveal tomorrow for him." A title that reflects upon this image is that cornerstone of the Socialist Realist canon, Ostrovskij's *How the Steel Was Tempered* (1935), where the "steel" that is "tempered" is the new man.[9]

We see the grotesque failure of this originally Platonic attempt to build the new man not only in Huxley's parody in *Brave New World* but also in Voinovich's *Moscow 2042*, possibly the strongest dystopian satire about the Soviet regime, where the scientist-created Communist Superman – Supey for short – is gradually reduced by the scientist bureaucrats to a debilitated, deformed, castrated golem.

LENIN'S "THE FUNCTION OF ART":
LITERATURE ON TRIAL

Moving from Plato to a chronologically closer precursor to the 1934 Guidelines on Socialist Realism, we turn to Lenin's famous 1905 pronouncement on the function of art, claimed to be a key document in the formation of the Guidelines.[10] In both its tone and its subject-matter Lenin's essay demonstrates the threefold phenomenon that came to form the central concern of all anti-utopian or dystopian critiques of the Soviet experiment.

To begin with, the speaker asserts absolute certainty about the future to be delivered, along the path delineated by Marx, by the forces of historical necessity. Second, the speaker asserts an equally absolute faith in one, and only one, Party that is to lead the "revolution from above" and maintain power after the revolution. Finally, self-justified in the scientific veracity of his convictions, the speaker is unashamedly intolerant of any voice in opposition: Lenin's essay reads like a trial where literature, or freedom of expression in general, is put in the dock, and the speaker figures as prosecutor, judge, and defence counsel in the same person: he simply brooks no opposition, whether engaged in politics or in literary criticism.

Lenin insists on the leader's responsibility to harness the energy of the arts – along the same lines he later suggests for the harnessing of electric energy – by making the artist "part of the common cause of the proletariat, a 'cog and a screw' of one single great social-Democratic 'mechanism' set in motion by the entire politically conscious vanguard of the entire working class. Literature must become a component of organized, planned and integrated Social-Democratic Party work."[11] Lenin's vocabulary, with its emphasis on utilitarian, mechanical imagery, is revealing, foreshadowing Stalin's much less eloquent but equally famous toast to the common people at the 1945 victory parade at the Kremlin: "I would like to drink to the people who are considered 'screws' of the great state mechanism, but without whom we, the marshals and commanders of fronts and armies, are ... not worth a darn. Some 'screw' is out of order – and all is finished. I raise a toast to people who are common, ordinary, modest – for 'screws' that keep our large state mechanism in a state of readiness in all areas of science, economics and the military to the common people who are considered 'screws' of the great state mechanism."[12]

Unlike Stalin in 1945, in 1905 Lenin still apologizes for the mechanical metaphor and foresees "hysterical intellectuals to raise a howl about such a comparison, which degrades, deadens, 'bureaucratizes' the free battle of ideas, freedom of criticism, freedom of literary creation, etc. etc." In Lenin's view such an objection is "hysterical," "nothing more than an expression of bourgeois-intellectual individualism." He does, however, make a conscious effort to search for a more inspiring organic metaphor when declaring that the writer must "infuse [into the literary process] the life stream of the living proletarian cause." In these pre-revolutionary speculations, more than a decade before coming to power, Lenin still goes back and forth between the metallic, mechanical imagery of state censorship and the organic image of a "natural" freedom of expression and creativity. He emphasizes that the change of all literature into party literature will not come easily. "Far be it from us to advocate any kind of standardized system or a solution by means of a few decrees," he interjects, an ironic statement in the light of the Stalin-Zhdanov decrees of 1934 and 1946, supposedly a continuation of the Leninist legacy. In the light of Stalin's ruthless enforcement of these decrees by publicly reprimanding, expelling, deporting, incarcerating, or executing writers suspected of subversive ideas, Lenin's words from 1905 receive a tragic illumination.

Yet, in spite of attempting to respond to the objections of an imagined liberal political opponent (repeatedly put down as an ultimately irresponsible "bourgeois individualist"), already in 1905 Lenin emphasizes the need for harsh Party control not only over literature but also over "science, philosophy, or aesthetics." Like a somewhat irritable schoolteacher who cannot get over the repeated mistakes made by his lazy or unimaginative pupil, Lenin points out the paradox in his opponents' clamour for the principle of democratic rights as the foundation of freedom when he promises that "we want to establish, and we shall establish, a free press," but he also adds that this free press "will also be free from [the opponents'] bourgeois-anarchist individualism" (25).

In other words, Lenin argues that the freedom the opponent – by now declared a bourgeois-anarchist individualist – may have in mind has never existed: true freedom can exist only in the Communist future, where the fundamental economic "unfreedom" of capitalism is eliminated. Lenin still insists here that no short-sighted opponent should mistake the leader of the Party for an autocrat, and emphasizes that, within the Party, discussion will always remain free: "Calm yourselves, gentlemen! First of all, we are discussing Party literature and its subordination to Party control. Everyone is free to write and say whatever he likes without any restriction."[13] At this point, however, he introduces a rhetorical twist that undermines what he has just said. He emphasizes that "freedom of speech and the press must be absolute, but so must the freedom of association. I am bound to accord you, in the name of *free speech, the full right to shout, lie and write* to your heart's content. But you are bound to grant me, in the name of freedom of association, the right to enter into, or withdraw from associating with people advocating this or that view" (my italics).[14]

It is worth noting that at this point the polemicist switches to the "I," the first person singular. Who is this "I"? Is Lenin here referring to himself as an ordinary Party member, a member of the Party leadership, or the one and only leader of the Party? If the "I" refers to the leader as the representative of the entire Party, his withdrawal from associating with the person in opposition carries the threat of that person's expulsion from the Party. In the one-party system of dictatorship, being expelled from the Party became tantamount to disenfranchisement and possibly liquidation.

As early as 1904 Trotsky observes that "it is essential to Lenin's position to substitute Party for class; the segment of professional revolutionaries for Party; and the Central Committee for the revolutionaries."[15] Trotsky also foresaw that this process would lead to the total power of one individual dictator.[16] In fact, the dictator is already here in the "I" that suddenly appears in Lenin's 1905 essay in the middle of his argument. And should one simply accept the sudden equation between the right to free speech and the "right to shout and lie"? What started as Lenin's vindication of the "absolute" freedom of speech has ended, within the same paragraph, as a condemnation of the very idea of free speech as nothing but "shouting and lying," to be punished by expulsion from the Party.

It is also at this point that the 1905 essay, written more than a decade before the revolution and almost three decades away from the Stalin-Zhdanov decree, comes to foreshadow Stalin's pre-war and post-war purges: "The party is a *voluntary* association, which would inevitably break up, first ideologically and then physically, if it did not *cleanse itself* of people advocating anti-party views" (my italics).[17] Although Lenin in 1905 might not have associated the purging or cleansing of the Party with Stalinist methods of punishing and persecuting intellectual dissent on the scale of keeping about one-tenth of the population in prison camps, the militant tone towards any opposition reveals intolerance.

At the end of the essay Lenin dismisses his opponent's "bourgeois individualist" argument by insisting that all his "talk about absolute freedom is sheer hypocrisy because the so-called freedom of the bourgeois writer or artist … is simply a masked (or hypocritically masked) dependence on the moneybag, on corruption, on prostitution."[18] (It is interesting that Orwell also reflects upon this point, admitting the limitations of the writer's freedom under capitalism; he argues, however, that these limitations are a great deal more severe in a country ruled by a one-party system.)[19] Lenin implies that the real freedom of literature can arrive only in the utopian future, when it will be openly linked with the proletariat, and by then "all social-democratic literature *must* become Party literature!" (my italics).[20]

It is worth noting how frequently Lenin repeats the term "must" in his essay on literature. It follows from the dictatorial imperative disguised as scientific certainty that once certain historical-political patterns are identified, the effect simply "must" (not will, or would, or may) follow from the cause. It is also at this point that we should examine Lenin's pejorative use of the word "utopia." He emphasizes Marx's point that there must be a sharp distinction between socialism in its "primitive utopian forms" and "scientific socialism."[21] In effect, the crucial difference between the naïve, self-deluding, or outright hypocritical opponents and the speaker of oracular wisdom should be located in the sharp distinction between their inferior, outmoded "utopia" and the speaker's genuinely Marxist "scientific socialism"; in the latter, socialism "must" follow capitalism, and Communism "must" follow socialism in the causal chain of the "scientifically" proven principles of the Law of History.

Since the speaker's picture of the future is "scientific" and therefore irrefutable, it is no doubt the opponent's naïvely unscientific or "utopian" way of thinking that is inferior, liable to be contaminated by infectious bourgeois liberalism: "We" – that is, scientific socialists – "are not utopian," Lenin emphasizes, "and we know the real value of bourgeois 'arguments.'"[22] This, in the context of the essay, means that the argument for free speech advocated by the opponent expresses a "bourgeois individualist" mentality and, as such, is nothing but sheer hypocrisy, indeed a hidden attempt at sabotaging the historical process that "must" lead towards the victory of the proletariat, and "must" do so under the leadership of the Party of professional revolutionaries.

Lenin's tone and strategies on these issues are polemical. The speaker seems totally oblivious of the definition of literature – or art in general – as an aesthetic creation; he simply wants to overcome an irritating opponent who would like to trap the speaker into agreement about a possibly non-utilitarian discussion on the function of art. At times in the essay Lenin's tone is already reminiscent of Stalin's, showing no sense of hesitation or speculation in the face of a complex problem, as if all questions about literature and the artistic process had already been established once and for all and with a logic that should be crystal clear for everyone. At the same time, he also implies that such clarity of reason can be attained only by those who are "politically correct," whose heart is in the right place and who place all their bets on the right goal: the achievement of Communism, the historical triumph of the proletariat.

From this stance of absolute certainty follows an acerbic, angry, often irritable tone, as if saying: "If you don't agree with my observations about, let us say, the colour scheme of Leonardo's Last Supper, it must inevitably follow that you are an enemy who, given the threats surrounding the cause of the proletariat's struggle, deserves to be expelled from the Party, silenced, or eliminated." Obviously, it would be naïve to expect that such intolerance of even the mildest form of opposition, a hostility deriving from the speaker's absolute certitude in the irrefutably "scientific" truth of his own principles, would get milder once the speaker has achieved political power. One can already hear the Lenin of the Tenth Party Congress: "We have no use for opposition. We must have an end to opposition, put the lid on it. We have had enough of it."[23] In Lenin's utilitarian position on the arts, whose energy he must harness in the service of the Communist future, the germs of severe state censorship and the persecution of dissent are already clearly present.

At other times, however, it seems Lenin took care to point out that even his judgment or aesthetic taste had its limitations. It is on record, for example, that he had the remarkable modesty to admit to Gorky in conversation: "I am not an admirer of [Mayakovsky's] poetical talent, although I admit I am not a competent judge."[24] How rare, however, even here, are the admissions of modesty, the admissions of the natural limitations connected with any individual's subjective tastes or opinions. In his discussion of modern art Lenin takes it for granted that a liking for the avant-garde is "pure hypocrisy and of course deference to the art fashions ruling the West."[25] With the mock humility of one who is absolutely certain of being superior to his "opponent" (in this case, one who loves avant-garde art), Lenin makes "bold to declare [himself] a barbarian": "It is beyond me to consider the products of expressionism, futurism, cubism and other 'isms' the highest manifestations of artistic genius. I do not understand them. I experience no joy from them."[26]

His utterances about the art of his contemporaries are old-fashioned and parochial, but, in spite of occasional instances of modesty, he seems to have been proud of these limitations as a sign of revolutionary purity, of his cunning vigilance against the bourgeois enemy within – and we have noted that he would label anyone standing up for the freedom of expression first a "bourgeois individualist" and then a "bourgeois individualist anarchist" – allusions to more and more dangerous and wider and wider representations of the intellectual opponent as "the enemy."

THE CENTRAL DRAMA OF UNMASKING THE ENEMY: THE MASTER PLOTTER

The ever-increasing oversimplification of aesthetic issues and the acceleration of hysteria about the more and more pervasive presence of this mysterious internal "enemy" of the Soviet system remain important elements in the militant pronouncements about literature of Stalin and his puppet, Zhdanov, first in 1934 and then in 1946: "We are put on the front of ideology, we have great tasks that have international significance, and this must increase every true Soviet literary figure's sense of responsibility before one's people, state, Party – the sense of the importance of the duty that is being fulfilled."[27] Stalin's own pathological obsession with enemies, spies, saboteurs – a staple ingredient in his virtually unchanging politics of terror over thirty years – is now imposed as a "must" on the writer when constructing a plot and establishing a cast of characters. Indeed, in a speech called "On the work in the countryside," delivered in 1933, Stalin reveals himself as a "master plotter," a mind that approaches the art of governance as a writer of a thriller would approach scenarios of conspiracies, intrigue, and villainy. The visual concretization of the ugliness of the enemy and the unmistakable delight the speaker takes in unmasking villains are obvious signs of his own temperament:

The class enemy is to be sought outside the *kolkhozes*, in the guise of people with beastly physiognomies, with huge teeth, thick necks, and sawed-off shotguns in their hands ... [yet today] *kulaks* and pseudo-*kulaks*, today's anti-Soviet elements in the village – these people are for the most part "quiet," "sweet," almost "holy" ... They are within the *kolkhoz* itself, as storeroom workers, accountants, secretaries, etc. [They are responsible for] sabotage and damage [making it] necessary to possess revolutionary vigilance – it is necessary to possess the ability to tear the mask off the enemy and show the *kolkhoz* members his true counterrevolutionary face.[28]

Stalin's political speech in this instance could easily be regarded as the scenario for the *kolkhoz* novel (with small changes of locale, of course, it is also the scenario of the factory novel, where the positive hero has to "unmask" the saboteur); it is also a demonstration of a political leader priding himself on literary invention, a natural legislator on genres, content, and style. It is not accidental that in this militarized atmosphere of aesthetics, the vision of trial and punishment lurks as a constant threat not only for the villain in the literary work but also for its author. As Dobrenko has pointed out, "variations on the 'enemies all around' theme occur as early as the 1920s" in Simonov's 'The Red and the White,' 'Friends and Enemies,' 'They and Us'; the positive and the negative heroes: this is the basis of our lexicon, attributes of a role-based, confrontational, mythologized consciousness."[29] Since Stalin's post-war political scenario returned very soon to pre-war methods of terror, inducing a veritable spy mania with show-trials staged within the Soviet Union and in the satellite countries, the tone of post-war literature did not introduce major changes: "It is impossible to find a single work of postwar literature where there are no clear or concealed enemies: the black-and-white scheme of those years simply could not exist without them. The literature at the beginning of the 1950s was engulfed by variations on the 'enemies all around' theme, in the anticosmopolite rendition [when] mass psychosis has reached its apogee ... Spy mania, as well as general suspicion which is at one with a militant anti-intellectualism of sorts, envelops many of the works of those years."[30]

The only thing the official literature of the day would not mention, of course, was the identity of the real enemy responsible for the trial of innocent people, for the hunt for more and more scapegoats, for new and ever newer human sacrifice at the altar of totalitarian dictatorship. Works that did not follow the official Guidelines – that is, works critical of the regime, thereby conveying the message of anti-utopia or dystopia – were simply not published, and writers suspected of subversive ideas were silenced.

Naturally, a certain kind of criticism was always permissible even within the framework of Socialist Realism. It was the task of the writer to draw attention to mistakes – but these mistakes were invariably traced to the vestiges of old, pre-revolutionary prejudices or a not yet fully enlightened class consciousness; these mistakes were committed *against* the Party or the regime. Criticism attacking mistakes committed *by* the Party first became possible after Khruschov's condemnation of Stalin's own "mistakes," at the Twentieth Party Congress in 1956. Consequently, more and more daring criticism, still under the brand name of Socialist Realism, became possible, introducing first an inversion and then gradually a rejection of some of the Guidelines.

INVERSIONS OF SOCIALIST REALISM: DUDINTSEV'S *NOT BY BREAD ALONE*

Novels that follow the aesthetic commands of Socialist Realism but end up inverting its utopian ideology, such as Vaculik's *Axe* and Klima's *An Hour of Silence*, already include elements of anti-utopias or dystopias. Examplary of the ambiguities of these inversions is Dudintsev's *Not by Bread Alone*, published in 1956 – that is, after the Twentieth Party Congress. At first it seems that the author still practises the kind of criticism associated with the officially approved "production novel," where after the discovery of certain mistakes that slow down production, villains are punished and eliminated, productivity is restored, and we are presented with a happy ending, the hero endorsing the Party's leadership in its invincible march towards the socialist future. However, what becomes clear from this novel is that "the methods associated with socialist realism could be turned against the party-state apparatus, portraying it as an obstacle to the building of socialism."[31]

At first glance it seems that Dudintsev observes most of the commands of Socialist Realism. Schoolmaster Lopatkin's characterization follows the larger-than-life heroism of the "positive hero": his faith in his invention, which is to advance socialism, is unbreakable. In his approach to life he is Spartan, to sexuality a puritan. In fact, his feelings for the heroine are far less passionate than his feelings for his invention and his Communist duty, and this, we are given to believe, is precisely why she loves him. A man of working-class origin, Lopatkin is passionately dedicated to perfecting his invention, a virtually miraculous machine for casting steel tubes, because the country cannot yet produce them in sufficient number or the right quality for its enormously accelerated process of industrialization. However, in the course of trying to have his excellent invention accepted, Lopatkin comes upon an involved, complex bureaucracy in the Institute for Scientific Inventions and unravels a consistent conspiracy among factory directors, bureaucrats, scientists, academicians, and Party officials, who envy anyone with original ideas and suspect anyone with moral integrity. The conspiracy manages not only to stall the acceptance of his invention but also to discredit him. As a result, he has to stand trial and is sentenced to years of hard labour in Siberia. The narrative by now reveals its essential affinity with what we have suggested to be the narrative line of dystopia: it is a critique of the elite's nightmarish conspiracy for the miscarriage of justice; the protagonist comes to understand the elite's motives for its conspiracy, but only at the point when he has to face a trial and take an unfair punishment.

Before the end of the novel, however, the narrative takes a turn that allows the author to return to the compulsory affirmation dictated by Socialist Realism. The prosecutor who sentenced Lopatkin to hard labour experiences a change of heart and reopens the case, only to confirm that Lopatkin was not guilty. Lopatkin is allowed to return from Siberia and is helped to break through the resistance of the whole cabal that had formerly been against him. His machine is accepted as a significant invention, and he receives an award. He believes he has earned the right to marry the woman who sacrificed everything for him throughout his years of hardship, and to settle down to a life of peace and comfort. However, at the last moment he recognizes that his former enemies are not only his enemies but also the enemies of socialism, and that they are still in position to sabotage or conspire against any honest but politically inexperienced inventor such as he used to be; he decides to dedicate his life to clearing the way for such new inventors by fighting against the machine of bureaucracy that almost succeeded in grinding him down. In other words, he regains his "optimistic" faith in the regime: it is still building socialism, and is worth fighting for.

Naturally, the first part of the novel, which unravels the elaborate conspiracy of the self-serving elite, is far more convincing than the ending, with its somewhat forced return to Socialist Realist affirmation. Eventually the novel that was first received with great enthusiasm at its appearance in Novi Mir became the centre of stormy critical debates instigated by the bureaucracy of the Party and the Writers' Union; the writer was expelled from "every possible organization" and prevented from publishing for decades; the Novi Mir editor responsible for the novel's appearance in print was dismissed (and advised to go into voluntary exile to Tashkent).[32]

DIRECT ATTACK ON SOCIALIST REALISM:
ABRAM TERTZ SINYAVSKI

In their combined effect, Abram Tertz Sinyavski's 1959 essay "On Socialist Realism" and its companion piece, *The Trial Begins,* are far more direct, more savagely ironic attacks on the Soviet regime than is Dudintsev's novel. Tertz was the first Soviet writer to attempt an in-depth analysis of the literary formula imposed on writers and critics by the totalitarian police-state in the name of building a utopian future. It is no accident that in the novel, set in 1953, the last year of Stalin's reign, Tertz presents us with an elaborate conspiracy of the elite to engineer another chain-reaction of show-trials, beginning with the trial of the teenage son of the Prosecutor himself. Tertz not only shows that the rigged trials and the deliberate persecution of the innocent were the very essence of Stalin's regime, but he also draws attention to the complicity of the self-serving state bureaucrats, who would, of course, still have been in power in 1959 – a point that would not have been lost on Tertz's Soviet readers. Since the book was smuggled abroad to be published, one wonders whether this point was equally clear to the Western reader at the time.

Both the essay and the novel go far beyond the limits of criticism permitted even in a period of a relative "thaw"; in fact, they challenge the very principles of Socialist Realism. Tertz defines the very term as a "strange and jarring phrase," an irrational concept that combines the "nightmare [of] Stalin's dictatorship" with "a crude propaganda trick of Zhdanov" and a "senile fancy of Gorky" (Stalin, Zhdanov, and Gorky being the three authors responsible for the 1934 coinage).

Tertz argues that, whether approached as "fiction, myth or propaganda," Socialist Realism is based on a paradox that goes far beyond the aesthetic problem of representing reality, to the paradox inherent in the contradiction between a secular versus a religious, or an idealistic versus materialistic definition of reality itself. What Tertz ironically calls the "innocent formula" of Socialist Realism contains the far from innocent "secret" of an unresolved contradiction to be located right in its 1934 founding document, which states that "the basic method of Soviet literature and literary criticism ... demands of the artist the truthful, historically concrete representation of reality in its revolutionary development" (116). The formula imposes a moral-intellectual straitjacket – literally a double-bind – on the writer, by declaring it the writer's "duty" to present reality truthfully, yet not the way it is but the way it should be. Can you present reality "truthfully" while you are forcibly directed to transform the readers' consciousness in the name of the compelling ideal of the future? Can you provide a realistic description of the present while being allowed to view it only through the fixed rear-view mirror of the imagined future?

Tertz defines this dilemma in the concept of a "Purpose with a capital P ... an all-embracing ideal, toward which truthfully represented reality ascends in an undeviating revolutionary movement. To direct this movement toward its end and to help the reader approach it more closely by transforming his consciousness – that is the Purpose of socialist realism, the most purposeful art of our time" (150).

In the name of this ultimate "purposefulness" of history that the true Communist is asked to embrace with the militant fanaticism of the Middle Ages, private morality and personal emotions simply disappear, until in the name of the "great ideal before us ... we free ourselves without regret from belief in afterlife, from love of our neighbour, from freedom of the individual and other prejudices." Although originally the revolutionary may have set out "to correct the universe according to ... the shining model of the Purpose" (162), once he condoned impersonal violence as a means to reach the paradise of the future, he had to come to a tragic realization: inhuman, cruel means dissipate the originally noble end: "So that prisons would vanish forever, we built new prisons. So that all frontiers should fall, we surrounded ourselves with a Chinese Wall. So that work should become a rest and pleasure, we introduced forced labor. So that not one drop of blood be shed any more, we killed and killed and killed" (141).

To see the poverty and brutality of Soviet reality the way it is, yet to depict it from the perspective of the Party, that is, the way it should be, demands the ability to practise what Orwell called Doublethink, an ability that in the true believer becomes the "right instinct." Ironically, Tertz praises Khruschov for demanding such a state of deliberately induced schizophrenia from every Communist writer, for whom "the question does not [even] arise whether he is free or not in his creative work ... [and who] need not conform or force himself, [because the true ... party spirit] is a *necessity of his soul*" (166, my italics).

To adhere to the Party line as "a necessity of one's soul" is a fundamental characteristic not only of the writer but also of the "positive hero," who, except for a few insignificant flaws to make him appear human, is in fact a creature crafted to be the Communist answer to Nietszche's Superman. The positive hero's most important emotion is his passionate and fundamentally religious commitment to that higher purpose defined by the Party line, but defined in a different way every day. In other words, once a fictional character has the right feelings for the current Party line, he becomes the positive hero, and it follows that all his emotional relationships must be exemplary: "To read the books of the last twenty or thirty years," noted Tertz ironically in 1960, "is to feel the great power of the positive hero," who "spread in every direction, until he filled all our literature. There are books in which all the heroes are positive" (174–5).

The blatant hypocrisy of the formula that demands that the positive hero should be virtually suprahuman is a reflection of the "insolvable contradiction," that "a socialist, i.e. a purposeful, a religious, art cannot be produced with the literary method of what the nineteenth century called 'realism.' And a really faithful representation of life cannot be achieved in a language based on teleogical concepts" (215).

Tertz concludes that "the result is a loathsome literary salad" that is ultimately "none too socialist and not at all realist" (215). To salvage Soviet fiction he recommends that writers "put ... hope in a phantasmagoric art, with hypotheses instead of a purpose," and he ends the essay with a wish: "May the fantastic imagery of Hoffman and Dostoevski, of Goya, Chagall, and Mayakovski ... and of many realists and non-realists teach us how to be truthful with the aid of the absurd and the fantastic" (218–19).

Although this sentence has been widely quoted by postmodern critics, it seems to me that none of them has noted Tertz's emphasis that the writer should be allowed to be "truthful," whether he uses the strategies of "realists [or] non-realists." In his novel *The Trial Begins* Tertz indeed presents us with a genuinely "truthful" picture of society the way the author sees it and not the way he should see it – a spirited challenge to the central formula of Socialist Realism and, simultaneously, a dark satire of the Party's ideology aiming to cover up for the horrible flaws of a dystopic society.

DYSTOPIAN FICTION AS A CRITIQUE OF SOCIALIST REALISM

To demonstrate one of the salient features of a dystopic society, let us take a look at the fate of some of those who refused to sing its praises. Our study deals with a selection of twenty-odd works expressive of the dystopian impulse, written in the USSR between 1920 and 1991, and in Poland, Hungary, and Czechoslovakia between 1948 and 1989.

Except for Koestler, who wrote and published his novel in the West, many writers on our list were either unable to publish their work in book form (Zamiatin, Zazubrin, Platonov, Grossman, Vaculik); had to wait ten to twenty years to have their work published (Ribakov, Dalos, Moldova); or had to smuggle their work abroad to have it published (Serge, Tertz, Daniel). They were silenced for a considerable period and exiled (Zamiatin, Serge, Zinoviev, Voinovich, Aksyonov); tried and sentenced to prison (Déry; Havel); tried and sentenced to hard labour (Tertz, Daniel); or executed (Zazubrin, Rodionov).

Of course, the fate of the writer or the text does not by itself qualify these works as dystopian fiction. Neither can one expect to classify all those works dystopian that were written, suppressed, or simply hidden away during the Stalin or the Brezhnev regime and brought to public attention between the 1960s and the 1980s. My aim has been to find works of fiction, written during the totalitarian regime, in which the dystopian impetus is the central thrust – that is, works that pay closer attention to the social-political criticism of the regime as a nightmare society than to psychological exploration, or that take a more direct interest in the utopian-dystopian discourse in the human drama acted out in the arena of history than in the human being's relationship to God or to the universe. This selection does not include Pasternak's *Doctor Zhivago* or Solzhenitsin's *A Day in the Life of Ivan Denisovich* or *Cancer Ward*, not because these works are not revelatory of the dystopic qualities of the regime but because they are probably primarily tragic explorations of their characters' spiritual life in the framework of psychological realism. In other words, although Pasternak's and Solzhenitsin's characters move about in a recognizably dystopic society, the writer's interest is not primarily social or political.

Naturally, some works more directly focused on the contemplation of history and politics, like Grossman's *Life and Fate,* for example, may also attempt psychologically dimensional characterization. Conversely, Pasternak and Solzhenitsin may also use some of the strategies of a dystopian critique of society. In another configuration, Solzhenitsin's *The Gulag Archipelago* is a comprehensive and compelling analysis of the Soviet Union under Stalin as a dystopic society – however, it is not a work of fiction.

The works we examine in the next seven chapters are simply a selection, not at all implying that works not on our list would therefore not qualify as dystopian fiction. I hope, however, that the selection will be found sufficiently consistent to display the maximum number of themes and strategies we defined as characteristic of the dystopian impetus: the interaction between tragic and satirical elements; the push and pull between utopian and dystopian perspectives; revelations about the barbaric state religion; the central drama of trial and retribution in the nightmare atmosphere of a society with a machinery for the organized miscarriage of justice. It has been my intention to show in this chapter that in the context of the aesthetic and political principles of Socialist Realism, both the literary work and the writer depicting the true face of a nightmare society behind the mask of the state utopia have themselves been put on trial.[33]

The Dystopia of Revolutionary Justice: Serge's *Conquered City*, Zazubrin's "The Chip," and Rodionov's *Chocolate*

While granting that "the interrelatedness of wars and revolutions as such is not a novel phenomenon," Hannah Arendt draws our attention to the fact that "in our own century there has arisen, in addition to such instances, an altogether different type of event in which it is as though even the fury of war was merely the prelude, a preparatory stage to the violence unleashed by revolution."[1]

Victor Serge's *Conquered City*, Zazubrin's "The Chip: A Story about a Chip and Her," and Rodionov's *Chocolate* juxtapose the protracted violence created by the First World War, the Russian Revolution, and the Civil War with the revolutionaries' faith "that the course of history suddenly [began] anew, that an entirely new story, a story never known or told before, [was] about to unfold"[2] out of the violence. The dramatic struggle between the unprecedented scope and intensity of the utopian hope in a radically new socialist society in the future and the machinery legitimizing violence and injustice in the present (which was gradually killing this hope instead of speeding it towards its realization) forms the central political and psychological dilemma in these three works of dystopian fiction. In each of these works dealing with the period between 1919 and 1921, the push and pull of utopian and dystopian perspectives recall, in an intensified fashion, the typical dynamics we have observed in the six novels that follow the classic futuristic structure of the Western tradition of dystopian fiction, in particular Zamiatin's *We*, Huxley's *Brave New World*, and Orwell's *Nineteen Eighty-four*. Unlike these, however, *Conquered City*, "The Chip," and *Chocolate* do not project their vision of a nightmarish society into the future: in the period between 1919 and 1921, the question of whether Russia was turning into a dystopic society or could still be redeemed by the original utopian dream of socialism was for the writers an unresolved and live issue, very much in the present tense.

The protagonists in these three works of fiction are members of the Cheka, the dreaded Special Commission for the Suppression of Counter-revolution and Sabotage, established by Lenin in 1917. The three works represent the dilemma of revolutionary justice and demonstrate the paradox behind the machinery of violence created to end all violence. The issue is the justification of "revolutionary justice" imposed on the "objective" or "class enemy," people declared guilty by birth and not because of individual wrongdoing. Although Marx was rather vague about the concept of the "dictatorship of the proletariat" and drew attention to the difference between the capitalist as a member of his class and as an individual human being,[3] in the name of the Law of History the revolution introduced the concept of merciless, accelerated class war against the class enemy, a "war" that came to justify virtually incessant violence against any group of targeted scapegoats.

These works, then, explore the protagonists' struggle to keep up with the currents of history that they believe will proceed inevitably towards the goal of socialism. What was the power of Fate in *Oedipus Rex* becomes here the inexorable power of History moving in a set direction. However, while Oedipus asserts his will and becomes an individual by challenging the superhuman power of Fate, the revolutionary in these works of fiction wishes to submerge his or her individuality in order to become one with the historical process, envisaged as a stream, a current, a raft moving down the river, or a train running on its rails.

Victor Serge's Riyik, Zazubrin's Srubov, and Rodionov's Zugyin are all committed Communists, ready to sacrifice their private will, their private conscience for what they see as historical necessity. As members of the Cheka they are given the task of upholding the legitimacy of "revolutionary justice" – in effect, a euphemism for injustice, the denial of the traditional or humanistic notion of justice – and are consequently destroyed by their own principles. Their faith in the revolution has a religious intensity; they are willing to sacrifice not only others but also themselves. Yet the violence and injustice involved in their task creates an intolerable burden for their psyches, and the battle between their commitment to the long-term justice upheld by ideology and their personal awareness that they are violating a humanistic, natural sense of justice in their everyday lives unhinges them mentally and undermines them physically as well. All are broken by this burden, the unresolved contradiction between their Messianic belief in socialism and their commitment to practise dictatorial methods.

VICTOR SERGE: *CONQUERED CITY*

Victor Serge's *Conquered City* has no individual protagonist, no central character, or rather, what emerges as the central character is a collective portrait of the inhabitants of the besieged city of Petrograd between 1919 and 1920, a time when, according to the young Bolsheviks in the novel, one could witness "the birth of a new kind of justice" (37).

Serge himself, like many of the writers we encounter in the next chapters, became a victim of the blatant injustice of the Stalin era. According to Orwell, Serge, together with Silone, Malraux, Borkenau, and Koestler, belonged to "the special class of literature that has arisen out of the European political struggle since the rise of Fascism."[4] It is unlikely that Orwell read Serge's novel about the Civil War, but he was familiar with Serge's *Memoirs of a Revolutionary*, which he made Serge send to his own publisher, Frederick Warburg. Orwell refers to Serge as one of the reliable critics of the Soviet regime, who was slandered by the Comintern as a traitor and a liar and whose works, therefore, would not be published in the Communist-controlled *Modern Quarterly*.[5] In his wartime diary of 1942 Orwell once more expresses his concern that "the Communists in Mexico are again chasing Victor Serge and other Trotskyist refugees who got there from France, urging their expulsion … Just the same tactics as in Spain. Horribly depressed to see these ancient intrigues coming up again."[6]

Serge's *Conquered City*, "his bleakest, most tragic novel," was written between 1929 and 1930 in Moscow before his exile, while the writer was under the surveillance of the Secret Police; the manuscript was smuggled abroad in instalments, and published in France by a press that was destroyed by the Nazis when they invaded France; the only English translation was made from a copy preserved by the French underground.[7] Writing ten years after the events he lived through as a committed Bolshevik, Serge had by then been "expelled from the Communist Party and the Writers' Union, deprived of means of livelihood, tracked and arrested by the G.P.U. … He had seen the best of his comrades of the Revolution decimated through their reckless heroism during the Civil War or purged by the new bureaucracy of Stalinist opportunists and office seekers who were making his own existence a living hell."[8] He was first exiled to Central Asia, then expelled from the Soviet Union in 1935, after which he moved first to Brussels, then to Paris, and finally to Mexico.

The novel begins in 1919 in Leningrad, in the guardroom of Cheka headquarters. The starving city is beleaguered by disease, treason from within, and the enemy without. Like Rodionov's *Chocolate*, the novel makes the cold, the scarcity of food and fuel, vividly palpable. Serge's composition of the collective portrait of the people of Petrograd is sketched in, as it were, layer by layer. At no point does he pass his own judgment on the action, or guide our perceptions in any way other than by juxtaposing vignette to vignette, scene to scene, and by letting us catch snippets of conversation among the characters who emerge on and disappear from our horizon in the whirl of events. Some of the historical characters – without names – also make their appearance in a series of quick, impressionistic sketches. For example, Serge makes reference to Lenin's face as the "pale, flabby, self-satisfied face of the dictator" (41), whom we see receiving letters from the front about the battles between Whites and Reds, dictating military orders, receiving committees, while also trying to appease hungry and disgruntled actors, singers, old comrades, as well as various members of the Party Committee.

Readers not familiar with the historical background may find the novel's choppy, impressionistic brushstrokes, episodic composition, and swirl of characters hard to follow at times; instead of the linear approach of a traditional narrative structure, the novel's aim is to re-create the atmosphere of this besieged city, expecting us to pick up the story-line from visual fragments and short, disconnected episodes, using the techniques of experimental cinema. The novel begins with a long, detailed, visually sensitive description of the city: "Not a single light in whole quarters. Prehistoric gloom."

The mood is established by describing the geography of the city, at the same time alluding to its history. The city lies "criss-crossed by broad, straight arteries and winding canals, surrounded by islands, cemeteries, and huge empty stations, sprawled over the tip of a narrow gulf on the edge of a white solitude" (2). The gulf of historical destiny, the solitude of its isolation may suggest symbolic connotations, but these images are never continued, repeated, or explained, not even indirectly. In fact, the method of composition evokes both the refreshing spontaneity and the frustrating lack of focus of the *cinéma vérité*: suggestive images appear and disappear altogether – when, for example, "skiers armed with heavy Mauser pistols, carrying fifty lovely pointed bullets, a flask of brandy, five pounds of black bread, twenty lumps of sugar, a well-forged Danish passport, and a hundred dollars sewed into the lining of their trousers, moved resolutely, with long strides into that desert where nothing was worse than meeting another man; and women clutching their children ... likewise entered that desert of ice led by traitors and spies, guided by hate and fear, sometimes hiding their diamonds, like convicts their money, in the secret and obscene folds of their flesh" (2).

The evocative images set the mood for these violent and hungry times, and the reader might expect to see a close-up of at least some of these characters or witness their fate enfold on the following pages, but the director is eager to move on to more vignettes. So next he takes us to the interior of the city, to one of the many former palaces that are now occupied by the revolutionaries. After a quick glimpse at "machine guns squatting in the vestibules" and the typewriters clattering all over, the author gives us our first view of Comrade Ryjik, one of the central characters in the collective portrait.

As a member of the Cheka, Ryjik finds his work exhausting; he is in charge of thousands of "humbled captives," members of the former aristocracy and bourgeoisie waiting in the cellars to be transferred to the Cheka offices for interrogation or to be taken out for summary execution. Ryjik also keeps receiving a variety of curt messages and orders: he should requisition clothing, cut back his men's rations, and "arrest the first ten hostages on the list."

These are turbulent times that blunt the participants' compassion for other human beings. When Ryjik finds out that Gorbunov, a fellow Chekist, was shot in the groin, his comrades at headquarters listen to the news by commenting that Gorbunov has always been known as a hustler, requisitioning everything that fell in his way. The men show no compassion for the victims of "socialist justice" in the cellars, or for their own wounded comrades, and Riyik feels uncomfortable about the only sign that he still has vestiges of his private self: he is attracted to eighteen-year-old Xenia, one of his comrades.

While on duty in the guardroom of Cheka headquarters, Xenia is writing a modern poem, comparing the revolution to an enormous fire and celebrating its destructive-purifying power: "Burn out the old. Burn yourself. Man's renewal by fire."

We realize that the city is besieged by starvation, as the last passage of the first chapter refers to the condition of Petrograd objectively and without emotion, like an item in a newspaper: "That night only seven cars of food supplies arrived in the city. (One was pillaged.) Forty suspects were arrested. Two men were shot in a cellar" (7).

Having seen the haphazard, chaotic conditions at Cheka headquarters, and having witnessed the casual, indifferent attitude of the Chekists, whose job is the meting out of revolutionary justice, the reader realizes that the "suspects" must be "class enemies" assembled at random. Whoever does or does not get shot among those arrested is simply a matter of chance. One of the few recurring images in the book is the grey sheets of newsprint pasted all over the walls where people assemble to read the latest announcements, the barrage of newly formulated decrees, and the long and haphazardly assembled lists of those recently executed.

Young Xenia appears several more times in Serge's imagistic plotline. We find out that she is an idealist, undaunted by the lack of food and fuel and the aggravations of living in a formerly comfortable middle-class apartment she now has to share with several other families.

She is friendly with two old intellectuals "huddled in their furs ... happy not to be under arrest, discuss[ing] the news of the day" (12). One of these old men even carries on a conversation with Xenia, complaining to her about the destruction of works of art by the revolutionaries. The girl's answer reveals an attitude that we had already observed from her poem: "We would smash all the porcelains in the world to transform life." And she reproaches the old man, "You love things too much and men too little" (13). Their conversation summarizes the two characters' political position in very few words, also presenting us with the conflict between the humanist and the revolutionary ethic with the brevity of an epigram, as the old man retorts to Xenia's reproach: "Men? But look what you are doing to them." Xenia still feels she can justify the violence of the revolution and murmurs to herself, "It is necessary to burn. Burn. That's what he can't understand," while concluding the conversation with another reproach addressed to the old man: "You love men too much, men and things, and Man too little" (13). Serge points out, without comment, the naïve cruelty of the young girl's idealism: in the service of that lifeless abstraction Man, with a capital M, she turns her back on the suffering of all live human beings around her.

Although Serge deals with individual characters only in a fairly impressionistic way, the recurring vignettes about Xenia indicate that she is central to the narrative development. She is, for example, one of the links in a chain when the Chekists are told to investigate the case of a spy, a young White officer who arrived in Petrograd in disguise under the assumed name of Daniel. It happens to be Xenia who discovers that one of their own comrades, Arkadij, has recently examined Daniel's false papers and released him. Gradually the Chekists also find out that Olga, the young woman Arkadij is in love with, happens to be the fugitive's sister. Once the real identity of the young White officer is found out, it could be suspected that, driven by his feelings for Olga, Arkadij had spared her brother; if this could be proved, Arkadij would be guilty of aiding and abetting a spy. All of Arkadij's comrades realize that these charges would probably be unfounded; Arkadij released Daniel simply because he was deceived by the young officer's false papers. Nevertheless, in the eyes of his comrades Arkadij's fate is sealed: nobody suggests examining evidence before laying charges.

The Chekists conduct a trial by forming a jury, and for once Serge describes the scene in some detail. It is a crucial scene for revealing the mentality of the revolutionaries and points out the irrational working of the machinery of injustice. All of Arkadij's comrades understand that he is not guilty, but even those who are fond of him don't dare to vote against his execution. In fact, the stronger their feelings for their young comrade, the more they insist on doing their duty by ignoring their hearts and escaping into reason and logic. Their logic is dictated by the danger of the besieged revolutionary city, their justice by martial law: Arkadij had the opportunity to corrupt his revolutionary principles; he had an opportunity to place personal considerations over those of his Bolshevik duty. What makes him suspect, of course, is merely circumstantial evidence. But being a member of the Cheka, he himself had been given the power to execute anyone who could be called a "suspect." In fact, when the Chekists get orders like "Clean out the rooms of hostages in category one" (167), they accept that "category one" refers to the class enemy who is personally innocent. Members of the former aristocracy or bourgeoisie may not have done anything against the revolution, but it would be in the interest of their class if the revolution failed. Therefore, they are "objectively" enemies, all of them "suspects." And to "clean out" their rooms in the prison is a euphemism for an order to shoot all of them, without trial, without even an investigation. Now Arkadij himself has become a "suspect," and according to the spirit of revolutionary justice, he has to pay for his former power to kill others by being killed by his own comrades. One by one all of his comrades vote for his execution: "One must pay with one's blood for being pitiless" (152).

Of course, for those who do not belong to the Cheka, it seems that "revolutionary justice" is simply another name for ceaseless terror: "With that kind of logic you could execute anyone. Nobody counts anymore. Even the numbers don't count any more" (139). The grey newsprint lists announcing the names of those outlawed for minor offences or no offences at all, and of those who will be shot without trial as "spies and counterrevolutionists," get longer and longer: on the last list we read the name of the history professor who gave shelter to Daniel, whose identity he simply could not have known; of Olga, Daniel's sister, who in fact had no idea that her brother was a spy; and of Egor, an acquaintance of Daniel. They were all guilty by association.

Serge describes a world driven insane by the long war that has just ended, the revolution, the lack of food and fuel, the threat posed to the revolution by the Whites and their foreign allies. It is a world where the supply commissar's job to requisition food from the countryside for the starving workers in the city in effect condemns the peasants to starvation. Naturally, supply commissars can expect resistance. When the newspaper reports these events, the Bolshevik term for the resister is *kulak*, ostensibly a rich, fat peasant who is another "objective" enemy of the revolution. But suddenly all hungry peasants who resist are termed *kulaks*, and the papers report that in their despair, "when the Kulaks rebelled they cut open the stomachs of supply commissars and stuffed them with grain" (19).

Parfenov, a young revolutionary, has a job not much more rewarding than that of the supply commissars. His task is to prevent the starving workers from stealing from the newly nationalized factory. He has the same conviction as does Xenia: "The workers have to live, but the Revolution must not be killed" (23). He justifies his role to himself as Hamlet does; he feels he must be cruel to be kind. In conversation with the history professor young Parfenov accepts the professor's statistics, that "the death rate in Petrograd this year was higher than in the Punjab during the great plague of 1907" (11), but such details do not disturb his faith in the Communist future.

The young Chekists feel that, because they represent the forces of historical necessity, they must ignore the principles of justice, which claim that the law is to protect the innocent. Working day and night for the distant future, each member of the Cheka finds it quite natural to act as "judges, jailers, and executioners" all in one. At the same time, even though they are convinced that they are executors of the Law of History, they are still haunted by reminders of a private conscience and wonder if they have followed the right path: "Everything and everything has slipped out of our grasp. We have conquered bread, and there is famine. We have declared peace to a war-weary world, and war has moved into every home. We have proclaimed the liberation of men ... and we are the bringers of dictatorship ... We have founded the Republic of Labor, and the factories are dying, grass is growing in their yards" (31). While they are ruthless towards the class enemy, they are also ruthless towards themselves. Thus they realize that being given extra food rations makes them "privileged in the middle of generalized misery" (31). This is one more reason why they feel they have to punish without mercy any Chekist comrade who offends against any of their own rules and abuses this privilege.

Following the fate of the various individuals in Serge's collective portrait of Petrograd makes us realize that the city is besieged not only by the enemy outside but also by the enemy within. Even those revolutionaries who consider themselves defenders of Petrograd and of the revolution are preying on the city by preying on one another, and on themselves.

By the end of the novel, most of the characters with whom we have become acquainted are dead, among them young Xenia, who is mortally wounded while executing a raid with her comrades. Riyik, Xenia's lover, alone is left to ponder the further junction in history, the failure or the success of the Russian Revolution and the other revolutions all over Europe:

And he walked out. He was suffocating. The freezing night cooled his face. Crystallike bells continued to jingle in the distance, far off. Ryjik said aloud the three magic words: "It is necessary. It is necessary." The bells covered them. It is necessary. It is necessary ... The world was empty like a great glass bell.

That night only twenty-one carloads of food supplies arrived in the city (three of them were pillaged). Just as long as we hold out until spring! The proletariat of Europe ...   (185)

The novel is enclosed by "bookends"; both the first chapter and the last end with an item in the newspaper about conditions in Petrograd. Also (like a revolutionary *La Ronde*) the novel suggests the completion of a circle: Riyik was the first member of the communal portrait we were introduced to; he is the last one we see at the end. Yet Serge also suggests that Riyik is only a fragment, or rather one of the many reflections of the besieged city that is being torn between the pain of violent revolutionary injustice and the faith that violence serves the higher purpose of historical necessity.

Richard Greeman, the translator of *Conquered City*, suggests that we should look to the circumstances of the novel's composition to explain its episodic structure: the book was completed bit by bit and sent abroad in great haste, in secret, and in instalments. I believe that, in addition, the overall effect of the quick, impressionistic vignettes, the episodic composition, and the emphasis on atmosphere is part of the author's aesthetic intent to enact the tumult and the haphazardness of revolution, the impersonality of its forces, as well as the elements of chaos and chance.

There is another factor we should probably take note of when discussing Serge's style. Writing in 1930, the time of the consolidation of Stalin's one-man power and four years before the rigid codification of literature by the Guidelines of Socialist Realism, Serge was already able to foresee the persecution of artists and writers who followed the experimental styles of the modernist avant-garde: "In 1929 full power in the literary field was placed in the hands of the RAPP (the Russian Association of Proletarian Writers), which became the instrument for the extirpation of all that was still independent in Russian literature. By campaigns of vilification, by pressure on journals and publishers, by calls for police methods, it sought to bend everyone to the requisite line – service to the party."[9]

Serge's style is deliberately experimental, imagistic, combining effects of impressionism and expressionism, in many ways following the same modernistic aesthetics that inspired Zamiatin's *We* in 1920, and the metaphorically foregrounded language of Zazubrin's "The Chip," written in 1923. By 1930 this style was not only a deliberate attempt to express the revolutionary spirit of the early twenties but an equally deliberate attempt to challenge not only the political but also the aesthetic climate of Stalin's regime.

VLADIMIR ZAZUBRIN: "THE CHIP: A STORY ABOUT A CHIP AND ABOUT HER"

Vladimir Zazubrin's novella "The Chip," written in 1923, "was rejected by the editorial board of *Sibirskie ogni*; a later reworking of the story as a novel also remained unpublished, and the manuscript has been lost. Zazubrin was arrested at the height of the purges and shot ... in 1938."[10] The novella was not published before 1989, in the literary journal *Eisney*, and was first published in English in 1991.

Like Serge's *Conquered City*, "The Chip" takes place during the first few years of the revolution, but unlike Serge, Zazubrin focuses on a more detailed portrait of the central character, Srubov, head of the Cheka Central Committee in a small town. Srubov is in charge of the operations of the Cheka, responsible for the mass executions that take place in the cellars of headquarters, which produce hundreds and hundreds of corpses. Shooting former cavalry officers, priests, gangsters, their own comrades who had made a mistake, men and women of all ages, the Chekists keep hauling up more and more bodies, while priding themselves on the fact that "the whole thing runs like a machine ... like a factory" (13).

Srubov justifies the practice of dispensing with trials and holding only perfunctory hearings. At one of these hearings he asks the name of the prisoner in his office but does not even bother to write it down. Paying no attention to the answer, he repeats the same question three times. By the third time, the prisoner realizes that nothing he – or thousands of others – could say will deter the Chekists from shooting him. Srubov simply closes his eyes to human beings as individuals. He is devoted passionately to the revolution and justifies the idea of defying legal tradition and keeping the hearings and the executions secret. This way thousands of the revolution's "enemies" will disappear without a trace, without a chance to turn up as martyrs.

Srubov believes in the revolution not only as a principle but as an animated spirit with a will and a soul of her own. He asks himself: "But does She really find any of this interesting? All She has to do is make some people kill, and order others to die. That's all. The Chekists, and Srubov, and the condemned prisoners are merely insignificant pawns, tiny screws in the huge mechanism, already hurtling out of control. In this factory coal and steam feed Her anger. She is the only boss here, at once cruel and beautiful ... For Her and for Her sake [Srubov] was prepared to do anything. Even murder, if it was in Her interest, filled him with joy" (15). He thinks of the revolution as if it were alive though larger than life, the archetype of the Terrible Mother: "As for Her. She is not an idea. She is a living organism. She is a pregnant peasant woman, a woman who wants to bear Her child, to bring it into the world" (22).

As the head of the local Cheka, Srubor receives hundreds of denunciations a day and develops a deep contempt for human beings; the only passion he has is his passion for the revolution. He is becoming so different from the person he used to be that his wife, who feels horrified of being married to an executioner whom everyone avoids in dread, decides to leave him and take their young son with her. He barely shows emotion: he is preoccupied with his commitment to the revolution and to socialism, her unborn child.

He prides himself on following reason and not emotions, and wishes to suppress everything personal. His friend from school, Kats, who fought together with him in the underground, works for the Cheka also. Srubov's father, an old physician who declares that Bolshevism is "a fit of madness" that people should be cured of, falls into Kats's hands. Kats signs his death warrant because the old man has organized an Association for Ideological Struggle against Bolshevism. Kats explains that he has to do his Bolshevik duty in spite of his friendly ties with Srubov and his genuine affection for Srubov's father. Srubov denies his feelings to such an extent that he himself believes that he respects Kats's dedication to the revolution; deep down, however, he holds an understandably deep resentment against his old friend and fantasizes about his death. Srubov lives a life where he has to deny all natural human instincts, and so do his subordinates. One of these admits that he was driven to drink after he had to shoot his own brother in one of the Cheka cellars.

No doubt, the Chekists carry out a job that is dehumanizing, but we also see them genuinely joyful when they believe they can spare some lives. A hundred peasants have participated in an uprising against their local Soviet; when they are given clemency from above, the Chekists celebrate with a snowball fight in the freshly fallen snow, suddenly feeling alive and full of lust for life.

On the whole, however, Srubov lives like an automaton engaged in endless executions. When Ivanov, one of the Chekist interrogators, wants to take advantage of his position and make a pass at a female prisoner during interrogation, Srubov orders them both shot; Ivanov first, to convince the prisoner that the Chekist who abuses his position will not be left without punishment; then the prisoner, simply because she happens to be a class enemy.

Srubov can feel no love or empathy for human beings anymore. He feels contempt for the prisoners' relatives who come to him to beg for the life of a son, a husband, a father awaiting execution. He looks at them indifferently as "pinheads," and cannot be deterred: like a train, or like the grey wagons that keep carrying the corpses from the Cheka cellars to the cemetery, he cannot be jolted out of his course; he sees himself as a chip of the raft carried on by the revolutionary current – he is as impersonal and as indifferent.

When one of his comrades argues that a particular suspect is not guilty, Srubov reprimands him: "Shut up, you sentimental fool. The Cheka is a tool in the class war. Understand? If it's war, then there can be no courtroom hearings. We do not dispute the principle of personal accountability, we just operate it differently from an ordinary court or a revolutionary tribunal. What matters most for us is the position an individual occupies in society, the class he belongs to. This, and only this, is what counts" (61).

With the concepts of the "class enemy" and the unstoppable stream of history, any personal sense of justice or compassion is beside the point. "Suspects" do not have to be put on trial; it is unnecessary for the prosecutor to prove their guilt: they are guilty by birth, for belonging to a class that must be swept away by the torrent of historical forces. By the end of the story Srubov himself will be swept away by this same stream.

Still, although Srubov seems to be convinced that he is simply performing his duty, the life he lives is beyond human endurance. We see the psychological decline leading to his collapse, although he denies this process even to himself. He is unable to sleep in the dark, and starts drinking heavily and cannot be cured even by long stints in the hospital. Finally, when confronted with Kats at a hearing whose aim is to warn Srubov, he vents his rage on Kats, who then signs a warrant for Srubov's arrest. By this time Srubov is delirious with anger and feelings of guilt accumulated over his months as head executioner: he breaks the mirror in his bedroom because he cannot tolerate seeing his own face. When he closes his eyes, he sees himself as a chip separated from the raft of the revolutionary current, and by now he sees this current boiling with the blood of the people he has executed. His mental balance is gone; he sees visions that spell out to him his sense of guilt and of being irrevocably lost: Srubov was going down "a blood-red river. Only this time he wasn't on a raft. He had broken away from this raft and like a solitary chip was now bobbing up and down on the waves."

Following organically from the mental landscape of this particular protagonist, these images also happen to be archetypal in expressing the revolutionary's sense of the historical process. In the words of Arendt, "in the decades following the French Revolution, this association of a mighty undercurrent sweeping men with it, first to the surface of glorious deeds and then down to peril and infamy, was to become dominant. The various metaphors in which the revolution is seen not as the work of men but as an irresistible process, the metaphors of stream and torrent and current, were still coined by the actors themselves, who ... no longer believed that they were free agents."[11] What is said here about the French Revolution could be said equally about those dedicated to the Russian Revolution, since, "if it is true, as Marx said, that the French Revolution had been played in Roman clothes, ... the October Revolution was enacted according to the rules and events"[12] of the French Revolution.

Srubov is destroyed by the very law of historical necessity that he deified through his work as an executioner. By the end of the narrative his contemplation of historical forces turns into a vivid hallucination, a sure sign of a psychotic breakdown:

What he heard was not the stamping of feet, nor the beating of drums, nor the blare of trumpets – it was the earth shaking, rumbling, crushing down around him, a volcano erupting, blinding him with its red-hot, bloody lava, its black, burning ash raining down on to his head and on to his brain ... He had to cover his scalp with his hands to protect his brain from the black, scalding liquid. Yet he could still see what was flowing out of the fire-breathing crater: a river, which was narrow, and a dull, blood-red colour as its source ... and which, at its mouth, spilled over into the vast gleaming emptiness, flowing out into a boundless, radiant sea.   (68–9)

The novella ends with the protagonist's animated vision of the revolution. He is still overwhelmed by the power of this vision, but understands that he has been destroyed by its violence: "She stood tall. Her naked feet planted on the great plain, watching the world with vigilant, hate-filled eyes" (69).

ALEXANDER RODIONOV: *CHOCOLATE*

Rodionov's *Chocolate,* the first novel about a conceptual trial, appeared in 1922 in a literary magazine, *Molodaja gvardgyija,* and created a world-wide sensation. However, it was not published in book form before 1925, and even then in so few copies that it was kept virtually inaccessible within the Soviet Union; its fate was not affected even by the thaw under Khruschov, when works of Babel and Plinyiak were readmitted into circulation. The truth the novel revealed about the everyday activities of the Cheka under Lenin was simply unacceptable to the Soviet regime, regardless of the many changes in literary policy after 1956.

The writer, Alexander Tarasov-Rodionov, was the famous Bolshevik officer who was instrumental in foiling the tsar's plans to escape to England. Having participated in the bombardment of the Winter Palace from the Peter-Paul Fortress during the October Revolution, Rodionov fought against the White counterrevolutionary forces in Tsaritsin, Petrograd, and Kronstadt. Like many Bolsheviks of his distinction, he was executed as a Trotskyite in 1938, and his literary works were effectively wiped out of the consciousness of his countrymen.[13]

The novel deals with a conceptual trial based on a preconceived idea: the provincial capital is surrounded by the Whites, and the starved, overworked population is ready to revolt against Bolshevik rule. There are "whispering rumours" that Zugyin, the head of the local Cheka, eats chocolate when everyone else is starving, and that he accepts bribes, even gold, from potential victims of the executioners' squads, and then he signs papers of acquittal. These rumours create strong hatred against the Bolsheviks among the population, and his comrades, in the presence of a comissar sent from the Central Committee, decide to make him stand trial. At the trial it never occurs to anyone either to request or to provide evidence to the most dangerous allegation, that Zugyin accepted bribes and signed acquittals. The Special Committee decides they have no time for such minor niceties. The enemy is approaching the city; there is an urgent need to organize special workers' battalions and then take them to the front immediately – the execution of Zugyin will create the right impression to calm down the dissatisfied, starving population: "We must immediately move all the workers to the front. And for that reason, for precisely that reason, and not because he is guilty of anything, Zugyin will be shot" (271).

A fully committed revolutionary, Zugyin accepts the fact that the Party needs to sacrifice him: he is willing to accept his own role in the sacrifice. He himself has dealt with "revolutionary justice" in such a way that many who were personally innocent have been sacrificed to the revolution. For example, when he hears that a good comrade of his, Abram Katzmann, has been murdered by the enemy, in his outrage he peremptorily orders the execution of a hundred hostages held in the cellars of the Cheka. The hostages are of a mixed background: officers of the former tsarist army, members of the former middle class, professors, peasants who resisted the requisition of their grain, or simply people arrested on false denunciations for "conspiracy" or for "hoarding" food or valuables – men and women of all ages. Even if they had the motive, technically they could by no means have committed Katzmann's murder, since they were already in custody at the time. Of course, they are guilty not individually but *en masse*. It is not in their interest to see the revolution succeed; hence they are, by definition, counterrevolutionaries. The execution of a hundred hostages is to demonstrate the Party's power to exact retribution, and to act as a deterrent; it is not at all connected with the old-fashioned principles of justice based on punishing the guilty and sparing the innocent. Later Zugyin raises the question: "Is there such a thing as guilt? Is the bourgeois guilty of being born a bourgeois, and the crocodile that he was born a crocodile?" He declares that "guilt and innocence in [the] petit-bourgeois use of these words do not exist for [him]" (136).

Zugyin gives many signs that he is willing to sacrifice himself for the revolution. He works day and night, often until he is so exhausted that he falls asleep at his desk; if he goes home, he does so only to sleep, and barely notices that his own wife and children are undernourished, have no stockings or shoes, and suffer from the cold. In fact he refuses to notice, because he believes that while the masses are suffering, the family of the Cheka's secretary have no right to enjoy privileges.

It is ironic that it is precisely this puritanical revolutionary who will be trapped by allegations that he accepts bribes that interfere with his function as a totally impartial and ruthless executioner of the counterrevolutionary enemy. In the course of interrogating a group of suspects consisting of professionals and artists, he comes across Valc, a former ballerina who has prostituted herself for food and the necessities of life. Zugyin takes pity on her, gives her a job at his office, and does not interfere forcefully when Valc makes friends with his wife and takes a rare gift of chocolate and stockings to the family suffering want.

Although Zugyin is attracted to Valc, and the young woman makes sexual advances to further assure his good will, he is steadfast in turning down these advances. Nevertheless, Valc – a character the writer presents as a curious mixture of an almost childish vulnerability, sensuality, and lack of moral scruples – manages to take advantage of her position. She discovers that Chortkin, formerly one of the rich young men in her circle, has been languishing in prison in spite of the fact that he has been cleared of charges of conspiracy. Valc wants to use her influence with Zugyin to her own ends; she decides to blackmail the young man's rich parents to provide her with twenty pounds of gold if they do not want to see their son shot within twenty-four hours. The chaotic conditions at Cheka headquarters allow Valc to steal the documents relating to the case, after she has them signed by Zugyin.

Rodionov, just like Serge and Zazubrin, raises the question of the role of individual responsibility in a world caught up in the sweep of the revolutionary current of history. Is Zugyin responsible at all? He is unaware of Valc's activities; still, he is made responsible for them when the rumours leak out, probably through the young man's parents and the lawyer whom they engage to assist them. Zugyin does not admit complicity in Valc's blackmail of the Chortkins; neither does anyone offer evidence that the blackmail was successful: the gold, we hear, simply disappears from Valc's room, and we never even find out whether young Chortkin is let go, as Valc has promised. Zugyin hears when he is already in custody that Valc has been arrested and will also be executed.

Since it is discovered that Valc had received the chocolate she gave to Zugyin's wife from a White officer, the rumours of Zugyin's sexual misconduct are combined with rumours of his accepting bribes from the enemy. These rumours become the focus of Zugyin's trial, conducted by a Special Committee, including an investigator sent from the capital and Zugyin's own Chekist comrades. He is sentenced to death.

There is a moving scene in which Zugyin is allowed to see his family for the last time. He convinces Lena, his exhausted, frightened wife, who has been his companion since their involvement in the underground Communist movement before the revolution, that he is not going to be executed. He tells her that the Party will simply assign him to another post – maybe in Australia. He admits to her, however, that his family might never see him again. Shattered, his wife and children leave. They all know that the family not only will lose its provider and protector against the violent upheavals of the times but also will be stigmatized as the family of a traitor; they are all guilty by association.

Still, the condemned man's last thoughts do not belong to his family: he confronts his death as part of the process of historical necessity, his last sacrifice to the cause of socialism. In spite of personal bitterness against the investigator who has humiliated him at his trial, he believes that his sacrifice is not meaningless, and that his fight – the Party's fight – will go on.

His position is similar here to that of another controversial Bolshevik, Rubashov, in Arthur Koestler's *Darkness at Noon*: the good Communist accepts the false accusations and goes to the rigged trial without embarrassing his former comrades because he accepts that at that particular juncture the Party needs scapegoats from its ranks; he is willing to play the role assigned to him, even if that role is that of the traitor, whose name will go down in ignominy in history. It is important to note here that in the secular religion of the revolutionary, the outcome of the historical struggle takes the place of the eschatological promise of heaven for the religious believer. Therefore, to give up hope of ever being admitted among those who have died for the utopian dream, the Communism of the future, is the most devastating blow for the true believer. The psychological tragedy that follows from the protagonist's total disregard for the guilt or the innocence of the individual, from the fanatical commitment to what he sees as the unswerving course of history, is rendered here with convincing power.

Rodionov reveals his sympathy for Zugyin; nevertheless, he also shows the "satanic mechanism" (210) of the system that at first compels the Bolshevik to follow the Party's corrupt position that the end justifies the means, and then to die for the purity of the original ideal by taking on the Party-assigned role of the despicable traitor. This "satanic mechanism" becomes truly memorable in light of the fact that Rodionov, the committed revolutionary, was himself caught by the much more advanced version of the same mechanism at the height of the Stalinist terror in 1938, and denounced and executed as a Trotskyite.[14] But what all three stories about the Cheka's activities between 1919 and 1921 illustrate is that the principles of Stalinist terror were already well established under Lenin's leadership. The message of Rodionov's dystopic novel had to be suppressed even after Khruschov's admission of Stalin's mistakes and in the ensuing waves of de-Stalinization because it raised an uncomfortable question. If even the heroic Leninist period of the revolution could be regarded as a dystopic society, where the ideology propagated by a one-party system demanded new and ever newer enemies, not only from the outside but also from within the Party, and this "satanic mechanism" was an essential part of the regime right from its foundation, where could one look for the pure Leninist revolutionary tradition the Party was to return to after the admission of Stalin's "mistakes"?

There is no doubt that there were several models for Zugyin's character during the chaotic, brutal years of the Civil War. It is interesting to note, though, that Chocolate was allowed to be published in 1923: its message then was not found objectionable. It was also translated into several foreign languages. I am aware of a Hungarian translation from 1930 by a Hungarian Communist, Frigyes Karikás, who later found asylum in the Soviet Union. It is a tragic irony that both writer and translator fell victim to the purges and show-trials of the late thirties, the principle of which Rodionov was first to describe. Even if on a much smaller scale, Chocolate anticipates the gigantic machinery of the show-trials stage-managed by Stalin himself. The Chekists of the "heroic age," the revolution and the Civil War, almost all fell victim to these purges; Stalin wanted a new guard of functionaries and bureau-crats who owed their position to him alone. In his excellent epilogue to the novel's Hungarian translation,[15] M. Kún suggests that there is evidence that Stalin himself would not have respected such puritans as Zugyin, who rejected his hungry wife's and children's pleas for the privileges a Chekist could easily have acquired. In fact, as the Com-missar of Nationalities in 1918, Stalin organized a special train unit at the front of Tsaritsin whose responsibility it was to take care of the Commissar's provisions. Both Budyonnij and Voroshilov imitated the aristocrats of the previous regime in sending expensive gifts to Fyodor Chaliapin so that he might entertain "the red gentlemen" with his singing.[16] It is probably worth a footnote that Victor Serge in *Conquered City* describes the actual scene when Chaliapin, in his white shirt and black tails, appeared on the stage of the Opera to sing for the starved, unwashed, ragged population of Petrograd.

After reading *Conquered City*, "The Chip," and *Chocolate*, all describing Russia between 1919 and 1921 as a nightmare society, one is strongly reminded of Orwell's description in *Animal Farm* of the "original sin" of the newly won revolution, the first offence against the revolutionary faith of equality in a classless society preached by the leaders. At first the animals agree that no animal should drink milk – it should be sold to other farms in exchange for provisions for all. At one point, however, both Napoleon and Snowball decide that since the pigs perform intellectual work indispensable for the survival of Animal Farm, they – and only they, among all the animals – are entitled to drink the milk. Gradually, once the first privilege of the new ruling class is legitimized, Orwell shows us, more and more examples follow, until the very spirit that inspired the revolution disappears, so that its creed that "all animals are equal" becomes negated by what seemed at first like a harmless addition, that "some animals are more equal than others."

Rodionov's *Chocolate* irritated the revolutionary leaders, who were, by the late twenties, abandoning the principles of class equality they had once preached. Gradually, most of them started accepting privileges supposedly in accord with their social position. As described in M. Kún's sketch on the novel's historical background,[17] Stalin manipulated this situation with great gusto. On the one hand he encouraged those on top to enjoy the trappings that used to go with top positions in the previous ruling class – good food, the sexual services of attractive younger women, elegant apartments and furniture – while on the other he used their weaknesses against them. When Kirov's wife engaged a special train for the transportation of their valuable furniture from Baku to Leningrad, Stalin made Zonyin, a leading journalist, write a scathing article about it in *Pravda*; then he had Zonyin expelled from the ranks of the Party for spreading rumours about the leaders of the Party.

The question of privilege was undoubtedly a burning issue during the Civil War, with its siege mentality, where people could be executed for "hoarding" two kilos of lard or flour. The chocolate Zugyin's wife accepts from Valc thus assumes tremendous significance in the imagination of the starving people. It is interesting that we never see Zugyin eat from the chocolate: it is enough that his wife and his two hungry children do. The rumour that he has partaken of this small privilege has, in effect, a much graver significance in the protagonist's fate than the far more serious allegation, the accepting of gold as a bribe to acquit the enemies of the people.

All three stories dealing with mass executions by the Cheka also offer insight into the mentality of the people; they show how mechanically, how inertly, the onlookers accepted as routine the executions, rarely resisting or even questioning the rationale behind them. If these three works read today as dystopian fiction, I believe their description of the mentality of the masses who accepted slaughter without resistance for years is just as important in re-creating the nightmare atmosphere of a dystopic society as is the tragic fate of the central characters.

No doubt both Zazubrin's protagonist, Srubov, and Rodionov's Zugyin have a tragic fate. But can we speak of tragic heroes without recognizing the concept of the individual? We are faced with a paradox: what these protagonists sacrifice at the altar of the Communist future is precisely their individual freedom, the very concept of having an individual personality, a private conscience, a private morality. They accept without a second thought the Party's rules of political exigency, that the end justifies the means, that universal justice in the Communist future justifies the violence, the injustice, the human being's inhumanity to another human being in their everyday life in the present. Admitting that the individual has no power to influence events except by becoming part of the "raft," the "train," the "current" of the historical process, they are all swept away by the same forces to which they have sacrificed their private lives.

Yet, in spite of the carnage and the "satanic machinery" that requires new and even newer scapegoats – the essential dynamics of a dystopic society – none of these three works dealing with the period 1919 to 1921 renounces the original utopian dream of the revolution: the image of the new society may have become tarnished, but the image of the "radiant future" that inspired the revolution remains, somehow, still unclouded.

Although the tone of the works creating a dystopic nightmare atmosphere will change in the course of the thirties and forties, the writer's voice will remain, for a very long time, the voice of the critic from within, implying harsh protest against the various phases of the regime that offended against the original ideal, yet not until the late seventies renouncing the ideal itself. In 1958 Pasternak's is still a lonely voice as he tries to explore the source of the dystopic society by turning to the mentality of the revolutionaries themselves: "It turns out," Zhivago announces to Lara, "that those who inspired the revolution aren't at home in anything except change and turmoil: that's their native element; they aren't happy with anything that's less than on a world scale ... And do you know why there is this incessant whirl of never-ending preparations? It's because they haven't any real capacities, they are ungifted. *Man is born to live, not to prepare for life.*"[18]

CHAPTER SEVEN

The Legalization of Terror:
Platonov's *The Foundation Pit*,
Ribakov's *The Children of the Arbat*, and
Koestler's *Darkness at Noon*

ANDREI PLATONOV: *THE FOUNDATION PIT*

In a world where the building of the socialist utopia has moved to the very centre of political reality and consequently into the mainstream of its "realistic" literary reflection, it is difficult to set the parameters of dystopian satire as a genre of its own. A case in point is Andrei Platonov, "one of the most original writers of the century ... a proletarian and dedicated communist. He produced a more profound refutation of Soviet ideology than any anticommunist author in the Soviet Union or abroad."[1] Another difficulty for the Western reader is the need to be intimately familiar with the historical political context in order to get the references and often subtle allusions to the reality the writer is *forbidden* to criticize openly. Without these references it would remain "difficult for the Western reader to appreciate what may be the most profound work of Soviet literature."[2]

Platonov's *The Foundation Pit* (1930) mixes the spice of folkloristic elements, surrealism, and the allegory of the parable into the bland state-prescribed diet of Socialist Realism (still to be codified in the Guidelines of 1934), not only to make this diet more palatable but also to camouflage the pungent, bitter flavour of biting satire. Still, this novel was not allowed publication in the Soviet Union in spite of Platonov's repeated entreaties to Gorky for his help. It was first published in 1987 in the Gorbachov era, more than a quarter-century after Platonov's death.

It is important to notice that the novel does *not* take us to the future. The central metaphor, the foundation pit, refers to the present generation's *dream* about the future, "of constructing one single building in which the entire local class of the proletariat would take up living quarters – and that common building would tower above the entire city made up of separate buildings and residences and courtyards, and the small individual homes would fall empty and would be covered over impenetrably by the plant world, and there people of a forgotten time, wasted away, would gradually cease breathing" (81).

In this dream, individual, private life is to be eliminated completely. The people come to resemble the Trade Union representative, who, "in the hustle and bustle of rallying the masses and organizing auxiliary joys for the workers, did not remember about satisfying with satisfaction his personal life, and he grew thin and slept deeply at night ... But he could not come to a halt and possess a contemplative consciousness" (18).

In fact, contemplative consciousness is forbidden by decree: Voschev, a labourer who is known to be making periodic attempts at thinking, is fired from his first job for this very reason. He is pleased to be allowed to assist in digging the pit, surrounded by people who feel that "the pit must be dug and the house built more [and more] swiftly, for otherwise you could die without having finished" (31). True to type, Voschev still mutters that "no matter what, we are never going to dig to the bottom of the whole world," but he is surrounded by men like Chiklin, who "hurriedly broke up the age-old earth, channelling the entire life of his body into blows at the required places" (21).

The pace of work is accelerated to the point of turning the entire project – the creation of physical and spiritual dwelling for the new socialist man – into a phantasmagoria. The planned economy is driven by the hysterical will of the "Main Person in the city" from above, but it is a hysteria that is contagious. Thus, the worker's foreman, Pashkin,

kept constantly thinking bright thoughts, and he reported to the Main Person in the city that the scale of the house was too *narrow*, for [surely] socialist women would be replete with freshness and full-bloodedness, and the whole surface of the soil would be covered with the sown seeds of childhood. Would the children then really have to live out in the open air, in the midst of unorganized weather?

"No," replied the chief, knocking the nourishing sandwich off the table with a sudden movement. "Dig the main foundation pit excavation *four times* bigger." (80)

The megalomania of the Main Person in the city becomes clear when Pashkin bends down to pick up the sandwich: "'It wasn't worth it to bend over,' said the Big Man. 'For next year we have projected agricultural production in this district at half a billion'" (81).

Half a billion of what? we may ask. And compared to what? Of course these questions never receive answers. In light of the novelist's description of a country where people are dying of starvation and fever, the irrationality of the planning process is clearly absurd. But does Platonov put the blame entirely on the shoulders of the Big Man in the city? No. The local big man, Pashkin, participates in the hysteria by translating such a cold, lifeless abstract term as the "Party Line" into a flesh-and-blood incarnation of the omniscient Godhead: after his talk with the Big Man, he is "weighing the idea of increasing the foundation pit not *four* times in size but *six* times, and thereby forging ahead of the main Party Line so as subsequently to greet it joyously on open ground – and then the Party Line would see him, and he would become impressed upon it in the form of an external dot" (81).

The novel was written during the first Five-Year Plan, the irrationally accelerated rate of industrialization in the cities and the brutal, forced collectivization of the peasants in the villages. According to the memoirs of Victor Serge, one of Platonov's contemporaries and author of *Conquered City*, by 1928 the Russian Revolution reached a new stage. In effect, "a Bureaucratic Counterrevolution had obtained power and a new despotic state had emerged ... From the depth of his exile in Alma Ata, Trotsky affirmed that this system was still ours, still proletarian, still socialist, even though diseased."[3]

This, in effect, is *the* question historians have been debating. Was the requisitioning, the forced collectivization, the terror, and the deportation of millions simply a flaw in the building of socialism, or were these atrocities the inevitable consequences of a process that, in the name of eliminating the oppression of the past, gave birth to a new ruling class, a new bureaucracy, that resorted to oppression on a scale and at an intensity unprecedented in Russian history?

"Will it be ever known," asks Victor Serge, "how terrible was the disorganization of agriculture that resulted from the requisitioning and forced collectivization? Rather than hand over their livestock to the kolkhoz, the peasants slaughtered the beasts, sold their meat and made boots out of the leather. Through the destruction of the livestock the country passed from poverty to famine."[4]

Around the foundation pit, Platonov tells us, the workers are suddenly puzzled by the fact that clouds of flies appear, in the middle of winter. The flies have come to feast on the slaughtered livestock rotting away, hidden in the barns by the desperate peasants. Platonov also presents us with another vivid, folkloric image to capture the inhumanity of this era: the workers decide to construct an enormous raft to send the scapegoats singled out by the regime, an entire class of landed peasants called *kulaks*, "down the river into the sea and further" (107). Victor Serge describes this mass deportation thus: "Trainloads of deported peasants left for the North, the forests, the steppes, the deserts. These were whole populations, denuded of every-thing. The old folk starved to death in mid-journey, new-born babies were buried on the banks of the roadside and each wilderness had its crops of little crosses of boughs of white wood. Other populations dragging along their mean possessions on wagons, rushed towards the frontiers of Poland, Romania and China and crossed them – in spite of machineguns."[5]

It is worth noting here that the village Platonov describes is passive; people hide in the snow, in the barns, but they know they will be caught, and find it quite natural to submit to superior forces they don't understand and don't even dream of resisting in an organized fashion. But the lack of organized resistance does not mean a lack of violence. Two workers among the pit diggers go out to the village to requisition food and agitate the peasants to join the *kolkhoz*. Both men are murdered.

In the words of Serge, "the Central Committee [of the Party] decreed requisitions, applying ... Article 107 of the Penal Code [death] for concealment of stocks. Detachments of young Communists scoured the countryside [only to be found] on the roadside with their skulls split open."[6] In retaliation, "the peasants were arrested in thousands and made to appear in huge sabotage trials so that the responsibility might be unloaded on somebody."[7] When trouble followed in the city, in the factories, the accusation of sabotage was "directed at thousands, or rather tens of thousands of technicians," and the accusation "was in general a monstrous slander justified solely by the need to find culprits for an economic state that was insupportable."[8]

In Platonov's novel it becomes clear that no one can be free of the fear of being accused of sabotage, including the Engineer who designed the foundation pit and the Activist responsible for the plan's execution. According to Serge's personal experience of the era, "the Politburo knew the truth perfectly well ... Some of the technicians were promptly rehabilitated. Once I had dinner with an outstanding expert in ener-getics who, in the space of 20 months, had been condemned to death, pardoned, sent to a concentration camp [and then] rehabilitated, and even decorated."[9]

Platonov's novel makes it clear that in this period of chaotic mis-management, the semblance of justice is achieved by totally haphazard scapegoating, so that the blame can always be placed on someone. After the two workers are murdered in the village, their comrade, Chiklin, carries on an investigation. He summons one of the weak, hungry peas-ants, called Jelisey, from a group around him: "'Was it you who killed them'? asked Chiklin. Jelisey pulled up his trousers and did not let them drop anymore, and without answering anything, concentrated his pale, empty eyes on Chiklin. – 'Well, who then? Go and bring me someone who is killing our masses.'"

At random, Chiklin picks Jelisey and another starved peasant with yellow eyes to be declared the murderers. The latter dies of his beating, but Jelisey, totally unexpectedly, gets off the hook. All of a sudden Chiklin, this self-appointed executioner, remembers a little girl, Natalia, for whom the socialist future is being built. And so, instead of killing his second scapegoat, Chiklin says: "Here is a ruble for you. Go over to the foundation pit and look to see whether the girl Nastya is still alive and buy her some candy. My heart just began to ache for her" (89).

It is totally unpredictable who does and does not get accused, executed, or pardoned. Thus the Activist, the Party's local representative, lives in continual fear that he may have missed some of the many absurd Party directives, issued often in retrospect, about "mobilizing the nettles on the front of socialist construction," about "cutting off the manes of horses," or about "the accumulation of the snow on the fields." He fears that he could be charged, as other activists have been, of being underactive, overactive, or deviationist, for "putting the cart ahead of the horse and falling into the leftist swamp of rightist opportunism."

When the Activist sees the corpses of the peasants Chiklin has executed, he concludes that they must have been guilty – that is, they must have belonged to the rich *kulaks*. He does not question Chiklin's judgment; he simply wants to take credit for it: "'In any case, I would have discovered him in another hour,' said the Activist. 'There is not a crop of unregulated elemental force in our village anymore, and there is nowhere to hide either. And who is *this* extra one lying here?' 'That one I finished off,' explained Chiklin. 'Very correct, too: in the district they would never believe that there was only one murderer'" (206).

Of course, the reader realizes that neither of the two starved peasants beaten to death had anything to do with the crime; nor did they belong to the formerly well-off peasant class of *kulaks*, as the Activist just claimed. But the workers are like children; they resort to the myths of class guilt. If the proletariat goes hungry, this has to be attributed to the diabolical "fat" *kulaks*; here is their explanation for all the shortages, disease, famine, and terror. If they are able to believe in class guilt, the absurd chain of events may take the semblance of justice, a guarantee of the redemptive power of the collective hope for the future. In fact, when the workers want to curse, they simply say: "You devil of a *kulak*"; then whoever is contemptible turns automatically into a *kulak*, appointed the devil's representative for the day.

Of course, the directives, slogans, and the designation of scapegoats appear from above, from the Big Man in the city, but there is something in the blocked consciousness of the characters themselves that makes them uncritically accept and internalize the way of thinking imposed on them from above. It has been observed that, in a curious way, Platonov's own language[10] is so stark and barren that it is as if the narrator himself were struggling with the blocked, censored consciousness of his characters, with the very process of articulation and reasoning his characters find so difficult. At first the reader has the impression of reading a strange version of William Faulkner's *The Sound and the Fury*, where the consciousness of each character functions at the mental level of the retarded child, but a child who has picked up the rudiments of speech from state bureaucrats. Apropos of this sense of a blocked, benumbed consciousness, Platonov even introduces an animal character, a tamed striking bear who is trained to work in the village smith's workshop. A traditional character from Russian folktales, Misha the bear becomes here representative of the good will, strength, and inarticulate suffering of the Russian people.

Throughout the novel we are aware of invisible, anonymous forces behind the fictional characters, just as we are when reading *Conquered City* or *Chocolate*. In *Foundation Pit* these forces are perceived as the ambling movement of faceless, degraded, semi-literate masses who do not even have a language of their own and therefore use the language of the bureaucratic terror imposed on them. There are only a few characters whose name the author reveals to us, as if to bring them into some kind of close-up. Even here, however, the close-up does not reveal an individual, only a particular social type. As for the functionaries, most are described without a name: the Big Man in the City, the Activist, or the Trade Union representative.

The first person we meet by name is Voschev, the man aware of the need to ponder. He is befriended by Chicklin, a strong, muscular man, who also reveals that he has a soul: in the middle of back-breaking labour he suddenly remembers that when he was a youth, he was kissed by a young girl, the daughter of his employer, a capitalist. The lonely, middle-aged engineer, Prushevsky, also remembers his desire for a girl in his youth: now the two men ponder whether they indeed remember the same girl. Then, when later in the working process they find a middle-aged woman dying of starvation and disease next to the foundation pit, they wonder whether this woman could have been the object of their youthful desire. The woman leaves behind a little girl, Natalia, and the two men take her under their wings. In effect, so does the entire workgroup. "'Comrades!' Safranov began to define the general feeling. 'Before us lies unconscious a *de facto* inhabitant of socialism ... a small human being destined to constitute the universal element. It is for the sake of that we must complete as suddenly as possible the foundation pit'" (71).

Participating eagerly in the general feeling for the child, Voschev responds in his own way. He "looked her all over just as in childhood he had looked upon the angel upon the church wall: this weak body … would some day feel that warming flood of the meaning of life, and her mind would see a time which was like the first primeval day" (71).

Not unexpectedly, by the end of the novel Natalia, who is weakened by starvation and the cold like all the workers around her, succumbs to a fever and dies. With her dies the hope for the foundation pit, for the entire structure; the collective utopian future has turned into the burial ground of the present *and* of the future generation. Platonov leaves the reader questioning who is responsible for the failure of such an ambitious experiment. Who are the guilty ones? The Big Man in the city? The Bureaucracy at his command? The Activist? The worker's foreman, Comrade Pashkin? And how about the workers themselves?

According to Hungarian Béla Hamvas, whose works, like Platonov's, were also repressed by the regime in his lifetime, dictatorship can come about only in "low-level societies, where the people cannot distinguish between the systems of lies and those of truth."[11] Platonov's novel fits Hamvas's definition of mob mentality: "The rule of the mob means that individual, clear, intelligent and sober activities are taken over by the mob's confused, blind, hazy and non-conscious activities, and in the process the human experience becomes blurred and sinks under. This was something the revolutionaries had not thought about."[12]

Platonov shows us a striking affinity between the concepts of justice in the mass mind and in the mind of the child. Thus, the little girl, Natalia, wants to believe that there must be a kind of justice in society. To her this means that anyone who has to lie naked in the earth and had to suffer as much in life as her mother did must have been guilty. She reasons that her mother's guilt must have been that she belonged to the guilty class of *kulaks* and capitalists. The child vehemently urges the men around her to keep killing the *kulaks*, the enemy. One of the men praises the little girl for her "class consciousness," and explains that "'For us only one class is precious – and we will soon purge our class of the politically unconscious element.' 'Of scum,' the girl guessed easily. 'And then all that will be left will be the very most chief people. My mama also called herself scum for having lived, and now that she has died, she has become good – it's true, isn't it?' 'True,' said Chicklin" (76).

Clearly, the child identifies with the aggressor out of her own deep anxiety: she wants to be a part of the proletariat; she justifies the mistreatment of her own mother, and the workers celebrate her childish mentality, admiring "the warm place from which emerged this intelligence and charm of a small life." Is Platonov being ironic here? Or is he simply showing the loss of human values when the individual's natural sense of justice is constantly being violated? In the interaction between Natalia and the workgroup Platonov shows us that all these adults accept and celebrate cruelty with the fear-driven irrationality of the child.

Platonov's irony raises a number of similar questions because, unlike Zamiatin's or Orwell's dystopic vision, which emerges through the fate of the protagonist, in Platonov's novel there are no individual characters with memories of failed alternatives; here no one has memories of a more humane past, or hope for a more humane future. Platonov's novel offers no "window on history"; at no point do we see what it was in the past that could have led the people of Russia to undertake the inexpressible suffering involved in building that enormous foundation pit, or why, instead of developing into a magnificent structure, the pit becomes a place of burial. Therefore, instead of finding that the dystopian satire opens up to us the constructive possibilities of changing our predicament, the novel reads more like a dirge sung over the great utopian experiment in universal justice, over the masses' failure to distinguish between the Messianism of socialism and the terror of dictatorship.

ANATOLIJ RIBAKOV: THE CHILDREN OF THE ARBAT[13]

Like Platonov's *Foundation Pit*, Anatolij Ribakov's *The Children of the Arbat* takes place in the early thirties (between 1933 and 1934). The atrocities committed in connection with the forced collectivization of the peasantry and the extermination of potential resisters as *kulaks* are still in the background, but the novel focuses on Moscow, and explores the effects of the forced industrialization and the consolidation of Stalin's power after the first Five-year Plan and before the beginning of the Moscow trials. Unlike Platonov's opaque style, with its evocative combination of visionary and folkloristic elements, Ribakov's transparent, "realistic" style could not be found objectionable even by the strictest Guidelines of Socialist Realism, which, by the way, were fully in place by the time Ribakov began writing. Of course, the novel deviates from the Guidelines in that its mood is not optimistic but tragic, and the central characters' faith in the Soviet Union as a socialist utopia is shaken to its very foundations. In fact, Stalin's regime is described here quite directly as a nightmare state of dystopia characterized by the deliberate miscarriage of justice and a gigantic network of conspiracy by the leader against his own people.

Ribakov completed the novel in 1966, but it was suppressed for twenty years. Rosalind Marsh points out that during this long period

Ribakov "chose not to circulate his work in samizdat or to send it abroad for publication, since he felt strongly that he wanted it to come out in Russia; 'I wanted my people to have it.'" He believed that the book was to be cathartic: "We have to free ourselves of this psychological legacy so that the country can move forward and be what it should be." In other words, Ribakov believed that by revealing the truth about the thirties as a dystopic society (he does not use the term, naturally) his novel would have a powerful effect on current developments in the greater openness of the Gorbachov era. Indeed, "since Gorbachov's approval must have been required for the novel's publication, its appearance suggested that the current leadership was contemplating a more radical reappraisal of Soviet history than ever before."[14]

The novel is set in a formerly fashionable central district of Moscow, the Arbat, which leads in a direct line to the Kremlin, that close yet mythically distant place that represents the goal of all ceremonial parades and demonstrations, as well as being the home of Stalin. Appropriately, the book is structured along two parallel lines. We are introduced to a group of young teenagers living on the Arbat, with special emphasis on the harrowing fate of an enthusiastic young Communist, Sasha Pankratov, who for reasons equally mysterious to him and to his friends and relatives is dragged through the legislative quagmire of expulsion from the university and the Communist Youth Movement, followed by arrest, imprisonment, and a three-year sentence to exile in East Siberia.

Parallel to the maze of these events in young Sasha's life, Ribakov gives the reader a close-up of Stalin in the Kremlin, in different mental states ranging from paranoia to self-congratulation, as he keeps convincing himself of the need to manufacture ever newer excuses for setting traps for various colleagues and friends, the former Bolshevik guard who had fought the revolution and the Civil War. At this point in history Ribakov presents Stalin concentrating on one particular man he considers his potentially most dangerous opponent and rival, the popular and highly respected Communist Kirov. Stalin's ongoing internal monologues elucidate the surprising insinuations against the people around him, as well as the unexpected promotions and demotions of members of the Politburo, the Central Committee, and the security organ the NKVD. All these together spell out a vast network of conspiracy: Stalin is preparing for the assassination of Kirov in 1934 as a prelude to the first great wave of terror, the Moscow trials of prominent Party members, vast purges in the rank and file of the Party, to be followed up by millions of mass arrests. In preparation for these events he first transfers people loyal to Kirov to other positions. Alfieri, a bright and loyal member of the NKVD, for example, gets a post in East

Siberia, where young Sasha meets him at an interview; his post in Leningrad is given to Zaporozsec, a man of weak character and easy to control with bribes and threats. Stalin's agents also select a weak, intimidated young man, Nikolaev, who is systematically pressured until he announces in a letter that "he is ready for anything." As those who are familiar with this era of history will realize, Stalin is stage-managing his first great theatrical in the political arena: Nikolaev is groomed to be Kirov's assassin; Zaporozsec is the head of the bureaucracy prepared to assure the would-be assassin's success.

What is the connection between the two story-lines, the fate of Sasha and his friends from the Arbat, and Stalin, the "mastermind" setting the political scenario for the era? The connection is made clear in the way Ribakov sets the scene for the nightmare of the persecution mania induced by the police-state to justify its own existence, by the myth of being surrounded by an omnipresent enemy outside and armies of traitors within. "The newspapers talked about virtually nothing else but machine wreckers, saboteurs and deviants. 'Unmask them! Punish them mercilessly. Destroy them. Stamp them out. Exterminate them by the roots! Wipe them off the surface of the earth!'" (123) These sentences sound like "pistol shots," making the population tremble. The mystique of the trial, heavy-handed slogans turning into personal accusations to be followed by decades of hard labour or even death, haunt the people's consciousness.

Sasha's uncle, Mark Rjazanov, is a chief engineer in charge of the construction of an enormous new industrial complex in the north. He labours on his task without the proper resources and equipment, trying to meet a forced, unrealistic deadline. The planning process relies on the tremendous sacrifice of young Communists, who at first must sleep outdoors, often in the mud, while the new structures are being erected at break-neck speed. All, of course, are aware of the "sabotage" trials, where engineers and workers unable to deal with their unrealistic tasks have been sentenced to death or long years of hard labour. Mark Rjazanov, however, is able to achieve outstanding results. Not only does he complete the construction of the steel works for the deadline; he even undertakes the building of workers' apartments, clubs, cinemas, and sanatoria to assure humane conditions for all those who have participated so enthusiastically, often as volunteers after their working hours, in the building process. Still, when Rjazanov is summoned at various points to Moscow, he can never foresee whether he will receive Stalin's congratulations or be arrested and tried for sabotage for acting on his own initiative.

It is while the chief engineer's career is still on the upswing that his nephew, Sasha, gets into trouble with the corrupt authorities at the university, and is expelled and arrested. At the interrogation Sasha is not told what he is accused of; the interrogator wants him to implicate himself and others. Could the interrogator trap Sasha into admitting that after the former rector of the university was dismissed, he expressed his bitterness to Sasha in an informal conversation, this admission – two people exchanging remarks critical of the authorities – would count as evidence that rector and student had participated in an "anti-Soviet conspiracy." But the specific cause for Sasha's arrest remains a secret to Sasha not only throughout his interrogation but also throughout his exile.

Only an old Bolshevik, Bugyagin, guesses the solution to the mystery. It was not an accident that Sasha was arrested while his uncle's career was on the upswing; it is characteristic of Stalin, who is described here as a feudal potentate, to choose someone like Rjazanov's young nephew to become Rjazanov's "Achilles's heel that will force [Rjazanov] to serve faithfully [precisely because his leader had so generously] disregarded this circumstance" (128). In other words, Rjazanov should feel personally indebted to the leader that he has not been declared guilty by association, as so many others have been.

Stalin's circle know that, like an oriental potentate, he wants the adulation of the masses and, like a feudal lord, demands unconditional personal loyalty from his retainers by making them depend on him for life and favours. Through his internal monologues that follow us through the novel, we see him as a small man with physical defects and a pock-marked face who suffered from people's rudeness in his impoverished childhood. Consequently, he came to believe that all people are rude and brutal, and can be easily reduced to a bestial level by cruelty and to mindless obedience by fear. Therefore he justifies his own brutality and cruelty, using the slogans of Marxism only as a camouflage: "the rude forces could be oppressed only by force; this force is called dictatorship" (183).

The overlord extorts the blind loyalty he craves from his retainers by finding out their flaws, weaknesses, their "Achilles heel." Thus, Ribakov suggests, Stalin is aware that Yagoda, whom he appoints to the office of Minister of Internal Affairs, the head of the NKVD, is not a Communist by conviction; on the contrary, Yagoda was most likely involved with the tsarist Secret Police as an informer. Stalin assumes that it is precisely the shameful secret in his past that will keep Yagoda in continual fear, hence in a state of abject obedience to his Master. Stalin is convinced that he can count on Yagoda's eternal loyalty because "one's conviction may change but fear never disappears" (247). As the head of the NKVD Yagoda will execute Stalin's wishes, even those Stalin does not care to put into words.

As for those who cannot be easily broken or reduced to servility, Stalin feels challenged and frustrated by their integrity. An old-time Bolshevik, Bugyagin, with whom Stalin spent years in exile before the revolution, has returned from a diplomatic assignment in Germany and wishes to warn Stalin against the dangerous rise of fascism. However, Stalin's *idée fixe* is that the Soviet Union's real capitalist enemies are England and France. Consequently, he believes that Germany, an enemy of England and France, cannot be dangerous for the Soviet Union. Anticipating that Bugyagin wants to warn him about the dangers of German fascism, Stalin refuses to see his old friend for a year, and when he finally admits Bugyagin to the Kremlin, he dismisses his old comrade-in-arms in a manner that makes the man realize that pretty soon it will be his turn to join in the fate of other "oppositionists" and "traitors."

Bugyagin is a man of conviction, with an invincible faith in the revolution, "who assumed every action was his action, every mistake his mistake; he had the supreme courage of the revolutionary; he took personal responsibility for the fate of individuals thrown into the shockwave of social upheaval. People dropped around him, guilty and not guilty, but he was convinced that he was breaking the way for a new generation" (127). Yet even this man of high principle makes excuses for the brutality of the political process, arguing that "the greatness of the revolution does not depend on who is overthrown and who is crushed, but on whom it creates" (127).

Ultimately, it is Bugyagin's faith in the "new socialist man" created by the revolution that Stalin cannot tolerate, just as he could not tolerate Bukharin's "oppositionist" warnings against the mass atrocities Stalin committed against the peasantry, the deliberate starving, imprisoning, and executing of millions of alleged *kulaks* in the late twenties. In fact, everyone who dares to express an opinion that deviates from Stalin's most recent whim, incarnated in the slogans of the ever-changing Party line, is inevitably declared an enemy of the people.

In 1933, Ribakov suggests, all of Stalin's jealousy and hatred was focused on the most popular, most talented leader of the time, the head of the Leningrad Soviet, Comrade Kirov. In the novel their various disagreements in policy boil down, once more, to their different attitudes to socialism, based on their different conceptions of human nature. Stalin, who considers himself a realist, is suspicious of Kirov's personality and convictions:

Kirov is a dangerous idealist, he demands material welfare for the working classes, does not understand that the person living well is not capable of sacrifices, of enthusiasm, he will become petty bourgeois. Only suffering evokes the great energy of the people. Human suffering leads to God, the people were imbued in this axiom for centuries, it is absorbed in their blood. This is what we have to make use of also. The terrestrial Heaven of Socialism is more attractive than the mythical celestial Heaven, but even this can be reached only through suffering. Of course, the people's conviction should be kept alive that their suffering is only temporal ... the supreme leader sees everything, he is omniscient and omnipotent.   (332)

Ribakov portrays Stalin's character as shrewd, suspicious, and totally without a sense of shame. He takes advantage of the mentality of the militant Church, the Church as an institution, in following the methods of self-perpetuating power. But unlike Dostoevski's Grand Inquisitor, who claimed to bring happiness to the people by denying them freedom, in Ribakov's interpretation Stalin does not pretend, even to himself, that he is concerned about anything other than the perpetuation of human suffering because the suffering of the masses is the basis of their willingness to sacrifice. Whether we find Stalin's self-justification here psychologically acceptable, Ribakov's portrait of Stalin explains that questions of right or wrong, of human justice, don't even enter Stalin's consciousness. His mind works as judge, investigator, and prosecutor at the same time. He believes in guilt by association: if Bugyagin had the same kind of training in technology as had Kirov, this means that Bugyagin must also be an "enemy" to be dealt with. Seeing Rjazanov in the company of Ordzsonokidze and Kirov after a Central Committee meeting, Stalin's resolve that these men must also be enemies and therefore eliminated is born. Finding out that a most knowledgeable and skilled dentist who has just recently treated Stalin had a pleasant conversation with Kirov on the seaside, Stalin immediately gives orders that the dentist should be dismissed from his job in Moscow. From his conviction that the friend of his "enemy" must be his enemy also, it follows that he punishes anyone speaking up for or interceding on behalf of his potential victims. Hence he demands that former friends, colleagues, even members of the same family renounce the one who is in trouble with the authorities and publicly repent, exercise self-criticism for their own errors.

Ribakov suggests that, by accepting an underlying philosophy about the baseness of human nature, Stalin's regime of fear and intimidation does indeed corrupt human beings. It is the encouragement to be vigilant and to "unmask" the enemy, together with the tacit understanding that the informers will receive their rewards, that encourages "little Stalins" at the workplace, or those unashamed careerists, Sasha's enemies at the university, the Party secretary, the dean of his faculty, Glinskaia, his interrogator Diakov, and his former schoolmate, Yura Sarok, who becomes a cunning, ruthless official at the NKVD. They use the latest slogans issued by Stalin, first to win their posts and then to maintain their positions, ready to execute the slogans of "unmasking" friends, lovers, family members as conspirators and traitors, all the time well aware that they are persecuting the innocent. In a legal system where one is guilty by association, circumstantial evidence is considered sufficient (397). In his exile in Siberia, Sasha notes the proliferation of laws announcing that anyone attempting to escape abroad will be shot by a firing squad, that family members left behind by the dissident will be sentenced to ten years, and he reads the news about ever more trials and retaliation (394).

This nightmare atmosphere penetrates even the most intimate relationships. In his exile Sasha develops a relationship with a young teacher, Zena. He is fairly distant, even callous in his treatment of her because he is continually aware of the risk to which she would be exposed if he were charged with misdemeanours; he also suspects that she would not be able to withstand torture if interrogated about secrets he had entrusted to her. In effect, Sasha realizes that human relations must be kept distant when any lover, spouse, or friend could be used either as a hostage or as a witness against him, especially while he is in exile, not only thrust outside the protection of the law but also stigmatized as an enemy of the Soviet people.

Ribakov does not raise the question of who or what is responsible for the mass rule of fear and intimidation, for the hysteria for "unmasking" traitors, saboteurs, enemies at all corners. He simply presents the symptoms, as if he wanted us to draw our own conclusions from the vast range of characters who allow us to examine this question in a number of ways. In addition to describing the paranoia and megalomania of the dictator, the increasing powerlessness of the old guard of revolutionaries, and the shameless careerists who perform their tasks out of self-interest, there is another group of people to whom Ribakov draws our attention. These are the people around the victim, particularly the people in Sasha's circle. Former friends, schoolmates, at times even his maternal uncle, feel sorry for him but are also ashamed or afraid of letting their feelings be known. They hide behind the hypocritical shrug, claiming that under socialist justice no one is punished without reason, and if Sasha has been punished, surely he must be guilty. One is reminded here of the chorus in *Oedipus Rex*: to admit that the powers above are instruments of injustice and therefore the hero's suffering is unjust would be a blow to the whole system of beliefs that provides the foundation for the people's security, for their faith in order.

Sasha himself refuses to believe that the dream of socialism to which he has dedicated his young life may be a sham. In spite of the revealing stories he hears from the other exiles around him, he does not want to understand that he lives in a dystopic state where injustice is legalized. He has hopes to return to a normal, constructive life after he has served his sentence. Yet, as the novel ends on an ominous note, announcing the dark consequences of the news about Kirov's assassination, Sasha is awakened to the truth that the miscarriage of justice in his case was not an exception to the rule, that now the entire country is in the throes of a Kremlin-directed conspiracy against the population.

The essential characteristics of the "bad place" we associate with dystopian fiction have been, clearly, the essential characteristics of the Soviet Union that Ribakov describes in his "realistic" historical novel. When, at a 1987 interview, Ribakov was asked whether the novel suggests that the murderers of Kirov were members of the Secret Service obeying Stalin's orders, he gave an elusive answer: "To be able to state that Stalin had Kirov assassinated, we would need written proofs. These proofs do not exist and will never exist. Or we would need eyewitnesses; but even these were murdered. We are left, then, with logic. Who benefited from this act? Most likely the reader will conclude that it was Stalin who benefited the most. Others might believe Stalin did not need this murder. In other words, in this case the reader must decide for himself or herself."[15]

There are historians who share Ribakov's caution about blaming Kirov's assassination on Stalin with any certainty. The novel, however, makes a stronger case for conspiracy than Ribakov's interview reveals. In the meantime, more discussion on the question followed. In the year of the interview there appeared a documentary film, scripted by Dinkevich and directed by Cherentsov,[16] supporting the conspiracy theory that informs Ribakov's narrative. This film makes clear that Kirov was a man of integrity who enjoyed great popularity, and that Stalin resented this heartily. Stalin also aimed to wash his hands of the murder by introducing the farce that he was searching relentlessly for Kirov's assassins. "We are going to answer Kirov's murderers with blows at our enemy," declared posters all over the country, and the newspapers announced: "Anyone who has had the crazed audacity to challenge the historical process and put a stop to it, to step in the way of the triumphant advancement of socialism, will be crushed to bloody pulp."[17] The vocabulary and the rhetoric here say a great deal about the actual style of the legal process involved in pursuing and investigating the "criminals," not only Stalin's close personal friends but also thousands picked up at random.

In 1971 the prominent Soviet historian Roj Medvedev shed light on significant details in connection with Kirov's assassination: Nikolaev, who eventually succeeded in shooting Kirov, had been considered suspect and arrested twice by Kirov's bodyguards. Zaporozsec, the recently appointed head of the NKVD in Leningrad, let the suspect go both times. He got his orders from Yagoda; Yagoda, directly from Stalin. Kirov's bodyguards objected to Nikolaev's release, but were warned not to meddle with the work of the NKVD. When, shortly after the assassination, Stalin arrived at Leningrad with his entourage, he immediately took the investigation into his own hands. He asked Nikolaev why he had shot Kirov, and the young man pointed at the members of the NKVD around him: "But they forced me to do this." According to Medvedev, Nikolaev was beaten almost to death at the investigation; he was revived only in order to stand trial.[18]

The details of the historian's account are, in effect, far more hair-raising than those introduced in Ribakov's novel. These details also include the murder of Borisov, Kirov's bodyguard, killed while on his way to the investigation; and the attempts to get rid of Borisov's widow, who was first locked up in a mental institution and then, when she managed to obtain her transfer to a regular hospital, "accidentally" poisoned. Later, the account goes, Borisov's murderers were also murdered. As for those members of the Leningrad NKVD who were involved in the investigation, they were given a lenient punishment at the time; they were executed only in 1937. Yagoda, head of the NKVD at the time of Kirov's murder, was executed in 1938 in connection with the so-called Rightist Trotskyite Bloc's trial, which also claimed Bukharin's life (a trial analysed in depth in Koestler's *Darkness at Noon*). One of the phantasmagorical charges against Bukharin was that he was responsible for the assassination of Kirov.

The conspiracy Ribakov touches upon in his novel was based, then, on historical evidence; as for the historical event itself, its circumstances spell out the spiral of treachery, deceit, and terror, the conspiracy of the ruler to cause deliberately the miscarriage of justice. It enacts that nightmarish reversal of the pursuit of justice familiar to us from the essential "formula" of the dystopian novel in its traditional Western structure.

Ribakov's novel ends in Siberia, with Sasha and his fellow exiles commenting on Kirov's assassination, apprehensive of ensuing terror – as this event indeed marked the first wave of mass arrests and mass deportations of millions in the camps in what was referred to as the "Kirovian stream."[19]

In *The Children of the Arbat* Ribakov presents us with the anatomy of a dystopic society that was gradually revealing its shocking resemblance to another dystopic society at the opposite end of the ideological spectrum – Hitler's Germany. When Anatolij Ribakov was asked in an interview whether Stalin could have regarded the political murders in Nazi Germany as a model for the purges and show-trials, Ribakov answered: "It is always difficult to determine who gave an example to whom. Stalin had started the elimination of his political opponents in 1926, maybe in 1925. With the help of Zinoviev and Kamenev he eliminated Trotsky; then, with the help of Bukharin and Rikov, he got rid of Zinoviev and Kamenev in 1926 and 1927. [Then] it was the turn of Bukharin and Rikov. At this time the contributors were other members of the Central Committee, who then [naturally] were also liquidated. By the time the Nazis started the 'night of the long knives,' Stalin had long since begun the process of liquidation."[20]

The shock of recognizing how the Party's stifling of opposition ushered in an endless stream of treachery,[21] denunciations, show-trials, and false confessions under the mask of Messianic socialism is the central theme of Koestler's *Darkness at Noon* in its fictional exploration of Bukharin's trial; the equally overpowering shock that the USSR under Stalin bore an uncanny resemblance to its mirror-image in Germany under Hitler is the central theme of Vassili Grossman's *Life and Fate*, the next two works in our discussion of the dystopian novel.

ARTHUR KOESTLER: *DARKNESS AT NOON*

Arthur Koestler's *Darkness at Noon* (1940) is probably the most widely known work of fiction dealing with Stalin's show-trials in the years following upon Kirov's assassination, a work that "helped to deliver [many a Western reader] from the platitudes of the Thirties, from [their] organized self-deceptions."[22] More specifically, the novel explores the unique, to many still mysterious psychological dynamics of the show-trials from the point of view of the defendant. As Koestler himself explains in his "Soviet Myth and Reality," "the dictatorial regime, committed to its own infallibility, could not afford to let the masses realize that in political matters there was scope for different opinions within the same camp. Hence the accused in the Moscow trials had to belong to the 'black' side; they could not appear as *bona fide* politicians at variance with the government, but had to play the role of counterrevolutionary agents of foreign powers who had acted not out of conviction but for pay and some undefined satanic motives."[23]

The regime's commitment to its own infallibility may indeed explain the motives of the prosecution. Still, the fact that the accused made public confessions during which they heaped crime upon crime on their own heads was not as easy to explain. In 1973 Solzhenitsyn wrote that, "although much appears to have been clarified since then – with particular success by Koestler – the riddle continues to circulate as durably as ever."[24]

In Koestler's own explanation of the case of Bukharin, the model for his protagonist, "the victims lent themselves to this game for reasons which varied according to their personality. Men like Bukharin who shared their accusers' philosophy acted their role voluntarily in the conviction that this was the last service they could render the Party after they had been politically defeated and had, according to the all-or-nothing law of totalitarian policies, forsaken their lives."[25]

Koestler's Rubashov is a victim at this "highest level": "Others, worn out by a life-long struggle, hoped to save if not their own, at least the lives of their families held as hostages ... Others, still on a lower level, had been broken by physical and mental torture alternating with promises to be spared to which they clung against better reason; and finally there were the *agents provocateurs* who had nothing to lose."[26]

Irving Howe may be correct in saying that Koestler "omits the ... gradual destruction of [Rubashov's] will and energy,"[27] but clearly, the psychological "riddle" Koestler is most interested in is the motivation of the first and highest order of victims, those who wanted to do one last service for the Party while also contriving to leave behind a message at the public trial. In a 1973 study that examines the court record of the trial, American Sovietologist Stephen Cohen argues that "although Bukharin had formally admitted the accusations against him – he had to do so to save his family – he had essentially denied any criminal activity of which Vishinsky and Stalin had accused him. [And in] the final rebuttal he is not simply defending himself. Practically it is he who accuses his accusers."[28] George Katkov also suggests that at his trial Bukharin spoke in code; in spite of his admission of guilt, he intended to let the people know that he was innocent, and used terms like "anti-Soviet conspiracy" and "counterrevolutionary activities" in quotation marks, as it were, to indicate to his audience that the only "sin" he had committed was to think differently from Stalin, and it was this "sin" that was called treason and conspiracy.[29]

Of course, at the time the public had no access to Katkov's or Cohen's reading: Bukharin's confession – and the confessions of many others at the show-trials – created a shock in Russia and abroad for long years, and it is the unique psychology of these confessions that Koestler explores in *Darkness at Noon*.

There are several details about the actual trial or about Bukharin's personality that Koestler does not use in his novel. For instance, Bukharin was a loving husband and a father of a young son; he was deeply concerned about his family's fate. In the novel Rubashov is a bachelor who does not leave anyone behind: his only serious attachment, Arlova, has already been eliminated by the Party a year before Rubashov's arrest.

Another interesting difference between the novel and the historical reality is that the language, the expressions, the invective, the brutal rhetoric directed against the accused in the show-trials would probably be unimaginable to a Western reader. As a result, Koestler does not refer to the language of the articles in Soviet papers at the time. This is, for example, a quote from the *Literaturnaya Gazeta* reproducing the words of Vishinsky, the Public Prosecutor at the trial in the year prior to Bukharin's, in its number of 16 January 1937: "Look at them; they are malformed, bald, wearing glasses – they are the adjutants of Trotsky's parallel Committee. Look at him – this is Radek, who since the nineteen hundreds has been leaving behind and betraying one country after another ... he is rootless and harmful, he roams over the whole of Central Europe, until in the Soviet Union they catch him and crash down upon him."[30] It was acceptable for a Party member to refer to the defendants as "Jackal Pjatakov, Jackal Radek ... after their birth father, that disgusting, uncanny wild animal, Jackal Trotsky, who is roaming, screaming in the deep forests of Hitlerian fascism."[31] It was in the spirit of this language that Vishinsky, "the chief director of the mystery play, called Bukharin 'the cursed mixture of fox and swine.'"[32] It was also in the spirit of these trials that the accused – people who had dedicated two or three decades of their lives to the working-class revolution – were described as criminals, with a program "to murder the workers, flood their mine shafts and choke them to death, to tear them to pieces in deliberately fabricated accidents."[33]

Neither does Koestler make reference to the irony that Bukharin made a significant contribution to the articulation of the Soviet Constitution, a most eloquent document of the humanistic spirit of socialism that was being inaugurated while he was already in investigative captivity. Nor does Koestler refer to the psychologically exhausting cat-and-mouse game Stalin played with some of his victims for long months before their arrest. While the hearings before the Central Committee were already going on with such outrageous accusations as Bukharin's participation in Kirov's assassination, Stalin would casually phone Bukharin, asking: "What is new with you, Nikolai?" And when Bukharin cried out bitterly, "They've just arrived to move me out from the Kremlin," Stalin dismissed the whole issue jovially: "Well, then, send them to hell."[34]

Notwithstanding some common characteristics that Rubashov shares with certain historical figures (Koestler mentions both Bukharin and Radek), Rubashov is a fictional character and not a portrait of any particular politician. I believe Jenni Calder is somewhat unfair in calling him a "schematic" character of fiction; Koestler referred to his novel as a parable, and Rubashov is an allegorical representation of a spiritual dilemma faced by the disillusioned revolutionary who has dedicated all his life to the spectre of an idea. He risked imprisonment and exile under the tsarist regime, death in battle in the years of the

Civil War, arrest and torture by the Gestapo while on a secret Party mission abroad. In this process he also appropriated the principle of revolutionary justice whereby the end justifies the means; "he sacrificed morality to expediency in the interest of the Cause." In the novel, while awaiting his interrogator, Rubashov is compelled to revert to his own private conscience, his personal morality, his personal sense of justice: before his public trial he stands trial within his private conscience.

Koestler selected certain biographical details from Bukharin's life and eliminated others because he wanted Rubashov to stand as a representative of the complex spiritual dilemma at the heart of twentieth-century dystopian fiction: the tension between the long-term utopian hope in universal justice inspired by socialism, and the exigencies of temporal, revolutionary justice; ultimately this is the tension between the Messiah and the Dictator.

The title, *Darkness at Noon*, is an obvious allusion to the Crucifixion: "Now from the sixth hour [noon] darkness fell upon all the land until the ninth hour," (Matt. 27:45) and "when the sixth hour came, darkness fell over the land until the ninth hour" (Mark 15:30). It is appropriate to ask at this point what the significance is of the consistent biblical imagery throughout the novel. There is no doubt that Koestler, steeped in Freudian psychology, is engaged in creating a credible, psychologically "realistic" portrait of a Bolshevik who would dismiss religious "idealism," who prides himself on being a man of reason, a materialist, an atheist by definition. Yet unlike Ribakov's *Children of the Arbat*, with its cinematic composition and transparently realistic style, Koestler's novel is based on a consistently religious symbolic structure, with a cluster of recurring metaphors in a clear line of development.

There are numerous allusions to the Pietà, used as an emblem of the cold, rationalist Rubashov's increasingly powerful sense of pity and grief over the suffering of human beings. There is also a reference to the Last Judgment that foreshadows Rubashov's thoughts about his ultimate trial at the Judgment Seat of History. There are recurring references to a photograph with a white circle of light, like a halo, over the head of each martyr of the revolution – that is, the old Bolshevik leaders who have been executed by Stalin. At various points in the novel Rubashov's fate is also elucidated by allusions to Moses and the forty years of wandering in the desert, to Moses who was not to see the Promised Land, to the people looking back to the fleshpots of Egypt. The voice of Ivanov, the first interrogator, is compared to that of Satan, the seductive voice of pure reason without feelings, and also echoes the haunting message of the Grand Inquisitor arguing for the legitimacy of the institution of the Party, even if this institution stifles the original spirit of socialism. At the end of his second hearing, still unwilling to sign his confession, Rubashov bursts out that he refuses to play Satan in the Party's Punch and Judy show; at a turning-point in the third and last interrogation, turning directly to Rubashov to sign the false confession as a sacrifice to the Party, Gletkin also makes a reference to Christ as a "voluntary scapegoat" for humanity. Finally, the humiliating scene of Rubashov's trial reveals to an old friend the similarity of this trial to the mocking of Christ with the crown of thorns.[35]

Koestler's parable is divided into three hearings, an allusion in this context to the three temptations of Christ. The novel ends on the final image of the "oceanic sense" of the union between the human soul and the universe, an image that Koestler was aware Freud considered the basis of religious feeling. The inner consistency of Koestler's biblical allusions carries special significance when he is articulating Rubashov's spiritual dilemma and the characteristics of his atheistic "religion" – that is, his invincible faith in the Law of History, which will bring forth the victory of socialism in the future.

Still, having read the novel, the reader may well wonder who the Messiah – or the failed Messiah – that the title alludes to is. Is it Rubashov himself, with his courage, tenacity, and willingness to sac-rifice his personal life to the revolution? But we also see him in the mirror of Koestler's insightful psychological analysis as a flawed, tor-mented human being unable to love or commit himself morally to his friends or his mistress. Also, he abandons and betrays his erstwhile comrades when directed by the Party to do so; he falsely recants his oppositionist platform because he believes that otherwise he would be immediately destroyed and of no further use to the Party; in fact, he has no personal morality, no personal loyalty, no private conscience – all these are devoured by the loyalty demanded by the Party in the name of the dictatorship of the proletariat. Is it then the cause of the revolution itself, the original revolutionary promise to bring universal justice and freedom to the people that is being crucified in the death of Rubashov? Is the Messiah the original faith in the revolution? "After all," Rubashov himself recognizes, "one can only be crucified in the name of one's own faith" (157).

Like the peasants to be executed in Platonov's *Foundation Pit*, and like Ribakov's Sasha at the interrogation that results in his exile to Siberia, at the time of his arrest Rubashov has no idea what the crime is that he is accused of. In the first scene of the novel he finds himself in a prison cell; he recalls the experience he has dreamt about many times in the past, always in connection with imprisonment abroad following from his secret missions on behalf of the Communist International: in his nightmare, under the watchful eyes of those who have arrested him, he is trying to put on his clothes and fumbles with his sleeve.

This time, however, the nightmarish scene is more than a nightmare. At his arrest he realizes that he is fully awake, that he is being imprisoned in his own country, and by the same Party he has been serving for forty years. Waiting for his first interrogation, he ponders the concept of justice, his own acts of summary revolutionary justice in the name of the dictatorship of the proletariat, his own acts of cruelty dictated by the Party in the name of future universal justice.

While Rubashov is awaiting his interrogation, repressed memories come to the surface, triggered by images of the Pietà on a painting he had seen in Germany in the year Hitler came to power. As a secret agent of the Communist International, Rubashov was sent there to get in touch with the German Communist Party, which had been forced underground. It was under a painting of the Pietà in a museum that he was to meet Richard, a young German Communist whose pregnant wife had just been arrested by the Gestapo. It was Rubashov's duty to reprimand Richard for not having followed the instructions sent to all German Communists by the Comintern, whose line was established in Moscow: at the darkest hours of the fascist dictatorship's coming to power in Germany, Richard refused to distribute pamphlets with flowery slogans about the triumph and victory of the Communist Party, dictated in Moscow. Instead, Richard wanted to appeal to the Resistance by calling attention to the reality of persecution, arrest, and torture rampant in Hitler's dictatorship. Ruthless in his uncritical obedience to the Party line, Rubashov announces Richard's expulsion from the Communist Party, takes a taxi to the train station, and leaves Richard standing alone on the sidewalk. By this gesture he leaves Richard exposed to the inevitable wrath of the Gestapo, for the secret agent within the Party will denounce Richard once he is expelled and declared an enemy of the Party. Ironically, the taxi driver refuses to accept any fare from Rubashov; he regards the Soviet Communist as the strongest ally of the German Resistance. Now, in a dream in his cell, Rubashov realizes that he has to pay: following the ever-changing Party line, at that train station Rubashov ruthlessly betrayed the trust of the taxi driver and Richard – the German worker and the German Communist; he had participated in the Party's unconscionable betrayal of the original spirit of the International.

While still waiting for his first interrogation, Rubashov becomes aware of a tapping from the neighbouring cell. He discovers that his neighbour is a former White officer, and Rubashov now recalls the White prisoners he had shot in the Civil War. He is pondering further on the principles of revolutionary justice: "How many of you have I shot?" he asks himself, arguing that here he has no reason to feel guilty: "To you I owe no fare." Then he recognizes the awakening of a more humane sense of justice, his individual private conscience over the cruel communal justice of the revolution: "But do I perhaps owe you the fare all the same? Must one also pay for the deeds which were right and necessary? ... Was there another measure beside that of reason?" (44)

In his subconscious Rubashov carries out the interrogation of Rubashov; he explores further and further the question of justice by reassessing the major events in his past. He recalls that while still in Germany he was arrested by the Gestapo. Although thrown into prison and tortured, he did not give away his comrades' names and he was eventually returned to Russia. Soon after his return as a celebrated hero, Rubashov recognized the tremendous change that had taken place while he was abroad: Stalin had consolidated his power, encouraged the personality cult around himself, and started to wipe out the former leaders of the revolution as "enemies of the people." Rubashov keeps remembering the changes by focusing on a well-known picture from the early twenties, "the delegates of the first congress of the Party ... Above each head was a small circle enclosing a number corresponding to a name printed underneath" (46). Rubashov remembers these martyrs as "an entirely new species: militant philosophers." With the disappearance of each victim from the political arena, a new circle appears, empty of name and number. Eventually the old group portrait disappears altogether, leaving a light spot on the wall, which carries now nothing except Stalin's single portrait.

Rubashov ponders the defeat of those "militant philosophers" who died indeed as martyrs, but martyrs to the cruelty of pure reason. He sees himself among them, as one of the false prophets to his people: "We brought you truth and in our mouth it sounded like a lie. We brought you freedom, and it looks in our hand like a whip" (46). Thinking about the fate of these leaders in the first few years of Stalin's reign, Rubashov's thoughts turn into a dirge, or rather into the bitter words of a jeremiad, full of religious paradox: "They dreamed of power with the object of abolishing power; of ruling over the people to wean them from the habit of being ruled ... Their brains, which had changed the course of the world, had each received a charge of lead. Some in the forehead, some in the back of the neck" (46).

Witnessing the cruelties connected with Stalin's consolidation of power, "after a fortnight, when ... still walking on crutches, Rubashov [asked] for a new mission abroad" (47). The Party sent him to Belgium. Here, in spite of his disillusionment with Stalin, he still followed the

Party line to the letter. His mission was, once more, to deal with the members of the Communist International. He had to make contact with Loewy, the leader of an underground Communist cell in a Belgian port, and make him realize that after years of advocating the Popular Front and the boycott of the fascist war machine to Communist parties abroad, the Soviet Union had started trading with the fascist countries, driven by the expediencies of economic self-interest and the game of *realpolitik*, not by the spirit of solidarity with Communists around the world. Consequently, Rubashov had now to convince the Belgian comrades to give up the idea of a boycott and start unloading the Soviet ships that were to arrive with "the flag of the Revolution [but] carrying petrol for the [fascist] aggressor" (54). Rejecting Rubashov's instructions and realizing that he and his comrades had not only been seduced and abandoned by the world's only socialist country but were also to be betrayed to the Belgian police, little Loewy hangs himself.

Now in his prison cell Rubashov admits to himself that he is personally responsible for little Loewy's suicide, that at the trial conducted by his private conscience he has to pay for that betrayal as well. Each time he touches upon a shameful episode in his past, Rubashov's sense of personal guilt surfaces in the shape of a violent toothache. When the prison doctor examines his infected tooth and diagnoses that "the root of the right eye-tooth is broken off and has remained in the jaw" (59), this announcement describes not only Rubashov's physical condition but also his spiritual condition of being "infected" by his past sins, haunted by his awakening private conscience, by a new sense of guilt.

It is only after making Rubashov come to a mature assessment of his past, as well as allowing the reader to see the unresolvable contradictions in his political position, that Koestler introduces the interrogator, Ivanov, into the story. He is an old friend and comrade of Rubashov. At first Ivanov seems to be the very voice of reason, the same voice Rubashov recognizes as his own cold, emotionless voice from the past. Now he ponders whether, under different circumstances, he would not be acting the same way as Ivanov does now; he admits to himself that "they could be in reverse position" (70). Ivanov is the Shadow, a mirror-image of Rubashov, challenging, taunting Rubashov with his own former position, stating, "We can't afford to lose ourselves in judicial subtleties. Did you in your time?" (71).

Ivanov is also a mirror-image in the sense that as a steadfast member of the old guard, he must be going through some of the same doubts as Rubashov. Thus Rubashov observes that his interrogator also looks on the light spot left by the removal of the former leaders' portrait, and he, too, has a "tormented look in his face, a fixedness in his eye, as though he were not focusing on him, Rubashov, but at a point at some distance behind him" (71).

The only thing revealed at the first interrogation is that Rubashov no longer thinks of the Party as "we"; he has become the voice of the outsider, of the opposition. Ivanov points out that by referring to himself as "I" and to the Party of Stalin and his followers as "them," Rubashov has already passed sentence on himself. Cynically, Ivanov explains that "for the public, one needs, of course, a trial and legal justification. For us, what I have just said should be enough" (62).

To get the full impact of Ivanov's words here, we should probably recall that Bukharin, the model for Rubashov, had been participating for long years in the political games of the Party autocracy that aimed at "the suppression of all opposition movements arising within the Communist party."[36] At the Tenth Party Congress, Bukharin also accepted the resolution whereby "in order to achieve maximum unity by eliminating all fractional tendencies, the Congress empowers the Central Committee to apply in all cases of breach of discipline ... every kind of Party disciplinary action, including expulsion from the Party."[37] With the help of this resolution, Bukharin himself was instrumental in getting rid of former opponents. In fact, Ivanov's cynical words are simply an echo of the circular logic in the words of Bukharin's ally, Rikov, when declaring Kamenev an oppositionist, something that in the spirit of the resolution was becoming identical with being declared an enemy of the Party, punishable by expulsion, arrest, and execution: "'The traditions of Bolshevism do not allow any member of the Party to defend views which have been recognized as anti-Party and anti-Bolshevik,' said Rikov. 'The very fact ... that oppositionists are ignoring and by-passing this resolution is the best demonstration of how far they have deviated ideologically from the Party'" (43).

Knowing this procedure from earlier show-trials, Bukharin recanted and admitted his mistakes so that he would not be declared in opposition to Stalin's latest policy, of which he did in fact disapprove. With each move he made in his last years, Bukharin became more and more entangled in the contradictions of his position – just as Rubashov is in the novel.

Rubashov repeatedly realizes in the course of his interrogation that he has to pay for his formerly ruthless adherence to the Party line; it is what made him betray young Richard and abandon crippled little Loewy, and more recently, while he was serving as head of the Trade Delegation, his secretary and mistress, Arlova. As his sense of guilt rakes up more and more detailed memories of the young woman, as compliant a mistress as she was a subservient secretary, Rubashov again becomes aware of the painful aching of his tooth.

The chapter on the second hearing begins with Rubashov's diary entry about the distinction between objective and subjective good. He still believes that the end of a socialist future justifies the means, the ruthless acts of cruelty committed in the present, that the only objective good is the long-term good of the Party. "For us," he writes, "the question of subjective good faith is of no interest. He who is in the wrong must pay, he who is in the right will be absolved." In this contemplation, the only judge is History, and each individual will receive justice according to the success or failure of his actions.

At the beginning of his second interrogation Rubashov is still a utilitarian, not a moralist. He still believes "History has taught us that often lies serve her better than the truth; for man is sluggish and has to be led through the desert for forty years before each step in his development. And he has to be driven through the desert with threats and promises, by imaginary terrors and imaginary consolations, so that he should not sit down prematurely to rest and divert himself by worshipping golden calves" (74).

In their contempt for the masses, Rubashov's words echo those of the Grand Inquisitor. He acts out the drama between Messiah and Dictator in his own soul, and in many instances the words of his first interrogator, Ivanov, simply remind him of his own voice from the past. After these talks, previously repressed memories about Arlova come to the surface, and he relives their love affair, remembering her expression of unconditional devotion (like a gesture from the Pieta): "You will always be able to do whatever you like with me" (86). (There is an interesting echo of this scene in Orwell's *Nineteen Eighty-four*, when Winston's repressed memories come to the surface and he recalls his mother's gesture of unconditional love.)

Rubashov's affair with Arlova took place in the mid-thirties, when Stalin was already engaged in the rewriting of history to ensure that he would appear to have been Lenin's closest associate and spiritual heir. This was also the era of great cultural upheavals. Earlier works of history, for example, were removed from the library shelves and replaced by more "up-to-date" versions of the same period. In the novel, to undermine Rubashov, at the Trade Delegation the security organs arrange a conspiracy against Arlova, who is in charge of the Delegation's library; some Party members accuse her of sabotaging the rearrangement of the library, hinting that she must harbour critical thoughts about the Party's re-evaluation of history and should be unmasked as an oppositionist. Already under a cloud for being an oppositionist and knowing that standing up for Arlova would only

enhance the likelihood of charges against him, Rubashov fails to come
to his mistress's defence. "He has sacrificed Arlova because his own
existence was more valuable to the Revolution" (94). Of course he
realizes that Arlova was singled out by the Party because of her
connection with him. Yet, while Arlova is tried on charges of anti-
Soviet conspiracy, Rubashov feels it incumbent upon him to publicly
recant his past mistakes, which also implicate his secretary. He confesses to former oppositionist tendencies and begs the Party's forgiveness. His recantation seals Arlova's fate; she is sentenced to death.

In his prison cell Rubashov relives these events with increasing
sensitivity and empathy for Arlova, who had accepted and loved him
unconditionally, and he is aware of his mounting sense of guilt. At this
point he is made to witness an execution: he sees a former comrade
and disciple being dragged along the prison corridor to his death. The
man is Bogrov, a brave soldier from the historic battleship *Potemkin*
and a bearer of the first revolutionary order. The formerly heroic figure
is broken physically and psychologically, and Rubashov suddenly
imagines the last minutes of Arlova's life as she must have been dragged
to her execution. Suddenly, for the first time, he can hear "how Arlova
whimpered" (106).

Himself a "military philosopher" of reason, "formerly Rubashov
had not imagined Arlova's death in such detail. It had always been for
him an abstract occurrence." It was this rational attitude that allowed
him to stay convinced of the "logical rightness of his behaviour" (106).
Now, in shock over Bogrov's execution, Rubashov collapses on his cot
and has a vision of Bogrov and Arlova, the horrifying effect aggravated
by his recurring nightmare of being arrested in enemy territory. At this
nadir of the Dark Night of the Soul, Ivanov appears in the cell as his
Saviour, with a bottle of cognac. Ivanov explains that it was his
subordinate, Gletkin, who staged Bogrov's execution so as to shock
Rubashov and extort his confession. Ivanov claims that he has far
greater respect for Rubashov's logic than to resort to such brutal
methods. In fact, Ivanov announces, he is confident that Rubashov will
see the logical reason why he should sign the confession Ivanov has
prepared for him, implying that upon signing, Rubashov can count on
a reasonably reduced punishment. Undermined by his own sense of
private guilt and his still invincible loyalty to the cause of the revolution, Rubashov is left to ponder Ivanov's proposal in a far more pliable
frame of mind.

Rubashov's next shock comes at the third hearing. He finds himself
in the presence of Gletkin, "the Barbarian of the new age," who has,
unlike Ivanov, an extremely simple notion of the human personality:
"Human beings able to resist any amount of physical pressure do not

exist," he declares to his superior. "Experience shows that resistance of the human nerve system is limited by Nature" and the success of an interrogator with a prisoner "is all a question of constitution" (76). It develops that, when Ivanov explained to Gletkin that Rubashov was on the verge of signing the false confession expected from him, Gletkin declared Ivanov a cynic, and in the course of his third hearing Rubashov is given the shocking news that Ivanov has been removed from his case, arrested, and promptly executed for being a "cynic," for not showing that he was sufficiently convinced of Rubashov's "guilt."

Gletkin is a "barbarian," a product of Stalin's new bureaucracy who no longer has any ties with the idealism of the old guard born before the revolution, with no ties to "a world which has vanished" (228). He also knows that Rubashov is not guilty of the charges levelled against him. But Gletkin is able to believe in Rubashov's innocence and guilt at the same time; he is performing the mental acrobatics of the "methodical lunacy of schizophrenia" (137) that Orwell came to call Doublethink.

A gloating Gletkin reminds Rubashov of his previous recantation, which had the effect of abandoning Arlova to her fate, as though Rubashov had not been pressured to recant. Gletkin also confronts Rubashov with a false witness tortured into a state of "animal helplessness" until he "confesses" that Rubashov hired him to poison Stalin.

Gletkin's method is fairly straightforward: for weeks he does not allow Rubashov to sleep, and he uses a glaring, blinding light at the interrogations. Exhausted by the glare, the lack of sleep, and his personal guilt and toothache, Rubashov admits to the most phantasmagorical of accusations, realizing that "powerlessness had as many grades as power [and] Gletkin forced him down the ladder" (156) step by step. (There is another echo of this scene in *Nineteen Eighty-four*, when Winston is finally taken to Room 101, a place "as deep as it was possible to go.")

It is at the lowest grade of his victim's powerlessness that Gletkin makes the plea: "Your testimony will be the last service you can do to the Party" (171). By making people see that opposition is paramount to treason and conspiracy, Rubashov would do a service for Party unity. Gletkin openly admits that "mankind could never do without scapegoats" and refers to Christ as a "voluntary scapegoat" (171). And so Rubashov accepts the role of being crucified "in the name of [his own] faith" (157).

The image of the Crucifixion gains further resonance in the scene where Vassily, the old porter of Rubashov's apartment house, who admired Rubashov as his heroic commander in the Civil War, listens to the humiliations visited upon Rubashov at his trial and to his confession to outrageous crimes. The old man begins mumbling to himself the words from the New Testament: "And the soldiers led him away, into the hall called Praetorium; and they called together the whole band. And they clothed him with purple and they smote him on the head with a reed and did spit upon him; and bowing their knees worshipped him."

Intimidated by the thought that he might be denounced for his sympathy for Rubashov, the old man does not dare to speak up for him even to his own daughter, and consequently he feels bitterly ashamed, identifying himself with Peter, who denied his Master (179). The words Koestler puts into the mouth of Rubashov at his trial echo Bukharin's declaration that judgment is in the hand of History: "If I ask myself to-day, 'For what am I dying?' I am confronted by absolute nothingness. There is nothing for which one could die, if one died without having repented and reconciled with the Party and the Movement ... I have paid; my account with history is settled" (182).

After settling his account with History, Rubashov awaits his execution; he gratefully accepts the words of empathy of the White officer in the next cell, who taps on the wall his final words of consolation. Rubashov recalls once more the image of the Pietà and also the landscape with the poplars and the blue sky he used to contemplate in his childhood, and experiences a sense of ecstasy, an "oceanic sense" that he is becoming one with the cosmos – an experience repeated at the moment of his execution. In the end Koestler leaves us with Rubashov at peace, after he was able to "pay" for the crimes of violence and betrayal he had committed in the name of the Party. Koestler suggests that in the face of all his disappointments in the present, Rubashov reaffirms his faith in the socialist dream of the future, a dream originally inspired by humanism.

Yet for the reader, just as for the old soldier Vassily, Rubashov's execution marks "darkness at noon," the descending of the darkness of universal mourning over the eclipse of the sun of Lenin's "radiant future."

After reading Rodionov's *Chocolate* and Ribakov's *The Children of the Arbat*, the reader finds that the Rubashov-Bukharin show-trial is a further continuation of the same themes. Hungarian-born Koestler, a former Communist, had travelled in the Soviet Union in the mid-thirties, at which time he noticed but still made excuses for the obvious signs of Stalin's terror. "The decisive event which led to" his final break with the Party "was the trial of the so-called 'Anti-Soviet Bloc of Rightists and Trotskyists,' which surpassed in absurdity and horror everything that had gone before ... it made the preceding show trials appear invalid, because the alleged evidence had been supplied by the self-confessed saboteur and poisoner at the head of the GPU; ... if one was to believe the accused men's confessions, both the Soviet Union and the Communist International had been, during the first fifteen years of their existence, headed by agents of the German and British Intelligence Service."[38]

Koestler adds another note here about the nightmarish miscarriage of justice: in the persons of Yagoda, Yeshov, and Beria "all the heads of the Russian police state during these twenty-five years were successively executed as poisoners, spies and traitors."[39] Koestler recognized, as Orwell had, the "satanic machinery" of denunciations, recantations, purges, trials, and false confessions operating in the Soviet Union at the time. Although *Darkness at Noon*, written in 1940 in Paris, had a profound influence on Orwell's *Nineteen Eighty-four*, the Western dystopian model *par excellence*, Koestler's novel does not embody the futuristic structure associated with the Western tradition of dystopian fiction. In 1940 Koestler was exploring the dynamics of Stalin's show-trials in the recent past. The novel offers no fictional hypothesis about the future, but concentrates on the political and psychological analysis of what had already taken place.

This does not mean, of course, that Koestler was not preoccupied with the question of the future of socialism, but, as the consistent allusions to the Crucifixion of the new Messiah indicate, in *Darkness at Noon* he was focused on the sense of spiritual loss modern man experiences after turning to socialism as a secular religion: "The age of enlightenment has destroyed faith in personal survival; the scars of this operation have never healed. There is a vacancy in every living soul, a deep thirst in all of us. If the socialist idea cannot fill this vacancy and quench our thirst, then it has failed in our time."[40]

On the evidence of the dystopic reversal of the pursuit of justice in the Soviet Union, Koestler challenges the Western reader to re-examine the question of whether "the basic trend in Russia is still towards socialism"[41] or whether Stalin's dictatorship has irrevocably betrayed the dream. In his overview of Koestler's works Orwell called Koestler a "short-term pessimist"[42] who no longer believed in the success of revolutionary socialism in the present of the 1940s, though he had not given up hope for the distant future. Yet Orwell would have agreed with Koestler that "the spreading of Russian pseudo-communism over Europe can be stopped only by a true Socialist movement. The antidote to eastern Byzantism is Western revolutionary humanism."[43]

It is the message of a return to humanism that Koestler advocates in *Darkness at Noon*, a message that also comes to us loud and clear through the political and psychological plight of the protagonist in the dystopian fiction of Zamiatin, Orwell, and Huxley.

Terror in War, Terror in Peace: Grossman's *Life and Fate*, Tertz Sinyavski's *The Trial Begins*, and Daniel's *This Is Moscow Speaking*

VASSILY GROSSMAN: *LIFE AND FATE*

At the end of *Darkness at Noon* Rubashov looks at the insignia on his torturer's uniform, and for a moment he cannot tell whether he is looking at the red star or the swastika. This moment of sighting a sinister political Doppelgänger is extended further in Vassily Grossman's *Life and Fate*.

The novel is a panorama of the Soviet Union in the throes of the Second World War, focusing on the heroic Battle at Stalingrad, which turned the tide of the war against Nazism. At the same time, the novel also provides a powerful statement about the shocking resemblance between Nazi Germany and the USSR, ostensibly the greatest of ideological enemies, both one-party states ruling through terror and intimidation. Grossman also presents a compelling illustration that the world is moving towards totalitarianism, whose essential principle is embodied in the German and Soviet concentration camps, which aim to transform humanity by debasing human nature. By this argument, Grossman taps into a central theme informing twentieth-century dystopian fiction in the Western tradition, sharing Arendt's and Orwell's diagnoses, inspired by a tragic humanism.

However, unlike Orwell and Arendt, who concentrate on the parallel between the two versions of totalitarianism based on the psycho-historical effects of ideological thinking, when analysing the effects of the victory at Stalingrad, Grossman also introduces a new angle: he draws a parallel between the two dictatorships on the basis of their mutual whipping-up of nationalistic fervour to advocate the superiority of their own culture, language, and "race," a chauvinistic fervour expressing itself in xenophobic hostility towards its own ethnic minorities and in anti-semitism. The novel indicates that Stalin's revival during the war of a "state-sponsored Russian nationalism could [and did] lead to results very similar to German National Socialism."[1]

Because of its epic proportions – the book consist of almost a thousand pages, and has more than one hundred and forty characters referred to by name – Grossman's novel has been called the *War and Peace* of the twentieth century. The comparison between Tolstoy and Grossman is indeed inevitable: along the Tolstoyan example, Grossman's extensive cast of characters are all interconnected, directly or indirectly, through various members of one particular family, the Shapolnikovs. This device provides a veritable panorama not only of Soviet society but also of the complex philosophical argument about the most divergent manifestations of the regime amplified by these characters.

It is indeed a symphony composed and orchestrated on the Tolstoyan model, yet it adheres to the central theme of twentieth-century dystopia, even if it has the dimensions, the tempo, and the pace usually associated with the nineteenth-century novel. In terms of its often painstakingly detailed realism, aimed to re-create the Soviet Union of the era with utmost verisimilitude, Grossman's novel could be regarded as the perfect model along the Guidelines for Socialist Realism, were it not for the fact that the Soviet Union as it emerges from Grossman's pages undermines the very foundation of the compulsory optimism and cheerful celebration of Party spirit prescribed by Socialist Realism. As demanded by these Guidelines, all the characters are shown in their interaction with the forces of society; but in Grossman's rendering these are the forces of a pathological society, wherein the characters – soldiers, officers, engineers, scientists, students, men and women of all ages – habitually teeter on the brink of being denounced, expelled from their jobs, arrested, and sent to camps.

The novel's structure at first seems cinematic or episodic. On closer reading (and this is a book that requires – and deserves – not only close reading but also rereading) the individual scenes between characters add up to a structurally imposing social panorama, or, to return to the musical metaphor, the various bars form a diversity of individually recognizable motifs, until these converge in a rich assembly of typically dystopic themes powerfully, albeit "traditionally," orchestrated: the concept of the concentration camp as the essence of totalitarianism; the war with the enemy who, upon closer inspection, is one's own mirror-image; spying and denunciation at the heart of the police-state; rampant nationalism inducing xenophobia; the individual's doomed struggle for "Life" against the deadly forces of his or her political "Fate."

The main structural device intertwines these various themes in a central thesis that has the shock effect of the mirror-image, a sinister political Doppelgänger. The novel begins in a German concentration camp near Poznan, among Soviet prisoners of war. An old Bolshevik, Mostovskoy, is summoned for interrogation by Obersturmbannführer Liss, the SS representative of the camp administration. Liss calls the old Bolshevik his "teacher" and asserts that "when we look one another in the face, we're neither of us just looking at a face we hate – no, *we're gazing into a mirror.* That's the tragedy of our age. Do you really not recognize yourselves in us ...? You may think you hate us, but what you really hate is yourselves – yourselves in us. It's terrible, isn't it? Do you understand me?"(395; my italics).

In fact the voice of the fascist enemy is identical to an inner voice in Mostovskoy; it refers to his acquiescence to Stalin's unconscionable betrayal of the Communists abroad, to the betrayal of the ideals of the International (the same betrayal Rubashov had been an instrument of in *Darkness at Noon*, until he recognizes a sense of justice in the fact that he has to "pay" for it by his imprisonment and execution). In the words of Liss, "The German Communists we've sent to camps are the same ones you sent to camps in 1937. Yezhov imprisoned them: Reichsführer Himmler imprisoned them ... Be more of a Hegelian, teacher" (398).

The fascist state presents a sinister foreshadowing of the anti-semitic terror in connection with the plot that Stalin and his followers concocted in the early 1950s: "Today you're appalled by our hatred of the Jews. Tomorrow you may make use of our experience yourselves ... I have been led by a great man down the road. You too have been led by a great man ... Did you really believe Bukharin was an agent provocateur? ... I knew Roehm himself. I trusted him. But that is how it had to be" (399).

The old Bolshevik is trying to deny the validity of the comparison between Hitler's and Stalin's regimes, but Liss unmistakably articulates Mostovskoy's own doubts; the old man finds it almost impossible to dismiss this voice as a "hallucination." What he finds unbearable is not only that, if Liss is right, "he would have to hate Stalin and his dictatorship" but that he also "would have to condemn Lenin!" the founder of the one-party state. This is "the edge of the abyss ... that makes him think he is about to go mad" (399–400).

Liss's argument is merciless and compellingly logical in showing that "in essence we are the same – both one-party States. Our capitalists are not the masters. The State gives them their plan ... Your State also outlines a plan and takes what is produced for itself" (401). Liss also argues that Stalin's slogans of Russian nationalism, which have taken the place of the original ideals of the International, are in fact quite similar to the slogans of National Socialism in Hitler's Germany.

"Nationalism is the soul of our epoch," he argues, "and your 'Social-ism in One Country' is the supreme expression of nationalism" (403). The slogans of nationalism gain their momentum by inciting hatred against the outsider, justifying the victimization of millions: "Stalin ... liquidated millions of peasants ... Hitler liquidated millions of Jews ... You've kept silent when I've been talking, but *I know that I'm like a mirror for you – a surgical mirror*" (402–3).

Mostovskoy no longer objects; in the 'mirror' that at first seems to drive him insane he recognizes his own moral flaws, his responsibility for acquiescing to the deliberate miscarriage of justice as a Party member: "If I believed in God, I would think that terrible interrogator had been sent to me as a punishment for my sins" (403).

The same sense of mirroring is pointed out by various characters throughout the novel. An old Tolstoyan, whom his mates in the concentration camp call the "Holy Fool," articulates the writer's own condemnation of any orthodoxy, any ideology. He regards the "good" of Christianity and Communism as mirror-images:

The Christian doctrine caused more suffering than all the crimes of the people who did evil for its own sake ... I have ... seen the unshakeable strength of the idea of social good that was born in my own country. I saw the struggle during the period of general collectivization and again in 1937. I saw people being annihilated in the name of an idea as good and fine and humane as the ideal of Christianity. I saw whole villages dying of hunger; I saw trains bound for Siberia with thousands and thousands of men and women who had been enemies of a great and bright idea of social good. This idea was something fine and noble – yet it killed some without mercy, crippled the lives of others, and separated wives from husbands and children from fathers.   (405–7)

The old man compares the fanatic idealism of fascism to other dan-gerous forms of idealism: "Now the horror of German Fascism has arisen ... The air is full of groans and cries of the condemned ... And even these crimes, crimes never before seen in the universe – even by Man on Earth – have been committed in the name of good" (407). Like the voice of Satan in Andzrejewski's *The Inquisitors*, the old man blames the fanatical pursuit of the ideal of the "good" as the cause of pain and suffering. Having seen throughout history that evil is com-mitted in the name of the greatest good all the time, he is left with a terrible question: "Is it that life itself is evil?"

His answer is surprising. It is not the "good" organized in any rational system but the irrational, instinctive "good" in the depth of the human heart that bespeaks the only hope for our species: "Yes, as well as this terrible Good with capital "G," there is everyday kindness.

The kindness of an old woman when carrying a piece of bread to a prisoner, the kindness of a soldier allowing a wounded enemy to drink from his water-flask" (407). The old man concludes: "This kindness, this stupid kindness, is what is most truly human in a human being. It is what sets man apart, the highest achievement of his soul. No, it says, life is not evil!"(409)

It is worth noting that this expression of hope comes from an old man everyone else in the camp considers a Holy Fool, an ineffectual and confused thinker because he dismisses any form of political ideology and religion: Christianity, Communism, and fascism. Yet, this "confused" apolitical thinker is the only one who has the courage to stand up against the overwhelming coercion of the concentration camp. When he finds out that the construction the inmates are made to work on is a crematorium for the mass murder of other victims, he refuses to work; he has the courage to overcome the slave mentality of all the others, although he knows full well that the prize for asserting his free will is execution.

There can be no doubt that here the words of the Holy Fool are the words of Grossman himself, but at times he also announces his own personal views quite directly, without the dramatic persona of a fictional character. Although Grossman was probably not familiar with Hannah Arendt's incisive anatomy in *Totalitarianism*, or with Orwell's *Nineteen Eighty-four*, he comes to a definition of the totalitarian state essentially similar to those of Arendt and Orwell by declaring that "the violence of a totalitarian State is so great as to be no longer a means to an end; it becomes an object of mystical worship and adoration" (215). Like Arendt and Orwell, Grossman articulates the proposition that the ultimate purpose of the totalitarian state is the transformation of human nature: "Does human nature undergo a true change in the cauldron of totalitarian violence? Does man lose his innate yearning for freedom? The fate of both man and the totalitarian State depends on the answer to this question. If human nature does change, then the eternal and world-wide triumph of the dictatorial state is assumed; if his yearning for freedom remains constant, then the totalitarian state is doomed."

Like Orwell's Winston Smith, who insists that as long as he has his own voice the "Spirit of Man" must ultimately triumph over the spirit of Big Brother, Grossman also believes in a "religion of humanity," where the human spirit is identified by an innate, unchangeable yearning for freedom. Against the weighty evidence of the various cases of betrayal, denunciation, and inner breakdown presented to us in the novel, he asserts that "man's fate may make him a slave, but his nature remains unchanged" (216).

The words of Grossman's philosophical contemplation constitute an often artificial voice-over throughout the novel, as if the characters' "Life and Fate" were not sufficient evidence for a philosophical assertion of optimism. He concludes that society under totalitarianism is enslaved by the terror of "eternal, ceaseless violence, overt or covert," yet it remains an essential attribute of human nature "not to renounce freedom voluntarily" (216). Although totalitarianism makes human beings carry the burden of the slaves' "Fate" relentlessly, the yearning for freedom, even when this yearning is stifled by coercion, remains eternal: it is the principle of "Life."

In introducing the life of the inmates in the German concentration camp and in the Russian labour camp as mirror-images, Grossman makes the reader realize that the conflict between the coercive forces of the police-state and the human being striving not only for physical survival but also for a sense of inner freedom is essentially the same in both.

To further the effect of the mirror-image, Grossman also introduces a series of scenes within the German and Soviet armies involved in the protracted Battle of Stalingrad: Nazi security officers spy upon German soldiers and officers; political commissars scrutinize the men and their officers in the Soviet Army, visiting even the hold-outs literally shot to pieces, to spy on the mood of each unit, each individual, in pursuit of "unmasking" "anti-Soviet" intentions in any remark that can be taken to be critical of the leader or of the Party line. These observations find their way into detailed reports that the political commissars manage to send back to Moscow even in the midst of the siege, to be securely stored in the enormous central file the police-state keeps on everyone – including on the political commissars themselves. The process is illustrated in full by the case of Krymov, the ex-husband of Zhenia Shapolnikova. As a political commissar in Stalingrad, Krymov sends a devastating report to Moscow about the dangerous precedent of free expression that the heroic commander Grekov encourages among his people, while political commissar Getmanov sends a devastating report on Krymov that eventually results in Krymov's arrest. In the course of his interrogation and torture at the Lyublianka prison, Krymov is astonished about the extensively detailed information on him held in the central file, including every step he has ever taken, every chance remark he has made or that has been made about him, throughout his public and in his private life, before and during the war.

But the role of the "political instructor" as a fully empowered spy preying upon each human being in his sphere is best illustrated in the relationship between Colonel Novikov (Zhenia Shapolnikova's lover) and political commissar Getmanov. Every word uttered by Novikov, every gesture, every detail of his public or private life becomes the target of Getmanov's scrutiny. Getmanov, who has no military training or rank, feels fully entitled to ingratiate himself with Novikov's superiors by offering them the colonel's cognac; a careerist always in step with the latest Party line, Getmanov is also a fervent Russian nationalist, stopping Novikov from promoting a valiant Kalmyk officer so that "in the name of the friendship of peoples we [shouldn't] keep sacrificing the Russians" (142). Getmanov also feels entitled to question Novikov on his military decisions as a commander of the army's tank unit, when, for example, Novikov begins the offensive five minutes later than his orders specify. Although Novikov receives Stalin's commendation for the successful execution of his orders, and his five-minute delay allows him to reduce casualties to a minimum, Getmanov immediately reports on Novikov's dangerous insubordination; to Novikov's face, however, he expresses his heartfelt congratulations.

Getmanov also feels entitled to taunt Novikov affectionately about his infatuation with Zhenia Shapolnikova, whose family includes several people in camps, not to mention her ex-husband Krymov, now under a cloud. A consummate hypocrite, Getmanov severely reprimands other officers for sexually loose conduct, while Getmanov, himself a married man, quite shamelessly conducts an affair with an attractive young woman army doctor. By pretending to be on most affectionate terms with Novikov, Getmanov provokes the colonel to reveal his thoughts to him: thus when Novikov repeats Zhenia's chance remark that her ex-husband Krymov had been considered a brilliant man by Trotsky during the revolution, these word seal the fate of Krymov, weighing more heavily than his courageous conduct during the revolution and the Civil War. Novikov's brave and efficient leadership of the tank unit has been cited on the radio by Stalin himself; still, by the end of the novel Novikov himself is asked to report to Central Security – often the first step to investigative arrest.

Getmanov, like all political commissars, is expected to be "vigilant," to "unmask" the potential enemy of the state, and he can expect promotion and further privileges only if he fulfils his quota of denunciations. The same structure, in much less detail, of course, is also shown in the German army, where the agents of the Secret Service have all the privileges and wield power over the officers and soldiers. Even in the process of its disintegration, Nazi Germany functions as a formidable police-state; so does Stalin's regime, regardless of defeat or victory. In this panorama, whether in the concentration camp or in the army, human beings have to exert all the forces of "Life" to overcome the overwhelming burden of their political "Fate."

But it is through the fluctuations of Viktor Shtrum's personal pre-dicament[2] that we get the fullest explanation of what Grossman meant by the title *Life and Fate*. Viktor's life is the linchpin of the novel, interwoven with those of the Shapolnikov family through his wife, Lyudmilla Shapolnikova. Viktor's character contains many elements from the life of the writer, who, like Viktor, lost his mother when the Germans occupied Ukraine and exterminated the Jews. Viktor's troubled married life and his emotional fluctuations are also closely observed. Grossman makes Viktor go through the psychological anxiety of a successful professional who at one point is presented the highest award available in his profession, and in the next minute is forced to recant his previous intellectual position as a "mistake" and beg for forgiveness – another experience derived from Grossman's life. In the novel Viktor is not a writer but a prominent scientist, whose professional life is modelled on that of the famous nuclear physicist Landau, who worked under Kapitza – Sokolov in the novel. During the war, when the Institute is transferred to Kazan, Viktor becomes the centre of a group of scientists who are encouraged to advance the international scientific reputation of the USSR but who could be dismissed, arrested, and sentenced to long years of prison at the drop of Stalin's latest whim about any theory, discovery, or invention he deems contradictory to the spirit of the latest Party line.

For a while, Viktor's career is under a cloud: his friends and col-leagues avoid him from afar, and his family fear his imminent arrest. Then, all of a sudden, his theory on nucleo-physics receives the highest approbation; he gets a congratulatory telephone call from Stalin him-self. Basking in the warmth of his success and popularity, Viktor immediately forgets his recent fears and the humiliations he has suf-fered. At this point his superiors at the Institute ask him to sign a personal letter as one of the prominent physicists with an international reputation. The letter is a response to Western scientists' protest against the continued imprisonment of two Soviet physicians, Levin and Pletnyev, implicated in the Bukharin trials of 1938 and convicted of the phantasmagorical crime of having poisoned Gorky and his son. The Party-designed letter rejects the Western scientists' indignation and publicly reaffirms the guilt of these two distinguished Jewish doctors. The language of the letter reminds Viktor of a regression to medieval witch-hunts – it is the same language and imagery that the Party condemned only yesterday as the anti-semitic language of fascism: "There was something medieval about these accusations. Assassin-doctors! The murderers of a great writer, the last Russian classic! What was the purpose of such slanders? The Inquisition and its bonfires, the execution of heretics, witch-trials, boiling pitch, the stench of smoke

... What did all this have to do with Lenin, with the construction of Socialism and the great war against Fascism?" (834).

Viktor experiences now what Mostovskoy experienced in his dialogue with the Nazi camp commander: the shocking effect of mirroring, the emergence of the political Doppelgänger. While it is clearly an incitement to anti-semitism, the letter addressed to Western scientists still insists that the Soviet state stands in staunch opposition to fascism: "Your defence of Pletnyev and Levin – degenerates who are a disgrace not only to medicine, but to the human race as a whole – is grist to the mill of the anti-human ideology of Fascism ... The Soviet nation stands alone in its struggle against Fascism, the ideology that has brought back medieval witch-trials, pogroms, torture-chambers and the bonfires of the Inquisition." Like Mostovskoy, Viktor also feels ready to cry out: "How could one read this and not go insane?" (835).

In the last moment, remembering his mother's tragic death for being born a Jew, Viktor gathers enough courage to refuse to sign the letter, with its slander of the Jewish doctors, even if this may mean the loss of his job and further retribution. In fact, at the end of the novel the fortunes of all the major characters are in decline. They grieve over those killed in the war: Viktor's stepson was killed in the Battle of Stalingrad and Viktor's wife, Lyudmilla, cannot get over her depression; Viktor's mother has been murdered by the Nazis; Marissa, Viktor's sister-in-law, was killed in Stalingrad; Marissa's daughter, Vera, lost the father of her newborn son. But just as frightening, the hope that the hardships and bloodshed suffered through the war will result in a freer world, without terror, seems also increasingly distant: "The war had given way to peace – a poor, miserable peace that was hardly any easier than the war" (858).

The major characters realize that they are still in danger of being denounced, imprisoned, or sent to the camps. Viktor's brother-in-law, Dmitrij, died in a camp; Dmitrij's wife has been sentenced to ten years of hard labour for refusing to denounce her husband; Marissa's widowed husband, Sidorov, acted bravely throughout the long Battle of Stalingrad as the Director of the Power Station but is now demoted and sent to Asia in disgrace. We understand he should be glad he was not sent to prison. Another of Viktor's brothers-in-law, Krymov, is arrested on the denunciation of Getmanov, probably to be sent to camp for long years.

The book begins in a Nazi concentration camp. Mostovskoy's gradual discovery that the one-party system in the Soviet Union has created a society in many ways strikingly similar to that created by Hitler completes the first major thesis of the dystopian theme. This is also the note on which the book is brought to an end. After a three-day-long interrogation in the Lyublanka, where he is coerced into signing a false confession, Krymov concludes that the totalitarian state has misappropriated the ideals of socialism, something he had refused to acknowledge during the show-trials of the thirties:

The amazing confessions of Bukharin and Rykov, of Kamenev and Zinoviev, the trials of the Trotskyists, of the Right Opposition and the Left Opposition ... all these things no longer seemed quite so hard to understand. The hide was being flayed off the still-living body of the Revolution so that a new age could slip into it; as for the red, bloody meat, the steaming innards – they were being thrown onto the scrapheap. The new age needed only the hide of the Revolution – and this was being flayed off people who were still alive. Those who slipped into it spoke the language of the Revolution and mimicked its gestures, but their brains, lungs, livers and eyes were utterly different. (841)

In this instance Grossman uses Krymov as his mouthpiece, introducing the idea that by depriving human beings of their freedom, the slave-driver also enslaves himself (an idea also vividly illustrated in Orwell's early essay "Shooting an Elephant"). In the context of Grossman's novel this means that the Master's "Fate" is not superior to that of his subjects: "Stalin! The great Stalin! Perhaps this man with the iron will had less will than any of them. He was a slave of his time and circumstances, a dutiful, submissive servant of the present day, flinging the doors before the new age" (842).

In the past Krymov himself has denounced people whom he suspected of being "oppositionists," of maintaining independent ideas. Now he condemns the police-state's notion of human beings: "The unity of man's physical and spiritual being was the key to the investigators' almost uninterrupted run of successes. [By breaking body and soul they] force him into unconditional capitulation" (842).

Krymov shares a cell with an old Chekist, whose celebration of the lasting enslavement of the masses echoes the position of Dostoevski's Grand Inquisitor: "The world of the camps planned and gave birth to mines, factories, reservoirs and giant power stations. The headlong pace of its development made old-fashioned penal servitude seem as touching and absurd as the toy bricks of a child" (844). The old man's explanation is a severe shock to Krymov, especially when he comes to understand that life inside the camps is really the essence of the totalitarian state, "an exaggerated, magnified reflection of life outside ... If one were to develop the system of camps boldly and systematically ... the boundaries would finally be erased. The camp would merge with the world outside" (844). Grossman shows that the madness of the old Chekist who welcomes the elimination of the boundaries is not really madness. It is simply the tragic conclusion of an originally quasi-religious faith in the historical process. The old man admits: "Yes, I believe in God. I am an ignorant, credulous old man. Every age creates the deity in its own image. The security organs are wise and powerful; they are [the force] that holds sway over twentieth-century man" (846).

Mirror-images abound. Between Hitler and Stalin; between slavery inside the camp and slavery outside; between the victim and his former self that justified working in the service of the victimizer – these shocking revelations encompass the novel in a bookend structure. Only in the very last chapter does Grossman feel the need to contemplate if not exactly an upbeat ending, then at least something like a ray of hope. The last chapter introduces a nameless young couple with a child: the man has just returned, wounded, from the war. On a sunny, late winter morning they take a walk in the fields and, stopping at a forest, become aware of the ruthless, merciless, but eternal life-process in nature: "Somehow you could sense spring more vividly in this cool forest than on the sunlit plains. And there was deeper sadness in this silence than in the silence of autumn. In it you could hear both a lament for the dead and the furious joy of life itself … They stood there, holding their bags, in silence" (871).

Although the book ends with this weak affirmation of the continuity of the forces of "Life" through nature, the silent determination of the nameless young couple does not balance the weight of the "Fate" suffered by Grossman's named characters in the war and in the years to come. The novel leaves us with a tragic vision: the twentieth century as the dystopic world of totalitarian dictatorship. Like tragedy, the novel also validates the nobility of fighting against "Fate" – through small, irrational gestures of goodness, through the assertion of individuality and the human being's inner freedom. Yet the young people in the last scene, "holding their bags, in silence" carry a weight far too heavy: the "Fate" of the many millions who are confronted by the radical injustice inherent in the machinery of totalitarianism, a conspiracy against the forces of "Life."

ABRAM TERTZ SINYAVSKI: *THE TRIAL BEGINS*

Written at about the same time as Grossman's *Life and Fate* (1960), Abram Tertz Sinyavski's *The Trial Begins* (1959) develops further the theme only hinted at by the end of Grossman's novel – the Jewish doctors' plot, and the emerging design of further show-trials. Although *The Trial Begins* also deals with the recent past and does not project the dystopic nightmare society into the future, in several ways it is still closer to Western expressions of the dystopian genre. A relatively short narrative, it develops along a single, clear story-line amplifying one central dsytopian theme: the machinery for the deliberate miscarriage of justice in the preparation for show-trials. It is the tragic irony of history that this dystopian novel about unjust trials (smuggled abroad and published, with its companion piece "On Socialist Realism," in 1962) became the reason its author was put on trial in 1966, and sentenced to seven years of hard labour.[3]

In the novel Tertz deliberately challenges the formula of Socialist Realism by not making a division between positive and negative characters based on the degree of their passionate commitment to the Party, by not having a positive hero, and, unlike Grossman, by making occasional use of such modernist, experimental techniques as the metaphorical foregrounding of language, a filmic use of flashbacks, and, intermittently, a stream-of-consciousness narrative. Nevertheless, even when openly challenging Socialist Realism, Tertz still moves within its boundaries. *The Trial Begins* still offers a "realistic," that is, a straightforward and palpable story-line, and the characters are seen in their interaction with social forces. The realistic touch turns into a satirical attack on Socialist Realism only when we realize the tremendous gap between compulsory optimism about the emotional aspects of human nature and Tertz's dark portrayal of the emotional life of Soviet man, emphasizing the fear, hypocrisy, and aggression instilled in everyone by the political regime.

Set in Moscow in 1953, the last year of Stalin's reign, the novel deals with the careful rehearsal of the last of those gigantic political theatricals Stalin was so fond of stage-managing. Golub, the Public Prosecutor, decides to "crack down" on a prominent old Jewish doctor, Rabinovits, for performing abortions, and so to begin an anti-semitic and anti-intellectual campaign, including false accusations and show-trials against "cosmopolitan" elements. In the course of this campaign the Prosecutor learns that his teenage son, Serjozha, has raised some politically unorthodox questions in his history class and carried on discussions with his classmates about how to return Soviet society to the originally humanistic ideals of the revolution. In the hysteria of the hate campaign generated by his own father, Serjozha is arrested and accused of conspiring with the phantomlike omnipresent enemy, convicted, and sentenced to long years of forced labour.

Thinking only of his own career, Prosecutor Golub distances himself from his son's case and does not intervene on his behalf with his influential friend, the Interrogator. Even the death of Stalin and the ensuing de-Stalinization initiated by Khruschov are of no help to Serjozha, who, together with the old doctor and the writer of the novel, is considered a "thinker," still seen as the most dangerous enemy of the Soviet system. In spite of the "thaw," the three "dissidents" must serve their full term even as less dangerous "criminals," the majority of the prisoners, are being released.

At his trial in 1966 Tertz was reprimanded on the grounds that his novel had no positive hero. Of course, those who are familiar with the production novel in post-war Socialist Realist fiction will recognize Golub as an eminent candidate for the positive hero, who, by definition, must be an outstanding practitioner in his own field; of a correct, that is working-class or peasant origin; a class-conscious member of the Party, vigilant about "unmasking" the class enemy – saboteurs, spies, and other "masked" elements of the former bourgeoisie or the rich peasant class of kulaks. Indeed, Golub is presented as a man of courage who fought in the Second World War, a peasant cadre who knows how to work with his own hands, a man passionately dedicated to the Party and his profession. Yet probably precisely because Golub comes so close to the Guidelines' criteria of the positive hero, Tertz memorably makes his character an emotional cripple, happiest in the silence of the empty courtroom at night while rehearsing his lines for the next day's show-trial. Golub is incapable of loving his mother, his wife, or his son because the only emotion he is able to feel is the worship of power.

In fact Golub is a personification of that brutal purposiveness and militancy of spirit that Tertz challenges in his essay on Socialist Realism, the same spirit that dominates every moral-psychological aspect of Soviet society, the spirit Tertz associates with the blind force of the tank, ready to destroy both the enemy and the innocent victim who happens to find himself in its way. When Serjozha's grandmother begs Golub to interfere with the crushing legal process destroying her grandson, Golub's own child, whom he must know to be innocent, Golub turns to the old woman with a question: "Do you know … what happens when tanks go into attack? Whatever's in their way, they crush it. Sometimes even their own wounded. A tank simply cannot turn aside. If it went out of its way for every wounded man it would be shot to pieces by antitank guns blazing at it point-blank. It just has to crush and crush" (80). He describes himself as such a powerful but blind, mechanical weapon when he proudly states that "With these two hands I've plowed the soil and I've sent people to their death," and then he pushes his fists, "like two tanks, to the middle of the table" (79).

Yet Tertz also makes us realize that Golub is not quite honest with himself when justifying his conduct in the name of his passionate commitment to the higher "purpose" of History. When he tells his mother-in-law that "spy centers had been discovered in X-garia and

Y-akia" and "a group of criminals in Z Regional Committee had been plotting to seize power" (80), he may or may not realize that the satellite countries are being prepared for Stalinist show-trials. But there can be no doubt in his mind that it is he himself who came up with the accusations against Rabinovits in order to initiate another Stalinist hate campaign in the USSR, and he is clearly aware of the falseness of the accusations that are to follow. In fact, in Tertz's novel Stalin – to whom Tertz refers simply as the Master – is no longer solely responsible for masterminding the machinery of terror: people like the Public Prosecutor have internalized Stalin's persecution mania; they enjoy the war against the fictitious enemy and do not mind at all seeing innocent victims hurled in the irreversible path of tanks. Of course the Prosecutor also has a professional interest in the process: "The Prosecutor's ears were flushed with blood as thick and dark as oil. His neck bulged over his collar. It was time, my goodness, it was high time for a good bloodletting, for a sensational public trial to clear the air!" (80)

The cynicism of those in power knows no bounds when it comes to accumulating merit points in the eyes of the paranoid and anti-semitic Master. "It was your notes that put us on the track," the Interrogator congratulates Prosecutor Golub: "and needless to say [Rabinovits] is not the only one ... It is on a country-wide scale, my dear fellow ... Medicine! Doctors! ... See what I mean? And all of them, you know, fellows with long noses ... cosmopolitans! Every one ..." (87).

Given the cynical opportunism camouflaged as passionate commitment to the Party, the Prosecutor has no desire to intervene on his son's behalf; nor does the Interrogator offer to make an exception for Serjozha. When, after his arrest, Serjozha is taken to the Interrogator's office, arguing that he has done nothing and therefore cannot be put on trial, the Interrogator takes the boy to the window to look down on the multitude of people on the square: "'That's where they are, the people who are on trial. See how many of them?' The Interrogator pointed at the crowds milling below. Then he stroked Serjozha's short hair and explained gently: 'You're different now, my boy. You're not on trial, you're condemned'" (102).

Both the Interrogator and the Prosecutor agree that in a society where everyone is continuously on trial, once a person is accused, he is already condemned. By this circular logic, the fact that the boy has been punished means automatically that he must have been guilty. Therefore, Golub gets more and more angry with Serjozha's grandmother as she begs him to help his son: "There's a big roundup going on. I can't ...," he says weakly. Then, more aggressively, he states: "I am a prosecutor and my conscience would not let me. Think of all the people I see every day, people who are still less guilty and whom I have to ..." (103). It is his unadmitted public guilt as Prosecutor and his inadmissible private grief over his son's fate that makes him repeat: "No traitor can be a son of mine!" (103) It is his need to justify his self-serving motives that makes him repeatedly emphasize his passionate commitment to the Purpose, to the relentless, irreversible path of the tank.

The extreme images of battle, defeat, death, conquest, and domination are also central in describing the male-female relationships of the novel, between Golub and his beautiful but frigid wife, Marina, and between Marina and her lover, Yurij. Tertz refers to the scene in which Marina admits to her husband that she has had an abortion as a scene after "an atomic explosion" (38). Their conflict is deadly: "Not to have to kill her, he slapped her face. Not to be killed, Marina ran into her room" (39). After he loses control over his wife, Golub turns away from her coldly, indifferent to her later entreaties.

Yury, Marina's lover, also thinks of her only as an object to dominate. Even when, in his loneliness and fear of death he conjures up the image of the beautiful Marina, all he dreams about is his "victory over" her. He is determined to "turn her own weapons against her," to use "all means, fair or foul, to prove his superiority." Even in his dreams about her, he murmurs: "Goddess, how humiliating will be your downfall!" and when at long last she allows him to make love to her, he feels neither love nor lust: he proves impotent. Still, being able to humiliate Marina by asking her to leave his bed, he feels he has been able to dominate her and thereby to score a victory: "He felt that he would live a long, long life, survive everyone, perhaps even that he would never die" (37).

The same obsession with an all-pervasive enemy and the need to dominate are the central emotions of the two sinister plainclothesmen, Vitya and Tolya, two look-alikes who appear several times in the novel. Their entire emotional life is centred on their compulsion to trap, to ambush the enemy – primarily the dissident thinker who may want to hide or destroy incriminating manuscripts. Totally without personal emotions, the two young spies even dream in unison about inventing the ultimate dystopic weapon against the enemy by devising a psychoscope, "so that you can tell what people think about and feel. So that even those who don't say anything and don't put down their thoughts in writing should be automatically subject to control. At any hour and at any distance" (95).

Tertz's analysis of the legal system in *The Trial Begins* could be used as a political illustration of Kafka's *The Trial*,[4] a society where, "in the end, out of nothing at all, an enormous fabric of guilt will be conjured up." Tertz's psychoscope would also be the perfect apparatus for detecting thought criminals for Orwell's Thought Police, and the writer character in the novel has a premonition of his own arrest for having written the novel we are in the process of reading: "Silence. Two men in plain clothes stroll through the city streets ... One is named Vitya, the other Tolya. And I am frightened" (97).

In describing the atmosphere of the police-state, Tertz alludes to the all-pervasive presence of Stalin, the Master. His hand, like "the chastising hand of God will reach any mortal, wherever he or she may steal away and hide." The enormous chastising hands and the larger-than-life presence of the dictator recall Zamiatin's image of the Benefactor. Indeed, Edith Clowes suggests that "as a researcher at the prestigious Institute of World Literature [Tertz] must certainly have known and read ... Kafka and Zamiatin."[5] Others suggest that he also had read Orwell. Whether or not the official readers would have recognized Tertz's allusions to any of these writers, they would definitely have caught Tertz's reference to Stalin as the Master, worshipped like a deity, a reference that functions as a satirical reversal of the genuinely exalted place the Socialist Realist writer would have to offer Stalin, the ultimate model of any positive hero. But there is no trace of the positive hero in Tertz's other characters either. All of them are infected by the general psychological disease spread by the corruption inherent in a totalitarian system, by the opportunism of the self-serving elite, their own fear, and their acceptance of the amoral conviction that the end justifies the means.

Even young Serjozha, the martyr for the originally high ideals of revolutionary socialism, cannot avoid the notion of violence. Naïvely he dreams about a "new world, Communist and radiant," where "top wages would be paid to cleaning women [and] Cabinet Ministers would be kept on short rations to make sure of their disinterestedness [until] perfect liberty would dawn, and ... no one would put anyone in jail and everyone would receive according to his needs" (60). Yet all of a sudden the notion of justifiable violence raises its head even in this seemingly innocent, childlike daydream of utopia: "The slogans in the streets would be mostly by Mayakovski; there would also be some by Serjozha, such as 'Beware! You might hurt the feelings of your fellow man!' This was just as a reminder, in case people got above themselves. Those who did would be shot" (60).

Tertz makes it clear that in the atmosphere generated by totalitarianism, even the most innocent, like young Serjozha and his love-stricken girlfriend, Katya, are not heroes, only victims of the corrupt, hypocritical system. That the system is truly dystopic, unable to renew itself, is represented by the fate of the children in the novel. Marina and Golub's child is aborted; young Serjozha's life is destroyed; and

Katya dies at the funeral of the Master. She is trampled to death by the hysterical crowd come to worship their idol, who seems to demand new sacrifices even in death.

The crowd itself becomes a character in the novel. Seeing the young girl trampled to death (in reality there were hundreds killed this way at Stalin's funeral), voices from the crowd immediately start asking for scapegoats, representatives of the all-pervasive "enemy" who should be "unmasked" and punished for the disaster.

Fear, guilt, and aggression are the dominating emotions of all the characters – they are held up to reflect the pathology of totalitarianism. The state's demonization of the enemy and its justification of violence insinuate themselves into the psyche; they become internalized and dominate the emotions even of those who would like to fight against the system. And so, even in challenging the Socialist Realist formula and mounting a convincing dystopian critique of its allegedly utopian purpose, the characters' – as well as the writer's – emotions remain essentially political. The combination of Tertz's novel and his essay "On Socialist Realism" harshly illuminate the psychologically crippling effects of the Socialist Realist formula, and demonstrate how the forcible politicization of fiction and the fictionalization of politics beget the Absurd.

JULIJ DANIEL: *THIS IS MOSCOW SPEAKING*

The publishing histories of Tertz's and Julij Daniel's dystopian satires, written during the "thaw" in the wake of the Stalin regime's deliberate miscarriage of justice, still read like scenarios for dystopian fiction. Like Tertz, Daniel also smuggled his dystopian satire abroad and had it published under the name of "Arzhak" in *tamizdat*. When the Soviet authorities discovered the identity of Arzhak in 1966, the writer was put on trial together with Tertz. Tertz was sentenced to seven and Daniel to five years of hard labour; their rebuttal at the end of the trial forms a memorable document in the historic struggle for freedom of expression.[6]

This Is Moscow Speaking (1960) is one of those dystopian satires that render a Kafkaesque nightmare in vividly realistic brushstrokes. The novella is a bitter satire on "the mentality of a people whose political reflexes have for so long been conditioned by terror"[7] that they find it quite natural when the government announces "Public Murder Day." The narrative is set in Moscow in 1960 – at the time and place of its writing – in the friendly circle of a group of young intellectuals. It raises the question of public responsibility, the complicity of the people in the systematic miscarriage of justice during the long years of Stalin's totalitarian dictatorship. Daniel's satirical strategies suggest that, after decades of terror during which the Soviet people accepted the fact that those in power could commit millions of political murders with impunity, nobody would find it shocking if the government suddenly declared a murderous free-for-all of legitimized killing for a day. Concentrating on the response of the narrator's circle of friends, a group of professional men and women in their thirties, Daniel's satire draws specific attention to the moral responsibility of the new generation in understanding and repudiating the pathological mentality of the Stalin years. Of course, the satirist's point is that these young intellectuals are so self-centred, inured to terror, and politically apathetic that they would not find even the declaration of Public Murder Day shocking or objectionable: "After all, we had 'Artillery Day' and 'Soviet Press Day,' so why not 'Public Murder Day'? Bus and train services would be operating and the police were not to be harmed – that means everything was in order" (270).

The satire's target becomes more and more unmistakable: Daniel makes bitter fun of the people's deference to authority, even to the authority that so obviously offers to the population no protection from violence but is in fact the perpetrator of violence. Public opinion is usually an instrument of common sense and hence a significant factor for any government to consider: here public opinion reflects the pathological mentality that accepts even extreme forms of violence as long as the authority of the police and of the government are not challenged. Daniel also raises the question of whether celebrating militarism at "Artillery Day" or state propaganda at "Soviet Press Day" is really all that different from celebrating citizens killing one another. Institutionalized murder has been condoned and celebrated throughout Stalin's different waves of terror, ever since "our great Party seized the Trotskyists by the collar."

The most opportunistic among the narrator's friends is Igor, a dedicated member of the Party: almost as if by conditioned reflex, he immediately starts blaming the mysterious enemy. Surely the government declaration of Public Murder Day must be a trick perpetrated by the enemies of the Soviet regime, the "transatlantic gangsters" responsible for the Voice of America. Once he confirms that it is indeed the Soviet government that stands behind the decree, Igor immediately accepts it as an expression of great wisdom and a sign of democratization. He lavishes praise on "the Party's wise policy," pointing out "that the Decree confirmed the development of the creative initiative of the popular masses" (271). In addition to making fun of Igor's kowtowing to authority, Daniel relishes the delicious absurdity of the mind that would regard the invitation of a murderous government to its people to engage in grass-roots murder as a sign of democratization.

Another of the narrator's friends, Volodya, is outraged by the decree and by Igor's attitude. The narrator points out, however, that Volodya himself is not much better than Igor because, during the Doctors' Plot in the early fifties, Volodya parroted the Party's accusations of "Zionist nationalism" against the Jewish doctors – an attitude equivalent to condoning their murder by the government. Feeling guilty about this memory, Volodya decides that, if Public Murder Day ends up in a pogrom against the Jews – a thought that comes quite naturally, given the long history of government-sanctioned anti-semitism – this time he will stand up for justice and fight against those who are always after the same scapegoats.

The narrator's greatest shock about his circle's reaction comes when he realizes that Zoya, his mistress, wants to take advantage of Public Murder Day to make him murder her husband. The narrator understands that in Zoya's mind, "hatred gives one the right to murder." He suddenly recalls the recent leaders of the USSR, the "fat-faced masters of our destiny, our leaders and teachers, true sons of the people," the murderers who pretended to be "the best friends of Soviet gymnasts, writers, textile workers, colour-blind persons, and madmen." In this invective Daniel mimics the pious tone of government propaganda in the papers and the ever-present posters of Stalin; he also juxtaposes the deceived and the deceiver, suggesting that those who believe in the good will of the leaders smiling on the posters are like the colour-blind and the insane. They simply cannot recognize that these are the very leaders responsible for brutal mass murders at the time of the show-trials, purges, and mass liquidation through the thirties; these were the same leaders still in the new wave of terror in the "postwar insanity when the country was possessed by the devil, thrashed about in the throes of a fit, and became hysterical and began devouring itself" (278). The narrator again raises the question of public responsibility in accepting, condoning, and celebrating the spirit of scapegoating; he explores the individual's responsibility in internalizing the spirit of legitimized murder. This is the spirit, the narrator feels, that de-Stalinization in itself will not heal; it is something each individual has to face within him or herself: "Do they think that once they have desecrated the grave of the Mustached One, that's all that's required of them?" (278). The truly uncanny question of personal responsibility recurs when the narrator's friends, and the narrator himself, realize that one cannot simply blame everyone else for the murderous spirit that permeates society as a whole. Before Volodya leaves the narrator's apartment, he announces: "'They won't take me easily.' When he had finally left, I stood for some time in the middle of the room. Who are 'they'?" (273)

Some of the narrator's friends gradually develop a certain understanding of the true significance of the decree in historical context. Volodya, for example, comes to see that this "weird business was not only inevitable but [it] lay at the very basis of socialist teaching." He explains that during the revolution and in the thirties, "it was the same thing. Complete freedom of extermination. Only at that time there were trimmings to go with it, while this time there's nothing. Kill and that's all! And anyway, at that time there was a complete apparatus with tremendous personnel at the service of the murderers. Now you do it yourself. Self-service" (290).

Daniel's novella is a powerful satire against the regime as an intrinsically corrupt, dystopic society, due to the pathological personality of the dictator and the pathological mentality the dictatorship inculcates in the population. Of course, accepting Volodya's summary of the legitimization of murder since the revolution would be equivalent to repudiating the entire Soviet regime, not only the "mistakes" of the Stalin era. At this dangerous point the narrator steps in and expresses his disagreement with Volodya's "anti-Soviet monologues." The narrator claims that he is still ready to stand up for "a real Soviet regime," inspired by the purity of his father's commitment to socialism during the Civil War, in which he fought as a commissar. He also recalls – and this recollection considerably diminishes his inspiration – that his father was among those millions of committed Communist fighters who were destroyed by Stalin's purges: "he was taken away in 1936, one of the first" (290).

In awaiting the frightening "Judgment Day" announced by the decree, practically everyone in the narrator's circle reveals complicity in the murders legitimized in the various scapegoat hunts endemic to the system. The narrator's neighbour in the communal apartment is an old lawyer who saw "hundreds, thousands, tens of thousands of people [passing] through [his] hand" during the thirties' purges. He still justifies his actions by regarding the spirit of the decree as "nothing else but the logical continuation of a process already begun – the process of democratization." He is sure that the only people in danger on that day will be "hoodlums, spongers, and the dregs of society" (274).

The much-feared day goes off fairly uneventfully for the narrator and his friends, although everyone feels paralysed by what could happen. Afterwards, with a sense of relief, the young people get together once more for a party and discuss the events that took place on Judgment Day all over the Soviet Union. In this conversation Daniel foresees the deep-seated forces of nationalism and ethnic hatred that could be suddenly released in the aftermath of totalitarianism. On the day that allowed the unleashing of spontaneous hatred, "the Georgians

went for the Armenians, the Armenians went for the Azerbaijanians,"
and in Central Asia, where "there was no fighting among themselves
... they killed all the Russians" (303). (This statement, written in 1960,
foreshadows the eruption of ethnic hatred after the collapse of the
Soviet Union in 1991.)

Although everyone in the group of friends is relieved that the Public
Day of Murder is over and they can now get ready to celebrate the
Anniversary of the Great October Socialist Revolution (one holiday is
as good as another), the narrator's new girlfriend, Svetlana, suddenly
cries out: "It was terror!" She is the only one who dares to put this
thought into words, and her courage suddenly changes the narrator's
world completely: "She thought she had spoken this word to me alone,
but she had inadvertently thrown it in the faces of huge government
buildings, confronting the miles of black-and-white newsprint which
crisscross the country every day. She had challenged unanimous opinions of general meetings, and all the diabolic clatter of tanks which
carry the gaping muzzles of guns to ceremonial parades" (305).

After Svetlana's audacity in calling a spade a spade, admitting that
she realizes what terror is, the narrator's life changes radically. He
comes to hear the real voice of the people, the voice of life, the voice
of hope, which, by identifying and repudiating the terror of the past,
can stop terror and prevent it from taking hold again. Suddenly he
can hear the real "Moscow speaking," and realizes how he "loves this
damned, this beautiful country." Like Svetlana, who had the courage
to voice her own feelings and her own opinion, the narrator tells
himself: "'You should not allow yourself to be intimidated. You should
answer for yourself, and thereby answer for others.' And the endless
streets and squares, embankments and trees, and the dreamy steam-
ships of houses, sailing as a gigantic convoy into obscurity, answer me
with a low hum of unconscious assent and surprised approval. – This
is Moscow Speaking" (306).

The political decline of totalitarianism, Daniel suggests, does not by
itself heal this pathological mentality. The government-decreed Day of
Public Murder is simply a pale, tired version of the original murderous
spirit of totalitarianism. This spirit itself, Daniel suggests, is not healed
unless it is fearlessly explored and repudiated by people like Svetlana
who have the courage to speak their own minds and not what they
think is expected from them.

Unlike the Western representatives of dystopian fiction, Daniel's does
not project the dystopic society into the future: the chronotope is here
and now in the writer's – and the Ideal Reader's – present of 1960.
The dilemma is how to get rid of an unmistakably dystopic society of
the past that has not quite relinquished its hold over the present.

Nevertheless, in a way Daniel's work could already qualify as speculative fiction: it begins with the question: What if? What if the government decreed a Day of Public Murder? How would the people – our friends, ourselves – respond?

According to Edith Clowes, Daniel's *This Is Moscow Speaking* belongs to the genre of meta-utopia; she argues that, "in contrast to the dystopian 'either/or,' [meta-utopia] countenances and challenges all kinds of authoritarian ideologies, each with its own vision of the ideal society, that insist on their own version of rightness, justice and truthfulness to the exclusion of all others."[8]

A close reading of Daniel's novella reveals that the difference between dystopia and meta-utopia in this case is not that significant. In fact, Clowes's definition of meta-utopia would comfortably cover such classics of dystopian literature as *Brave New World* and *Nineteen Eighty-four*. Neither of these novels suggests an "either/or" conclusion concerning the most acceptable form of society. Both Orwell and Huxley would reject the "vision of the ideal society that insists on its own version of rightness, justness and truthfulness"; they would insist, however, on our right to the unhampered *pursuit of justice*, the free, truthful expression of thought in a functional, vital society. In a way, one could even say that the central issue of justice or injustice in the dystopian critique of society is inextricably linked with the issue of free speech, freedom of expression. Significantly, when Winston Smith starts writing in his diary, he is full of fear about the consequences; he knows that what he is doing is punishable by death in Oceania. Still his vital need for freedom of expression in the pursuit of truth overrides his fear. This issue of the pursuit of truth through freedom of expression is also central to Daniel's *This Is Moscow Speaking*. However, the novella further implies that after the long and traumatic reign of the mental tyranny characterizing a dystopic society, there is a delay before people awaken to their desire – and ability – to claim this freedom.

Part Three

Dystopia East: The Soviet Bloc 1950s–1980s

István Örkény   Tibor Déry   Alexander Zinoviev

György Dalos   Vasily Aksyonov   Vaclav Havel   Ladislas Fuks

Vladimir Voinovich   Marek Hlasko   Ivan Klima

CHAPTER NINE

Collective Paranoia:
The Persecutor and the Persecuted:
Andzrejewski, Déry, Fuks, Hlasko,
Örkény, Vaculik, and Mrozek

The post-Stalin years in the Soviet bloc saw the revival of the dystopian impulse in literature, with special emphasis on a particular pathology: the disease of paranoia shared by the persecutor and the persecuted as a consequence of the elite's deliberate miscarriage of justice in totalitarian regimes. Instead of projecting the vision of such a dystopic society into the future, writers looked at their own societies in the present through the mirrors of parable, allegory, the grotesque, short satirical pieces, or the "false" or quasi-historical novel to be read as political allegory about the present.

QUASI-HISTORICAL NOVELS

A quasi-historical novel, Jerzy Andzrejewski's *The Inquisitors*, was written in 1957 in Poland, just a year after Khruschov's revelations about Stalin's "mistakes" at the Twentieth Party Congress, including hints about certain "abuses" of the socialist legal process in Stalin's last show-trials in the USSR in 1952 and 1953, and in the various show-trials in the satellite countries between 1949 and 1951. The latter were staged by the Kremlin following "Tito's defiance, in whose wake the need to demonstrate Soviet power and Stalinist infallibility became all the more imperative."[1] The show-trials in Poland, Hungary, and Czechoslovakia had many similar objectives, such as "Stalin's arranging for the wartime 'Muscovites' to eliminate the 'local undergrounders' or authorizing the Communists who belonged genealogically to the eponymous state-nations to liquidate the Jewish and other ethnic minority ones."[2] Each campaign was characterized by a marked "anti-Zionist" or "anti-cosmopolitan" angle to incite anti-semitism and to resuscitate the traditional scapegoats, on whom the frustrated population could fix the blame for the serious economic and political mistakes committed by the centralized police-state directed from the Kremlin. Although Poland may have suffered somewhat less than the other satellite countries in this phase of terror, "the net outcome" of the show-trials everywhere "was to render the surviving Communist leaders of the 'loyal' people's democracies dependent, insecure, and utterly subservient to Moscow for the rest of Stalin's lifetime."[3]

Andzrejewski's[4] *The Inquisitors* is like a key-novel, a one-armed equation in which it is up to the reader to complete the parallel between the methods of the Inquisition in fifteenth-century Spain and the methods applied by the Communist parties in the rigged trials and purges all over the Soviet bloc in the early fifties. The strategies of the novel are primarily those of political satire tending towards allegory, yet the writer shows a somewhat deeper interest in psychological analysis than is usually associated with this genre. Nevertheless, Andzrejewski's interest in his characters' motivation also remains fairly two-dimensional; the only psychology he is interested in exploring is the psychology of power, the persecution mania spurring on the persecutor and paralysing the persecuted.

Sexuality, male-female, or child-parent relationships are beyond the writer's scope. Women scarcely appear in the novel (a fairly general characteristic of works of the dystopian impulse in this area). King Ferdinand and Queen Isabella make a brief appearance, but their role is simply to demonstrate that Inquisitor Torquemada is able to challenge, confront, and overpower even the will of royalty. The royal couple are reluctant to expel the Jews from Spain as Torquemada demands they do, especially after the Jews offer a huge amount of gold to help Ferdinand finance his next war. Torquemada reproaches Isabella and Ferdinand for being mercenary, ready to betray their Christian duty, comparing them to Judas, who received thirty pieces of silver – they would receive 300,000 pieces of gold. Using his rhetorical powers to good effect, Torquemada manages to shame the royal couple into submitting to his will. Yet Torquemada's own greed is greater than that he preaches against: he knows that the property left behind after the expulsion of the Jews will yield incomparably more than their original offering.

It is through invoking shame and fear that Torquemada wields absolute power over the souls of royalty, nobility, the clergy, and the poor. To his secretary, Diego, Torquemada admits that making people afraid is the key to the Inquisition's power, an admission that is probably the central psycho-historical insight into dictatorship in general. Like Dostoevski's Grand Inquisitor, Torquemada justifies keeping the masses subjugated, but, like Orwell's O'Brien, he no longer pretends that he does this to keep them happy: "because man is wretched, his fear is not only necessary but indispensable. If evil is to be rooted out we must keep showing it up in all its naked ugliness so that it evokes repugnance and above all fear. That's the truth of power!" (47)

Torquemada's self-justification as a man who has the right to use any means to uproot evil also informs the system of justice pursued by the Inquisition. It is a jurisprudence that metes out justice according to guilt by analogy, by association, and by belonging. At every instance Andzrejewski alludes to parallels to Soviet jurisprudence. Like Stalin, Torquemada is not beyond having his associates assassinated and using this atrocity to charge those he wants to eliminate with the crime. In the process, anyone ever associated with the scapegoat also becomes tainted. Guilt by belonging to another denomination in Torquemada's case is parallelled by the guilt of belonging to another social class or adhering to another mode of thinking in the Soviet system.

Continually serving up details of the methods of the Inquisition that the reader should recognize as comparable to those of the Soviet regime, Andzrejewski sets in motion a lively machinery of satire. However, the philosophical-political argument claims the writer's nearly undivided attention; it is rarely embodied in the closely observed interaction of psychologically convincing characters. The novel reads like a thoroughgoing but somewhat abstract illustration of the writer's central argument, hammering home the essential resemblance between the miscarriage of justice in Spain during the Inquisition and in the Soviet bloc at the time of the writing of the novel.

Compared to Arthur Miller's *The Crucible,* for example, a complex analysis of the sexual, spiritual, and political dimensions of the mass hysteria of witch-hunts in seventeenth-century Salem, Massachusetts, the limitations of Andzrejewski's fiction become apparent. Miller also uses an event from the past to make a political point about the dystopic process of terror in the present, the McCarthy era of the 1950s. Nevertheless, his characters have a vitality, complexity, and psychological credibility that is probably also connected to Miller's shrewd use of Freudian depth psychology, then a well-respected intellectual currency in North America. The Polish novelist does not seem to be interested in "psychologizing": the passions he is exploring are purely political. Not that the work does not make interesting reading as political satire, especially as one knows that the writer is severely restricted in expressing his political views. This restriction itself creates an interesting sense of suspense with not only political but also spiritual and aesthetic implications; the struggle for clarity and intensity of expression when expression is being denied adds an extra dimension to the novel.

The parallels are worked out with great skill and care. The author shows that the self-flagellation, humble admissions of guilt, and helpless acquiescence in the will of the Holy Church are unmistakably parallel to the behaviour of the accused in the course of Stalin's show-trials. In fact, the novel includes a fictitious "transcript" of the Inquisition's court proceedings, including the confession of an ordinary citizen who is tortured as a heretic because he has questioned the existence of the Devil on earth. The transcript is uncannily similar to the court transcripts of the interrogation of "heretics" in the Soviet regime, who were charged with conspiring with a satanic enemy, and tortured and "converted" until they signed false confessions admitting their guilt and asking for severe punishment. The tortured man in the novel confesses that, "having put my trust in Satan, I had to follow his devilish ways; having committed one crime I had to go on committing other and worse crimes ... I don't deserve mercy, reverend fathers, and if I dare to make a request, it is that my punishment be as severe as possible so that it helps me to purge myself of my sins and gives the community a just compensation for the harm I have done" (121).

This is the same suicidal self-incrimination so familiar from Rubashov's confession in Koestler's *Darkness at Noon*, or the confessions of the victims of the show-trials in the USSR and in the satellite countries. The transcript also refers to the Inquisition's insistence that the victim under torture name names – that is, that he implicate a wide circle of other innocent people who, in their turn, will also be forced to name others – a chain-reaction masterfully described by Orwell in *Nineteen Eighty-four* as a feature of the actual show-trials.

Torquemada is obsessed by the spiral of fear that motivates human beings to denounce one another, betray their nearest and dearest, succumbing to his unlimited power:

One day if we run out of culprits, we shall have to create more. We need them so that crimes can be seen to be publicly humiliated and punished all the time. Until the truth finally triumphs it cannot exist without its opposite – falsehood. Our power, my son, is based on universal fear. With the exception of a handful who are obedient from choice, everybody must be so afraid that no one is capable of even imagining an existence free of fear. A wife must mistrust her husband, parents must fear their children, superiors must be afraid of their subordinates, and all of them must tremble before the all-knowing and omnipresent punitive justice of the Holy Inquisition. (47–8)

Torquemada's speech here is a summary of the methods used by the Party during the show-trials and the purges, never allowing the courts to "run out of culprits." Rich in literary echoes, the passage recalls the Grand Inquisitor's statement about the contemptibility and weakness of human nature. It also recalls Gletkin's speech to Rubashov in

Darkness at Noon, when Gletkin explains why the masses need to be vividly shown that anyone who would oppose the dictator's will must be conspiring with a satanic enemy. In many ways the speech also follows the rhetoric of self-justification in O'Brien's speech to Winston in *Nineteen Eighty-four*. However, there is one significant exception: Torquemada still argues that he is creating fear as a means to a higher good, that ultimately the aim of the Inquisition is to root out evil.

Only at the end of the novel, when he confronts death, will Torquemada reach the recognition that by being obsessed with uprooting evil, he has himself become the source of evil. He finally recognizes that fear and terror are corrupting human nature and wishes he could "put an end to terror that has already moulded men and made itself the sole reason for their existence" (14).

His Shadow, whom normally we would call the voice of Satan, introduces himself as the spirit of the ideal. He explains that originally people lived in paradise, which meant no consciousness, no sense of excitement. It was Satan who gave them ideals. From humanity's fanatical belief in ideals came violence and bloodshed – a new sense of excitement and a new consciousness. This ideal given to man by Satan was, paradoxically, the ideal of God. If the ideal is the ultimate source of evil, the ultimate "ideal is faith itself" (146).

Like Grossman's Holy Fool, who argued that Christianity and social-ism, like all great systems of belief that set out to accomplish ultimate good, ended up as terrible instruments of evil, Torquemada's Shadow reveals to him that "the work of building and strengthening the kingdom of God on Earth will go on, the task of introducing general slavery for the sake of future freedom, and terror for the sake of future justice, will not be interrupted" (144).

It is in the name of the Communist future that the Party enslaves the population in the present. It is in the name of the "good" of mankind that the Party needs to exterminate more and more scape-goats as the symbols of evil, just as it was in the name of Heaven that Torquemada lit up the pyres of the Inquisition. When Torquemada regrets his past deeds and wishes to change his Testament, he cries out to Diego, his secretary, closest assistant, and spiritual heir: "Put out the flames!" But to live without evil it will be necessary for human beings "to learn to live without God and without Satan ... They don't exist" (158).

As he revokes his earlier Testament point by point, he instructs Diego that "we must destroy what we built misguidedly at the cost of the greatest tragedies and sufferings" (157), even if this destruction results in temporary chaos. Most important, Diego "must also write a decree abolishing fear" (158). It is a tragic irony that in the novel Diego starts out as an opponent of Torquemada, horrified by his ideas. In the meantime, however, Diego has become even more fanatical in extirpating heresy by fire than was Torquemada himself. Diego's transformation demonstrates that the lies and cruelty practised by the tyrant are contagious: on his deathbed Torquemada faces his own duality and sheds his old self; Diego is unwilling or unable to change because this would mean admitting that all his life's work has been wasted. Crying in his frustration, he slaps the dead man's face. The parable is complete.

Political satire of the present system practised through the quasi-historical narrative was a strategy well known in all three satellite countries under review. In Czechoslovakia, Jiri Sotola, for example, wrote a novel under the title *The Society of Jesus* (*Tovarisstvo Jezisovo*) in 1969, during another wave of re-Stalinization following the defeat of the 1968 Prague Spring, in which he describes the techniques of coercion used by the Jesuit Order in Bohemia in 1620, expecting his readers to draw parallels with the methods used by the foreign conquerors of the present.

Hungarian Tibor Déry's *The Excommunicator* (1966) deals ostensibly with the life of St Ambrose, a bishop of Milan in the early Middle Ages, only to draw attention to the parallels between the tyranny of the medieval Church and the contemporary Party, both of them subjecting the individual to the "anthill" of the community; the crowd to the authorities in power; and the creative individual mind to the tyranny of dogma. Like Andzrejewski's and Sotola's novels, Déry's focuses on the parallels between the Church and the Party.

In two other novels from Czechoslovakia, Ladislav Fuks's *Mr Theodore Mundstock* (1968) and *The Cremator* (1967), the author[5] goes back to the more recent past, the historical period of the Nazi occupation, to make the reader look for parallels with the present. Mr Mundstock's character represents the total passivity of a Jewish victim who wants to prepare himself for the horrors of the concentration camp. During the long months that he awaits his inevitable deportation, he tries to train himself to get used to the deprivations he associates with life in captivity. The outcome of all his efforts is a study in tragic irony: before being able to put his training as a professional victim to the test, he is accidentally killed by one of the trucks that has come to deport him, like millions of others, to the concentration camp. The paralysis of the will that characterizes the victim who knows that his last moments are approaching also alludes to the mental state of thousands of victims of various terror cycles under Communist rule who could do nothing but passively face their inevitable fate.

The Cremator is a novella cast in the form of the grotesque, about a sycophantic undertaker in Czechoslovakia under Nazi occupation.

He is so eager to please his Nazi masters that he eliminates first his beloved wife, because she is of Jewish origin, and then his own son and daughter, whom he considers also "contaminated" – all this to prove his purity of blood, which is the condition of his advancement. A grotesque story where blood-curdling details are rendered with a seemingly cool objectivity, the novella also alludes to the careerist under the Soviet regime who has to show his "purity" and absolute faith in the Party by shedding – that is renouncing, denouncing, in effect destroying – his friends and even his family if they are not from the right class background.

PARABLES

The theme of the overlap between the persecutor and the persecuted in a dystopic society is also characteristic of the quasi-realistic short novel that works, in effect, like a parable, in Marek Hlasko's *Graveyard* and Andzrejewski's *The Appeal*.

The Appeal (1968) returns to the theme Andzrejewski introduced in *The Inquisitors*, of the all-pervasive fear that arises, in the totalitarian state, from being watched, denounced, and persecuted. This time, however, the writer examines this fear from the point of view of the persecuted. Koniecki is a simple, uneducated labourer, born on the northeast frontier of Poland. At the age of seventeen, during the German occupation of Poland, he is captured and tortured by the Gestapo. Subsequently, in the course of his working life as a meat-packer in Communist Poland, he feels compelled to denounce people and is himself denounced. At twenty-two he is imprisoned for political reasons; about ten years later he gets into political trouble once more for "sabotaging" the Five-Year Plan when, in an outburst of temper, he tears up the factory's plans for the next season.

The political reversals in Poland between Nazi and Communist rule, then the constant shifts in the Communist Party line, followed by waves of persecution, undermine his mental balance. He has several breakdowns and is repeatedly admitted to the Clinic of Psychosomatic Diseases. He is tormented by paranoia, convinced that he is under constant surveillance by secret agents and a mysterious Electric Brain that follow him everywhere. Feeling continually guilty and convinced he is under suspicion, he composes a long and elaborate appeal to the First Secretary of the Party, asking for a thorough examination of his case in the hope that he can clear his name. He declares: "I am not and never have been a Party member, I have always loyally served People's Poland, have never been anybody's agent or a traitor, and if I have committed mistakes, it was from ignorance because I did not complete my schooling, although I wanted to do so very much indeed and have tried all my life to improve my education" (11).

In many ways like the workers bewildered by the twists and turns of propaganda phrases in Platonov's *The Foundation Pit*, Koniecki, with his limited vocabulary, uses the ready-made rhetorical formulae of Marxist bureaucratese with telling awkwardness; he even talks about his mother, wife, and children in formulaic terms. The slogans and clichés he reads on the posters and hears on the radio penetrate his mind, depriving him of the chance to develop a language expressive of his private self. So often has he heard that the accused confessed themselves to be foreign agents and traitors during the show-trials that he wants to make sure he is not considered to be in that category. In fact, he does not really know why the police agents would think that he is guilty, yet he is overwhelmed by a childish insecurity about his position in the state, in the factory, and in his family, where he does not know quite what his role should be. He has seen so many people denounced, tried, and imprisoned that he is totally preoccupied by the process, which, due to his mental condition, he cannot understand at all. Like an insecure child feeling continually guilty of a crime unknown even to himself, he seeks the reassurance of the Father, the Party Secretary. Ironically, it is his fear of the omnipresent watching eye of this authority that also makes him draw the authority's attention to himself. He cannot help the spiralling insecurity he feels and begs the cruel but authoritative Father "for the great favour to pass a just verdict after getting acquainted with the present material, because I am suffering a great deal innocently and have no strength to suffer any longer" (12).

Yet, no matter how painful his fear of persecution must be, fear has become the vital substance of his life. At the end, when he receives a letter from the Party Secretary's office informing him that there are no denunciations, no reports, in fact no information on him in their files whatsoever, Koniecki is so disappointed about his lack of importance that he collapses into another, possibly a final breakdown, taking on the position of the helpless child: "Sister Irena, worried by Koniecki's disappearance, found him … and began to comfort him with maternal tenderness like a small child, but he did not recognize her, refused to get up, did not allow her to pull his hands from around his head, only cried and cried" (118).

There is something in the atmosphere of the novel that reminds one of the Kafkaesque grotesque, particularly *The Trial*, in the way Koniecki perceives that the whole legal system is closing in on him, and in many ways the protagonist reminds one of Kafka's Joseph K, except that Koniecki feels compelled to seek out the authorities he is most afraid of. Also, unlike Kafka's K, Koniecki is not mysterious or distant enough to become the symbolic centre of parable; neither is he quite fully enough realized for a character of psychological realism (as are Andzrzejewski's characters in his powerful *Ashes and Diamonds*). Undoubtedly written as a dystopian satire of the pathological political system that functions on a pattern of paranoia, *The Appeal* falls between the genres of psychological case-history and parable.

Marek Hlasko's[6] *Graveyard* is another dystopian satire that demonstrates a somewhat uneasy combination of parable and psychological realism. Frantisek Kovalski, a former partisan who as a young man fought against the Germans occupying Poland and welcomed the liberating Red Army introducing Communism, is a true believer. Years after the war – he has a grown son and a daughter at university – he meets an old partisan friend. The men get drunk, and Frantisek is arrested for disturbing the peace and making some unacceptable remarks. In the cell he shares with several others he stands on his Communist dignity and rejects the suggestion that he could have been arrested because someone had denounced him: "I am a former partisan, and I didn't fight through the whole occupation to hear people like you sneer at everything. I made a hash of people like you with my own hands in the underground. You offend against everything I believe and our country believes in. Understand?" (27).

Irritated by the true believer's earnestness, his cellmates retaliate by threatening to denounce him for trying "to make a dash for the West." Bewildered by this unfounded accusation, Frantisek is summoned to interrogation. Like Sasha in Ribakov's *The Children of the Arbat* or Rubashov in *Darkness at Noon*, Frantisek is not told by his interrogator what crime he is charged with. All the police officer tells him is: "You've unmasked yourself, Kovalski … That's the way it looks … You've unmasked yourself and that's that."

Very much like Parsons, Orwell's true believer in *Nineteen Eighty-four*, Frantisek Kovalski simply can't imagine what he could have said in his drunkenness that could be considered "unmasking himself" as an enemy of the regime. In his bewilderment he tells his boss and the local Party Secretary what happened. Although they are ready to make a simple phone call and settle the whole affair with the police, Frantisek insists that he wants a formal investigation and a formal acquittal that will prove his innocence and vindicate his good Communist name.

His tragedy is that, precisely because he is a true believer, he cannot see that he is by himself. When the Secretary jovially tells him that next time he should keep his opinion about the regime to himself,

Frantisek threatens to reveal the man's cynicism at the open meeting the following day. The Secretary, as a result, has no choice but to discredit Frantisek at this meeting, and Frantisek's children will never see their father vindicated.

As a result of having "unmasked" himself as an enemy critical of the regime, Frantisek is expelled from the Party and is fired from his job. His son, who is a shameless opportunist, leaves his father the moment the old man is politically disgraced. Frantisek's beautiful daughter is expelled from the university because she will not denounce her father: she is abandoned by her careerist fiancé, and in her despair commits suicide.

In his grief Frantisek goes out once more to get drunk and runs into the same policeman who arrested him earlier. He asks the policeman what horrible thing he had uttered when he was drunk, whereby he had "unmasked himself." To his utter surprise he hears: "You're the biggest fool I've ever met ... You didn't say anything, and that's why we let you go ... We saw you were a party man, soft-spoken, quiet – we just put a bit of a scare into you and let you go in the morning ... We scared you for your own good, so that next time you'd stay sober ... Go home and pull yourself together." But Frantisek, overcome by grief, blurts out: "there are no homes any more ... There are only graveyards" (125).

The novel shows the tragicomic fate of the true believer who fails to see through the corruption of all the authorities, all his colleagues, all the people who have learned to lie cynically about being faithful to the Party if they want to survive in the police-state. Like a pointed anecdote about an incorrigible fool, or a parable about the incurable disease of being a true believer in the socialist dream even with all the evidence to the contrary, the narrative shows that Frantisek has not learned much from his tragedy. Separated from the policeman by a crowd, "he forced a passage toward him: 'Give me your hand!' he cried. 'Give me your hand, or I'll lose my way again'" (126).

Hlasko's dystopian satire, which reads like a parable about the childlike true believer who refuses to see that dishonesty and injustice are central to the police-state, is transparently clear. This clarity is partly responsible for the two-dimensional nature of Frantisek Kovalski's character. He is less a psychological credible character than a caricature – although an excellent one at that. (In another, considerably longer novel of a dystopian inspiration, *Next Stop Paradise*, Hlasko attempts a psychologically more multi-dimensional portrayal of his characters, but the essential contradiction between the unifying theme of parable and a longer, more complex, and somewhat sprawling plot-line is not fully resolved.)

SHORT PIECES

In addition to the false or quasi-historical novel, the allegory, the grotesque, and the parable, the critique of the dsytopic reality in Eastern and Central Europe is also represented by shorter pieces such as short stories, feuilletons, or in the case of Hungarian István Örkény, even in the form of "one-minute" pieces consisting of no more than one or two paragraphs.

Örkény's short story "Café Niagara," published in 1988, offers a wry comment on the mentality of everyday people who have become so deranged by living too long in a deranged system that they actually seek torture and humiliation. A middle-aged couple from the provinces, the Nikolitses, arrive in the capital and want to see the Café Niagara, which, recently remodelled, "was becoming *the* place in town." (57) In fact the restaurant functions more like a theatre, the "guests" waiting patiently for their turn to appear on a stage "behind the curtain," in a performance where, to our shock, their role is to be beaten, abused, and humiliated by thugs.

When it is Mr Nikolits's turn to come face to face with the three thugs, one standing there with a truncheon, another with a bamboo cane, while the third, barehanded, suddenly moves forward and slaps him in the face, he realizes that "he was neither scared nor surprised since he always had the feeling – no, he knew – that something like this was going to happen to him one day" (63). After he is beaten up, one of his torturers opens the door for him with impeccable courtesy: "This way, sir, if you please." The horrible treatment followed by the signs of everyday courtesy has such an effect on Mr Nikolits that he wonders "whether it was customary on such occasions to leave a tip."

Clearly, Örkény's grotesque is a reminder of a dystopian reality in which victims are put on trial, tortured by their interrogators to confess to crimes never committed, imprisoned, and then, for reasons equally unpredictable, released, rehabilitated, and expected to go on with their lives as if nothing had happened. But Mr Nikolits's character also suggests that we must question our own complicity in tolerating organized violence as if it were a "normal" part of the civilized fabric of life, some kind of perverted theatre.

That the atrocious trials have changed since Stalin but that dissenters, particularly writers and artists, can still expect to be stripped of their basic human rights if they "go too far" in their critique of the regime, and that this practice is often accepted as an unchangeable fact of life, is satirized by the Czech Ludvik Vaculik's feuilleton, "A Cup of Coffee with My Interrogator." This seemingly low-key, matter-of-fact account of a few casual, friendly sessions between the writer and an interrogator, written in 1982, is about Vaculik's involvement in Charter 77, a human and civil rights movement. The narrator knows that his interrogator is no longer permitted to use the violent methods that were customary under Stalin; still, as an interrogator, Lieutenant-Colonel Noga has the right to summon the narrator to testify every day; he is entitled to examine and requisition the narrator's briefcase, his manuscripts, and threaten him with incarceration. Of course, instead of depriving the narrator of sleep or threatening him with brutality, the interrogator treats the narrator with courtesy, takes him to lunch in the cafeteria, and repeatedly offers him a cup of coffee. Nevertheless, the narrator refuses to testify. The fairly informal atmosphere between interrogator and detainee is carried to an absurd conclusion: when Noga offers the narrator an apple from his own apple tree, the narrator feels like reciprocating with a bag of apples from his own garden. The "climax" of the story is fairly understated: after a reassessment of his situation, the narrator concludes that, in spite of all the informality and civilized politesse displayed by his interrogator, he is still in the hands of a system that has the power to incarcerate him, his friends, and his colleagues; ultimately, he decides not to offer the interrogator the gift of the bag of apples.

In another feuilleton, "Glassnost," written in 1987, Vaculik gives a cynically disrespectful assessment of each of Gorbachov's reforms, expressing his anger and contempt for the Soviet Union as a mindless bully that has deprived Czechoslovakia of its independence for too long, and imposed on it a backward regime's mental tyranny for decades: "To manufacture quality goods: what a revolutionary and daring idea. More than one candidate to stand for election: now there's a discovery for you ... There are still more amazing discoveries waiting to be made: for instance, the separation of legislative, executive and judicial power. But whatever you may discover, just leave us alone, especially if you don't feel like it" (126).

Another master of the short, terse satirical touch about totalitarianism as a "mad-hatter's world, the pinnacle of absurdity" is Slawomir Mrozek,[7] whose play Tango is well known in the West. In his "Elephant" he presents a parable about the emptiness behind the promises made by the Communist regime, the Potemkin village created by Socialist Realist literature, the contrast between the glossy world of propaganda and the shabby, artificial, disappointing reality. A group of schoolchildren are looking forward to a trip to the zoo to see the elephant; but to save money, the zoo decides to float a huge balloon of an elephant and pretend that it is the real thing. The children are disappointed and will never again believe in what the adults tell them.

In another two-page piece, "The Lion," Mrozek makes fun of the violent somersaults in the party line as power-group follows power-group in unpredictable succession. The persecuted of today can become tomorrow's persecutor, and so it goes, it seems, *ad infinitum*. Gaius, the keeper of the lions in the Coliseum, notes that one of the lions is reluctant to enter the arena and refuses to participate in the devouring of Christians. Should readers expect to see this reluctance as an example of moral resistance to evil, they will be disappointed. What the lion explains to Gaius is, actually, quite natural in the context of the frequent swinging of the political pendulum, in the post-totalitarian regime, between thaws and crackdowns, de-Stalinizations and re-Stalinizations. The lion is already counting on the Christians' coming to power with Constantine the Great, and when, at that time, every other lion is punished for having participated in devouring Christians, our lion wants to have an alibi. Won over by the lion's caution, Gaius allows him to stay away from the arena on condition that at the next change of regimes the lion will testify that Gaius "had not forced anyone to do anything.".

To mention only one more of the many expressive short pieces, we should take a look at Mrozek's "The Trial," a seemingly light-hearted but incisive satire of the nightmare society, with its make-believe trials followed by retribution in earnest. The Writers' Union in this story is organized like an army, with writers "ranked" according to their political standing. (This is a reference to the militarization of literature in the Guidelines of Socialist Realism, as well as to the "ranking" of the dullest, least imaginative writer who is ideologically correct above the one who has talent and therefore has to resist dull conformity – a notion also exploited by Voinovich in his *Moscow 2042*.) In this army of writers an insignificant writer-private fails to notice that a ladybug has settled on his hat. The tragedy is that the ladybug, an innocent creature of nature, also happens to serve as a symbol of the highest military rank among the writers. When the writer-general sees our private's hat, "respect for authority [is] so deeply embedded" in him that he inadvertently salutes the man of lower rank. Having precipitated such a flagrant reversal of military etiquette, the writer-private is put on trial. Although in the increasingly more humane atmosphere of the thaw he is acquitted, the tiny ladybug, who is also brought to trial, is found guilty, sentenced to death, and promptly executed by the full force of the law; they drop on her "four thick and well-bound volumes of the latest novel by the writer-marshal of literature." Now, for expressing his spontaneous sympathy for the fate of the guilty ladybug who has been declared an enemy agent, the writer-private becomes a suspect again, and thus possibly a candidate for yet another trial. (Again, Voinovich uses similar images to make fun of the heavy, dull works produced by Socialist Realism, and the ranking of the ghost-written multi-volume autobiography of Brezhnev, undeniably the "writer-marshal" in the Writers' Union in Moscow, as being among the greatest masterpieces of Soviet literature.)

As these selections from Poland, Hungary, and Czechoslovakia indicate, here the dystopian impulse is bound less by form, structure, and genre than in the classics of the Western tradition. Writers also experiment more freely with the absurd and the grotesque to explore the dominant pathology of the totalitarian system: the paranoia affecting both the persecutor and the persecuted.

Trial and punishment are also at the very centre of satirical commentaries on the dystopian society in yet another genre. In the gradually more relaxed atmosphere of the theatre in the years preceding the Prague Spring, playwrights in Czechoslovakia composed satirical variations on the political theatricals of the early 1950s for the stage of the 1960s. A selection of three of these plays will be discussed in the next chapter.

CHAPTER TEN

Kafka's Ghost:
The Trial as Theatre:
Klima's *The Castle*,
Karvas's *The Big Wig*, and
Havel's *Memorandum*

After Stalin's death in 1953 the entire Eastern bloc underwent a process of de-Stalinization. In Czechoslovakia this process was exceptionally slow,[1] since the Party leadership was caught up in a truly Kafkaesque situation: the same leaders who, on Stalin's orders, had set up the atrocious show-trials against Slansky and his circle were now, on orders from Khruschov, to "investigate" who had been responsible for the "mistakes" and "excesses" in the "distortion of socialist legality," and to rehabilitate their victims.

Corollary to the Stalinist "excesses" in politics were the excesses in the cultural-literary world, such as the imposition of an utopian strait-jacket of Socialist Realism on literature and the condemnation and imprisonment of writers who resisted this straitjacket. It is therefore not an accident that "in 1963 the rehabilitation of Kafka's work became an important test of de-Stalinization in Prague: as so often when the communist intelligentsia faced a test of policy, it was decided to hold a conference to discuss the issue ... on May 27–28 at Liblice, a recreation centre of the Czechoslovak Academy."[2]

The changes in cultural politics that once more permitted appreciation of Kafka's individual vision and experimental style were a direct reflection on the changes in the political mainstream, and so "it was appropriate that the Czech convenor [of the Kafka conference] was himself a recently rehabilitated victim of the political trials ... In restoring to Kafka his due position the conference was ceremonially annulling the literary policies of Stalinism."[3]

This chapter takes a closer look at three of the many plays written in the ensuing literary revival of the 1960s, when allusions to Kafka's works and vision became a major instrument of political satire. In Ivan Klima's *The Castle*, Petr Karvas's *The Big Wig*, and Vaclav Havel's *Memorandum*, dissent is voiced in the form of allusions, allegory, or parable to reflect upon the Kafkaesque absurdity in the reality of the 1950s and 1960s. In this new wave of political satire, Kafka's works become central texts, central metaphors: *The Castle* of the new Communist ruling class; *The Penal Colony* of torture in the police-state; and *The Trial* of the totalitarian legal system, where everyone is guilty until proven innocent.

As the legal profession exerted more and more pressure "to restore the rule of law in its classic sense, [that is] without the Stalinist presumption of guilt by probability, analogy, or class background,"[4] in the horrifying evidence of the earlier "distortions of socialist legality" the writers of the period were compelled to recognize the crazed legal system of Josef K's trial. I would suggest that the trial engineered to perpetrate injustice in fact becomes the organizing metaphor in this period, and in the three plays in question the sinister effect of the Kafkaesque is further enhanced by the unique combination of the metaphor of trial with the metaphor of theatre.

By the mid 1960s it was increasingly obvious that the 1949–53 trials of former leaders of the Party had indeed been "show-trials" – that is, organized and well-rehearsed theatre, where both accused and accuser wore masks. The accused were cruelly broken, the witnesses threatened, blackmailed, or bribed, until they were all ready to commit to memory their "confessions." The text of these was dictated by the interrogators, prosecutors, and judges – the supporting cast – who were held responsible, together with the accused, for the success of a smooth "public performance" stage-managed by the Czech Party leadership, directed from the Kremlin, scripted by Stalin himself.

There is a striking connection between the show-trials and the theatre: "Before the actual trial, judges, counsel, prisoners, all went through elaborate rehersals so that the performance would be perfect. The teams that had worked on the prisoners vied with each other in the excellence of their preparation: during the hearing accuser and accused met in the corridors, congratulating each other on their performances ... From the absurd confessions to the childish recitations they were a spectacle of unreason and unreality: the final macabre stroke was the verdicts, and the hanging of all but three of the accused."[5]

Indeed, one could best describe this political phenomenon as a combination of the Theatre of Cruelty and the Theatre of the Absurd; this ritualization of injustice did not change fundamentally even after 1953 because "a dogmatic Czechoslovak Stalinism endured intact long after Stalin's death," largely due to the fact that "all surviving Czechoslovak leaders were tainted by direct implication in the Stalinist terror and purges, toward which they nursed a custodial attitude."[6] Ironically, it was this same leadership that was assigned the duty under Khruschov to stage the farce of a search for the criminals by the criminals themselves, a situation bitterly satirized in Klima's *The Castle.*

While in the political life of the fifties the dramatized miscarriage of justice assumed the shape of macabre theatre, conversely, in the sixties theatre often assumed the role of public tribunal, dramatizing the tormenting political questions of crime and punishment, of a whole generation on trial. In Karvas's *The Big Wig* the Minister's talentless son plays the role of an extra at a performance of *Hamlet,* and it becomes clear that, just like references to Kafka, in the Czechoslovakia of the sixties references to *Hamlet* are explosive. In the political context of the "theatre within the theatre" of Karvas's play, the audience understands that the corruption of contemporary Czechoslovakia is indeed like the corruption of Denmark, with an illegitimate ruler at the helm – to be more precise, with a Claudius who submits to public self-criticism, admitting that it was indeed something of an "excess" or a "mistake" to poison his brother, but now solemnly promises that for the rest of his reign, while still enjoying all the privileges of power, he will do his best not to commit the same "mistake" again. Therefore, when in "the play within the play" Hamlet finally kills Claudius, the audience is jubilant; it is the victory of justice over the lies and tyranny of the contemporary regime.

Just so, as the trial as theatre is enacted on the stage in the sixties, the numerous allusions to the absurd world of Kafka demonstrate the "fantasmagoric reality"[7] not only of Stalinism but also of the de-Stalinization period in Czechoslovakia.

IVAN KLIMA: *THE CASTLE*

Even in its title, Ivan Klima's *The Castle* pays open tribute to Kafka. The allusion becomes unmistakable when we realize that Josef Kan, who arrives uninvited to the castle, is a clear allusion to Kafka's Josef K, the land surveyor (albeit K was never allowed to enter the castle of his desires). In the play that takes place in the 1960s, the castle is still a virtually inaccessible place of class privilege, even if its residents, a number of gifted intellectuals, insist on being dedicated Communists. The building and the grounds are a take-off on Dobros, where the government set up a Writer's Residence, or of Liblice itself, the recreation centre for members of the Academy. The residents live in this castle on a never-ending creative holiday. The irony is, of course, that once they move into the castle, supported and supervised by the state, they are no longer creative: Emil the research biologist does no more research; Bernard the philosopher no longer produces philosophical works; and Ales is described simply as a "non-writing writer." In proportion to their creative impotence is their fear of losing their privileges, and consequently they fabricate exaggerated lies about their own creative output, and resent youth, purity, and talent. In fact, the play begins with a prolonged, horrible scream: Ilya, the youngest, most promising resident of the castle is murdered.

The "plot" consists of a criminal investigation in which everyone wears a mask. Of course, the guilty wear the mask of innocence. But even the investigators who arrive on the scene after the murder, the Doctor and the Inspector, are playing theatre: they know the murder must have been committed by the residents in the castle, and indeed they know all about the "shameful and repeated crimes" (19) that have been committed here, but like the Party "investigators" who are themselves guilty, they are careful not to stumble upon the truth.

At this point a new resident arrives in the castle, the young Josef Kan, whose consciousness is still uncorrupted by privilege and who immediately understands that everyone within the castle is complicit in Ilya's murder: "They were all here, in vain are they trying to prove … And they hated him … They were possessed by their awaresnss of their superiority – their glory … They are trembling with fear that anyone could take this away from them … that's why they had to" (213).

As Josef Kan is trying to explain to the investigators that all the other residents must have participated in the murder, or at least must have aided and abetted the murderers, he fails to notice that the investigators themselves are not acting in good faith. Inspector Haba's final words are full of veiled threat and ambiguity: "Undoubtedly at this place regrettable errors have been committed," he begins, with the typical understatement of the Party practising self-criticism about the serious atrocities it committed, and "keeping silent about the responsibility of those practising self-criticism."[8] Then Insperctor Haba changes direction: "I hope you won't regard this statement as an attempt to slur the glory of the castle … at this glorious aspect of history." Haba's speech implies that, although many intellectuals have behaved abominably during the show-trials, in order to save its own prestige the Party not only acquits but also reinstates the criminals in their privileges. What is more, the Inspector now insists on a a theatrical re-enactment of the murder in question, thereby preparing the inhabitants of the castle for their next crime. Indeed, the very moment the Inspector leaves, the residents – all middle-aged or aging members of the Establishment – surround young Josef Kan, the only innocent one among them, who insists on a fair legal process; they prepare to strangle him. A hand turns off the light; we hear a prolonged horrible scream – exactly the same scream we heard at the play's opening.

PETR KARVAS: *THE BIG WIG*

The *Big Wig*, by Slovakian writer Petr Karvas, is also based on allusions to a Kafkaesque society, full of violent and gratuitous political reversals: six years of German occupation; occupation by the Soviet Union in 1945; de-Nazification led by the Communist Party under the leadership of Slansky; the show-trials of Slansky and his circle as enemies of the people; the death of Stalin and the rehabilitation of Slansky; various phases of de-Stalinization and neo-Stalinism in the form of thaws and crackdowns.

The setting of Karvas's play is a fictitious country where the all-powerful military ruler of the occupying force, called simply the General (a composite portrait of Stalin, Khruschov, and Brezhnev), summons the servile Prime Minister of the occupied country to announce his impatience with the current political thaw for its policy of "democratization": "To rule in a democracy," the General grumbles, "is a task for a murderer, my respected sir. You slap someone on the face and right away you are saddled with a parliamentary debate. An untenable situation – something was bound to happen to stop this" (222). To reintroduce the respect for authority he used to get in the former days of undisguised dictatorship, the General announces a new campaign of scapegoat hunting. All the bald people in the country are suddenly declared traitors, guilty of poisoning the wells, corrupting the national culture, and collaborating with the enemy. As such they have to be arrested, sent to camps, and exterminated.

Together with the baffled Prime Minister of the occupied country, we may also ask: "But why single out the bald ones?" In a country such as Czechoslovakia that had been occupied by Germany, the General's reference to the bald ones is clearly an allusion to the Nazi's victimization of the Jews. But as the General makes clear right away, the current government's urgent requirement for new scapegoats regrettably can be supplied neither by Negroes, who never lived in this country, nor by Jews, who no longer live here: "Had you treated your Jews with greater economy, my dear," the General explains to the Prime Minister, "we would have no problem today. But you have been profligate, did not think of the future" (223). The satirist's point is that, in a totalitarian state, one group of scapegoats should be as good as another, whether it is identified as an inferior race by fascism or as the bourgeois "class enemy" by Communism.[9]

Karvas's plot is based on the invention of a lotion by Hanjo Phabsem, the wigmaker in the local theatre. It is a lotion that can restore hair growth. Since everyone, even the General, is understandably afraid of going bald, the invention seems to be extremely valuable. Hanjo's scoundrel of a brother-in-law, Mike, therefore steals and then starts selling Hanjo's invention. Unfortunately, he has overlooked an important issue: although at the beginning the lotion stimulates hair growth, within three weeks it causes total and irreversible baldness (the more you try to cover up your ethnic or class origins, the more likely you will betray yourself).

Hanjo the wigmaker, who has always shown sympathy for the bald people singled out for victimization, now is declared a criminal and has to stand trial. Mike becomes the key witness in incriminating Hanjo, and at Hanjo's trial delivers a speech that has obviously been written for him, to be memorized word for word, with all the grotesque clichés familiar to any member of the audience who ever read the "confessions" made at the show-trials: "'Defendant Hanjo Phabsem,' Mike opens up the customary catalogue of false charges, 'came to our country on the orders of a foreign power ... he unveiled his dirty plans [to me], and since ever since my childhood I have been a person with a weak character showing clear signs of a tendency for criminality, he succeeded in winning me over to his anti-state ... anti-state ... anti-state ...'" (287).

The State Prosecutor interrupts impatiently and tries to prod him: "Let's say goals, eh?" But Mike is genuinely astonished that someone else is interfering in his delivery of his well-rehearsed lines, and corrects the Prosecutor: "No. No. Designs." Then he rattles on with the words he has memorized, heaping condemnation after condemnation on himself for having co-operated with the mysterious "foreign powers," a line of confessions familiar from all the show-trials of the 1930s in Moscow and the late 1940s and early 1950s in the satellite countries: "This is the way I have become the supporter of the international treachery of the bald ones ... It is only our terrific hairy nation's vigilance and determination that we can thank for the failure of their rotten design" (287).

After a short pause, the State Prosecutor prods gently: "Go on?" Mike, who was obviously allowed a longer pause during the rehearsals of this scene, is confused: "Already? Aha ..." But then he goes on reciting the rest of his speech word for word, pause for pause, exactly the way he has been taught at the rehearsals for his role at the trial.

The final irony in Karvas's plot is that the General finds out that, having used the lotion against baldness, he will inevitably go bald himself. Therefore he suddenly announces that from now on persecutor and persecuted will simply change roles: the bald ones become the good guys; those with hair will be called traitors. In the meantime the accusations about poisoning wells, corrupting national culture, and conspiring with foreign powers remain the same; they are simply the same vignettes transferred from one target of hatred on to another – reminiscent of the uncanny similarity between the texts of "confessions" in the anti-Trotsky, anti-Zionist, anti-Tito show-trials in the 1930s, 1940s, and early 1950s respectively. (The scene is also reminiscent of the Party's decision to switch the enemy's name in the middle of the demonstration at Victory Square during Hateweek, while the masses go on with their hysterical expression of hatred, in *Nineteen Eighty-four*.)

Although in The *Big Wig* some members of the ruling class inevitably fall victim to the political reversal, the top brass manage to brazen it out, simply ignoring the fact that the people persecuted today were their best friends yesterday. At this point Hanjo, the bald wigmaker who at his trial spoke up against the persecution of the bald ones, could expect to be rehabilitated. However, he refuses the admiration of the new bald regime, which by now has begun persecuting its former persecutors. Because Hanjo condemns the persecution of *any* group of scapegoats, of course he has to die: regardless of which extreme is on top at the moment, as a man who refuses to hate a pre-set target, he is an embarrassment to those in power. His death signifies that the opposite of the regime that persecutes the bald ones is not the one that persecutes the hairy ones: it is the regime that practises tolerance. Hanjo dies with our full sympathy, a martyr to human decency, with the words of reason on his lips.

The play, however, ends on a cynical note: the General finally comes to understand that the real enemy of the military dictatorship is neither the bald one nor the hairy one: it is the individual who has the courage to think his own thoughts. However, the General also realizes that, even if he could do so, he should not eradicate all individual thinkers, because then he would run out of much-needed scapegoats; consequently, he prepares to introduce a new wave of war hysteria, the most efficient way to eradicate thought itself.

In tone, both *The Castle* and *The Big Wig* are dramatic dystopias with a tragic intensity. In *The Castle* the innocent is murdered as a sacrificial victim in a recurring ritual; in *The Big Wig* the one who stands up for all the persecuted has to face martyrdom. By contrast, in the third play, Vaclav Havel's *Memorandum*, the tone is considerably lighter. Here the character who represents innocence happens to be an attractive young woman, and she is not put to death – she merely loses her secretarial job in an office.

VACLAV HAVEL: *MEMORANDUM*

Its lighter tone notwithstanding, Havel's *Memorandum* offers yet another illustration of the Kafkaesque by concentrating on the absurdity of bureaucracy, as two rival office managers jockey for power. Havel's play takes place in an office, but an "office" that really represents the state. Although most Western critics consider Havel's play a satire on the inevitable ambiguities of language, I agree with A. French's point that "behind Havel's satire on modern comunication theory [we should recognize] the rather terrible allegory of a power game."[10] To be more precise, we should recognize Harvel's allusions to the jockeying for power among the various leaders and teams of leadership after Stalin's death. We should also recognize that, as one regime followed another in rapid succession, each had another agenda, other slogans, other vocabulary, and each time before a change of positions took place, the population was presented with a strikingly new kind of torrent of political jargon. Thus, in the

first few days after Stalin's death, *Pravda* [announced] Malenkov [as the new head of state]; then it announced the members of a troika, Malenkov, Berija, and Molotov ... At the top of the hierarchy – and in the leadership of the satellite countries – one could distinguish three directions. The first one crystallized around Molotov and Kaganovich ... who regarded the maintenance of the Stalinist model as their goal. The second direction was represented by Malenkov and ... Beria, recommending radical economic reforms and a certain degree of liberalization in political life ... The third direction, which we would call middle road, was centred on Khruschov ... an advocate of de-Stalinization, but claiming the first power priority to the Party apparatus.[11]

No doubt, the first sign of the new leadership's emergence to the top was signified by *Pravda's* condemnation of those leaders "who offend against the principle of collective leadership and decide by themselves on important questions, without asking for the opinion of other leaders."[12] This was clearly a condemnation of Stalin and his autocratic ways:

But it was easier to preach collective leadership than to realize it. In 1953 ... Malenkov, Molotov, and Khruschov advised the Communist leaders [of the satellite countries] that they too should apply the model of collective leadership introduced by the Kremlin. But ... the Kremlin did not set a good example. At the end of June 1953, the troika fell apart. On July 10 the Central Committee released a communiqué accusing Beria of "criminal manipulations against the Party and the State" with the purpose of "undermining the Soviet State in order to serve foreign capitalism." Shortly after, Beria was arrested and stripped of all his functions. In the same year, Beria and several of his partners were condemned and executed in the course of a secretly conducted trial, [and it was announced that] "after Beria became the Minister of Internal Affairs in the Soviet Union, he made attempts to assume power, and with tenacious attempts tried to place members of his conspiratorial group into leadership positions."[13]

Clearly this catalogue of "crimes" was so general and exaggerated that none of them was possible to nail down – very much like the announcements about those condemned under Stalin. It seems, then, that the Party's sanctimonious, rigid, and jargon-ridden style was a façade for the literally cutthroat race for power among the members of the troika, each of them a rival and not a partner. (At first Malenkov came to power alone; then emerged the troika of Malenkov, Beria, and Molotov; then the two in unison managed to get rid of the third "partner," Beria. Each time a new set of slogans about economic or political isses appeared, it was tantamount to a shift in the power structure carried out behind closed doors.)

But the hypocrisy behind the principle of "collective leadership" was revealed not only by the rapid changes among "partners" in Moscow; the principle also came into conflict with the interests of "little Stalins" who held the power positions in the satellite countries. In spite of the ever-changing language about the new leadership's agenda and the ever-changing leadership style, the fundamental political structure remained the same: the leaders' naked thirst for power, for the elimination of rivals, and for the taking of scapegoats in large numbers.

Havel's *Memorandum* describes three reversals in the language of an "office" that represents the state – that is, three reversals in the power structure. The play begins with Mr Gross, the middle-echelon manager, finding out that behind his back his deputy, Ballas, has introduced an entirely new language of office communication called PTYDEPE. To his dismay Mr Gross discovers that, by having been kept in ignorance of the new language, he has also been shafted by his own deputy, who has "unmasked him" to the whole office as an offender, an enemy of the people (typically, the charges are so general that they do not need the proof of evidence). Mr Gross quickly goes through the ritual of public self-criticism (just as each leader who had fallen out of grace with the new leadership had done both before and after Stalin's death), but this ritual in his case comes too late. Ballas announces himself manager, and Mr Gross is demoted. And how the mighty have fallen! Being forced to give up his managerial office at the top, Gross is to occupy the lowly crawlspace the architect had designed for the official spy, a job considered the lowest of the low, although needless to say in the police-state, a position with job security guaranteed for eternity.

Yet Mr Gross does not remain in this lowly position for long; he is rehabilitated. The pragmatic reason for this reversal is that the operations of the entire office are breaking down in utter confusion:

PTYDEPE is found impossible to learn (the Party's new economic directives camouflaged in the goobledy-gook of ideology did not work). Now it is Ballas's turn to practise public self-criticism: he promises that he will be a loyal deputy of Gross, now reinstated as manager, will practise the high principles of collective leadership, and will never again promote that irritating language PTYDEPE. In fact, Ballas insists that all employees must attend lectures on the evil ways of PTYDEPE and unlearn it. But as soon as Gross is ready to re-enter his leadership position as manager, he discovers that behind his back the cunning Ballas has by now introduced another synthetic language: it is called CHORUKOR; it is as absurd as PTYDEPE was, and it is being taught by the same teacher. (The new Party directives are preached by the same people who advocated the previous ones; in the name of the unchanging ideology of socialism, the same self-serving elite takes advantage of power under each change of regimes.)

We are led to expect that the procedure of absurd reversal in the blind-man's-bluff of top bureaucrats will go on indefinitely, and always with the same participants, until we find out that the process has already had at least one casualty. It is young Maria, a junior secretary who fell in love with Mr Gross during his misfortune and made then an attempt, although Ballas had strictly forbidden this, to translate for Mr Gross a memorandum written in PTYDEPE. Now, even after the change of regime, Ballas insists that Maria acted as a subversive and therefore has to be fired for insubordination. Naturally, Maria turns to Mr Gross for help: "I hate to bother you," she approaches Gross shyly, "but couldn't you perhaps reverse [Mr Ballas's] decision? Or perhaps put in a kind word for me?" (128).

Havel's satire here hits another target: the fact that Mr Gross has suffered at the hands of Ballas in the previous regime does not yet make him a man of integrity. Once rehabilitated and reinstated as manager, Mr Gross shows himself to be as manipulative and ruthless as any other politician. In fact, Mr Gross is a member of the same crew of opportunist bureaucrats as his opponent Ballas. And so Gross refuses to stand up for Maria, explaining to her that since it is his task to "salvage the last remains of man's humanity" from Ballas, he consequently cannot afford to weaken his position by interfering on behalf of an individual victim. His speech is full of political cliché, his own hypocritical language of leadership that is as harmful as PTYDEPE or CHORUKOR, called "socialism with a human face":

Dear Maria! You can't begin to guess how happy I would be if I could do what you've asked me to do. The more am I frightened therefore that in reality I can do next to nothing for you, because I am in fact totally alienated from myself: the desire to help you fatefully encounters within me the responsibility thrust upon me – who am attempting to salvage the last remains of man's humanity – by the permanent menace to our organization from the side of Mr Ballas and his men; a responsibility so binding that I absolutely may not risk the loss of the position on which it is based by any open conflict with Mr Ballas and his men (129).

Mr Gross ends his cowardly speech with an empty rhetorical flourish that only a child would not see through: "What matters now is that you must not lose hope, your love of life and your trust in people! Chin up my girl! Keep smiling! I know it is absurd, dear Maria, but I must go and have lunch. So – goodbye! be good!" (129)

Like the dystopian plays of Klima and Karvas, *The Memorandum* leaves us with a final glimpse of the sacrificial victim, the only pure soul in the bureaucracy of bullies and opportunists. Havel, however, ends his parable on a note of ambiguity when, in the last words of the play, Maria responds to Gross's speech: "Nobody ever talked to me so nicely before," she says softly.

Is the audience to feel compassion for Maria's loving, innocent nature? Or are we to recognize that, in her naïveté, she fails to see through her boss's blatant ingratitude and hypocrisy, his clichés of "socialism with a human face"? Havel's play, then, ends on a bitter but also a constructive note: the first step in breaking out of the absurd maze of corrupt state bureaucracy is that the victim should not be bamboozled by the pious language of those in power.

In *The Memorandum* the ritual "masque" of the theatre takes the form of a repeated, ritual changing of partners in the power game. It is a kind of sinister blind-man's bluff played among the top bureaucrats enjoined in the farce of "collective leadership," where the winner of the partnership is the one who succeeds in introducing the new language code more quickly, more unexpectedly, using it to denounce, demote, and destroy his hoodwinked erstwhile partner, his very best friend of yesterday. This was the way Malenkov and Molotov managed to get rid of their partner Beria; the way Khruschov managed to get rid of his partner Malenkov, and Czech Party Chief Novotny managed to get rid of his partner Zápotocký, whom he could simply declare a "Malenkovite." The Kafkaesque absurdity of the high-falluting political slogans that bear the strangest, most unpredictable relationship to the things they describe creates the tone for all three Czech dystopian dramatic satires.

There is no doubt that the Kafkaesque assumed a significant role in the intellectual ferment provided by political satire in Czechoslovakia in the 1960s. Yet in Kafka's work, written in the 1910s and 1920s, the absurd had a tendency to foreshadow, to anticipate the very real horror of future totalitarian police-states in the 1940s and 1950s. By contrast, in the case of the parables of Klima, Karvas, and Havel, the absurdity of the world depicted is an unmistakable reflection on the writer's political present in the 1960s. Also, while Kafka's heavily encoded language emphasizes the tenuous link of communication between writer and reader, in the three plays in question the satirical targets are designed to be easily decoded, as if Klima, Karvas, and Havel wanted to compel their audience to admit unanimously how absurd their world *has become*, to admit that they have been led to a hellscape by the excesses of a totalitarian mentality. Making their allusions politically transparent, the dramatists assume that the audience will respond with appreciation to allusions to these political excesses that must have been familiar to all but were so far forbidden to articulate. While Kafka's stories characteristically convey the individual's anxiety and fear of a world where human beings are inevitably victimized by overwhelming, rationally incomprehensible forces, an absurd world without perceptible meaning, in the plays of Klima, Karvas, and Havel the references to Kafkaesque absurdity still function as a public warning *against* the demonic power of the irrational, a power that the satirists imply could and *should* be defeated. In other words, I would suggest that in these plays about the three dramatists' truly Kafkaesque present, the absurd has assumed a clearly delimited goal: it has come to function within the framework of the traditionally rational norms of dystopian political satire.

CHAPTER ELEVEN

From Terror to Entropy:
The Downward Spiral:
Konwicki's *A Minor Apocalypse*, Déry's *Mr G.A. in X*, and Zinoviev's *The Radiant Future*

"We have built Socialism," the slogans declare all over the nightmare city of Warsaw in Tadeusz Konwicki's[1] *A Minor Apocalypse*, in glaring contrast to a panorama of "our contemporary poverty [that] is as transparent as glass and as invisible as the air. Our poverty is the kilometre-long lines, ... lives without any hope whatsoever ... the grace of the totalitarian state by whose grace we live" (43). In the monotony of hopelessness the proletariat is dehumanized; the frustrated young turn into hooligans, and even the most basic emotions become brutalized, witness "a rather tipsy woman ... pushing a baby carriage with a child in it ... To break the monotony, she would let go of the handle and then catch up with the carriage, pretending that she was about to kick it" (72). As if all this were perfectly normal, the narrator and the tipsy woman watch together as the famous Poniatowski Bridge slowly sinks into the river, its collapse caused by decay and neglect. "Houses have collapsed in front of my eyes, but bridges – never," he observes matter of factly, while "the slogan 'We have built socialism' [is] floating down the center of the current" (72–3).

The horror over decay, neglect, and apathy is also a keynote in Tibor Déry's *Mr G.A. in X*, published in Hungary in 1964: "The picture of destruction was not horrifying, only boring. The irritating monotony was not diminished by the fact that the houses had not been destroyed all of a sudden, but in the course of several decades ... that the destruction was not caused by war ... but human neglect. G.A. was a calm, contemplative kind of man ... [but now] he became agitated" (20).

Both the Polish and the Hungarian dystopias present us with the manic-depressive pattern of a nightmare city that demonstrates the cause-effect relationship between two spiral movements: the demonic fury of totalitarian terror followed by the equally demonic dimension of entropy, the irreversible tendency of an organism to disintegrate.

What makes the downward spiral even more sinister is the fact that this death-bound society masquerades as a vital and triumphant fulfilment of that dream that called it into existence, the utopian dream of socialism.

Zinoviev's Moscow in *The Radiant Future* (1978) belongs to the same map. Like Konwicki and Déry, Zinoviev presents us with the unforgettable image of entropy in the erection, destruction, and repair of a gigantic slogan reading "Long Live Communism – the Radiant Future of Mankind!" It is worth noting that this slogan is displayed "where the Avenue of Marxism-Leninism meets Cosmonaut Square" – that is, at the convergence of two enormous lies. The first lie is that the Soviet regime of the 1970s still follows in the footsteps of Marxist-Leninist ideology; the second, that Soviet advances in space travel stand for scientific advances achieved in the interest of a better future for Soviet society as a whole.

In the course of the novel the gigantic letters are destroyed or vandalized until the words become indecipherable, and the lacklustre, garbled slogan becomes a parody of itself, a telling comment on material and spiritual decline, on the inevitable process of entropy that the protagonist observes around him. While the shabby physical condition of the gigantic slogan undercuts the meaning of the celebratory words, Zinoviev's description lacks the passion of Konwicki's grotesque, or the quiet intensity of Déry's allegorical vision. Zinoviev's comment on the entropy of the system is manifest in the contrast of the utopian promise of the slogan about the radiant future and the dirty, wasteful world of contemporary reality, and in the direct, matter-of-fact language of a political journalist's commentary: "The Slogan was created at the request of the workers. It was a long time in building, mainly in winter, when costs are higher. A huge amount of money was poured into it – no less (it is rumoured) than was invested in the whole of our agriculture during the first five-year plan. But today we are very rich, and such expenses are a mere nothing. We have spent even more on the Arabs without breaking ourselves. What we spent on the Arabs was a complete waste, while the Slogan is a source of undoubted benefit" (7).

The profound ironies in this introduction draw immediate attention to the Doublethink practised by the regime. The creation of the slogan – a monstrous structure of gigantic proportions – is a waste of money and labour; the government pretends to be following the workers' "request" in order to cover up for its ineptitude in wasting enormous sums. Wasting money is also the keynote of its irrational foreign policy and of its blatant neglect of the city where playgrounds turn into garbage dumps.

Each in his own way, Konwicki, Déry, and Zinoviev, delineates the dynamic of a dystopic regime on its downward spiral. Unabashedly ignoring all evidence to the contrary, the streamer in Warsaw declares that socialism has been built. The slogan in Moscow celebrates the next phase, Communism, after Brezhnev's joyful declaration that socialism has already been accomplished. The three novels demonstrate that when people accept the government's lies, they accept the unacceptable. Resigned to the chronic shortages, the corruption and insolence of office, the paralysing red tape, the chaotic network of propaganda woven by the self-serving ruling class, the people's state of apathy turns into an unnatural denial of life, an absurd, insane, suicidal acquiescence in their own extinction. Each novel demonstrates the inextricable fusion of the economic and political entropy of the regime as an ideological construct, the apathy of the people as a whole, as well as the overwhelming death-wish of the individual. In *A Minor Apocalypse* the narrator sets himself on fire; in *Mr G.A. in X* the narrator's fiancée, Elizabeth, refuses to escape with him from X because she is irresistibly drawn to the Excursion, a grotesque parade ending with mass suicide; in Zinoviev's *The Radiant Future* the narrator's teenage daughter commits suicide.

TADEUSZ KONWICKI: *A MINOR APOCALYPSE*

Written as a *roman-à-clef* of the 1979 political-intellectual scene in Poland, Konwicki's *The Minor Apocalypse* is a work that readers outside of Poland may at times find difficult to follow. With its reliance on political allusions and its often rhapsodic style, this decidedly postmodern text is uninterrupted by chapters, sections, partitions – clearly a novel not only about but also for intellectuals.

The central character is an aging writer who is strongly critical of the establishment, the Soviet-serving Polish apparatchiks. At the same time he also believes that those in the reform movement are simply "dissidents with lifetime appointment. The regime has grown accustomed to them and they've grown accustomed to the regime ... they're part and parcel of each other" (36). The story begins in the morning as two dissident fellow writers appear on the narrator's doorstep and introduce the outrageous central premise of the narrative: "'We have a proposition for you. On behalf of our colleagues' – 'What is it you wish to propose?' – 'That tonight at eight o'clock you set yourself on fire in front of the Central Committee Building'" (15).

The grim Hubert and the "now balding" "blond angel" (2) Rysio may seem unlikely candidates, yet here they assume the role of the angels of the apocalypse, even if at first the narrator challenges their authority. Testily he asks why he was selected for this public sacrifice – a protest against Soviet oppression – instead of a world-famous Polish film director – a take-off on Andrzew Wajda. He is told that the film director "would be too high a price to pay ... You're just right" (6). Understandably piqued by being intellectually belittled even in his command performance as a martyr, the narrator asks defiantly: "And what if I don't do it?" The answer is very simple, very poignant: "Then you'll go on living the way you've lived till now" (24).

Since from this point the narrative follows the furtive ramblings of an indecisive, hesitant narrator in a chaotic nightmare city, at first reading the text appears to be almost impenetrable. There are, however, three threads to remind us of that principle of continuity and structure that, I claim, even the most deconstructionist postmodern text cannot – or would not seriously attempt to – deconstruct.

First, the action starts in the morning and we know it will have to culminate at eight o'clock in the evening, at the end of the meeting between the Soviet and the Polish Party secretaries. We are reminded of this time-frame by numerous television announcements throughout the day: the Soviet Party Secretary's plane has landed at the Warsaw airport; he emerges to embrace the Polish Secretary to the swelling music of the *Internationale*; they discuss the cheering prospect of incorporating Poland into the Union of Soviet Republics; they receive sincere well-wishers; the protester who publicly removes his clothes on the platform is carted away tactfully by the Secret Police; the two secretaries repeatedly exchange congratulations, embraces, kisses, and decorations.

The second thread that creates a sense of continuity is the narrator's repeated breaking away from his mysterious follower, Tadzio, who has volunteered to carry the matches and the can of gasoline, standard equipment for acts of self-immolation. An awestruck young poet from the provinces with an angelic face, Tadzio metamorphoses into a balding government spy in his middle age, then into Judas Iscariot, yet he also remains the angel of the apocalypse, with the would-be-martyr narrator under his wings, in charge of the sacrificial liquid that will set the corrupt Earth on fire.

The third thread in the seemingly haphazard ramblings of narrator and narrative is a symbolic device we are allowed to identify only at the end: the ramblings consist of seven episodes. After the two shabby angels of the apocalypse announce the necessity of his martyrdom, the narrator visits a dairy bar to meet some more of the confused and aimless intellectuals. From here he moves on to the conspirators' headquarters, where he meets, makes love to, and is separated from a beautiful young woman of Russian origin whose name is Nadezhda – Hope. Afterwards, he goes on to a reception where he meets some

more leading intellectuals, but then he is suddenly arrested and subjected to the subtle cruelty of an interrogation by the Communist Secret
Police, who want to find out more about the conspirators in charge
of public protests. Released as unexpectedly as he was captured, the
narrator finds himself in the Restaurant Paradiso, where he participates
in a "Kremlin lunch" of pilfered champagne and caviar, followed by
the beginnings of an orgy featuring the Scarlet Woman of Warsaw. It
is also in this "Paradise" that he meets the head of the reform movement, Caban – a recognizable take-off on Kuron, the predecessor of
Lech Walencza. The narrator finds an uncanny resemblance between
Caban and the brutally arrogant representatives of the Communist
regime Caban is supposed to be fighting against. Now the narrator
has a surreal dream vision of all the women he has ever made love to
sitting at the same campfire, and in a rather brutal moment of awakening he comes close to being mugged by a gang of young hooligans.
Learning that the narrator is on his way to set himself on fire, the gang
disappear, but at this point public transportation breaks down entirely.
The narrator is offered a ride by a straitjacketed dissident who is just
being carted away in an ambulance to the madhouse reserved for
political offenders. The offer of a lift is repeated by the driver of a
police van, who first wants to fine him for taking a walk but then
offers to drive him to the scene of his martyrdom in exchange for a
bribe or a hand-out. The narrator refuses both lifts and arrives on foot
at the appointed place – now identified as the seventh stage of his
journey, the seventh stage of the Cross.

Even Caban approaches him to kiss his shoulder, according to old
Polish custom, and beautiful Nadezhda-Hope also reappears. The
narrator bids farewell to all: "Goodbye, Hope. If freedom does not
come after me as suddenly and surprisingly as the beginning of
summer, then it will come after one of the next poets, workers,
students" (230).

Having realized that "the Antichrist is in every one of us" (158), he
is now ready for the vision of a new heaven and earth. His "minor
apocalypse" allows him to die with "the sudden, all-embracing certainty that it is we, people, the biological river flowing from nowhere
into the next, who have created God ... the God of Mercy, the God
of the People" (230–1).

The novel is a literary grotesque where the reader is trapped in a
no-man's land between objective descriptions of Warsaw, recognizable
allusions to Polish politics, and a vision of a hallucinatory Kafkaesque
nightmare. Of course, Konwicki's point is that the world he describes
can be approached only as a hallucination: the newspapers of Warsaw
have been so full of lies, omissions, and distortions that it is no longer

possible to determine even the year, the date, or the season. Objective reality is dead, and so is common sense.

TIBOR DÉRY: *MR G.A. IN X*

Elements of the surreal and the phantasmagorical are also important in Tibor Déry's *Mr G.A. in X*, even though here the narrative method is more traditional. In fact, if Konwicki's dystopia is a literary grotesque, Déry's employs the devices of parable: allegory and allusion.

A major Hungarian novelist of his era, Déry achieved the ironic distinction of being imprisoned for the same offence – freedom of expression – by two allegedly opposite regimes. In 1938 he was imprisoned by Horthy's right-wing government; in 1957, after the Hungarian Revolution, by an allegedly socialist, left-wing government. In fact *Mr G.A. in X* was written in prison. The Western reader may therefore find it rather surprising that Hungarian literary critics of the calibre of Mihály Sükösd and George Lukacs have read *Mr G.A. in X* as a parable about "the threat of total freedom."[2] Indeed there is no sign of coercion in X. The spirit of disintegration comes from within, a spirit perpetrated by a people "ambling slowly" in the cold winter streets of a crumbling, dilapidated city, wearing "no overcoats, in shabby and torn clothes," displaying a spirit of ease and contentment one would associate with a pleasant excursion. Still, written in prison, the novel is not about freedom at all: it is about a society that has lost its goal, its soul, its will to live, a society suspended in a state of entropy. It is about the self-imprisonment of people in a life-denying society, a people whose "mind-forged manacles" make them regard their lives in X as normal, acceptable.

The importance of the prison theme becomes clear if we look at Déry's account of his own prison term: "if, looking at the door, I saw that there was no doorknob on the door, that could be tolerated only [if] I kept [writing] from morning alarm to evening curfew for close to three years."[3] The door that has no doorknob from the inside becomes an important symbol in G.A.'s description of X. We should point out here that our hero arrived in the City of X of his own free will. In effect, he risked his life on a tremendously difficult, life-threatening journey from the capitalist Hungary of the 1930s to reach X – undoubtedly the city of his dreams. Upon arrival, utterly exhausted, he has unexpected difficulty when asking for transportation, food, and shelter, not only because these are in short supply but also because the people of X seem simply to be unable to give anything but vague, evasive, misleading answers. At last he finds a hotel and a porter at the desk, but it still takes a painfully long series of aggravations and misunderstandings before he gets a room and is finally ready to lie down, only to find out that electricity is turned off at night; it works only in the daytime, when it is not needed. What's more, there are no knobs on the doors from the inside: the "guest" of the hotel is locked up in absolute darkness.

By now we realize that the hotel is a metaphor for a prison – a crazy, irrational, claustrophobic structure that is not, however, *called* prison. In fact, imprisonment is accepted by the inhabitants as a natural part of life. The narrator observes that the "district prison is higher even than the Hotel, the only forty-two storey high sky-scraper, with towers and porthole-like dark openings." It is the only intact and fully completed building in a city of rubble and half-finished or dilapidated structures. The city of X is so designed that every street leads to the prison. When G.A. first bumps into this building, a little boy innocently asks him whether he would like to enter:

"That's what I have been desiring, son, all my life," said G.A.
"Are you sentenced already?" the child asked.
"Of course," said G.A.
"For how long?" asked the child.
"For life," said G.A.
The child looked at him for a while. "It does not matter that you are not sentenced yet, they would still take you in," he said after a while. "Just press the bell under the doorplate."
G.A. did not press the bell.
"What are you waiting for, sir?" asked the child. "Are you not going to press it?"
"I am still going to wait a while ...."
"How long?"
"Until the gates open by themselves," said G.A. (56)

At the end of the narrative the gates of the prison indeed open by themselves. Both G.A. and his beloved, Elizabeth, find out that they will be called to testify in a murder case. By now G.A. also finds out that, in the absurd system of X, there is no difference between witness and accused: one turns, imperceptibly, into the other. Neither is there a difference between being accused and being condemned: "Honourable Council: the accused is always guilty." That the legal system of X represents the Stalinist system, with its conceptual trials and purges, should be quite clear even to the most casual student of the USSR or Eastern Europe, let alone to Hungarian critics of the period. In fact, when these critics say that Déry's novel deals with the "threat of total freedom" instead of saying that it deals with the threat of a people

choosing their own imprisonment, they demonstrate the same phenomenon that Déry ridicules among the citizens of X. That in X you can
hint at, allude to the truth but cannot speak it openly becomes clear
from the words of the merchant in charge of the empty shop, who
draws G.A.'s attention to a discoloured patch on the crumbling wall:

> "I have been looking … at it, sir, and feel truly moved by it. Its sophisticated
> radiance has conjured up an age when the people still enjoyed being alive."
> G.A. pricked up his ears. "They do not enjoy it anymore?" he asked.
> The merchant lifted his hand … "Why should they not enjoy it?" he asked.
> G.A. looked at him.
> "If my words could be misunderstood, naturally I withdraw them," said the
> merchant shortly. "At any rate, I have no right to make declarations in the
> name of others."
> G.A. rested his gaze on him. "Your words were unmistakable," he said.   (60)

Obviously, the merchant is afraid to speak clearly. But what is he afraid
of? We don't hear about a dictator or a dictatorial upper class in X.
The only sign of the ruling class consists of a group of overweight,
overfed "riders" who are expected to ride piggyback on their thin,
half-starved servants. Yet, even though these servants can be seen to
collapse from exhaustion, they are not only willing; they are literally
dying for the privilege to serve as beasts of burden for their overgrown,
lethargic masters.

But if there is no sign of dictatorial terror in X, why is the merchant
afraid to admit that, whereas in the past people enjoyed being alive,
they clearly no longer do so? The answer lies in the web of lies that
the legal system, the entire subtle prison system is based on. "To my
knowledge," the merchant explains, "our laws are all in favour of the
survival of the human species. It is true, of course, that laws can be
interpreted in a variety of ways" (61). Déry here pokes fun at the
hypocritical split between the humanistic spirit of the law in the Soviet
Constitution and its unpredictable, absurd, inhuman application. It is
well known that in the rigged political trials of the Eastern bloc, judges
were forced to pronounce cruel and dishonest verdicts or they themselves would have shared the fate of their victims. Déry alludes to this
when explaining that in X "the judges are … appointed from among
the prisoners"; they are part of the same system that denies human
rights to everyone.

Both the Polish and the Hungarian dystopias indicate that in the
totalitarian state the fury of terror is followed by the apathy of
disintegration. To accept this process as normal is tantamount to
deliberate self-imprisonment and, ultimately, the greatest absurdity of

all, denial of the value of being alive. In *Mr G.A. in X* the symbol that unifies these themes is the Great Excursion, a periodically recurring ritual of mass hysteria where the inhabitants take part in a death-march that culminates in mass-suicide. It is this massive death-wish ingrained in a society that has given up providing the basic necessities of life that prevents the narrator's escape with the beautiful Elizabeth. Elizabeth is torn between her desire to escape her trial by going abroad with G.A. and the sinister attraction of participating in the Big Excursion. At the end G.A. is left alone to undertake the arduous journey back to the world abroad, the world of capitalism.

ALEXANDER ZINOVIEV: *THE RADIANT FUTURE*

Compared to Konwicki's grotesque and Déry's allegory, Zinoviev's style is relatively straightforward, often discursive or plainly journalistic. However, its ironic method of composition – foregrounding the indifferent detail and paying little attention to more emotionally charged themes – makes the satirical target often just as elusive as that of Déry or Konwicki.

The introductory paragraph of *The Radiant Future* not only sets the tone for the central theme of entropy, apathy, and suicidal feelings but also prepares us for the discursive, often essaylike meditations and snippets of conversations on various aspects of Communism, displaying the effects of an "intellectual pointillism."[4] Keeping our eye on the opening image of the enormous concrete structure where each letter of the slogan "Long Live Communism" is cast in heavy concrete, quickly we realize that the slogan's function is to conceal reality. It "had to be completely repaired at least three times a year: once for the May Day celebrations, once for the November celebrations, and on every occasion when Moscow entered the All-Union contest for the model communist city" (7). Undoubtedly, both the gigantic letters of the slogan itself and its companion piece, the enormous concrete-framed portaits of the members of the Politburo, have the same purpose; they are for show, for a cover-up, to add to "the splendid architectural ensemble of Cosmonaut Square and the wasteground adjoining it," mainly to "be able to conceal the ugliness of the wasteground from the eyes of foreigners" (8).

The enormous "wasteground" of Soviet reality, the failure of the hypocritical concealment of this dystopic reality with the gigantic portraits and slogans, is the central theme of the novel. Parallel to this, the concealment of the unpleasant aspects of one's personality even from oneself has become a psychological need for those who want to "make it" in this system of empty façades. The stage is set right away:

our narrator is an intellectual, head of the Department of Theoretical Problems of Methodology of Scientific Communism, a doctor of philosophy and a potential candidate for the Academy – a well-situated professional who has a great deal at stake to maintain his position in the power structure.

The narrative is a curious combination of four voices: first, savage satire against the system and all those who benefit from the absurd lack of ethical or moral principles; second, contempt for those who toe the party line and cover up for their self-serving motives; third, self-irony for being part of the same system and trying to make it within the parameters of a dishonest, hypocritical institution; and finally, cynical self-justification. These four voices combine to create the unique resonance of the narration. It is this fugal tone rather than the actions the narrator performs in the novel that creates his unique persona.

We hear these voices in various combinations as he tries to get home from the opening ceremony celebrating the repair of the Slogan. His boss, Kanareikin, takes off with the institutional automobile. As a Communist, the narrator feels uncomfortable about tipping the cab-driver, who naturally expects to be tipped. Therefore, he decides to "drag [himself] home" via public transport. "Again," he admits to himself, "I could walk. It's not very far. But that would be against my principles. A professor, almost a corresponding member [of the Academy] – and walking home! It's ruled out by my rank!" There is no doubt that there is a great deal of self-irony in the way he describes his dilemma. The self-irony is well founded; it serves to introduce a man who sees through the dishonesty of the power game in an allegedly classless society, yet is determined to play the game nevertheless.

Our sense of the narrator is based almost exclusively on the tone of his conversation with various members of his circle. We don't get a description of what he looks like, and even when it comes to the central events of his life and his interaction with those closest to him – his children, his friends, his drinking companions, his mistress, and his wife – the author favours a minimalist approach. Emotionally the language is that of consistent understatement, as if all the emotional energies of the characters were absorbed by the unending social-political disputations about the pros and cons of Soviet Communism. We hear, in brief intervals between political discussions, as it were, that the narrator's favourite conversational partner is his old friend Anton Zimin, a man arrested in 1945 who spent twelve years in the camps. We also hear, in passing, that when Anton was released it was the narrator who found him a job, first as a poorly paid research assistant in his own department and then as a technician who was to prepare manuscripts for the press. We are not told but we can assume that Anton must have abilities superior to many of the writers he edits; he becomes an indispensable, first-class editor. Of course, Anton's great manuscript about Communism – an original and therefore dangerous work – can never be published. The narrator seems to condone this fact, while shaking his head over poor Anton's inability to adjust to the realities of life. Yet he knows entire chapters of Anton's manuscript by heart, realizing that Anton's insights are sheer genius.

One of the most prominent characteristics of the narrator is that he considers natural the wide gap between his liberal, subversive private views and his politically orthodox views, which he reserves for public occasions. This duality has become second nature to him, to the extent that he barely notices that it determines his attitude even towards his own children. Both his son Sashka, a college student, and his daughter Lenka, still in high school, are typical of the rebellious youth of the seventies, strongly critical not only of Stalin's atrocities but also of the generation that condoned and co-operated with Stalinist terror. They have difficulty understanding the double-bind of their parents' generation, the narrator himself among them, who had to survive and struggle for professional recognition under the regime. Coming to understand more and more about the deep-seated moral pathology of their parents' generation causes an anxiety in both young people, particularly in Lenka. She repeatedly seeks assurance that the Brezhnev era – in spite of evidence to the contrary – will allow her generation to improve the country by unmasking the corruption, hypocrisy, and unfairness at the heart of the ruling class, still clinging to its obsolete privileges.

The texture of the narrative, which consists of long political-philosophical essays and essay-type conversations, is interrupted only by the long satirical poems declaimed by Lenka day by day as she bursts into her father's office. The poems, allegedly written by classmates, are full of harsh satirical condemnation of the political leadership past and present. On the one hand Lenka is told by her father not to bring these poems to the house because he is in a responsible position and, if the Secret Police should find them in his home, he could be in serious trouble. On the other hand, he laughs appreciatively at his daughter's and son's jokes at the expense of the hypocrisy and stupidity of the regime.

Gradually the narrator realizes that the poems are Lenka's own, a medium of venting her anger, her injured idealism, at those who have betrayed the pure spirit of the revolution. Clearly, she is bewildered by the atrocities committed in the past, as ever more revelations appear in the novels and poems of dissident writers. The narrator follows the intellectual pranks and the audacity of his children with unmistakable pride, but he does not stand up decisively for Lenka against her dogmatic grandmother when the old woman reprimands the young girl for offending against Party piety. He himself is concerned at times that his children's liberal attitudes may eventually interfere with his politically conservative, orthodox image, especially as his own jockeying for nomination to the Academy brings him more and more into the limelight. Finally, because, in spite of the great care he takes to appear politically orthodox, he is an incomparably more interesting and more original scholar than the many parasites, sycophants, and former KGB informers who lead the Institute where he is employed, his nomination session turns into a trial – a familiar landmark of dystopian literature. Expecting accolades for his scholarship that declare him worthy of membership in the Academy, he is publicly reprimanded instead for serious "theoretical errors" and instantly dismissed from his position at the Institute. At first he feels shattered, but slowly he recuperates, learning to face the fact that his wife, mistress, friends, and colleagues have all abandoned him in his misfortune. At this point he articulates the climax of the central drama in a most typically minimalist, emotionally understated way: "But troubles never come singly. Lenka died" (280).

The effect of this unexpected, unpredicted announcement is that of an accidental outburst. We hear nothing further about his grief or bereavement. We can guess the magnitude of his feeling for Lenka only indirectly when, in another understatement typical of his approach to essential emotions, he states: "Later I was ill for a long time." The only people still devoted to him are his son Sashka and his best friend Anton, who bring him out of the hospital. Because he is "still in such a poor state, Sashka decide[s] to come and live with [him] for a time" (281).

It is only after discussing a number of mundane everyday events that the narrator gathers the emotional strength to inquire what happened to Lenka:

> One day I asked Sashka how it had happened.
> "She did it herself," Sashka replied.
> "But why?"
> "She found out everything."
> "How?"
> "Quite by chance. She and some of the kids from her school went to the Military Affairs to invite some war veterans to the Victory Day celebrations. And they found out accidentally that you and Uncle Anton had been in the same regiment. I'd guessed that long ago. But I swear I never said a word about it to anyone. After all, I can understand. But she was only a little girl!" (281)

And here we come to the dramatic climax and the psychological centre of the novel. We have heard before that in 1945, while serving in the army, Uncle Anton was condemned to twelve years of forced labour because of a satirical poem he had written against Stalin, and the narrator, his best friend, had been trying to help him ever since his release by finding him jobs, even though Anton remained politically suspect as a writer. What Lenka and Shaska could see, throughout their childhood, was that the narrator and Anton were the best of friends imaginable. For Lenka to find out that it was her own father, Anton's best friend, who was responsible for denouncing him and causing him to be sentenced to hard labour, was, obviously a morally, psychologically unbearable shock. Her love for and trust in her father were the mainstay in her life, in spite of her jocular repartee with him and the mocking tone she adopted whenever she congratulated him for parroting the hollow Party slogans of the time.

It is interesting to take a look here at the strategies of Zinoviev; after hundreds of pages devoted to political-theoretical discussions, in only a few lines he summarizes the central drama – the central tragedy – in the narrator's life. The emotional effect of this disclosure is powerful precisely because of the brief, sketchy way the story is told, deliberately leaving out information the reader must reconstruct or infer. After our shock at Lenka's suicide and the dark secret of the narrator's betrayal, slowly it dawns on us that Anton must have known that it was his best friend who turned informer on him, and yet he remained a devoted friend, as if both had accepted that denunciations and hard labour were part of the natural order of things.

The fact that the narrator's older child, his son, understands his father and his father's generation, while the younger child, Lenka, could not ("she was just a little girl") adds to the tragic rift between the generations. That the young girl, full of promise, energy, and courage to find out the truth, feels she has no way out but suicide emerges as a significant theme in the novel: it suggests that the promise of the utopian future – in whose name all opportunism, betrayal, and cruelty is to be justified – is doomed. There will not be, there cannot be, a "radiant future" for the next generation, which must inherit the parents' corrupted world.

The images of waste, garbage, and physical decay are essential to describe the physical landscape of a society in a state of entropy. They are also symbolic of moral and psychological corruption. Throughout the novel Zinoviev makes us aware of the recurring figure of an old bag lady: She is an old woman, an alcoholic, without a home, who goes door to door with her little cart – a reminder of all those who were lost and destroyed by the indifference of a system designed to create the "new man," the new human being of socialism. What she drags along on her cart is the burden of past promises that turned into nothing but waste. Zinoviev returns to this image several times to juxtapose the promises of Paradise and the reality of the wasteland. By the end, although the narrator's professional "period in purgatory came to an end" and he is offered a chair in a Moscow institute, he still identifies himself with those pushed aside, like the bag lady. In the last scene, just as at the beginning of the novel, we see him standing on Cosmonaut Square, watching the letters of the Slogan being repaired yet again, covered in scaffolding. His meditation on this phenomenon forms the conclusion to the novel: "'Yet we will build it. We will build communism.' I thought I was talking to myself, but somehow the words came out aloud. I was afraid passers-by would look at me and laugh. But no one paid the slightest attention. I walked past them dragging my meaningless little cart, walked through them, in some sector of existence of which they were unaware. But where to? ..." (287).

The novel ends on a note of uncertainty: Dragging the "meaningless little cart," the burden of his disillusionment with the past, the narrator still ponders Anton's suggestion that the only way to improve upon this garbage dump of a system is to fight, to struggle against the obvious flaws of the regime according to one's abilities and courage. We don't really know until the last minute whether the condemnation of the system also means the condemnation of the original ideals of Communism. Or does the narrator, in spite of his defeat in the power game and in his role as father, still believe in the superiority of Communism over any other existing society? The Western world definitely does not enter the narrator's mind as a morally superior alternative to the Soviet system; does he still consider Communism a real possibility, after the Brezhnev, Khruschov, and Stalin eras?

The narrator does leave us with the question: "Where to?"

And does Déry or Konwicki suggest a hope that we could wake up from the dystopian nightmares of these death-bound cities, X, Warsaw, and Moscow? If there is hope, where does it come from? Should one abandon the failed dream of socialism and turn towards the freedom of democracy – which is tantamount to accepting the principles of capitalism? Should one salvage the dream by returning to the original model of socialism *as it should have been*, in the place of the corrupt, chaotic, life-denying system socialism has undeniably become? Or should one forget about ideologies altogether and simply return to the values of humanism, which have been forgotten or denied in both the Eastern and the Western blocs in the course of this century?

Konwicki's position is that of the old-fashioned humanist looking for moral regeneration. The Palace of Culture built in the Stalin era crumbles, like all the other structures in Warsaw. But the hero feels that "the last war also shattered the great Palace of Culture of European morality, aesthetics and custom. And humankind drove back to gloomy caverns and icy caves in their Rolls Royces, Mercedeses, and Moskviches" (7). The "caves" of Stone Age morality are the same in the Soviet bloc of Moskviches and in the Western bloc of Rolls Royces. Where is help to come from? It is Hubert, the first shabby angel of the apocalypse, who puts this hope into words: "Terror goes strong and then it grows senile ... How many freezes and thaws have we lived through already, how much of the regime's fury, and how much of its surprising apathy ... Your death will bring [the people] back to life to redeem them" (86–7). If there is renewal, it can only come from a return to the moral values of the autonomous individual, which transcend the *realpolitik* of Communists, reformists, and capitalists.

Déry's final position is more difficult to decipher. It was at the risk of his life that G.A. left behind the capitalist Hungary of the 1930s. In fact, the novel includes several references to the historical experiences of Hungarian Communists who, together with Communists from other countries, sought refuge in the Soviet Union, the country of their dreams, in the 1930s. In their memoirs some of these "Muscovites" even describe the store in Déry's novel that would open every day but have absolutely no merchandise.[5] Even more important, all of them describe the sinister hotel where Mr G.A. has to reside as the famous Hotel Lux in Moscow, where these foreign Communists lived as if in a prison, under the close surveillance of the Secret Police.[6] Indeed, for many of them this prisonlike hotel became a prelude to arrest, imprisonment, labour camp, or execution – they were absorbed by the waves of terror sweeping across the land in the 1930s. The residents never knew who would disappear from among them from one day to the next. In his X, Déry presents this sinister dystopic world, originally the world of Mr G.A.'s dreams, at a later stage, not at the height of the terror. Nevertheless, Déry also suggests that X assumed its essential shape in the time of terror and has been functioning ever since according to its strange, absurd logic – a logic accepted by its suicidal population as the natural order of things. Faced with the threat of imprisonment that awaits anyone in X, at the end the protagonist is compelled to undertake the return journey, even if his hair turns completely white in this painful process. But, as we learn from the frame story introduced in the first chapter, G.A. will never be able to stay away from X for good. He will be compelled to return there in search of the beautiful, elusive Elizabeth. Can one ever give up the elusive beauty of the socialist dream, or is one to return to it in spite of all the disappointments, aberrations, and dangers G.A. encountered in X?

Déry's conclusion is particularly problematic in light of the statements he made about his dystopian novel in 1963, after his release and rehabilitation: "What our future will be like, this is the fatal question of humanity; I simply wrote what it should not be. The fact that I wrote it bears witness to my faith in humanity and Socialism."[7]

But can we take Déry's statement at face value? In an interview given to a West German newspaper in the same year, Déry declared: "Today the situation is that I could write freely, except against Socialism. But then, I am a Socialist."[8] It is precisely because of the veracity of the first two statements that we have to be sceptical about the veracity of the third. It is the Doublethink of censorship imposed on the writer – and the critic – of the Hungary of the 1960s that suggests to Déry the allegorical genre of parable. Yet, even if the language of allegory can loosen the "mind-forged manacles" of the inhabitants of X, it cannot completely break these manacles; the strict code of allusions clearly opens the way, but it also sets a limit on our effort to identify the parameters and decode the utopian model for a vital society – if there is such a model – behind Déry's dystopian satire.

Ultimately all three novels leave us with Zinoviev's final question: "Where to?"

CHAPTER TWELVE

Speculative Fiction Returns from Exile:
Dystopian Vision with a Sneer:
Voinovich's *Moscow 2042*,
Aksyonov's *The Island of Crimea*,
Dalos's *1985*, and
Moldova's *Hitler in Hungary*

VLADIMIR VOINOVICH: MOSCOW 2042

Vladimir Voinovich's *Moscow 2042* (1986) opens a new chapter in the expression of the dystopian impulse in the Soviet bloc: it declares the termination of the Soviet utopian experiment, and, as if to fill the vacuum left by the disappearance of the state utopia, sixty-odd years after Zamiatin's *We*, Voinovich reintroduces the speculative structure of dystopian satire, inviting the contemporary reader along on the writer's private trip into the future.

We have left the narrator of Zinoviev's *Radiant Future* (1981) with the question "Where to?" The narrator of *Moscow 2042* (1986) no longer asks for directions for reaching Communism: instead, he raises the question of the Soviet Union's new directions *after the failure of Communism* has become a *fait accompli*. Voinovich develops Konwicki's, Déry's, and Zinoviev's image of the demonic spiral of disintegration to its logical extreme. By 2042 Moscow has turned into a place where food and waste – nourishment and excrement – have become indistinguishable. Unlike Konwicki, Déry, and Zinoviev, Voinovich states quite explicitly that "this society of pitiful paupers who can't even tell the difference between primary and secondary matter, ... [a] society whose entire spiritual life has been reduced to composing and studying Genialissimania" (400), does not present an aberration of the dream about the "radiant future." On the contrary, it is the very essence of the Communist system. In fact, as the deposed dictator, Genialissimo, argues, if one really wants to get rid of Communism, one should simply allow the process of material decline, mental confusion, spiritual degradation, and a pathological system of justice to take its natural course. In other words, left unhindered, Communism will prepare its own demise. Here Voinovich puts a satirical twist on

Marx's statement that it is the very pattern of growth in the capitalist system that will inevitably lead to its overthrow by the proletariat; Voinovich makes the dictator explain that "you have to build communism if you want to destroy it."

The point is no longer how to realize the dream. On the contrary, "when people start realizing their dreams in life, when they start moving *en masse* towards a single goal, something like what you've seen here is always the result" (401). This march *en masse* towards a single goal is the disease humanity has to be cured of, and fortunately, "all those people from Marx to [the dictator himself] who infected mankind with communism, also gave mankind the chance to come down with the disease and develop an immunity which will last for many generations into the future" (402).

But the destruction of one nightmarish dystopic system is no guarantee that it will not be followed by another. In Voinovich's novel the demise of Communism is followed by a nationalistic theocracy; the extreme left wing is overthrown by the extreme right wing. Voinovich's satire is a warning against both versions of the same nightmare.

Written in 1986, the novel begins in Munich in 1982. Vitalij, the protagonist-narrator, is the persona of the author himself as a down-to-earth observer of different kinds of human folly. Exiled from the Soviet Union (like Voinovich himself), in Munich, Vitalij is living a fully satisfying existence as a writer with his wife and two children when he hears about the latest luxury trip available at better travel agents: space travel into the past or the future. Still deeply drawn to his native land, and irked by curiosity about how his writing will be treated by posterity, Vitalij succumbs to the lure of adventure like a postmodern reincarnation of Gulliver: he reserves a trip to Moscow sixty years into the future. The book he is in the process of composing about the journey becomes the "text" lived in 2042.

Making his preparations, he says farewell to his acquaintances, including the prominent but insufferable fellow writer-in-exile Sim Simych, whom everyone considers a genius to be treated with reverence, including Simych himself. (This is an unrestrained satirical take-off on Solzhenitsyin, not only on account of his nationalistic views but also because of the tremendous political influence of his philosophy.) Imperiously, Simych passes on to Vitalij a computer disk containing a charitably high-tech metamorphosis of the heavy – monolithic – "slabs" of Simych's thirty-six-volume *œuvre*, and admonishes Vitalij to propagate these classics in the Moscow of the future.

Arriving in the Moscow of 2042, Vitalij notes that his native country has declared that it has achieved Communism, the highest stage in our historical development according to Marxist prediction. He sees that in the years between 1982 and 2042 Moscow has simply developed further along the path from where he left it. The common people live as badly or even worse than they did in the 1980s, and the "personality cult" is stronger than ever. The inhabitants, called "Communites," worship the narrator's old schoolmate, a former KGB man, a leader whose pomposity combines some of the worst features of Stalin and Brezhnev, the general of generals, called Genialissimo. He occupies such an exalted position that he literally leaves the earth to live among the clouds in some kind of space-station.

In Moscow all the statues of historical figures have been beheaded and replaced by the cheap plastic portrait of Genialissimo: the only books one is allowed to read consist of his works, speeches, and memoirs (obviously an allusion not only to Stalin's notorious authorship of theoretical treatises but also to the literary pretensions of Brezhnev, who craved – and received – the highest awards and critical accolades for his dull, ghost-written multi-volume memoirs). Yet, in spite of the piety of the personality cult, the Genialissimo has surprisingly little power: the top bureaucrats decided to place him in such an exalted position in order to get rid of him, and under the aegis of his icon take advantage of belonging to a most privileged ruling class in this ostensibly fully Communist society.

At the same time, living conditions for the average citizen are simply unbearable: the central joke in the novel deals with the deceptive closeness between primary and secondary matter – that is, between food and excrement. The bureaucracy and the secret police are stronger than ever, and since even the simplest pleasures of the senses are denied or perverted by the regime, the average Muscovite in 2042 lives the life of an inmate in a prison compound that has become indistinguishable from an insane asylum run by the insane.

Needless to say, as an intellectual from a capitalist country and from another time, the narrator is under strict surveillance. The Secret Service, SECO, assigns him a live-in companion in the person of the attractive young Iskrina, whose "duty to the Party" combines the services of call-girl and intelligence agent. Vitalij discusses his observations of the major institutions of the regime with Iskrina: the educational system, the position of science and scientists, and the position of literature and writers.

In the spirit of Swift's highly corrosive understatements the narrator explains that "in the cheery, natural settings of Pioneer camps, children learn to inform on one another, to report their parents' transgressions to their teachers and those of their teachers to the kindergarten principals" (227). These "character-building" skills are gradually developed further, until "children learn how to compose written denunciations," while their intellectual growth is assured by devoting themselves "to works by the Genialissimo and works about the Genialissimo" (227).

As for freedom of expression in literature, the narrator is told that "nothing had changed in that respect – every communist writer was perfectly free to write about his ardent love for the Genialissimo" (233). (This is an echo of Déry's statement that as a writer he is absolutely free as long as he does not write against socialism, but then he is a socialist.)

Voinovich lavishes his satirical invention on descriptions of the position of writers and literature under the regime. He describes the Writers' Union as strictly hierarchical. Iskrina takes it for granted that only writers of high rank can get published (an allusion again to Brezhnev), and she would like to find out why Pushkin was published at all since he was not even a general. She simply cannot understand how "in those days writers were not judged by rank, but by the extent of their talent" (254). (Voinovich here pokes fun at the same bureaucratization of literature as Mrozek does in "The Trial.")

But the central target of the dystopian satire is again connected with the way the regime concentrates its efforts on disarming dissent and stifling freedom of expression. In 2042 writers in Moscow work on computers in public writing rooms arranged in a hierarchical order. Designated to the appropriate room according to their rank and category, writers spend their days working on a variety of computers – all connected to a central computer that is, however, disconnected. In this way writers – potentially the most dangerous segment of eccentrics and dissenters in any dictatorship – are kept busy fighting over their meaningless privileges and punching up their work on keyboards that will never lead to readable written text, let alone to publication of the text.

The narrator also visits the state laboratory run by a crazed scientist, Edison Xenofontovich, who in the process of genetic experimentation has managed to produce Superman (Supey for short), the incarnation of the New Socialist Man heralded by Lenin and Stalin. Like Frankenstein's monster, Supey is turned into a freak; through the scientists, the fumbling state bureaucracy deprives him not only of his masculinity but also of his humanity. At the end of the novel, when the narrator visits the laboratory again, he realizes that Edison has altogether too much power. He rules over life and death, and doles out privilege, able to determine who can and who cannot partake of the elixir of life. The narrator manages to poison the mad scientist with the scientist's own poison.

Finally, while preparing for a major writers' convention to celebrate his Jubilee, the narrator realizes that he "didn't feel that [he] was at a celebration, but the sort of press conference which in [his] time was held for repentant spies and dissidents" (380). In effect, he is on trial. No matter how primitive this society's living standards are, the Secret Police possess the most sophisticated methods for finding out about the manuscript he is writing, the conversations he is having, even the dreams he is dreaming. He is reprimanded by the head of the editorial board of the Writers' Union for being repeatedly critical of the regime in his *Moscow 2042* and for referring to that dangerous character Sim Simych, who after a long sleep in the deep freeze wants to march into Moscow to become the new tsar of Russia. Vitalij is commanded to remove the character from his manuscript. First he tries to resist, but when he is deprived of all his privileges for a time, he sees reason and agrees to make a public confession and to practise self-criticism. He also announces that he has changed his manuscript, and "Sim no longer exists." He adds, though, that "I have renamed him. And now he will be known as Serafim, not Sim."

At this moment the audience breaks out in great acclamation; Sim-Seraphim has just sent an announcement that he is marching on Moscow. The Revolution of the Simites against the Communites erupts. For his role as a writer privileged by the Communite regime, Vitalij is for a time thrown into jail. To his astonishment, he finds himself in the same cell as the Genialissimo, who now bears the rare distinction of being the first mortal to have been "arrested in space." In their discussion the dictator explains his motives, and this, of course, is the crux of the satire: "No one understood one simple thing – that you have to build communism if you want to destroy it" (401). In other words, if you simply allow Communism to reach its own conclusion, it will self-destruct.

The discussion goes on about the crucial relationship between the leader and the people – another rendering of the Grand Inquisitor's self-justification. The narrator reproaches the defeated Genialissimo for having surrounded himself "with bureaucrats and yes-men who did not know how to do anything but applaud. Maybe you should have sent them all packing to hell and gone directly to the people. I'm sure that the people would have supported you." In response, the dictator explains what becomes the moral-emotional centre of the political satire: the regression of the individual to the mass man:

And who are the people anyway? Is there any difference between the people, the populace, society, the mob, the nation, the masses? What do you call those millions of people who run enthusiastically after their leaders, carrying their portraits and chanting their senseless slogans? If you mean that the people are the best of those millions, then you have to admit that the people consist of very few people. But if the people are the majority, then I should tell you that the people are stupider than any one person. It's much more difficult to convince an individual of an idiotic idea than an entire people." (403)

When the narrator reproaches the defeated Genialissimo for being a tyrant like Simych, the autocratic ruler of Russia, the former dictator responds that he was simply interested in seeing "how the whole thing will end" (404), and then, like an apparition, he disappears by the next morning.

The last few chapters deal with the reign of Autocrat Sim Simych, who represents the regressive, nationalistic tendencies of the extreme right that Voinovich associates with the political position of Solzhenitsyn. In the novel the Simites take over an evil system not to improve it but to turn it into something equally or, if possible, even more evil. The Autocrat declares: "The Empire consists of the territories formerly controlled by the KPGB, that gang of devils, and includes Poland, Bulgaria, and Rumania, each of which is to be a province" (405). Undoubtedly, in this case dictatorship follows dictatorship: "All former communists are called upon to surrender their party cards ... and to undergo confession and penitence in church" (405–6). Indeed, people are openly ordered "to display vigilance and *intolerance* for all signs of the false and abominable communist ideology." It is a regime that is ludicrously retrograde: "Steam, mechanical, electric and all other forms of transportation are to be abolished and gradually replaced by draught animals" (407).

The Autocrat also forces the population to go back to the Old Pravoslav tradition with a strict dress code: all men should grow beards; women should wear long garments. The prudery and misogyny of the new regime is shown in the ban on women wearing pants, in their having to appear in churches or other public places with their heads covered, and in the proclamation that "women found guilty of violating these rules will have their heads shaved and tarred and feathered" (8). To give a dramatic flourish to these new rules, the narrator ends his quotation of Simych's "ukases" with the most absurd one, "forbidding women to ride bicycles."

Voinovich satirizes Sim Simych as a right-wing extremist appropriating all the worst faults he has condemned in left-wing extremists. Significantly, the new regime takes over the stiff and violent epithets of its predecessors' language of propaganda, even though the barbs are directed at the predecessors themselves. The regime wants people to "unmask," to "denounce," "to expose all predatory communists and pluralists." Much as it hates its opposite extreme in communism, what it hates even more is the idea of a pluralistic, tolerant society. (We learn that Simych gives his dog the name of Plushka, a diminutive of Pluralist, to express his contempt for the concept.)

As the new Autocrat, Simych introduces a regime under which victims are selected at random and sent to medieval pageants of execution, and Vitalij's life is also in danger. Having just been put on a trial by the Communist regime – albeit under the guise of a Writer's Jubilee – now he is tried again, by the opposite regime. His trial is brief but fraught with the threat of summary execution when the megalomaniac Sim Simych (self-proclaimed Autocrat also as a writer) charges him with the "crime" of having failed to propagate the thirty-six-volume *œuvre* Simych entrusted to him sixty years before. When the narrator explains that the computer disk containing Simych's books was destroyed by the technically inept Communite authorities, he receives a pardon, and to his great relief he is allowed to leave Moscow in the year 2042 and return to his family back in Munich, on 24 September 1982.

After sorting out some of the nightmarish confusion that inevitably follows time travel over sixty years, back and forth, the narrator comes to the central point of most speculative fiction. He expresses his wish that both disasters – the full development of Communism to its own absurd conclusion, and the takeover by a right-wing, retrograde theocracy – are to be avoided: "May the reality of the future not resemble the one I describe here. Of course, in that event, my reputation for exceptional honesty will suffer some damage, but that I am willing to accept. To hell with my reputation. As long as life's a little easier on people. – And that, ladies and gentlemen, is the whole point" (424).

Voinovich's approach to plot and characterization is consistently satirical. The characters are caricatures, including the hard-drinking, lustful, but politically honest narrator, who is serious about only one thing: the trade of the writer – that is, the unhampered pursuit of freedom of expression.

In his *Anatomy of Criticism* Northrop Frye offers a definition of the "satire of the low norm, [which] takes for granted a world which is full of anomalies, injustices, follies, and crimes, and yet is permanent and undisplaceable. Its principle is that anyone who wishes to keep ... his balance in such a world must learn first to keep his eyes open and his mouth shut ... The *eiron* of the low norm takes an attitude of flexible pragmatism."[1]

Hasek's Schweik and Voinovich's Ivan Chonkin[2] would fit the behaviour of the protagonist of the low-norm satire. *Moscow 2042* no longer belongs to this type of satire entirely; the narrator, Vitalij, is fully aware of the advisability of Schweik's life philosophy, and he is definitely willing "to keep his eyes open," but he also has a manuscript to complete, and undoubtedly he is not willing "to keep his mouth shut" when anyone wants to interfere with that.

The world of Moscow 2042 that Voinovich describes fits Frye's description. Although the regime changes from one extreme to another, it retains something that is "permanent and undisplacable." No doubt, Vitalij also values "an attitude of flexible pragmatism," demonstrated by his making fun of the pieties and intellectual pretensions behind the slogans and high-fallutin' ideology of the Communites – as well as the Simites. But *Moscow 2042* also displays affinity with the structure of what Frye called the "second phase of comedy ... the comedy of escape, in which a hero runs away to a more congenial society without transforming his own."[3] Voinovich's narrator escapes the nightmare society of the Soviet Union: he starts the book in 1982, living in Munich with his family, and ends it in the same year and at the same place. He expresses tremendous relief at being able to return from the nightmarish trials and threats of capital punishment he had to face in Moscow under both regimes. Compared to the nightmare trip into the future, Munich offers tranquillity and peace, not to mention the presence of his family circle (although, like Gulliver, the narrator is still so deeply absorbed in the atmosphere of his voyage that he re-enters the family circle with an abstracted, absent-minded air). But did he run away to a more congenial society without making an attempt to transform his own? Does the writer see the emergence of any positive social model for his native land? Does *Moscow 2042* contain any hint at positive social and political change? Perhaps the only indication of hope in finding such a society is the reference to pluralism, which Voinovich seems also to connect here with tolerance, a principle abhorred equally by Communites and Simites in the Moscow of 2042.

To appreciate Voinovich's satirical focus on the fate of the writer, we should realize that in 1972 Voinovich was expelled from the Soviet Writers' Union. (Like Vitalij in the novel, he was fully aware of the consequences of expulsion.) He left the Soviet Union for Germany in 1980; was stripped of his Soviet citizenship in 1981; and wrote *Moscow 2042* in 1986. In spite of the greater openness under Gorbachov, the editor-in-chief of *Novy mir* still refused to publish the author's work in the USSR, and, when, at the Sixth Moscow International Book Fair in 1987, Ardis Books presented Soviet works of fiction written in exile, all the books on display, including *Moscow 2042*, were confiscated by the Soviet authorities – a telling comment on the fate of dystopian satire almost to the very last moment of the regime. In 1990 Voinovich was one of those exiled writers who was reinstated, encouraged to visit the

Soviet Union freely and publish his works there. In 1991 "the Soviet Union ceases to exist, thus putting an end to formal exile."[4]

VASSILY AKSYONOV: *THE ISLAND OF CRIMEA*

The return to the speculative futuristic structure of dystopian fiction is also exemplified by the dystopian novel of another exiled writer, Vassily Aksyonov's *The Island of Crimea* (1981). Like *Moscow 2042*, it presents a mirror-image of two different societies. Aksyonov juxtaposes a fictitious world – Crimea not as a peninsula but as an island, a pluralistic, multi-ethnic, affluent society – with the historical reality of a monolithic, drab, hungry police-state, the Soviet Union in the 1980s. The protagonist, Andrei Luchnikov, moves back and forth between this hypothetical society and the actual society of the Soviet Union – a pattern at some variance from the futuristic structure that creates a division between two time-periods in the same locale. By the end of the novel this hypothetical society is destroyed, precisely because the central character makes an attempt to bring it closer to the historical reality of the Soviet Union. What Andrei Luchnikov attempts is to reunite Crimea, the affluent, consumerist, pluralistic fantasy, with his sentimental idea of Mother Russia. By the end of the novel Andrei's image of the Russian Motherland proves to be a sham; the gigantic police-state reveals its historically real fangs: instead of a sentimental reunification of island and Motherland, the Soviet Union invades the island and destroys it in the process.

The narrative begins at an unspecified future date on the island of Crimea, close to but independent of the Soviet mainland. Although connected to Russia by historical and emotional ties, Crimea in the novel is a society whose origins go back to the victory of the Whites in the Civil War, a type of Soviet Taiwan that has developed into a democratic, capitalistic, and most importantly a pluralistic society. The narrative is structured around the adventures of three generations of a rich and cultivated Crimean family, the Luchnikovs. Arseni is the father of the central character, Andrei; Anton is his young son of twenty. The old man, Arseni, served in the White Army during the revolution; Andrei is a strikingly handsome middle-aged "Marlborough man," a media expert, a gifted journalist, and the owner of the island's major newspaper.

The characters are presented from an emotional distance that does not invite the reader to identify with any one of them. This fact creates a particular problem when it comes to the protagonist, whose traditional role is to guide the reader in decoding the maze of dystopian satire. There is, however, a lack of consistency in the characterization of Andrei Luchnikov. As dystopian novelists are wont to do, Aksyonov assigns a tragic fate to his central character. Yet in spite of the tragic ending, the mood of the novel and the methods of characterization express a great deal of ambivalence: the reader is at a loss to find the serious core of dystopian satire. Andrei Luchnikov is more a fantasy than a psychologically credible character: he is described as one of the most intelligent businessmen, journalists, film producers, and playboys of his generation. In the space of a newspaper article Luchnikov is, apparently, able to produce an incisive analysis of Stalin's reign, full of insights into the past and the politics of the present.

Luchnikov's article does present a provocative analysis of the tragic effect of Stalin's reign on the Soviet Union, proclaiming the Stalinist revolution in 1929 as that shift in the revolutionary movement that ushered in the reign of mediocrities. He argues that Stalin was simply inept and inefficient; hence all the mistakes in the planning process that cost millions of lives during the forced collectivization and the famine that followed. He also argues that the same ineptitude was responsible for the tragedies of forced industrialization, the Moscow trials and the purges, the colossal list of casualties during the Second World War, as well as the post-war terror up to the death of Stalin in 1953. In Luchnikov's opinion this reign of a mediocre and bungling leadership is by now over, and he feels confident that the Soviet people will not allow such a regime ever to return.

Having travelled in the Soviet Union, where he is welcomed warmly by people at all levels of society, Andrei is confident that there is a new spirit among the young people who follow Western music and the philosophy of the Western youth movement. Andrei is also moved by the spiritual-religious revival among the people. However, when the narrator describes Andrei's elaborate manipulations to bring about a reunification between Crimea and the Motherland, the reader is left bewildered. It is apparent that Andrei is not blind to the cynicism of the Soviet ruling class of self-serving apparatchiks, nor to the ruthlessness and amorality of the corrupt members of the Secret Service. When in Moscow, Andrei knows he is under constant surveillance, and he is also aware that the Secret Service keep an eye on his Russian mistress, Tana, who is compelled to inform upon him whether they are in Crimea or in the Soviet Union. In other words, Andrei is not a political innocent. Yet, when preparing the reunification of Crimea and Soviet Russia, Andrei accepts the guarantees of the Secret Service at face value. He even intends to produce a film about the reunification as an enormous pageant of celebration; he is planning the celebration and the film production together with the Soviet representatives of the project.

He is already in the midst of shooting the film when he realizes that instead of a magnificent tableau of celebration, the Soviet air force has staged an airborne invasion. The novel shows that Andrei's dream of a reunification is naïve and impossible: Andrei is right in assuming that the Soviet ruling class has lost its ideological conviction; he overlooks, however, that this ruling class still clings to power with unchanged tenacity in spite of the numerous thaws since Stalin's regime; it is overwhelmingly militaristic and nationalistic, bolstered by shameless displays of xenophobia and anti-semitism.

Andrei is convinced that the capitalist society in the West must move towards socialism while socialist society must approximate the political and economic agenda of capitalism; he believes that both regimes must see the logic of rapprochement or convergence. Going beyond political convictions, Andrei's blindness may have a psychological explanation. He feels guilty about his good life and, as an act of repentance towards Mother Russia, advocates the reunification of Crimea with the Soviet Union. This could contribute to his blindness to the militaristic Soviet Union when the latter is "unable to comprehend voluntary reunification."[5]

The savagery of the Soviet conquest of the affluent, pluralistic Crimea shows up Andrei's idea of unification as an illusion. The effects of this political naïveté are tragic: Arseni Luchnikov, Andrei's father, loses his life, as do Andrei's wife and his former girlfriend. Burdened by grief and guilt, Andrei goes insane. Only Anton, his son, escapes with his young family.

The reader is never quite clear about the psychological or political motivation of this seemingly well-travelled, sophisticated, but actually pitifully naïve "playboy of the Eastern world." Is Andrei a simpleton? The narrator wants to convince us of Anton's superior intelligence. How could he then so easily overlook the long periods of terror imposed on the Soviet population, and the lies that are demonstrably the central characteristic of the Soviet system? The answer is, I believe, that the novel is more of a fantasy than a clearly targeted satire of the Soviet political system; nor is it the result of a serious contemplation of the historical process. The narrative is playful, inconsistent, whimsical, and idiosyncratic – more like a political thriller than a well-thought-out dystopian satire.

Or maybe one should look at the novel as something pertaining less to dystopian satire than to an autobiographical reflection on Aksyonov's position as a writer in exile. According to Olga Matich, "although the novel contains dissident political ideas and satirical images of Soviet reality, it is first and foremost self-critical, demythologizing Aksyonov's own utopian motifs of the 1960s – the superman heroes and beautiful

ladies in western garb who put their faith in the magically simple convergence panacea."[6] In spite of Aksyonov's return to the speculative
futuristic structure of dystopian fiction, the overall effect is closer to
personal fantasy than to dystopian political satire.

GYÖRGY DALOS: 1985: A HISTORICAL REPORT

Dalos's *1985: A Historical Report* was written in Hungary at the end
of the 1970s and published first in Germany in 1982. The novella is
another return to the structure of speculative literature: it is set in
England in 1985, after the collapse of Oceania following its defeat by
Eurasia – a continuation of Orwell's narrative in *Nineteen Eighty-four*.
However, the story is only ostensibly about the future, and we discover
that it is not at all about England either. Dalos uses the year 1985 so
that he can make use of Orwell's novel as a frame of reference. He
argues that Orwell's dystopian novel is actually about the political situation in Eastern Europe and it should be read as such. Accordingly,
1985 takes us to the post-Stalin era in Hungary between 1953 and 1956,
the years of political ferment prior to the Hungarian Revolution of
1956, and of the political somersaults between waves of de-Stalinization
and re-Stalinization.

In his 1990 epilogue Dalos points out that, through his work in the
late seventies, he wanted to address the Western reader, and hoped that
by carrying the Orwellian narrative further he could realistically demonstrate to the West the existing reality of socialism in Eastern and
Central Europe. He expresses his dismay that, in 1990, "Western readers
[still] had not got any closer to the understanding of this reality [because
they still stubbornly insisted] on reading Orwell's anti-utopia as a satire
of today's Western society" (19). Dalos's novel is set in 1985 in London,
after the collapse of Oceania. To emphasize the fictitious historicity of
his fantasy, Dalos mentions Julia's memoirs as one of his sources, as
well as the archives of the Irkutsk Academy Historical Research Institution from 2035 (the date Orwell gives as the date of the completion
of the Newspeak dictionary in the appendix to the novel).

The atmosphere of lies and fabrications is developed further in the
novel. Right after the Oceanian press denies the defeat of its air forces,
the papers announce total military collapse and negotiations for peace.
The change of regime is introduced by the same kind of hypocrisy:
O'Brien invites Winston Smith to his office to make an apology for
torturing him, explaining that O'Brien has been a mere subordinate
obeying higher orders. He also asks Winston to become one of the
editors of *The Times*; Winston accepts and becomes one of the leading

intellectuals in the years between the death of Big Brother and the revolution. He becomes so popular and so busy that he virtually loses touch with Julia. When Julia takes over the narration, her opportunism becomes equally apparent: she makes excuses for Big Brother's reign, claiming that it was not without its economic and military achievements – the voice of the apologists in a period of re-Stalinization.

Each Orwellian character reappears in the "La Ronde" of political play-acting: O'Brien stages huge public confessions about the mistakes committed by Big Brother's regime, and the people responsible practise self-criticism. Ampleworth, the bad poet, celebrates the new regime in the same obsequious tone he used to celebrate the old one. Should Western readers be intimately familiar with the political events in Hungary in the years in question, they may enjoy Dalos's allusions to particular political events connected with the abuses of legality in the Stalin years, the attempts at de-Stalinization in the periods of thaw, and further abuses during repeated crackdowns.

Dalos gives a witty summary of the principles of the new legality that are meant to redress the miscarriage of justice under the previous dystopic regime, in two points: "1. Whoever is innocent will not be prosecuted. 2. Whoever is not prosecuted is innocent." At first sight the spirit of these principles seems to be in sharp contrast with those of the previous regime's announcement that "1. Whoever is guilty will be prosecuted. 2. Whoever is prosecuted is guilty" (145). However, on closer inspection, the difference between the two regimes is not highly significant. Dalos suggests that the rehabilitation of victims by the same people who are responsible for their murder is not to be taken too seriously; under the rule of the police-state any semblance of legality is only a farce.

The novel ends with the defeat of the revolution. Winston Smith, one of its leaders, is sentenced to death; his sentence is commuted to thirty years' imprisonment. O'Brien is on top once more: he classifies the potential opponents of the post-revolutionary regime – in fact, the entire population – into three categories: "1. Those who have to be locked up. 2. Those who don't have to be but could be locked up, and 3. those who should but cannot be locked up" (145). In other words, the police-state has not changed at all: it simply cannot change if it wants to sustain itself.

We have noted earlier that writers of Eastern and Central Europe were familiar with the strategies of the mock-historic or quasi-historical novel that used the past as an excuse to analyse the present. Here Dalos uses the framework of another novel's time and space as an excuse to analyse the events of what was then the recent past in his own country.

GYÖRGY MOLDOVA: *HITLER IN HUNGARY*

György Moldova's *Hitler in Hungary* was written in 1972 but published only in 1992, after the collapse of the Soviet regime. The time of the narrative is left somewhat indefinite at first; we realize simply that it is set in the future following 1945, the date of Germany's defeat in the Second World War. Moldova borrows the same device from science fiction as does Voinovich in portraying Sim Simych's travel to the future after years spent in deep freeze. In Moldova's plot, Hitler has slept twenty-five years deep frozen when he wakes up in the world of 1970. Awakening to a political situation in which Germany is divided, East Germany is a Communist country, and West Germany an ally of Israel, Hitler is so horrified that he agrees to transfer his seat from the former Reich to its friendly neighbour, Hungary.

The point of Moldova's satire is that Hitler is given a warm welcome in Hungary. Does this imply that the people of Hungary have essentially remained fascist in spite of accepting a Communist regime for over two decades? Or is Moldova suggesting that the people are fascistic because there actually is no real difference between those who uncritically follow the Communist regime and those who followed Hitler?[7]

The plot is based on a minor misunderstanding. In a small Hungarian village, Bánegeres, a historical film is being shot about the October night in 1944 when the Arrow Cross, the Hungarian Nazi Party, came to power. Because for this occasion the local council building flies the flag of the Arrow Cross Party, some people in the village assume that Communism has been overthrown and the old regime has returned.

Without any psychological difficulty, the people of the village simply return to the attitudes once advocated by fascism, all eager to show their support for the old regime. Those who were the most enthusiastic members of the Communist Party only yesterday are now the most eager to show their loyalty to Hitler and his entourage. As for the other villagers, they simply go along with the routinized rituals of constantly changing regimes: "In the school the old teacher removed the [portrait of] Lenin and put up the portrait of John Calvin instead: he had already performed this activity in October, 1956. The teacher had learned enough from that incident so now he did not destroy the portrait of Lenin – the last time he had to pay for the replacement [from his own pocket] – he was satisfied with hiding it in a corner of the attic" (120).

As a matter of course the workers remove the red star from the top of the factory, change the title of the local newspaper, and one of the neighbours, Mister Adam, makes his way to Hitler's headquarters at the house of the Barna family, wearing a shabby old leather coat that he puts on only for historic upheavals, such as 1949, the coming to power of the Communist Party, and 1956, the overthrow of the same Party during the Hungarian Revolution. In other words, the inhabitants of the village are fairly sophisticated; they revert to previous behaviour practised during takeovers. They simply deny their adherence to the previous regime and make every attempt to assure their survival in the new one. This technique actually assures social stability: the same cast of actors fulfil the same functions even though one political regime appears to be the diametric opposite of the other.

However, the young people of the village no longer want to follow the survivalist techniques of their parents' generation. Young Matyi Barna becomes the leader of the fascist youth group, and he makes it clear that the young people of the village are eager for violence. At first they enthusiastically embrace Hitler's advice about the "two stages in any revolution: the first phase concentrates on salvaging the appearance of a legal process by maintaining some of the previous conditions. In the second phase revenge takes over without any further camouflage." But young Barna becomes dissatisfied with the relatively slow pace of violence prescribed by Hitler's agenda, even though he is still inspired by Hitler's old adage that it is better to kill a hundred innocent people than to allow a single guilty one to escape. In the spirit of these words, the youth gang lines up groups of people to be shot summarily, without conducting an investigation or a trial. They also decide to have a night of book-burning combined with a ball in the local night club, to celebrate the event.

Matyi Barna suspects even Hitler of being "soft-hearted," and the former dictator admits, "I would not have thought that I have anything to learn in these areas." Finally, when young Barna wants to demote, fire, or exterminate everyone over thirty and is met with Hitler's mild disapproval, he comes up with the decisively devastating rebuttal: he insinuates that Hitler himself must be some kind of a liberal who may possibly even have Jewish blood. So zealous is this young man for the old cause of fascism that he is dissatisfied with the zeal of Hitler himself and proceeds to put *Mein Kampf* on the pyre, together with other books preaching the sickeningly mild views of liberalism.

Moldova, who is a powerful and sensitive writer of complex novels in the mode of psychological realism,[8] presents us here with a bitter and angry vision of Hungary as a dystopic society, and the satirical passion driving the composition is anything but subtle. By the end of the novel Hitler, who is to be pilloried for being a traitor to the fascist revolution, has to find an escape route. Smidelius, Hitler's steadfast

German disciple, admits that he should never have brought the Fuehrer "into this cursed country , where even [Hitler] is considered too liberal and too soft hearted" (143).

By the time the villagers find out that the Communist regime is not defeated and that the flag of the Arrow Cross was a mere misunderstanding, Smidelius is ready to smuggle Hitler out from Hungary: he gives him an injection to induce another twenty-five years of sleep in deep freeze. The writer leaves us with the warning implicit in this last image: Hitler's spirit is still not dead, only dormant.[9]

As we have seen in *Brave New World, Nineteen Eighty-four*, and *We*, the writer of the traditional Western structure of dystopian fiction projects his fear of a dystopic society into the future but makes the reader emphatically aware of the distinction and the interaction between two different time-planes. The reader can successfully decode the satirist's target only by recognizing those specific trends in the present that could but should not be allowed to lead to a nightmare society in the future.

This futuristic, speculative structure, with the two time-planes that allow for a sustained contemplation of history accompanied by the writer's exhortation about the future, disappeared for a long time from dystopian fiction in the USSR and the Eastern bloc during the period of totalitarian dictatorship. What Voinovich's, Aksyonov's, Dalos's, and Moldova's dystopian novels have in common is that they all make an attempt to reincorporate elements from this "classically" speculative, futuristic structure, where the process of describing a dystopic society gives the writer an opportunity to frame an exhortatory message, a warning, to the reader.

Although the speculative aspect of dystopian fiction made a return from its exile in the 1970s and 1980s, except for *Moscow 2042* the distinction between the two time-planes works as a warning only intermittently. No doubt Aksyonov, Dalos, and Moldova make use of fictional projection to develop the nightmarish features of a dystopic society. Nevertheless, even the Ideal Reader, one intimately familiar with the political-social reality of the authors' time, would have difficulty grasping the direction of these writers' warnings about the future. While Dalos wrote his dystopian novel, *1985*, more than a decade prior to the eponymous date, he uses it only to refer to *Nineteen Eighty-four*, because he wants to prove that Orwell's novel should be read as a reflection upon the events that took place in Hungary between 1953 and 1956. In this case the futuristic projection is actually used to analyse the past.

In his *Hitler in Hungary* Moldova uses futuristic projection in order to criticize, in the form of a parable, the deeply fascist sentiments that underpin the appearance of Communism in the dystopic society of the Hungary of his own time. Yet the novella lacks the dynamic satirical machinery that operates by making allusions to specific trends or events in the writer's present and projecting their fully nightmarish impact into the future. Thus Moldova too uses a quasi-futuristic technique to make a dramatic comment on the past.

The same holds for Aksyonov's political phantasmagoria, *The Island of Crimea*. The futuristic projection is not anchored by references to specific trends in the present. The message that emerges is that aiming for the unification of a pluralistic utopia with a dystopic police-state will lead to disaster. This message may mark a dramatic junction in the *œuvre* of Aksyonov (himself, like Voinovich, writing in exile), but it does not lead to the political-philosophical analysis of specific trends in the present associated with the speculative tradition of dystopian satire.

The return to the structural characteristics of the Western classics of dystopia as a speculative, futuristic genre suggests that writers from Eastern and Central Europe no longer deny the possibility of stopping the development of a future more horrible than the present. Ultimately, by throwing off the ideological and stylistic straitjacket of Socialist Realism, writers regain their freedom to perceive and portray humanity as searching for a way towards the future instead of being swept inevitably, by historic necessity, in an irresistible ideological current towards a fixed goal in a preordained direction.

At the same time, we have noted that much of the suspense in the intellectual drama of *We, Brave New World,* and *Nineteen Eighty-four,* prototypes of the classically structured speculative dystopias, emerges from the push and pull between utopian and dystopian perspectives. This tension between desire and fear, dream and nightmare, is no longer present in the four works we have discussed in this chapter. Compared to Zamiatin or Orwell, these four writers display a deeper sense of cynicism, perhaps more playfulness but also far less interest in creating a protagonist with whom the reader can identify. (In effect, neither Dalos's *1985* nor Moldova's *Hitler in Hungary* has a protagonist at all.)

If speculative political literature in this "other Europe" has returned from its exile, it seems it has returned with a sneer, even a rather cynical or bitter grimace about a dystopic society, instead of an impassioned warning against it. After the loss of utopian hope in socialism, and without a commensurate increase in trust in capitalist democracy, the writer of speculative fiction has been left somehow stranded. The outlines of dystopic satire are undoubtedly here, but the corrective "norm" of a sane and rational society, the image of a world better than the hellish landscape of dystopia, is not firmly in place. Consequently, these four novels suggest that while speculative dystopian fiction has reappeared on the horizon of Eastern and Central Europe, as a genre it has not yet regained its self-confidence and power to illuminate the future.

CHAPTER THIRTEEN

Dystopia East and West: Conclusion

What is truth? What is justice?

While tragedy raises the questions but postpones the answers, works of utopia ever since Plato and More have been rooted in the writer's conviction that it is worthwhile to pursue social justice here and now. By contrast, dystopian fiction depicts a society where justice is deliberately subverted by a small ruling elite who conspire against their own people, misleading them through the means of a powerfully deceptive state religion. In *We, Brave New World, Nineteen Eighty-four, Fahrenheit 451, Player Piano*, and *The Handmaid's Tale* this deliberate miscarriage of justice, represented by the protagonist's trial, becomes the essential theme that, in turn, also determines the symbolic structure of these dystopian novels. In the framework of the two time-planes of this speculative genre, however harsh the writer's warning might be, it also implies that, unlike the protagonist, we can still count on a suspended sentence: we can still prevent the transformation of our own society into the hypothetical monster state that defines itself through its deliberate miscarriage of justice.

Reading the dystopian fiction of the East about the abuses of legality by the totalitarian governments in the writer's present or his past, we are faced with a significantly different experience. Here the actual historical phenomenon and its ficitional representation combine to form a self-referential cycle. At centre-stage, in both fiction and reality, is the conceptual trial.

Discussing the transcripts of the Moscow show-trials of the thirties, in 1988 Alexander Jakovlev, a member of the Central Committee under Gorbachov, raised the question of whether we are faced here with aberrations in the justice system or with deliberate, systematic attempts at "antijustice":

Each participant in the trial, without exception, says the same thing. What's more, the defendants are willing to accuse themselves of the most weighty criminal activities; each flagellates himself, slanders himself, and shows repentance at the same time. No one argues with the prosecutor or the witness. No one even attempts to deny some of the accusations brought up against him; on the contrary, each even enlarges the list of his own crimes ... The prosecutor reveals and puts a stamp on ... the others simply agree with him. The defence, in the best case, begs for understanding ... One's impression is as if one saw a carefully prepared and rehearsed theatrical performance."[1]

When Jakovlev concludes that "the monstrous evil committed in the course of the people's enemies' trials cannot be regarded as the aberrations or abnormalities of the justice system [because] this was not justice but *antijustice*," essentially he defines the central feature of the dysfunctional society that is explored and deplored by the fiction expressive of a dystopian impetus.

DYSTOPIA EAST AND WEST: THE WRITER AND THE PROTAGONIST

The parallel between the fate of the protagonist in the dystopian novel and the fate of the author in the dystopic nightmare state demonstrates an uncanny interaction between fact and fiction. Let us focus on this parallel by introducing here three dates: 1953, 1959, and 1966.

In 1959 Andrei Sinyavski wrote a novel entitled *The Trial Begins*, set in the then recent past, 1953. In the early 1960s he had the book published abroad, under the name of Abram Tertz, "the audacious hero of an underworld ballad about a Jewish freebooter." The pen-name hints at the "extraordinary fact that under Stalin there was honor only among the thieves,"[2] and it also compares the courage demanded from the non-conformist writer to the *audace* of a rebel who also happens to be Jewish – none of these suggestions calculated to endear a writer to the authorities, under either Khruschov or Brezhnev. The title *The Trial Begins* refers to the virtually unstoppable chain-reaction of purges and rigged trials in connection with the last wave of Stalinist terror that came to an end only with the dictator's death in 1953. Although Stalin's abuses committed against "socialist justice" were condemned in 1956 by Khruschov himself, the "Prelude" to Tertz's 1959 novel still begins with an expression of the author's intense fear of arrest. He has a vision that Vitya and Tolya, two look-alike plain-clothesmen, may appear at any moment to begin eliminating the letters from each page of the manuscript – that is, to make it vanish forever, together with its author.

In the middle of the novel the author once more admits his fear of being found out. He overhears the same two faceless plainclothesmen discussing an invention that would outdo even Orwell's telescreen; it is a "psychoscope" that can monitor any vibration of a free soul, making each thinking, feeling human being easy to detect. Kafka's *Penal Colony* and *The Trial* anticipate the systematic torture and persecution endemic to the totalitarian state long before the emergence of Hitler or Stalin. Stanislaw Witkiewicz's *Insatiability* anticipates in 1930 the cause of the author's suicide: the simultaneous conquest of Poland, his native country, by Nazi and Communist forces in 1939. In 1959 Tertz-Sinyavski predicts his own future. He foresees his arrest, trial, and conviction for having written the novel we are still in the process of reading, and he is, ostensibly, still in the process of writing: "Silence. Two men in plain clothes stroll through the city streets. Two men in plain clothes. Softly, decorously, they advance along the sleeping streets, peering into lifeless windows, gateways, doors. There's nobody. One is named Vitya, the other Tolya. And I am frightened" (97).

The author had good reason to be frightened. His "dual existence" came to an end in 1965, when, possibly because of an indiscretion in the West, "the subversive Abram Tertz was found to be none other than the respected literary critic Sinyavski, member of the Gorky Institute, contributor to the *Novy Mir* and author of studies ranging from Picasso to Pasternak ... Through a little detective work, aided by the installation of listening devices which monitored conversations in Sinyavski's apartment, [the KGB] were soon able to gather all the evidence they needed"[3] for his arrest.

Does it not seem, then, that the two faceless plainclothesmen in the novel were indeed successful with their psychoscope in reality, as if the characters of fiction had jumped out from the pages of the book to take on their anticipated function in the writer's biography?

There are several more issues here relevant to the relationship between dystopian fiction and biographical reality. It is known that in his university years Sinyavski was an atheist and "an ideal Communist." In *The Trial Begins* the victim-protagonist, the teenager Serjozha, is clearly a projection of Sinyavski's own youthful persona. The young boy believes that Soviet society should return to Lenin's original dream of a great revolution leading to an egalitarian world order and asks some daring questions about Soviet imperialism in his history class. He gets caught, with millions of others, in the web of denunciations and betrayals instigated by his own father, the Public Prosecutor. When, upon his arrest, Serjozha protests that he is innocent and cannot be put on trial, the Public Investigator points out that in a society where the entire population is continuously on trial, once a person gets arrested, he is already condemned.

This exchange is clearly another uncanny foreshadowing of the author's own Kafkaesque "three-day trial, which eventually took place in February, 1966. [It] was unique [even] in Russian history: neither under the czars nor even under Stalin had there been proceedings in which the main *corpus delicti* consisted of the actual contents of works of imaginative literature."[4]

Later Sinyavski referred to his attempt to defend himself as "a dialogue with the deaf"; not only the prosecution but also the so-called defence used absurdly distorted or truncated quotes from the novel as evidence of his anti-Soviet activities, shamelessly arguing for the harshest punishment – seven years of hard labour in a "severe regime camp." Just as the novel's Serjozha, innocent of any crime, was used as political fodder in the terror of 1953, Sinyavski's sentence was decided in the Kremlin long before his trial in 1966, "to teach a lesson and give warning to the liberals and rebels among the Russian intellectuals."[5]

In the novel the author foresees not only his own arrest and trial but also the manner of his punishment. As a dangerous offender he was sentenced to hard labour in Dubrovlag, near Potma, one of the camp complexes still operational after the winding down of camps in the post-Stalin era.[6] When, at the end of the novel, the narrator takes a last look at his three victim-protagonists who serve their sentence in the same labour camp – Serjozha, the writer's own youthful double, the old Jewish doctor who keeps reciting Marx even while digging trenches, and the shadowy figure of the writer himself – Sinyavski makes clear an important point. Even after letting go of most of Stalin's victims, the new regime still refuses to let go of these three dissidents because they represent the ultimate enemy of any dictatorship: the freedom of conscience and expression.

FICTION OR BIOGRAPHY?

Is there an explanation for such an uncanny connection between fiction and biographical fact? Thomas Mann, one of the most prominent practitioners of psychological realism, has observed that in a way all great fiction is autobiographical. By this I assume he must have meant that since all significant works take their substance from the conflicts within the depth of the author's psyche, it is these conflicts that are, often subconsciously, projected on to the writer's characters.

But in utopia – and also in dystopia – characters are shaped and moulded by the writer's deliberate, didactic intent to show how a given ideology tends to influence, indeed determine, the individual psyche.

In a utopian novel the writer's purpose is to show that healthy social-political forces are synonymous with a healthy psyche; in a dystopian novel, no doubt, the writer's purpose is to show the opposite. Still, both utopian and dystopian novels belong to political literature aiming at social criticism, where the psychological complexity of the characters may be welcome but not obligatory. Hence there is a tension between psychological realism and the author's political-ideological "message," as Professor Beauchamp has observed.[7]

Nevertheless, I believe that autobiographical elements – that is, revelations about the author's own temperament and psyche – still find their way into utopian fiction. In this sense, the writer presenting us with the allegedly objective social model can still not wipe himself out of the centre of the picture: to give that old adage a new twist, *et in Arcadia ego*. Reading Karl Popper's critique of the closed city of Plato's *Republic*, for example, one cannot help but recognize the sharp profile of Plato the man; why should the philosopher of kings not find it quite natural to aspire to the role of the philosopher-king, that well-meaning teacher-dictator who rules in the name of Absolute Reason? In fact, the leader of any form of utopia tends to bear a recognizable likeness to the particular writer's personality and biographical experience. In dystopian literature there is an even greater, and probably far more exciting connection between the writer's personality and the allegedly "objective" picture of society he describes. After all, in dystopia the writer projects his worst fear of an evil society, and fear is definitely a more dramatic, more exciting literary ingredient than hope. While the utopian writer, shaping and structuring his work, tends to identify with the builder or leader of the model society as a matter of course, the writer of dystopian fiction attempts to convince us of the disastrous effects of the monster state on the individual. The writer's sympathies, again as a matter of course, focus on the protagonist, who often comes to embody many of the artist's likes and dislikes.

When it comes to the the Western writer's political message – this is the kind of society, dear reader, you should avoid – the impact of this message depends on the psychological credibility of the victim-protagonist. Hence it is our genuine sympathy with Huxley's young John the Savage that evokes our distaste for the society he detests; it is our psychological identification with Winston Smith that makes us feel the threat of Oceania as if it crawled on our own skin. (It may also be worth pointing out here that the Western writer of dystopian fiction does his or her best to create a psychologically complex victim-protagonist in order to carry the emotional weight of the political message: hence the well-worked-out elements of the Oedipus complex in the characterization of John Savage; of the childhood trauma leading to lifelong phobia in the case of Winston Smith; of the father complex of Paul Proteus in *Player Piano*; and of Offred's tortured love-hate relationship with her mother in Atwood's *The Handmaid's Tale*.)

Thanks to the evocative power of his fiction, Tertz-Sinyavski has been described not only as "deeply influenced by Zamiatin, Kafka and Orwell"[8] but also as a "spiritual brother of Orwell."[9] Unlike Zamiatin's D-503 or Orwell's Winston Smith, however, neither Sinyavski's protagonist-victim nor the other characters are described in terms of their psycho-sexual passions; their only passion is political. Probably just as importantly, Sinyavski's dystopia is not structured around a warning. Written in 1948, Orwell's *Nineteen Eighty-four* suggests to the reader that by 1984 a system like Oceania could but should not be allowed to come into being. Tertz-Sinyavski, however, does not project his message into the future: he focuses on the events of the recent past and extrapolates from these events the inevitably tragic consequences his writing will bring to him, personally, in the future.

FICTION OR PROPHECY?

How does one explain the mysterious power of prophecy, that is the reference to autobiographical fact *before* the fact, in the dystopian works of Kafka, Witkiewicz, and most specifically of Abram Tertz Sinyavski? Does Life indeed imitate Art? Should one take Oscar Wilde seriously? Or does the writer of this region have antennae more sensitive than most of the rest of humanity when it comes to extrapolating from the tragic past and present to the tragic future?

We have seen Tertz-Sinyavski foreshadow his own future with uncanny precision. We should also note, however, that the fate of the writer character in *The Trial Begins* is far from personal or private. In fact, the writer's figure in the novel is as shadowlike and faceless as that of the two plaincothesmen, Vitya and Tolya, who represent his Nemesis, as if we were watching an allegorical presentation of a ritual drama between the freedom of speech and the oppressive censorship of dictatorship. The real dramatic focus, the real protagonist, is not Serjozha, not the Jewish doctor, and not even the writer, but the Book itself. The writer is, *ex officio*, the creator and custodian of the manuscript, and his fate is important primarily, if not only, in connection with that.

Indeed, the manuscript had already been portrayed as the central character in Bulgakov's *Master and Margarita*, a novel published decades after its writer's death, but its motto well known even before its publication: even tyranny cannot destroy the power of the word: "manuscripts do not burn."

The case of Solzhenitsin, whose manuscript of *The Gulag Archipel-ago* was confiscated by the KGB, makes abundantly clear that in a one-party system the uncensored manuscript is considered the only kind of possible opposition; hence the great fear of the authorities of this manuscript, which, being forced underground, is in effect elevated to the status of a quasi-religious object.

Given the cat-and-mouse game between the KGB and the subversive writer in the Soviet system, one could say that in his 1959 novel Tertz Sinyavski's prediction of his own fate simply refers to the fate of any writer with the courage to voice his opinion. Vassily Grossman, for example, author of *Life and Fate*, considered by many critics the true *War and Peace* of this century, delivered his manuscript to the journal *Znamya* in 1960, but the editors handed it over to the Central Committee, who returned it to the author with a note that it was "anti-Soviet." In a year two KGB officers arrived in Grossman's home and confiscated not only the manuscript but "even sheets of used carbon paper and typewriter ribbons."[10] In fact, they behaved very much like the two plainclothesmen who are able to make the letters vanish from the written page in the "Prelude" to Sinyavski's work of fiction.

But if we concentrate on the fate of the manuscript and not on its old and devastated author, there is also something positive in this story. Years after Grossman's death, a microfilm copy of the manuscript was smuggled abroad by another dissident writer, Voinovich. Voinovich's dystopian novel *Moscow 2042* (1986) makes reference to such an incident with a satirical twist: Here the writer-protagonist smuggles back a disk including the *œuvre* of another dissident writer *into* Moscow.

Writing in the era of Khruschov, whose moods fluctuated between the urge to condemn Stalin and his own fear of too much liberalism, Tertz Sinyavski must naturally have been aware of the potentially tremendous impact of his manuscript published abroad, and of his own dangerous situation. One could even say that in his *Lyubimov* (also known as *The Makepeace Experiment*, and published abroad at the same time) the author anticipates the ensuing attack on writers such as Grossman, Joseph Brodsky, Voinovich, and himself when the narrator of that novel announces: "The investigation continues. Any moment there will be a new wave of arrests. If they search the house and find the manuscript under the floorboards, they will punish every single one of us. Will you hide the wretched book away for the time being?" (192)

Once more, the power of prophecy seems uncanny; yet the scenario is simply the ritualistic enactment of the perennial conflict between the shadowlike Secret Police and the equally shadowlike writer – a scenario central to the ritual drama in a dystopic society. In the words of

Czeslaw Milosz, "the fact that [Sinyavski] has decided to have his work published abroad shows his belief in the importance of what he has to say ... He knows full well the risk he runs should the authorities identify him as the author, while at the same time the preservation of his anonymity means that he can acquire neither fame nor money, even if his work is translated into many languages ... He lives in a state which forbids writers to publish without permission, and which regards violation of this rule as tantamount to ... treason."[11]

We began this discussion with three dates: 1959, the writing of *The Trial Begins*; 1953, the setting of the novel; and 1966, the author's trial, following his arrest and preceding his seven-year conviction for writing the novel. Unlike the Western writer of dystopia, in *The Trial Begins* Abram Tertz-Sinyavski describes not the future but the recent past, analysing the mechanism of rigged trials that no work of fiction had quite dared to analyse with the same boldness before him. Like any subversive writer in a dictatorship, he is in a unique position to foretell the tragic personal consequences of the act of writing, yet he is undeterred in his commitment.

It is the biographical fact of such exceptional courage demanded from writers living in the dystopic nightmare state where the Book itself is regarded as subversive that Zamiatin, Huxley, Orwell, Bradbury, and Atwood turned into one of the classic themes of the speculative genre of dystopia: what D-503, John Savage, Winston Smith, Guy Montag, and Atwood's Offred have in common is that they reflect each writer's own commitment to be the keeper of the Book – Shakespeare and the Bible, the fiction of the past, the protagonist's record of his or her own life; it is through making these characters psychologically credible that the writers of dystopian fiction evoke the reader's sympathy for the cause – freedom of expression – and warn against the dangers of dictatorship.

DYSTOPIA EAST AND WEST: THE FATE OF THE CHILD

In addition to the structural-thematic principle of the trial and the tragic fate of the writer-protagonist, is there another thematic common denominator shared by between Eastern and Western versions of dystopia? As we have noted in passing, the loss or the destruction of a child or teenaged youth is a recurring theme expressing the failure of the death-bound dystopic society, both in the East and in the West. The interaction between the satiric and the tragic dimensions in the exploration of this theme is also worth a closer look in each area.

Dystopian society evokes the horror of a nightmare. Approaching this horror psychologically, we should keep in mind that what most people would probably find the most harrowing experience would be to watch helplessly while children, reminders of our own helplessness and innocence as well as our instinct for the survival of our species, are exposed to danger – murder, abandonment, torture, or slaughter. There are examples of this horror in the Bible, in the murder of the Hebrew children at the birth of Moses and the slaughter of the innocents at the birth of Jesus; and in Greek mythology, in the exposure to death, with ankles pierced and tied together, of the newborn Oedipus at the mountainside of Cithareon. Of course, the fact that these incidents form an archetypally significant part in the birth of the hero, the mythical Saviour of his age or community, who incidentally overcomes these threats to his young life, does not lessen the horrifying effect of these acts. To evoke horror at the overwhelming menace of a nightmare society, it seems natural for the writer of dystopian fiction to introduce a helpless child or a still immature, innocent teenager as a victim, even a martyr, sacrificed to a monstrous state machine.

The child or the concept of childhood can also play a signficant role in the dystopian novel as social satire, when, for example, it shows that the mentality the ruling elite has prescribed for the masses is in fact the mentality of suggestible children. The inhabitants of Zamiatin's, Huxley's, and Orwell's nightmare societies are kept at the level of infantile dependence on the state embodied by the Dictator, ostensibly the archetype of the benevolent Wise Man but ultimately that of the Terrible Father.

Zamiatin, Huxley, Orwell, Bradbury, and Atwood are equally aware of the dual importance of the child character in establishing a satirical context for social criticism, and in evoking the tragic dimension of the hypothetical society in the future.

Huxley's World State ensures stability by producing five castes of children on the biological assembly line. Children in each group are subjected to a meticulously designed conditioning process appropriate to their caste, to make sure that no child will have the freedom to experience childhood and youth as a period of individuation, the awakening of the private self. John Savage, the teenaged outsider who regarded London as the "brave new world" of his childhood dreams of Paradise, commits suicide at the end of the novel. In a time warp between the Reservation (our distant and horrifying past) and the London of 651 AF (our distant and equally horrifying future), he is prevented from reaching maturity. But immaturity also happens to be characteristic of the rest of the childlike population of the World State: even the Alpha-pluses spend their entire life in infantile dependence on the Mastermind of the World Controller. As if kept in test-tubes for life, they are unable to "break through" to a comprehension of the self, of free will, of reality beyond the World State.

The corruption of childhood innocence, the fate of the child martyr, and the regression of an entire population to a mental state of protracted childhood also play an important role in Orwell's Oceania. Through the "Underground" of his dreams, Winston comes to remember that as a ten-year-old child he stole the last piece of chocolate from his starving mother, who was holding her dying baby daughter against her body. In fact the tableau of mother and child becomes an enigma tormenting the adult Winston until he realizes that there is only one way to redeem himself for the childhood betrayal of his nearest and dearest; it is by remaining loyal to Julia. When in Room 101 he is compelled to betray Julia also, Winston's old self is broken: newly born from that horrible womb, the Ministry of Love, Winston is reborn with coarse pink features, hanging on to his gin bottle – he becomes a creature who rejects any flashbacks to private feelings as "false memories." Only now is he able to return to the parental breast of Big Brother – in fact a monstrous, tyrannical father – with the emotions of a repentant prodigal son: "He loved Big Brother." In other words, Winston by the end is also reduced to the childlike level of the mass mentality where he no longer has an autonomous adult self, private memory, or a private conscience.

In *Fahrenheit 451* and *Player Piano*, each protagonist lives in a childless, barren marriage; society is unable to renew itself. In *The Handmaid's Tale* the United States faces a crisis whereby it is unable to reproduce itself biologically, and the theocracy of Gilead, a violent and death-bound society, can do little to change the situation.

The tragic figure of the child plays a role equally dramatic in the dystopian fiction of the East, the more so since here the nightmarish society of state tyranny is not a futuristic projection; it has become a *fait accompli*. In Zazubrin's "The Chip" (1923) and Rodionov's *Chocolate* the protagonists abandon their children to a dangerous world so that they can dedicate all their energies to the cause. In "The Chip," in Srubin's troubled mind the images of his own wife and his child are washed away by a hallucinatory vision of the revolution as a gigantic peasant woman, whose "womb was swollen from the child She carries, and from the hunger She endured. She is covered in wounds and blood – Her own as well as that of Her enemies ... watching the world with vigilant, hate-filled eyes" (69).

Ribakov's *The Children of the Arbat* focuses on the harrowing trial and Siberian exile of a young Communist, Serjozha; in Tertz's the *Trial Begins* Prosecutor Golub sacrifices his own teenaged son and does not interfere on his behalf to save him from trial and forced labour. The young boy's girlfriend is trampled to death by a fanatical crowd at the funeral of the dictator; the Prosecutor's child from his second wife, Maria, is aborted.

The miscarriage of the promise of the "radiant future" is acted out, once more, under most tragic circumstances in Zinoviev's *The Radiant Future,* where the protagonist's teenage daughter, Lena, commits suicide when she finds out about her own father's utter moral corruption. In Marek Hlasko's *Graveyard* Frantisek, a "true believer," is expelled from the Party. When his daughter has to pay the customary price of being expelled from the university, her "politically correct" fiancé also abandons her, and the young girl commits suicide. Her father is left to face the bleak image of the formerly promising Communist future as a "graveyard." Tibor Déry's *Mr G.A in X* also demonstrates the deathbound spirit of the nightmare society of X through the suicide of the young. Beautiful young Elizabeth refuses her lover's plea to flee the nightmare city with him because she feels the irresistible compulsion, with the rest of the population, to participate in the regularly recurring Big Excursion, a ritual of mass suicide of old and young alike.

Probably the most compelling example of the writer's society as a dystopia that devours the lifeblood of its own children is Platonov's *Foundation Pit.* At the site of the gigantic work pit dug to serve as the foundation for a new dwelling for the entire proletariat, the workers come upon a starving woman dying of disease. She leaves behind her little girl, Natalia. The workers take her under their wings and cherish her as someone who will become "a de facto inhabitant of socialism." When, weakened by starvation and cold, Natalia also dies, with her dies the hope for the foundation pit: the dream of a collective utopian future turns into the burial-ground both for the present and for future generations.

Undoubtedly, the fate of the child and the concept of childhood play a dramatic role in the Western representatives of the genre. Yet here it follows from the writer's clear distinction between the two time-planes of present and future that we are expected to distance ourselves from the emotional impact of the characters' tragic fate, as if saying to ourselves, "This work of fiction is only a hypothesis about our future; something that has not happened yet, something that still could, and should be prevented from happening."

By contrast, the works conveying a dystopian vision written in the East under totalitarianism offer no similar distancing mechanism to readers.[12] Here we are not given a chance to step back from the tragic ending by saying that this was merely a hypothesis, and possibly also an exaggeration, to wake up from the nightmare of history. Unaffected by the distancing mechanism inherent in the speculative structure, here the fate of the child assumes the dimension of tragic reality; in fact, it assumes the note of a dirge over the lost hope in socialism, that long-awaited offspring of the revolution that was to act out our century's version of the archetypal drama of the birth of the mythical hero or saviour.

It is the fate of the children and youth in the novels here examined
– imprisonment, forced labour, death, suicide – that conveys the dystopian writers' loss of hope in the feasibility of this utopian future,
their loss of faith not only in the original dream of socialism but also
in its chances for renewal or rebirth.

DYSTOPIA EAST AND WEST:
A MODERNIST GENRE
AND ITS POSTMODERN CRITICS

To find an even more comprehensive common denominator for the
dystopian impulse in the East and the West, probably we should look
at the fundamentally dystopic or anti-utopian tendencies of contemporary post-Marxist, post-Soviet, postmodern criticism. Two significant books have appeared in the past few years on the subject. In his
1992 *The Dystopian Impulse in Modern Literature: Fiction as Social
Criticism* M. Keith Booker takes an overview of dystopian works in
the West; he also includes several Soviet dystopian novels from
Zinoviev, Aksynov, and Voinovich. Welcoming the resurgence of political fiction, Booker does not raise the question of thematic or structural
variations due to the difference between writers who project their fear
of the totalitarian regime into the future and those who write about
existing conditions based on first-hand experience of dictatorship. In
her 1993 *Russian Experimental Fiction: Resisting Ideology after
Utopia* Edith Clowes deals exclusively with the Soviet Union, with the
post-Stalin years, focusing on aesthetic experimentation in the fiction
of Tertz, Daniel, Aksynov, Zinoviev, and Voinovich, among others,
whose works she describes as "metautopias." In her view meta-utopia
offers a wider range of imaginative possibilities than the Western
tradition of anti-utopian and dystopian fiction. In fact she suggests that
works in the dystopian genre tend to direct us towards a "nostalgic
revision of some past age" until they "deconstruct utopian schemes,
only to abandon the notion of beneficial social imagination."[13]

But is Clowes right in her assessment of the classics of the dystopian
genre? Of course, it is true that the protagonist in Orwell's *Nineteen
Eighty-four*, for example, feels compelled to reconstruct his past
through memory, to return to his childhood with his mother, to
remember a time where the distinction between private and public life
was not yet eliminated. As he gradually comes to understand, this was
a world with private feelings, private loyalties, a private conscience –
a world drastically different from the dehumanized nightmare society
under total state control in 1984. Winston feels that only by remembering a past that was more human than the world he is living in will

he ever have a chance to hope that, in spite of the slogans, the Party is not eternal. However, Winston's compulsion to return to the private universe of his childhood is not reducible to Orwell's nostalgia for the past. If we read Goldstein's Book at the end of part 2, with its account of the rising totalitarian mentality among the rulers and the ruled in the 1930s and the 1940s, it becomes crystal clear that Orwell is not encouraging us to return to the past for a political model; he makes it eminently clear that the political realities of Winston's childhood years in the late forties marked a time of political and spiritual confusion. In fact, it was the condoning of the totalitarian mentality at that time that allowed the ruthless elite of the Inner Party to come to power in the fifties and sixties. At no point does Orwell cast a nostalgic look at the past or urge us to "abandon the notion of ... the social imagination." On the contrary, it is essential to the strategies of the political satire to make us realize that the nightmarish world of the hypothetical 1984 in the future is *the direct effect* of the political choices made by the Ideal Reader's generation in 1948, at the time Orwell was writing the novel.

Neither is Huxley's Reservation, the world of our past, presented with nostalgia, although it is a counterpoint to the dehumanized World State six hundred years into our future. The satirist presents the Savage with two equally unacceptable extremes and thereby makes the reader actively search for a third, more viable alternative.

Nor does Zamiatin's green world of the Mefis outside the glass dome of the One State beckon with the promise of a return to an idealized past. If the green world behind the wall is indeed an escape route for some of the malcontents under the glass dome, it is so simply because it represents a condition of freedom from the uncanny stasis of the One State, the nightmare world of pure reason. We may turn to the green world to tap the resources of our natural instincts and passions, but only so that we can return to society, awaiting its revolutionary renewal and revitalization.

In fact, what Frye defined as the "militant irony" of satire, which "assumes [norms and] standards against which the grotesque and the absurd are measured," is inextricably intertwined with the moral imagination required to criticize and improve the present world. Dystopian satire, in most cases, is what Frye described as satire of the "moral type," where the norm consists of "a serious vision of society as a single intellectual pattern, in other words a Utopia."[14]

I believe both Clowes and Booker overlook or deliberately ignore the satirical impulse in the social imagination, an impulse just as significant in criticizing the social-political pathology of the writer's own society in the present in dystopian as it is in utopian fiction. Of

course, this is not merely an oversight. Both Clowes and Booker rely
on many of the concepts and much of the terminology of Mikhail
Bakhtin, taking for granted that Bakhtin's approach, with its emphasis
on the carnivalesque – the valorization of the dialogic versus the
monologic authorial voice, of the ambivalence of playfulness, of the
laughter of open-ended parody – is invariably the best approach when
examining *any* work of literature. Yet, as Caryl Emerson warns us, in
their attempt to "get a responsible politics out of Bakhtinian carnival,"[14] Western critics often tend to disregard the context of Bakhtin's
interpretation of social change and power. As George Hyde also points
out, Bakhtin's "dialogic principle [is] a phrase widely misunderstood
and misapplied in the Anglo-Saxon world," mainly because the Western critic tends to overlook the fact that Bakhtin's "'coded' writing
was intended to defy Stalinism, and when he makes extensive play
with the concept of 'carnivalization,' the suspension and subversion of
cultural codes, we should probably remember the cultural political
context of the Stalin years his theory was in defiance of."[16] More
specifically, we should also realize, as Léna Szilárd's excellent study
points out, that the place and value of satire is extremely problematic
in Bakhtin's theory because in his view "the unambiguously 'serious
laughter' of satire ... divides the world into two polarities – one of them
validated, the other denied – carnivalesque laughter does not know
about absolute denial or absolute affirmation."[17] In fact, what Bakhtin
sees as the "reduced forms of laughter, sarcasm, irony, and especially
satire, are often positioned in an antagonistic position with the principles of the carnivalesque, the ambivalent." It is precisely this antagonistic positioning, Szilárd points out helpfully, "that explains
Bakhtin's lack of understanding for the writers of the Enlightenment,
among them Voltaire,"[18] who, we should remember, happened to excel
in the genre of satire. As insightful as Bakhtin's response to the truly
"monological" dictatorial voice behind Socialist Realism may be, the
critic today should probably be careful to use his or her own discretion
and enter into "dialogue" with Bakhtin himself, especially when examining works, writers, or genres where Bakhtin's approach is not particularly illuminating. If, according to Bakhtin, "satire provides a
savage mockery of its subject, while carnivalesque laughter opens up
the dialectically dual truth of the universe," does it follow that we should
simply send to oblivion such dystopian satirists as Swift, Voltaire,
Zamiatin, Huxley, and Orwell, for example? Or, in another and to me
equally unacceptable response to this dilemma, should we simply choose
to examine the genre of dystopian fiction by overlooking one of its
most significant attributes, its satirical dimension? And since Bakhtin's

bias in this instance is quite clear, should we take his "monological" verdict about the inferiority of the "serious laughter" of satire and the superiority of the "carnivalesque laughter [that] does not know absolute denial or absolute affirmation"[19] as an article of faith?

When advocating "carnivalesque laughter" because it is "permeated by ambivalence," Bakhtin's postmodern followers should probably be asked to recall that the celebration of ambivalence or the indefinite parameters of meaning is not altogether a novelty in twentieth-century criticism. William Empson's *Seven Types of Ambiguity* (1947) comes close to affirming, even celebrating, the concept of ambiguity as a psychological indicator of particular stresspoints in the text that reveal what he calls "the hidden riches" of the controversial – often the most interesting – areas in a particular author's vision of reality. Empson also notes the antagonism of some critics in his own time who reject this concept of ambiguity or the "puzzle as to what the author meant" because they "do not like to recognize this concept they connect with depth Psychology."[20]

Empson's position suggests that ambiguity in the text draws the reader's attention to the complexity of a particular dilemma the writer has had difficulty coming to terms with. This concept of ambiguity also implies that in literature words, lines, entire works are expected to reveal meaning, and this meaning is often multi-dimensional. By contrast, there is a tendency in postmodern criticism to turn to Bakhtin as one of the authorities on the legitimization of the "ambivalence" of language in general. Their position implies that ambivalence should be equated with the futility of trying to define a text's central meaning, or meaning as such. While Empson's modernist approach to "ambiguity" acts as an invitation to the reader to join the critic in "puzzling out" a complex meaning, the postmodern critic's approach to "ambivalence" implies that, if a text reveals contradictions (as complex texts do), we should give up any attempt at old-fashioned "explication" – that is, at the exploration or interpretation of meaning. Insisting that language is, by definition, subversive of meaning seems to me particularly counterproductive when analysing dystopian literature, or indeed documentary descriptions of a dystopic society, where cynical obfuscation of the language in the interests of state propaganda is one of the most sinister strategies of the ruling elite. To say that one has to be extremely vigilant in observing how easily language can become the means of propagating lies – the warning implied in dystopian literature – is quite radically different from the position of some postmodern criticism, which argues that any language, anywhere and at any time, is deceptive. In fact this difference between the pessimistic shrug of postmodern criticism about *any* society stands in radical opposition to the impulse for political and social criticism informing the most powerful works of dystopian satire.

No doubt Bakhtin is right in drawing attention to the polarization inherent in the satirist's strategy; there is indeed a polarization between the irrational world of reality and the unstated "norm" of sanity and reason implied in satire. However, if great satire is rarely that "reduced form" of laughter that Bakhtin suggests, this is probably due precisely to the fact that the satirist's norm of sanity and reason is merely implied and not explicitly stated. It is by puzzling out this hidden, implied norm that readers are able to recognize the topsy-turvy logic, the irrationality, and the moral corruption of their own society, the society that is being criticized, and are therefore able to identify the object of the satire.

Undoubtedly, the "fun" suggested by political and social satire does not derive from the Dyonisian overflow Bakhtin associates with the laughter of carnival. To go even further, I would venture that when it comes to the laughter of carnival, both Swift and Voltaire, for example, would identify this with the land of Cockaigne, the archetypal dream of a fool's paradise. If we take a closer look at the crowd scenes not only in the works of Zamiatin, Huxley, and Orwell but also in what Clowes would identify as the "metautopian" novels of Abram Tertz Sinyavski, Julij Daniel, and Vladimir Voinovich, the group behaviour of the crowd in action demonstrates more of a brutal threat than a naïvely joyous or liberating promise to our humanity. In fact, in Tertz's *The Makepeace Experiment* it becomes clear that the dictator who comes to power by promising bread and circuses can succeed precisely by his "hypnotic" power over the mindless population of Lyubimov – that is, by knowing how to offer carnivalesque "fun" to the masses until they are deceived to the point of drinking water as if it were champagne and sampling toothpaste as if it were delicious caviar.

If we are looking for the "fun" offered by satire, even in the case of grim dystopian satire, we should probably settle for the fun of a game with stakes set up for a treasure hunt – the "hidden riches" of complex meaning responding to such timeless questions as: What does it mean to be human? What does it mean to be an animal capable of reason? And what does it mean to live in a society where we are deprived of the right to ask such questions?

It would be, I believe, regrettable to approach dystopian fiction without taking note of the strategies of political satire, whether we are studying the genre in the West or in the East. It may also be worth pointing out that the presence of a structural-philosophical "norm" or "standard" implied by satire is not contradictory to advocating a political system of pluralism. In *Moscow 2042*, for example, Voinovich uses the classical strategies of political satire when he juxtaposes a fanatical society of Communists with an equally fanatical society of right-wing extremists, and implies that only a tolerant pluralist society would be able to forestall the tragic consequences of either left- or right-wing forms of fanaticism.

Having observed that the works of dystopian fiction go back and forth between the tragic and the satirical perspectives of the aberrant society they are depicting, one is left to ponder whether the reluctance of the postmodern sensibility to acknowledge the strategies of satire does not also extend to a reluctance to address the tragic dimension as well. Taking a look at Sophocles' *Oedipus Rex* or, in our century, at works of Russian or Soviet literature by Pasternak, Solzhenitzyn, or Vasilij Grossman, for example, we find that works with a tragic vision deal invariably with irrevocable loss, but they also confer value on what is lost in the course of the tragic action. It is impossible to perceive the sustaining power and spiritual worth of Juliet's sacrificial love for Romeo, or Cordelia's love for Lear, without acknowledging a humanistic standard of moral-spiritual values. This humanistic standard – essential for the appreciation of both satire and tragedy – is something postmodern thought often rejects on the grounds that the values of humanism are too general, too abstract, or ahistorical. But postmodern criticism of literature itself tends to be extremely ahistorical. Neither Booker's political analysis nor Clowes's excellent aesthetic insights into the novels she approaches as "metautopias" intend to illuminate the historical moment in which the work they analyse was written, or the issues, problems, and values particular to that moment.[21]

It seems to me nevertheless extremely important to observe the increased interest the postmodern movement takes in the genre of dystopia, an interest most likely connected with the generally dystopic mood of such influential thinkers as Foucault, for example, who tends to see any society as a hellscape. Yet it is precisely because they tend to regard our entire civilization as dystopic that postmodern critics do not bother to search for the target of the particular writer's social-political criticism, which, I believe, constitutes the vital impetus for dystopian fiction. Maybe we should recall here that Dante defines the realm beyond the Gate of Hell as the region of those souls who had "lost the good of the intellect." It seems to me that when many a postmodern critic deliberately yields up "the good of the intellect" by arguing against any meaning whatsoever, he not only deliberately joins the damned but also invites us to concede that our entire world is, has been, and remains to be nothing but a hellscape. But if the whole world is inevitably a dystopian hellscape, why should we single out and try to forestall the further development of any particularly harmful trend in our society? If the whole civilized world is, by definition, already a prison, a madhouse, a concentration camp, is there any point in fighting against the rise of that most dangerous form of government, totalitarian dictatorship? To regard our entire civilization as "the worst of all possible worlds" implies that all societies are inherently dystopic, and this ultimately means admitting the utmost futility of social and political criticism. (One is reminded here of Arthur Koestler's argument with his long-term opponent, the self-deceived leftist intellectual in the West, who argued that if we observe the flaws of Western democracy, we should see that the flaws of Stalin's regime are neither better nor worse. In Koestler's view, his opponent committed the fallacy of equating the common cold with leprosy.)

It is at this point also interesting to note a curious parallel. The principles of Socialist Realism introduced in the USSR in 1934 and reinforced there and in the satellite countries in the late 1940s claimed to define a literary code in relation to the allegedly utopian purpose of the regime. All works of art were to be "realistic" in their style and optimistic in their content, based on an unquestioning faith in the future of Communism. Consequently, the mainstream of literature was to be pressed into service by the state-defined utopia, and became an expression of a utopian literature *ex officio*. Yet, under the aegis of Socialist Realism very few truly utopian works of the speculative imagination were created. By the same token, our postmodern age has a tendency to deal with all societies as dystopic, and to regard the lack of reason, the lack of fixed and communicable meaning in language as a given, a general condition of our human predicament. Yet precisely because the postmodern sensibility tends towards moral relativism and a pessimistic dismissal of the search for meaning, it is probably neither conducive to the writing of dystopian fiction of the impact of *We*, *Nineteen Eighty-four*, or *Brave New World* nor in tune with the critical appreciation of this genre that combines the dimensions of tragedy and political satire.

One sometimes wonders whether some historian in the future will not find a strict cause-effect relationship between the cynicism, bitterness, and moral and aesthetic relativism of the postmodern sensibility and the cynicism, bitterness, and moral relativism of our post-Marxist, post-Soviet, and to many our post-socialist political climate. Or maybe the postmodern sensibility, with its "deconstruction" of all meaning and all values, functions precisely as a psychological defence mechanism, so that we do not have to deal with the bewildering "meaning" of a phenomenon that stares us in the face: our post-Christian century's central experience of the loss of faith in our salvation by society, after the true face of state Dictatorship was revealed under the mask of Messianism.

Ultimately, dystopian fiction is probably a typically "modern" as opposed to a "postmodern" genre. The modern artist still bewails the loss of reason, emotion, individuality, and meaning; conseqently he or she still has the energies to criticize topsy-turvy societies in the name of the satirist's hidden "norm" of sanity; to criticize, in the name of individual freedom, societies that enslave their subjects; to criticize, in the name of the unhampered search for truth, societies that are built on the deliberate untruth of propaganda; to criticize, in the name of justice, societies with a machinery for deliberately miscarrying justice.

Notes

INTRODUCTION

1 Max J. Patrick suggests that "the opposite of eutopia, the ideal society, [is] a dystopia, if it is permissible to coin a word." Negley and Patrick, eds., *The Quest for Utopia* (1952).
2 Clowes, *Russian Experimental Fiction*, 4, 32.
3 A further distinction we may want to look at is the difference between dystopia and anti-utopia. According to Gary Saul Morson, "whereas utopias describe an escape from history, ... anti-utopias describe an escape, or attempted escape, to history, which is to say, to the world of contingency, conflict and uncertainty" (128). Yet some of the works Morson categorizes as "anti-utopias" others would categorize as dystopias. Clearly the anti-utopian and the dystopic may overlap.
   In his *Dystopian Literature: A Theory and Research Guide*, for example, M. Keith Booker suggests that "dystopian literature is specifically that literature which situates itself in direct opposition to utopian thought" (3), while Edith Clowes in her *Russian Experimental Fiction* states that "the term anti-utopian refers to a philosophy or worldview critical of positive utopian schemes. The term dystopia refers to a novelistic form of narrative that depicts a bad place, or 'dys-topia'" (10). For futher distinctions see Arthur O. Lewis's excellent essay, "The Anti-Utopian Novel."
4 Lyman Tower Sargent, in his "The Three Faces of Utopianism Revisited," gives the following definition: "Dystopia or negative utopia – a non-existent society described in considerable detail and normally located in time and space that the author intended a contemporaneous reader to view as criticism of that contemporary society." For a discussion of dystopia as a primarily mental construct, see Dennis Rohatyn's "Hell and Dystopia."

5 As M. Keith Booker points out, "Foucault reverses Pope to argue that whatever is is wrong, and he sees his role as a radical opponent of the 'system'; regardless of what system that might be [he] argues the need to oppose the existing order of society, but refuses to propose an alternative order as the goal of this opposition ... Foucault's emphasis on continual change arises from an intense sense of cultural crisis that might be termed 'dystopian' more rightly than utopian, embodying a fundamental suspicion of any and all idealized visions of society"(*The Dystopian Impulse*, 15). To demonstrate Booker's point, let me refer to Foucault's statement in *Discipline and Punish* that "prisons resemble factories, schools, barracks, hospitals, which all resemble prisons" (228). To say that society is an enormous prison camp – both within and without the barbed wire – is one of the strongest criticisms directed by the writers of dystopian fiction at a monster society that cannot – and should not – be accepted as normal (see, for example, Vassilij Grossman's *Life and Fate*). For Foucault any society, as it were quite naturally, exists under these conditions.

6 Hamvas "Poeta Sacer," *A Láthatatlan Történet*, 112; my trans.

7 For a discussion of this problem, see Kamenka, "Marxismus és politika," 37–9 (my trans.); and Hannah Arendt's *On Revolution*, 54–5.

8 Camus, *Actuelles II*, 48–52.

9 In "The Mechanism of Paranoia" Sigmund Freud suggests that "megalomania can by itself constitute a paranoia" (*Three Case Histories*, 175).

10 The public scrutiny of the most intimate details of President Clinton's private life conducted by a ruthless "Starr Chamber," the coercing of mother to testify against her own daughter, friend against friend, working associate against working associate is an alarming sign in the direction taken, or at least tolerated by, American society.

11 The 1986 version of *Hamlet* was directed by Kenneth Branagh, with Branagh in the title role.

12 The mechanism to establish the distinction between these two time planes – the World State of 651 AF and the London of the 1930s – is the Director's lecture about the past, which he delivers in many instalments to a group of eager students. Except for these lectures, these young people will stay cut off from all records of the past. The Director's only purpose in talking about the past is to convince them that the world of 651 AF is far superior to all the societies that ever existed – a major tenet of the state religion.

   The juxtaposition of the values of the present and the past is carried on by the characters throughout the novel, as a kind of debate between the utopian and dystopian aspects of technological progress. Finally, all these debates culminate in a "duel of ideas" between the Savage and the World Controller at the trial scene in chapters 15 and 16, the intellectual climax of the novel.

13 Stites, *Revolutionary Dreams*, 236, 229.

14 Philip Roth edited a series of translations from Eastern and Central Europe under the title "The Other Europe."

15 One should only mention Stanislaw Witkiewicz's *Insatiability,* an intriguing novel that foresaw, in 1929, Poland's catastrophe in 1939, and his dystopian plays, such as *The Shoemaker.* The Czech Kafka's *The Trial, The Castle,* and *In the Penal Colony* foreshadow the totalitarian nightmare more than a decade before its appearance, while Karel Capek's *RUR* and *War with the Newts* examine impending social catastrophe in the guise of science fiction. In Hungary, Frigyes Karinthy's *Travels to Faremido* and *Capillaria* are satirical fantasies in the framework of the Gulliveriad, and Sándor Szathmári's *Kazohinia* also belongs to this genre. Szathmári's *In Vain* is a dystopian novel speculating about the defeat of utopian aspirations throughout history – acknowledging the influence of Karinthy and Imre Madách's philosophical drama, *The Tragedy of Man.*

16 Zamiatin, for example, could have read "Valery Bryusov's *Republic of the Southern Cross,* written in 1905 ... about a metropolis of 50 million beneath a glass dome," as well as Nikolai Fedorov's *An Evening in the Year 2217* of 1906, about a society wherein citizens wear numbers on their arms and register for "sex-choosing sessions." (Stites, *Revolutionary Dreams*, chap. 1.)

17 Esslin, *Brief Chronicles*, 155.

18 For a more thorough discussion of this question, see Lanin, "Images of Woman in Russian Anti-Utopian Literature," 646–55; Gasiorowska, *Women in Soviet Fiction*; and her *Russian and Polish Women's Fiction* (1985), ed. and trans. Goscilio, and *Fruits of Her Plume: Essays on Contemporary Russian Women's Culture* (1998), ed. Goscilio.

19 Kumar, *Utopia and Anti-Utopia in Modern Times*, 124.

CHAPTER ONE

1 More, *Utopia*, 130.

2 Ibid.

3 For the connection between the fear of unprecedented technological advancement in modern warfare and the development of dystopian fiction, see Ignatius Fiedorow Clarke's *Voices Prophesying War.* For the "use of utopian [and dystopian] fiction as a means of influencing the political attitudes of the general public ... which had become signally important in party politics" in Germany, for example, see Samson B. Knoll's valuable study on "Socialism as Dystopia," analysing the findings of Claus Ritter's *Start nach Utopolis. Eine Zukunfts-Nostalgie* (1980).

4 Plato, *Republic, Book X* (ed. Bate), 48.

5 Steiner, *The Death of Tragedy*, 7–8.
6 Gorky's position is interesting to examine in this context. In the words of Robert Elliott, "at a writers' conference in Moscow in the early 30s André Malraux caused consternation by rising to ask: 'What happens in a classless society when a streetcar runs over a beautiful girl?' Gorky was hauled out of sickbed to deliver the answer, arrived at after long debate: in a planned classless (and hence perfect) society, a streetcar would not run over a beautiful girl." Quoted in Elliott, *The Shape of Utopia*, 105.
7 Frye, *Anatomy of Criticism*, 215.
8 Steiner, *The Death of Tragedy*, 305.
9 Ibid. 14.
10 Frye, *Anatomy of Criticism*, 215.
11 Steiner, *The Death of Tragedy*, 10.
12 Gottlieb, *The Orwell Conundrum*, 273.
13 Popper, *The Poverty of Historicism*, 73–4.
14 Djilas, from *The Unperfect Society*, quoted by György Litván, "Mi Kommunisták Különös Emberek Vagyunk," 150; my trans.
15 Litván, "Mi Kommunisták Különös Emberek Vagyunk," 152; my trans.
16 Popper, *Conjectures and Refutations*, 358.
17 Arendt, *Totalitarianism*, 168–9.
18 Popper, *Conjectures and Refutations*, 360.
19 Ibid., 360.
20 Popper, *The Open Society and Its Enemies*, 166.
21 Bracher, "The Disputed Concept of Totalitarianism," 30.
22 Stites, *Revolutionary Dreams*, 247.
23 Orwell, "Wells, Hitler and the World State," *Collected Essays, Journalism and Letters* (hereafter CEJL), 2:170.
24 Ibid.
25 Ibid.
26 Orwell, "Inside the Whale," CEJL, 1:564, 3:387–8.
27 Talmon, *The Origins of Totalitarian Democracy*, 254.
28 Lifton, "Death and History," 215.
29 Eliade, *Occultism, Witchcraft and Cultural Fashions*, 45.
30 Arendt, *Totalitarianism*, 25, 176.

CHAPTER TWO

1 Sándor Hevesi, the director of the Hungarian National Theatre between 1922 and 1933, considered the play the "Bible of the National Theatre."
2 For the stage history of Madách's play, see Tamás Koltai's *Az Ember Tragédiája a Szinpadon (1933–1968)*.

3 Abram Tertz Sinyavski, in his *The Trial Begins*, gives an ironic portrayal of the young protagonist Serjozha, who wants to return to an
egalitarian society where there is no coercion – and then adds that whoever disagrees with his non-violent principles will be shot. "Beware! You
might hurt the feelings of your fellow man! ... Those who did would be
shot" (60).

4 It is interesting that in arguing against the "clericalism" of the play,
prominent Marxist critics, including George Lukács, failed to take note
of this point at all. Banning the performance of the play between 1947
and 1954, they had a fourfold argument:

First, staged in the Hevesi tradition as a mystery play, *The Tragedy of
Man* had been successful in Nazi Germany and in Horthy's Hungary.
How could a work appreciated by these reactionary forces also be
appreciated in Communist Hungary?

The second consideration related to the play itself, its reflection of
Madách's historical pessimism – a mental attitude simply unthinkable for
those labouring in the optimistic straitjacket of Socialist Realism.
Authors had to resolve any historical question according to the Marxist
vision of Paradise Regained at the end of the dialectic process, in Communism. The wheel had come full circle: Marxism, which was to overthrow the limitations of the age of faith, had produced another faith.
And we should recall that in an age of faith, no tragedy is possible.

Third, doctrinaire Marxist critics also objected to the negative role
Madách attributed to the masses. Milthiades in the Athenian scene, the
heretics in the Constantinople scene, and Danton in the scene of the
French Revolution fall victim to destructive, primitive mass hysteria.
According to Marxist criticism, the people were to be represented,
under all circumstances, as the driving force behind historical change –
and of course, ultimately, historical change as such was to be seen as
progressive.

Fourth, the Marxist critic who opposed the staging of *The Tragedy*
objected most specifically to Madách's negative presentation of socialism
in the Phalanstery scene, although some also argued that since Madách
was dealing with "utopian socialism," the scene was an unrecognizable
caricature of true socialism, and as such it could bear no resemblance to
the socialism practised in the Soviet bloc. Still, the set in the 1937
Hamburg performance used Cyrillic letters to demonstrate such a resemblance, and in Stalinist Hungary it was regarded as too dangerous to let
such a resemblance suggest itself to the mind of the ordinary playgoer.

It was only after Stalin's death that the seven-year ban on the play
was temporarily lifted. In 1954 students of the Madách High School
decided to stage the play. Emboldened by this student performance, the

National Theatre asked for and was granted permission for its performance. But after Party Secretary Rákosi attended this performance, he angrily banned it once more. Eventually a compromise was reached between the theatre and the Soviet puppet dictator, and more critical debate followed. But it was only in the year after the 1956 revolution that the decisive argument was found in its favour, in a way typical of the spirit of the Kádár years. The point was that the play should be performed as invincible proof that the reactionary forces must simply fail in their wish to appropriate such a prominent example of the progressive national heritage. The director and the set designer were to emphasize the historical context in which the play was conceived; *The Tragedy of Man* had a right to be performed as an expression of Madách's sympathy with the defeat of the 1848 Hungarian Revolution–ultimately a sentiment in sympathy with progress.

5 Dostoevski, "The Legend of the Grand Inquisitor," *The Brothers Karamazov*, quoted in Krishan Kumar's *Utopia and Anti-Utopia in Modern Times*, 123.

6 Ibid.

7 Carr, *Dostoevsky 1821–1881*, 227.

8 Kumar, *Utopia and Anti-Utopia in Modern Times*, 125.

9 Arendt, On *Revolution*, 83, 79, 77, 82, 83.

10 Steiner, *Tolstoy or Dostoevsky*, 342.

11 Shelley, "On the Devil and the Devils," *Collected Works*, 7:94.

12 Steiner, *Tolstoy or Dostoevsky*, 33.

13 Ibid., 340.

14 Karinthy, "Barabbas," 39.

15 Ibid.

16 Tertz, *The Makepeace Experiment*, 30, 32.

17 Ibid., 33.

18 Voinovich, *Moscow 2042*, 403.

19 Steiner, *Tolstoy or Dostoevsky*, 33.

CHAPTER THREE

1 Rev. 21:21.

2 Stites, *Revolutionary Dreams*, 153.

3 Ibid., 149, 155.

4 Ibid., 147, 148.

5 In his "On Literature and Art" (1905) Lenin says: "Down with non-partisan writers! Down with literary supermen! Literature must become part of the common cause of the proletariat, a 'cog and screw' of one single great Social-Democratic mechanism set in motion by the entire politically conscious vanguard of the entire working class" (23).

6 Stites, *Revolutionary Dreams*, 150.

7 Ibid.

8 Ibid., 146, 148.

9 Ginsburg, Introduction to Zamiatin's *We*, xv.

10 Zamiatin, "On Literature, Revolution, Entropy, and Other Matters," 108.

11 Beauchamp, "Zamiatin's *We*," 57.

12 Ginsburg, Introduction to Zamiatin's *We*, xvii.

13 Kumar, *Utopia and Anti-Utopia in Modern Times*, 242.

14 In "Atavism and Utopia" Eric Rabkin states: "Often the utopian world is a pastoral one by virtue of the exclusion of technology, as we see in the Savage Reservation of Brave New World" (3). Also see Edith Clowes, *Russian Experimental Fiction*, 10–12.

15 Rabkin, "Atavism and Utopia"; Clowes, *Russian Experimental Fiction*, 10–12.

16 Clowes, *Russian Experimental Fiction*, 10.

17 Orwell, "Pleasure Spots," CEJL, 4:105.

18 Orwell, "Review of N. De Basily's *Russia Under Soviet Rule*," CEJL, 1:419.

19 Booker, *The Dystopian Impulse in Modern Literature*, 48.

20 Huxley, "The New Romanticism," 213–14.

21 Kumar, *Utopia and Anti-Utopia in Modern Times*, 262.

22 Ibid., 225.

23 Orwell, "Letter to Francis A.Henson" (extract), CEJL, 4:564.

24 Orwell, "Preface to *Animal Farm*," CEJL, 3:458.

25 Harold Nicolson, quoted by Nikolai Tolstoy in *Stalin's Secret War*, 278.

26 Orwell, "Letter to John Middleton Murry," CEJL, 3:237.

27 Orwell, "Raffles and Miss Blandish," CEJL, 3:257–8.

28 Arendt, *Totalitarianism*, 436, 344.

29 Camus, "The Failing of the Prophecy," 3.

30 Gottlieb, *The Orwell Conundrum*, chap. 4.

31 Ibid., 79–80.

32 Eliade, *Occultism, Witchcraft and Cultural Fashions*, 88.

33 Gottlieb, *The Orwell Conundrum*, 135.

34 Orwell, "Letter to Roger Senhouse," CEJL, 4:520.

35 Orwell, "As I Please" (*Tribune*, 29 Nov. 1946), CEJL, 4:289.

36 Orwell, "Burnham's View of the Contemporary World Struggle," CEJL, 4:370.

CHAPTER FOUR

1 Ray Bradbury, Introduction (1967), 14.

2 Ibid., 11.

3 Ibid., 12.

4 Jack Zipes, "Mass Degradation," 187.

5 Ibid., 190.

6 Darko Suvin, in his *Metamorphoses of Science Fiction*, calls science fiction "the literature of cognitive estrangement" (4).

7 Howard Segal, "Vonnegut's *Player Piano*," 171.

8 Mark Hillegas, *The Future as Nightmare*, 161.

9 Of course Vonnegut was not at all alone in the fifties and sixties in associating woman as wife and mother with the sinister powers of the establishment; she represents the demands society makes on the male. The only acceptable role, it seems, in which woman can join the male rebelling against the establishment is in the role of prostitute, who is by definition subversive of middle-class social values. Ken Kesey's powerful *One Flew over the Cuckoo's Nest*, another novel of utopian-dystopian inspiration, demonstrates these assumptions. The novel takes place in a psychiatric ward in the u.s. in the fifties. On the ward, which is a replica of a dystopic society, the role of Big Brother is taken by a female, Big Nurse (a conscious allusion to Orwell). Big Nurse represents all the author finds wrong with society: the obsession of Freudian theory with breaking the manhood of the patients, and the dictatorial insistence of the establishment on regarding these patients as damaged parts of the machine of society, who will have to be "repaired" only so that they can again fit the "Combine" of society. In Kesey's novel Big Nurse not only serves this evil machine; she is the machine.

Another possessive, tyrannical "Mom" in Kesey's novel is young Bibbit's mother, who makes her son, a psychiatric patient, feel so guilty about his sexual desires that she drives him to suicide – with the full co-operation of Big Nurse. The only "good women" who have a liberating effect on the male patients are two young prostitutes who give these men broken by the "Combine" a chance to experience their manhood, the basis for restoring their independence from Big Nurse. Just like Vonnegut, Kesey expresses profound hostility to woman as wife and mother, who deprives the male of his freedom by reminding him of his duties to her, thereby forcing the rebel to conform to the oppressive code of the establishment.

10 Stillman and Johnson, "Identity, Complicity, and Resistance in *The Handmaid's Tale*," 78–81.

11 Ibid., 81.

12 Booker, *The Dystopian Impulse in Modern Literature*, 166.

13 Quoted in Booker, *The Dystopian Impulse*, 166.

CHAPTER FIVE

1 Hayward, *Writers in Russia 1917–1978*, 150.

2 Ginsburg, Foreword to Zamyatin's *We*," xvii.

3 Hosking, *Beyond Socialist Realism*, 130.

4 Groys, *The Total Art of Stalin*, 35–6.

5 Chandler, Introduction to Grossman's *Life and Fate*, 9.

6 Ibid., 10–11.

7 Ruder, Review of Robin Regine's *Socialist Realism*, 179. See also Kathleen Parthé's "Introduction: Vulnerable Writers and Indestructible Texts," 217–23. Describing the 1960s, Parthé suggests that "Socialist Realism – the brittle heart of official Soviet literature – was in Yeatsian terms, a center that 'could not hold' ... The most interesting literature of this period defined itself against this hollow core; it is at the borders of the literary world that we will find what we need to fill in the blank pages" (221).

8 Plato, *The Republic*, Book X (ed. Bate), 48.

9 Shortly after the revolution a group of poets formed in Moscow a literary circle called Kuzhnitsa, "the smithy," referring to the poet's task: to forge the new man. Anton Makarenko, in the *Road of Life* (1935), relies on the same metaphor to define the role of the educator.

10 Lenin, "On Literature and Art" (1905), 24. Max Hayward, in his *Writers in Russia 1917–1978*, describes the debate introduced in 1956 about whether Lenin's essay "had been intended to apply only to political and publicist writing ... It was at once recognized that the removal of this keystone would have brought the whole edifice of Soviet literary doctrine tumbling down." Hayward believes that "Lenin probably did intend his words to appply to literature of every kind" (152).

11 Lenin, "On Literature and Art" (1905), 24.

12 Quoted in Evgeniy Dobrenko's "The Literature of the Zhdanov Era," 119.

13 Lenin, "On Literature and Art" (1905), 25.

14 Ibid.

15 Quoted in György Litván, "Mi Kommunisták," 152.

16 Ibid.

17 Lenin, *On Literature and Art* (1920s), 25.

18 Ibid., 26.

19 In "The Prevention of Literature" George Orwell points out that the "immediate, practical enemies" of intellectual liberty are "monopoly and bureacracy," and he speaks up against "the concentration of the press in the hands of a few rich men, the grip of monopoly on radio and the film" (82). Nevertheless, in the same essay he makes it clear that the enemy of intellectual liberty in the one-party system of a totalitarian dictatorship is even more powerful. CEJL, 4:81–95.

20 Lenin. "On Literature and Art" (1905), 27.

21 Ibid.

22 Ibid., 29.

23 *Proceedings of the Tenth Party Congress*, Leningrad, quoted in Katkov, *The Trial of Bukharin*, 43.

24 Lenin, *On Literature and Art* (1920s), 31.

25 Ibid., 30.

26 Ibid.

27 Zhdanov, "Doklad o zhurnalakh 'Zvezda' i 'Leningrad,'" 109–27. In *Writers in Russia 1917–1978* Max Hayward refers to the Zhdanov era of 1946 to 1953 as the "cultural pogrom begun by Zhdanov" (155), while Grigory Svirski, in *A History of Post-War Soviet Writing*, describes in some detail the "trials and mass murder of writers writing in Yiddish" (47) on 12 August 1952.

28 Stalin, "O rabote v derevne," 133.

29 Evgeniy Dobrenko, "The Literature in the Zhdanov Era," 132.

30 Ibid., 134.

31 Hosking, *Beyond Socialist Realism*, 130.

32 Dudintsev, Interview, 35; my trans.

33 For a more general discussion of this era see Mihajlov, *Russian Themes*; Matthewson, *The Positive Hero in Russian Literature*; Hosking, *The Twentieth Century: In Search of New Ways*; Moser, ed., *The Cambridge History of Russian Literature*; Clowes, *Russian Experimental Fiction*.

CHAPTER SIX

1 Hannah Arendt, *On Revolution*, 8.

2 Ibid., 21.

3 In discussing Communism as the end of history, Marx points out: "We do not mean it to be understood ... that, for example, the rentier, the capitalist, etc., cease to be persons; but their personality is conditioned and determined by quite definite class relationships, and the division appears only in their opposition to another class and, for themselves, only when they get bankrupt. [Communism as the end of History], "The German Ideology," 194.

4 Orwell, "Letter to Arthur Koestler," CEJL, 3:271.

5 Orwell, "Editorial to Polemic," CEJL, 4:191.

6 Orwell, "War-time Diary, 1942," CEJL, 2:476.

7 Greeman, Introduction to Serge's *Conquered City*, viii–ix.

8 Ibid., 190.

9 Ginsburg, Introduction to Zamiatin's *We*, xvii. In his *Writers in Russia 1917–1978* Max Hayward points out that "early attempts at innovation (e.g., the Serapion Brothers, the formalist critics, not to mention the many individual poetic and artistic styles of the 1920's) were destroyed and replaced in the late 1930's by an empty, bombastic pseudo-popular style" (148).

10 Chukhontntsev, ed. *Dissonant Voices*, 444.

11 Arendt, *On Revolution*, 43.

12 Ibid., 44.

13 Kún, Epilogue to Rodionov's *Csokoládé [Chocolate]*, 213–14.

14 Ibid., 207–29.

15 Ibid., 218.

16 Serge, *Conquered City*, 140.

17 Kún, Epilogue to *Csokoládé [Chocolate]*, 221. For the importance of holding on to the Lenininst legacy as the true basis of reform under Gorbachov's regime, see Gooding, "Perestroika and the Russian Revolution of 1991," 234–48.

18 Pasternak, *Doctor Zhivago*, 269. In *The Double Vision*, Northrop Frye draws a comparison between the attitude to the future in Christianity and in Communism. The "fixation on the future" in Christianity "usually takes the form of a fearful expectation of a second coming, or simply a postponing of spiritual life ... the assumption that death automatically brings enlightenment. Secular parodies of this take the form of beliefs in revolution or progress, and in their demonic form employ the tactic of sacrificing the present to the future. Such visions can be quite as horrible in their results as their fascist counterparts. It seemed logical in Stalin's Russia that that if hundreds of thousands of kulaks were murdered or sent to concentration camps right away, Russia might have a more efficient system of argiculture within the next century. But such means adopted for theoretically reasonable ends never serve such ends: they merely replace them, and the original ends disappear" (51).

CHAPTER SEVEN

1 Terras, *A History of Russian Literature*, 80.

2 Ibid., 82. In *The Shape of Apocalypse in Modern Russia* David Bethea suggests another angle by noting that "perhaps more than any other Russian writer, Andrei Platonov represents the collision of the Christian apocalypse and Marxist utopian models" (159).

3 Serge, *Memoirs of a Revolutionary*, 245.

4 Ibid., 246.

5 Ibid., 247.

6 Ibid., 246.

7 Ibid., 249.

8 Ibid.

9 Ibid., 250.

10 For a different focus on Platonov's language, see Joseph Brodsky's Preface to Platonov's *The Foundation Pit*. For a different focus on the plot-line ending with the child's death, see *Andrei Platonov: Uncertainties of Spirit*

by Thomas Seifrid, who suggests that for Platonov "being exists in subordination of the material body from which it is fundamentally estranged" (144), eager to find "a release from the sorrows of the flesh" (118).

11 Hamvas, "A Vizöntö" ("Aquarius"), in *A Láthatatlan Történet*, 18. My trans.

12 Ibid.

13 All quotations from Anatolij Ribakov's *The Children of the Arbat* refer to N. Elli's Hungarian translation of the Russian original; my trans.

14 Marsh, *Images of Dictatorship*, 81, 80.

15 Ribakov, Interview, 304; my trans.

16 Aleksander Plahov, "Jó Lenne élni," 305–6; my trans.

17 Mikhail Kolcov, "Gyilkosok a Leningradi Központból," 309; my trans.

18 Roy Medvedev, "Sz. M Kirov Meggyilkolása," 313–18; my trans.

19 Ibid., 317.

20 Ribakov, Interview, 303; my trans.

21 In their essay "Stalinist Terror: New Perspectives," J. Arch Getty and Robert T. Manning agree that there is no invincible evidence that Stalin was behind the shooting of Kirov. Still, they argue, Stalin took advantage of the events, even if he did not plan them from the beginning but only "stumbled into them."

22 Fiedler, "Toward the Freudian Pill," 162

23 Koestler, "Soviet Myth and Reality," in *The Yogi and the Commissar*, 133.

24 Solzhenitsyn, *The Gulag Archipelago*, 409.

25 Koestler, "Soviet Myth and Reality," in *The Yogi and the Commissar*, 133.

26 Ibid.

27 Howe, *Politics and the Novel*, 229.

28 Cohen, Interview, 333–5; my trans.

29 Katkov, *The Trial of Bukharin*, 181–92.

30 "Irók a Párhuzamos trotckista központ moszkvai peréről," 319–20; my trans.

31 Ibid., 320.

32 Vakszberg, "Bizonyiték őfelsége – Andrej Visinskijről," 348; my trans.

33 "Irók a Párhuzamos trotckista," 321; my trans.

34 Felix Medvedev, "Beszélgetés Buharin özvegyével," 325–6; my trans. See also Solzhenitsyn's *Gulag Archipelago*, 414–16.

35 John 19:2.

36 Katkov, *The Trial of Bukharin*, 36.

37 Ibid., 40.

38 Koestler, *Darkness at Noon*, chap. 15; *Bricks to Babel*, 180–1.

39 Ibid., 181.

40 Koestler, "The End of an Illusion," 204.

41 Ibid., 202.
42 George Orwell, "Arthur Koestler," CEJL, 3:282.
43 Koestler, "The End of an Illusion," 203.

CHAPTER EIGHT

1 Garrard, "A Conflict of Visions," 60.
2 The fluctuations of Shtrum's career, his anxieties about arrest and his joy over success and awards, are clearly based on Grossman's own experience. As Robert Chandler describes this, Grossman worked as a well-respected war correspondent through the Second World War, and as author of "The Hell of Treblinka" produced

> the first journalistic account of a German death-camp in any language. Together with Ilya Ehrenburg, Grossman was on the editorial committee of the *Black Book* ... of documents relating to the Holocaust ... As the Cold War began ... in 1946, Grossman was viciously attacked by several of the most authoritative Soviet literary critics [for] his play *If You Believe the Pythagoreans* ... In 1952 [his epic novel *For a Just Cause* was published and] Grossman enjoyed the full support of Tvardovsky, the editor of *Novy mir*, and Fadeev, the General Secretary of the Writer's Union ... In February 1953, however, as a new series of purges, directed particularly at Jews, gathered momentum, Grossman was again attacked, possibly at the instigation of Stalin himself ... Grossman was saved from almost certain arrest ... by the change in the political climate following Stalin's death in March 1953 ... In 1955 Grossman was awarded the important decoration 'The Banner of Labour.' (Introduction to Grossman's *Life and Fate*, 8)

For further details on the various waves of the Stalinist pogroms of 1946–53 that affected well-respected writers like Grossman and Ilia Ehrenburg, see Grigory Svirski's *A History of Post-War Soviet Writing*, 41–75.
3 About Tertz Sinyavski's trial, see Hayward, ed., *On Trial*.
4 Kafka, *The Trial*.
5 Clowes, *Russian Experimental Fiction*, 317.
6 About Daniel's trial, see "Witch Hunt," in Muchic, *Russian Writers*, 374–82; and Hayward, ed., *On Trial*.
7 Blake and Hayward, eds., *Dissonant Voices in Soviet Literature*, 262.
8 Clowes, *Russian Experimental Fiction*, 10.

CHAPTER NINE

1 Rothschild, *Return to Diversity*, 132.
2 Ibid., 133.

3 Ibid.

4 Jerzy Andzrejewskij wrote *The Inquisitors* in 1957, the same year in which he resigned his party membership "in protest against censorship." For a short biography, see Gillon and Kryzanowski, eds., *Introduction to Modern Polish Literature*, 225. On Andzrejewskij's works, see Milosz, *History of Polish Literature*, 490–3, 536; and Eile, "Moral Dilemmas in Andzrejewskij's Fiction."

5 On Ladislas Fuks's work, see Harkins, "The Czech Novel since 1956," 12–13.

6 On Marek Hlasko, see Milosz, *History of Polish Literature*, 526.

7 On Slawomir Mrozek's short pieces, see Helene Wlodarczyk, "The Telescopic World of Jeu de Miroirs," 119–141. Also see Milosz, *History of Polish Literature*, 513–15.

CHAPTER TEN

The Castle had its premiere in the Prague Theatre of the Armed Forces in 1964, and was published in 1966 (Hruby, *Daydreams and Nightmares*, 259). References to Klima's *The Castle* and Petr Karvas's *The Big Wig* are to these plays' Hungarian translation in *Mai Cseh és Szlovák Drámák* (*Czech and Slovakian Drama Today*), ed. András Zádor; my trans.

1 Longworth, *The Making of Eastern Europe*, 23.

2 French, *Czech Writers and Politics 1945–1969*, 179.

3 Ibid.

4 Joseph Rothchild, *Return to Diversity*, 168.

5 French, *Czech Writers and Politics*, 81.

6 Rothchild, *Return to Diversity*, 168.

7 Grayson, Review of *The European Foundations of Russian Modernism*," 309.

8 Fejtő, *A Népi Demokráciák Története* [*The History of the* People's Democracies], 2:11; my trans.

9 The fact that the "doctors' plot" and the 1967 anti-Israel propaganda revived the language of traditional anti-semitism, even if under the guise of Communist euphemisms, gives the fascist echoes in the General's scapegoat hunt particular significance in the satire. It should be also pointed out that in 1967 Czech intellectuals demonstrated against the Party's anti-Israel propaganda; they clearly identified with Israel, a small country, like Czechoslovakia, whose existence was threated by a powerful neighbour.

Through the echo of anti-semitic slurs in the General's denunciation of the "bald ones" Karvas also makes the point that the foreign dictator who rules in the name of socialism is really not that different from the foreign dictator who ruled in the name of fascism.

10 French, *Czech Writers and Politics*, 189.
11 Fejtő, *A Népi Demokráciak Törtènete*, 2:8; my trans.
12 Ibid., 9–10.
13 Ibid., 9.

CHAPTER ELEVEN

All references to Tibor Déry's *G.A. Ur X-ben* are to the Hungarian original; my trans.

1 On the works of Tadeusz Konwicki, see Hyde, "Tadeusz Konwicki"; Milosz, *History of Polish Literature*, 499–501; and Eile, "Between Absurdity and Apocalypse."
2 Ungvári. *Déry Tibor Alkotásai és Vallomásai Tükrében*, 249; my trans.
3 Quoted in ibid., 251; my trans.
4 Hosking, *The Twentieth Century*, 575. For further discussion of Zinoviev's work, see also Kirkwood, *Alexander Zinoviev*; and Hanson and Kirkwood, eds., *Alexander Zinoviev as Writer and Thinker.*
5 Háy, *Született 1900-ban*, 281; my trans.
6 Ibid., 204–6; my trans.
7 Déry, Előszó, *G.A. Ur X ben* hez; my trans.
8 Quoted in Ungvári, *Déry Tibor Alkotásai és Vallomásai Tükrében*, 224; my trans.

CHAPTER TWELVE

All references to György Dalos's *1985* are to the Hungarian original, *1985: Történelmi Jelentés*; my trans. All references to György Moldova's novel are to the Hungarian original, *Hitler Magyarországon*; my trans.

1 Frye, *Anatomy of Criticism*, 226.
2 Ivan Chonkin is Vladimir Voinovich's protagonist in *The Life and Extraordinary Adventures of Private Ivan Chonkin* (1975–79).
3 Frye, *Anatomy of Criticism*, 229.
4 Glad, *Conversations in Exile*, 294.
5 Matich, "Vasilii Aksenov and the Literature of Convergence," 643–51.
6 Ibid., 651.
7 In his 1993 book, *Free to Hate*, Paul Hockenos analyses the rise of extreme right-wing movements in Poland and Hungary, reiterating Moldova's fear of the chances for a fascist dictatorship not only in Hungary but in the entire region of Eastern Europe: "The problem of the right is not one of a couple of thousand skinheads, but of the latent prejudices and sentiments that they express in their most extreme forms, and that right-wing parties have shown themselves deft at exploiting" (318).

8 See, for example, Moldova's *Szent Imre Induló* (*The Saint Imre March*).
9 For a Western novel that deals with the dystopia of victorious Nazism in our times, see Robert Harris's *Fatherland*, written in 1993. For a Western author alluding to what he sees as Orwell's prediction about 1984, see Anthony Burgess's *1985* (1978).

CHAPTER THIRTEEN

1 Jakovlev, "Az Igazságszolgáltatás és mi," 336–40; my trans.
2 Lord, *Russian Literature*, 276.
3 Ibid., 277.
4 Ibid., 287.
5 Slonim, *Soviet Russian Literature*, 398.
6 Ibid., 279.
7 Beauchamp, Paper delivered at *Vite di utopia*.
8 Clowes, "Kafka and the Modernism-Realism Debate in Literary Criticism of the Thaw," 317.
9 Mihajlov, *Russian Themes*, 343.
10 Chandler, Introduction to Grossman's *Life and Fate*, 9.
11 Milosz, Introduction to Tertz Sinyavski's *The Trial Begins*, 133.
12 This is true even in the case of the Strugatsky brothers' science fiction novel, *The Ugly Swans* (1972), which focuses on the fate of the children in a nightmare society that bears an unmistakable resemblance to the USSR of the writer's time.
13 Clowes, *Russian Experimental Fiction*, 5.
14 Frye, *Anatomy of Criticism*, 223.
15 Emerson, "Bakhtin and Women," 3–20.
16 Hyde, "Poland," 205. In his "Russian Literary Resistance Reconsidered," Thomas Lahusen asks: "Also, doesn't one end up undermining Bakhtin in using him too much?" (680)
17 Szilárd, *A Karnevál Elmélet*, 105–6.
18 Ibid., 106.
19 Ibid.
20 Empson, *Seven Types of Ambiguity*, x.
21 While Edith Clowes's 1993 study on *Russian Experimental Fiction* reveals unquestioning adherence to the concepts of Bakhtin, a theorist of profound influence on postmodern thought and criticism, in her "Simulacrum as S(t)imulation? Postmodernist Theory and Russian Cultural Criticism," written in 1995, Clowes herself seems rather critical of "the collapse of valuative polarities and [the] stressing of epistemological and ontological shiftiness [that] has become a hallmark of what we have come with Lyotard to call the 'postmodern condition'" (333). More specifically, she questions whether concepts of Lyotard, Derrida,

Foucault, Baudrillard, and Lacan are indeed appropriate for the analysis of Stalinism or late Soviet and post-Soviet culture (333). Her analysis of Mikhail Epstein's critical works and Boris Groys's *The Total Art of Stalinism* ends with the important admission that "in the Russian experience" we will find "grounds for a productive dialogue with [but also a] serious critique of postmodernist thinking" (342).

Bibliography

Aksyonov, Vassily. *The Island of Crimea*. 1981. Trans. Michael Henry Heim. New York: Random House, 1983.

Aldridge, Alexandra. *The Scientific World View in Dystopia*. Ann Arbor: UMI Research Press 1984.

Amis, Kingsley. *The Maps of Hell*. London: New English Library 1969.

Andzrejewski, Jerzy. *Ashes and Diamonds*. 1948. Intr. Heinrich Boll. Trans. D.J. Welsh. Writers from the Other Europe, ed. Philip Roth. Harmondsworth: Penguin 1962.

– *The Inquisitors*. 1957. Trans. Konrad Syrop. London: Weidenfeld and Nicolson 1960.

– *The Appeal*. 1968. Trans. C. Wienewska. London: Weidenfeld and Nicolson 1971.

Arendt, Hannah. *On Revolution*. New York: Viking Press 1963.

– *Totalitarianism*. Part 3 of *The Origins of Totalitarianism*. New intro. New York: Harvest Book 1966.

Arzhak, Nikolai. *See* Daniel.

Atwood, Margaret. *The Handmaid's Tale*. Toronto: McClelland and Stewart 1985.

Barta, Peter, and Ulrich Goebel, eds. *The European Foundation of Russian Modernism*. Lewiston: Edwin Mellen 1991.

Beauchamp, Gorman. "Of Man's Last Disobedience: Zamiatin's *We* and Orwell's *1984*." *Comparative Literature Studies* 10 (1973): 285–301.

– "Zamiatin's *We*." In Rabkin, ed., *No Place Else*, 56–77.

– "All's Well that Ends Wells: The Anti-Wellsian Satire of Brave New World." *Utopian Studies II*, ed Michael S. Cummings and Nicholas Smith. Lanham: University Press of America, 1989.

– Paper delivered at *Vite di utopia*, Centro Interdipartmentale di Ricerca Sulla Utopia, Gargnano, Italy, 8–11 June 1997.

Beckett, Samuel. *Waiting for Godot*. New York: Grove Weidenfeld 1976.

Berkes, Tamás. *Senki sem fog nevetni.* Budapest: Gondolat 1990.

Bethea, David. *The Shape of Apocalypse in Modern Russian Fiction.* Princeton, NJ: Princeton University Press 1988.

Blake, Patricia, and Max Hayward, eds. *Dissonant Voices in Soviet Literature.* London: George Allen and Unwin 1964.

Boffa, Giuseppe. *The Stalin Phenomenon.* Trans. Nicholas Fersen. Ithaca: Cornell University Press 1992.

Booker, M. Keith. *The Dystopian Impulse in Modern Literature: Fiction as Social Criticism.* Contributions to the Study of Science Fiction and Fantasy 58. Westport, Conn.: Greenwood Press 1994.

– *Dystopian Literature: A Theory and Research Guide.* Westport, Conn.: Greenwood Press 1994.

Bracher, Karl Dietrich. "The Disputed Concept of Totalitarianism." In *Totalitarianism Reconsidered,* ed. Ernest Menze. Port Washington: Free Press 1981.

Bradbury, Ray. *Fahrenheit 451.* New York: Simon and Schuster, 1951, 1967.

Brodsky, Joseph. Preface to Platonov, *The Foundation Pit.* Ann Arbor: Ardis 1973.

Brooks, Maria Zagorska. "The Bear in Slavonic and Polish Mythology and Folklore." *Essays in Polish Literature, Language and History.* The Hague: Mouton 1975.

Buitenhuis, Peter, and Ira Nadel, eds. *George Orwell: A Reassessment.* London: Macmillan 1988.

Burdekin, Katharine. *Swastika Night.* London: Gollancz 1937.

Burgess, Anthony. *1985.* London: Hutchinson 1978.

Byron. *Manfred.* In *Selected Poetry.* Modern Library. New York: Random House 1951.

Camus, Albert. *Actuelles Chroniques 1944–1948.* Paris: Gallimard 1950.

– "The Failing of the Prophecy." In *Existentialism versus Marxism: Conflicting Views on Humanism,* ed. George Novack. New York: Dell 1966.

Capek, Karel. R.U.R.: *A Play in Three Acts.* 1921. Trans. P. Selver. London: Oxford University Press 1930.

– *The Absolute at Large.* 1924. Trans. W.E.Harkins. Westport, Conn.: Hyperion 1974.

– *War with the Newts.* 1936. Trans. M. Weatherall. New York: Bantam Books 1955.

Carr, Edward Hallett. *Dostoevsky 1821–1881.* London: Unwin Books, 1962.

Chad, Walsh. *From Utopia to Nightmare.* New York: Harper and Row 1962.

Chandler, Robert. Introduction to Vassily Grossman, *Life and Fate.*

Chukhontsev, Oleg., ed. *Dissonant Voices: The New Russian Fiction.* London: Harvill 1991.

Clarke, Ignatius Fiedorow. *Voices Prophesying War: Future Wars 1763–3749.* 2nd ed. Oxford: Oxford University Press 1992.

Clowes, Edith W. "Kafka and the Modernism-Realism Debate in Literary Criticism of the Thaw." In *The European Foundations of Russian Modernism*, ed. Peter I. Barta. Lewiston: Edwin Mellen Press 1991.

– *Russian Experimental Fiction: Resisting Ideology after Utopia*. Princeton, NJ: Princeton University Press 1993.

– "Simulacrum as S(t)imulation? Postmodernist Theory and Russian Cultural Criticism." *Slavic and East European Journal* 39, no. 3 (Fall 1995): 333–43.

Cohen, Stephen. Interview. In Szilágyi, ed., *Tovább*, 333–335.

Crick, Bernard. *George Orwell: A Life*. London: Secker and Warburg 1980.

Czigány, Loránt. *The Oxford History of Hungarian Literature*. Oxford: Clarendon Press 1984.

Dalos, György. *1985: Történelmi Jelentés (1985: Historical Report)*. [Budapest]: Uj Géniusz 1990.

Daniel, Julij (Nikolai Arzhak). *This is Moscow Speaking*. Trans. John Richardson. In Blake and Hayward, eds., *Dissonant Voices in Soviet Literature*.

– *On Trial*. In Hayward, ed., *On Trial*.

Déry, Tibor. *G.A. Ur X-ben (Mr. G.A. in X].)* 1964. Budapest: Szépirodalmi Könyvkiadó 1983.

– *A Kiközösitő (The Excommunicators)*. Budapest: Szépirodalmi Könyvkiadó 1983.

Djilas, Milovan. *The Unperfect Society*. Trans. Dorian Cool. New York: Harcourt 1969.

Dobrenko, Yevgeny. "The Literature of the Zhdanov Era: Mentality, Mythology, Lexicon." In Lahusen and Kuperman, eds., *Late Soviet Culture*.

Dostoevski, Fyodor. *The Brothers Karamazov*. Trans. Richard Pevear. New York: Vintage Books 1991.

Dudintsev, Vladimir. *Not by Bread Alone*. Trans. Edith Bone. London: Hutchinson 1957.

– "Beszélgetés Vlagyimir Dugyincevvel" ("Interview with *Uj Tükör*, 1986, 5, 42." In Szilágyi, ed., *Tovább*, 35–7.

Dumitriu, Petru. *Incognito*. Trans. Norman Denny. New York: Macmillan 1964.

Eile, Stanislaw. "Between Absurdity and Apocalypse: Contemporary Poland in Drama and Fiction, 1977–87." In Eile and Phillips, eds., *New Perspectives in Twentieth-Century Polish Literature*.

– "Moral Dilemmas in Andrzejewski's Fiction." In Eile and Phillips, eds., *New Perspectives in Twentieth-Century Polish Literature*.

Eile, Stanislaw, and Ursula Phillips, eds. *New Perspectives in Twentieth-Century Polish Literature: Flight from Martyrology*. Studies in Russia and East Europe. London: Methuen 1992.

Eliade, Mircea. *Occultism, Witchcraft and Cultural Fashions*. Chicago: University of Chicago Press 1976.

Elliott, Robert. *The Shape of Utopia: Studies in a Literary Genre*. Chicago: University of Chicago Press 1970.

Emerson, Caryl. "Bakhtin and Women: A Nontopic with Immense Implications." In Goscilo, ed., *Fruits of Her Plume*.

Empson, William. *Seven Types of Ambiguity*. 1930. 3rd ed. London: Chatto and Windus 1963.

Esslin, Martin. *Theatre of the Absurd*. New York: Doubleday, Anchor Books 1961.

- *Brief Chronicles: Essays on Modern Theatre*. London: Temple Smith 1970.

Fejtő, Ferenc. *A Népi Demokráciák Története*. Budapest: Magvetö Kiadó, 1991. Histoire des democraties populaires, 2 vols. Paris: Editions du Seuil 1953.

Fiedler, Leslie. "Toward the Freudian Pill." In Sperber, ed., *Arthur Koestler*.

Foucault, Michel. *Discipline and Punish: The Birth of the Prison*. Trans. Alan Sheridan. New York: Vintage 1979.

French, A. *Czech Writers and Politics: 1945–1969*. East European Monographs no.94. New York: Cambridge University Press 1982.

Freud, Sigmund. *Three Case Histories*. Trans. Philip Rieff. New York: Collier 1963.

Frye, Northrop. *Anatomy of Criticism: Four Essays*. Princeton: Princeton University Press 1957.

- *The Double Vision: Language and Meaning in Religion*. Toronto: University of Toronto Press 1991.

Fuks, Ladislav. *Mr Theodore Mundstock*. 1963. New York: Four Walls Eight Windows 1991.

- *The Cremator*. 1967. Trans. Eva M. Kandler. London: Marion Boyars 1984.

Garrard, John. "A Conflict of Visions: Vasilii Grossman and the Russian Idea." In Thompson, ed., *The Search for Self-Definition in Russian Literature*.

Garrard, John, and Carol Garrard. *Inside the Soviet Writers' Union*. London: I.B.Tavis 1990.

Gasiorska, Xenia. *Women in Soviet Fiction*. Knoxville: University of Tennessee Press 1985.

Getty, J. Arch, and Robert T. Manning, eds. *Stalinist Terror: New Perspectives*. Cambridge: Cambridge University Press 1993.

Gillon, Adam, and Ludwik Krzyzanowski, eds. *Introduction to Modern Polish Literature: An Anthology of Fiction and Poetry*. New York: Hippocrene Books 1964.

Ginsburg, Mirra. Foreword to Zamiatin's *We*. New York: Avon Books 1983.

Glad, John, ed. *Conversations in Exile: Russian Writers Abroad*. London: Duke University Press 1993.

Gleb, Stuve. *Russian Literature under Lenin and Stalin*. Norman, Okla.: University of Oklahoma Press 1971.

Goetz-Stankiewicz, Marketa. *The Silenced Theatre: Czech Playwrights without a Stage*. Toronto: University of Toronto Press 1973.

Gömöri, György. *Polish and Hungarian Poetry 1945 to 1956.* Oxford: Clarendon Press 1966.

Gooding, John. "Perestroika and the Russian Revolution of 1991." *Slavonic and Eastern European Review* 71, no. 1 (Apr. 1993): 234–45.

Goscilio, Helen, ed., trans. *Russian and Polish Women's Fiction.* Knoxville: University of Tennessee Press 1985.

– ed. *Fruits of Her Plume: Essays on Contemporary Russian Women's Culture.* Armonk, NY: M.E. Sharpe 1993.

Gottlieb, Erika. *The Orwell Conundrum: A Cry of Despair of Faith in the Spirit of Man?* Ottawa: Carleton University Press 1992.

Grayson, Jane. Review of *The European Foundations of Russian Modernism,* ed. Peter I. Barta and Ulrich Goebel. *Slavonic and Eastern European Review* 72, no. 2 (Apr. 1994): 309.

Greeman, Richard. Introduction to Victor Serge, *Conquered City.*

Grossman, Vassily. *Life and Fate.* Trans. and intro. Robert Chandler. London: Fontana Books 1986.

Groys, Boris. *The Total Art of Stalinism: Avant Garde, Aesthetic Dictatorship, and Beyond.* Trans. Charles Rougle. Princeton: Princeton University Press 1992.

Hamvas, Béla. *A Láthatatlan Történet (The Invisible Story: Essays).* Budapest: Akadémiai Könyvkiadó 1988.

Hanson, Philip, and Michael Kirkwood, eds. *Alexander Zinoviev as Writer and Thinker.* London: Macmillan 1988.

Harkins, William E. "The Czech Novel since 1956: At Home and Abroad." In Harkins and Trensky, eds., *Czech Literature since 1956.*

Harkins, William E., and Paul I. Trensky, eds. *Czech Literature since 1956: A Symposium.* Columbia Slavic Studies. New York: Bohemia 1980.

Harris, Robert. *Fatherland.* London: Hutchinson 1992.

Havel, Vaclav. *Memorandum.* Intro. Tom Stoppard. London: Methuen 1967.

– *Disturbing the Peace: A Conversation with Karel Hviazdala.* Trans. Paul Wilson. London: Faber and Faber 1990.

– *Selected Plays 1963-1983.* London: Faber and Faber 1992.

Háy, Gyula. *Született 1900-ban: Emlékezések (Born in 1900: Recollections).* Budapest: Interakt 1990.

Hayward, Max. *Writers in Russia 1917–1978.* Ed and intro. Patricia Blake. London: Harvill Press 1983.

Hayward, Max, ed. *On Trial: The Soviet State versus "Abram Tertz" and "Nikolai Arzhak."* Trans. and intro. Max Hayward. New York: Harper and Row 1966.

Hillegas, Mark. *The Future as Nightmare: H.G. Wells and the Anti-Utopians.* New York: Oxford University Press 1967.

Hlasko, Marek. *The Graveyard.* Trans. Norbert Guterman. New York: Dutton 1959.

– *Next Stop – Paradise*. Trans. Norbert Guterman. New York: Dutton 1960.

Hockenos, Paul. *Free to Hate: The Rise of the Right in Post-Communist Eastern Europe*. New York: Routledge 1993.

Hosking, Geoffrey. *Beyond Socialist Realism: Soviet Fiction since Ivan Denisovich*. London: Granada 1980.

– "The Twentieth Century: In Search of New Ways 1953–1980." In Moser, ed., *Cambridge History of Russian Literature*.

Howe, Irving. *Politics and the Novel*. New York: Meridian 1957.

Hruby, Peter. *Daydreams and Nightmares: Czech Communist and Ex-Communist Literature 1917–1987*. East European monographs 290. New York: Columbia University Press 1990.

Hutcheon, Linda. *A Poetics of Postmodernism: History, Theory, Fiction*. New York: Routledge 1988.

Huxley, Aldous. *Brave New World*. Harmondsworth: Penguin 1931.

– "The New Romanticism." *Music at Night and Other Essays*. London: Chatto and Windus 1932.

– *Brave New World Revisited*. New York: Harper and Row 1958.

Hyde, George. "Poland: Dead Souls Under Western Eyes." In Yarrow, ed., *European Theater*.

– "Tadeusz Konvicki: A Personal View." In Eile and Phillips, eds., *New Perpectives*.

"Irók a Párhuzamos trotckista központ moszkvai peréről" ("Writers on the Trotskyite Centre's Moscow Trial"). *Lityeraturnaja gazeta*, 26 Jan. 1937. In Szilágyi, ed., *Tovább*. 318–19.

Iskander, Fazil. *Rabbits and Boa Constrictors*. Trans. Ronald E. Peterson. Ann Arbor: Ardis 1989.

Jakovlev, Alexander. "Az Igazságszolgáltatás és mi." In Szilágyi, ed., *Tovább*. 335–40.

Kafka, Franz. *The Trial*. Trans. Villa and Edwin Muir. New York: Shocken Books 1968.

Kamenka, Eugene. "Marxismus és politika" ("Marxism and Politics"). In *Századvég* 6–7 (1988): 33–9.

Kamenka, Eugene, ed. *The Portable Karl Marx*. Harmondsworth: Penguin 1983.

Karinthy, Frigyes. *Voyage to Capillaria*. 1917. Budapest: Corvina 1965.

– "Barabbas." 1935. Trans. István Farkas. In *Grave and Gay: Selections from His Work*. Budapest: Corvina 1973.

Karp, David. *One*. New York: Vanguard Press 1953.

Karvas, Petr. *A Nagy Paróka (The Big Wig)*. 1965. In *Mai Cseh es Szlovák Drámák. (Czech and Slovakian Drama Today)*, ed. and intro. András Zádor; trans. from the Czech, *Velka Parochna*, into Hungarian, Ferenc Hosszú. Budapest: Europa 1967.

Kateb, George. *Utopia and Its Enemies.* New York: Free Press of Glencoe, Collier Macmillan 1963.

Katkov, George. *The Trial of Bukharin.* London: Batsford 1969.

Kesey, Ken. *One Flew over the Cuckoo's Nest.* New York: Signet–New American Library 1962.

Kirkwood, Michael. "Stalin and Stalinism in the Works of Zinoviev." In Hanson and Kirkwood, eds., *Alexander Zinoviev as Writer and Thinker.*

– *Alexander Zinoviev: An Introduction to His Work.* London: Macmillan 1993.

Klaic, Dragan. *The Plot of the Future: Utopia and Dystopia in Modern Drama.* Ann Arbor: University of Michigan Press 1991.

Klima, Ivan. *A Kastély (The Castle).* In *Mai Cseh és Szlovák Drámák (Czech and Slovakian Drama Today),* ed. and intro. András Zádor; trans. from the Czech, *Zamek,* into Hungarian by András Zádor. Budapest: Europa 1967.

– *Judge on Trial.* Trans. A.G.Brain. London: Vintage 1992.

Knoll, Samson B. "Socialism as Dystopia: Political Uses of Utopian Dime Novels in Pre–World War I Germany." In *Utopian Studies IV,* ed. Lise Leibacher Ouvrard and D. Smith. Lanham: University Press of America 1991. 35–41.

Koestler, Arthur. *Darkness at Noon.* London: Jonathan Cape 1940. New York: Macmillan 1941.

– *The Yogi and the Commissar: Essays on the Modern Dilemma.* New York: Macmillan 1945.

– *Bricks to Babel.* London: Hutchinson 1980.

Kolcov, Mikhail. "Gyilkosok a Leningrádi Központból" ("Murderers from the Leningrad Centre"). *Pravda,* 22 Dec. 1934. In Szilágyi, ed., *Tovább.* 309–10.

Koltai, Tamás. *Az Ember Tragédiája a Szinpadon (1933–1968) (The Tragedy of Man on Stage (1933–1968)).* Budapest: Kelenföld Kiadó 1990.

Konwiczki, Tadeusz. *A Minor Apocalypse.* Trans. Richard Louri. New York: Random House 1984.

Kumar, Krishan. *Utopia and Anti-Utopia in Modern Times.* Oxford: Blackwell 1987.

– "The End of Socialism? The End of Utopia? The End of History?" In Kumar and Bann, eds., *Utopias and the Millennium.*

Kumar, Krishan, and Stephen Bann, eds. *Utopias and the Millennium.* London: Reaktion Books 1993.

Kún, Miklós. "Epilogus Rodionoff' *Csokoládé* jához" (Epilogue to the Hungarian version of Rodionov's *Chocolate*).

Lahusen, Thomas. Review of Edith Clowes's *Russian Experimental Fiction. Slavic and East European Journal* 38, no. 4 (Winter 1995): 680.

Lahusen, Thomas, and Gene Kuperman, eds. *Late Soviet Culture: From Perestroika to Novostroika.* Durham: Duke University Press 1992.

Lanin, Boris. "Images of Women in Russian Anti-Utopian Literature." *Slavonic and Eastern European Review* 71, no. 4 (Oct. 1993): 646–55.

Lenin. "On Literature and Art." 1905. *On Literature and Art.* 1920s. In *Socialist Realism – Literature and Art: A Collection of Articles.*

Leonov, Leonid. "A Tale About the Furious Calaphat." From *Badgers* (1925). In *The Fatal Eggs and Other Soviet Satire.* Trans. Mirra Ginsburg. London: Quartet Books 1993.

Lewis, Arthur O. "The Anti-Utopian Novel: Preliminary Notes and Checklist." *Extrapolations* 2 (1961): 27–32.

Lifton, Robert Jay. "Death and History: Ideological Totalism: Victimization and Violence." In Menze, ed., *Totalitarianism Reconsidered.*

Litván, György. "Mi Kommunisták Különös Emberek Vagyunk: A sztálinizmus lélektana" ("We Communists are Unusual People: The Psychology of Stalinism"). *Századvég* (Bibó István Szakkollégium Társadalomelméleti Folyóirata) 6–7 (1988): 150–9.

London, Jack. *Iron Heel.* London: Macmillan 1908.

Longworth, Philip. *The Making of Eastern Europe.* London: Macmillan 1992.

– "1989 and After." *Slavonic and Eastern European Review* 71, no. 4 (Oct. 1993): 703–11.

Lord, Robert. *Russian Literature: An Introduction.* London: Kahn and Averill 1980.

McLuhan, Marshall. *The Gutenberg Galaxy: The Making of Typographic Man.* Toronto: University of Toronto Press 1962.

Madách, Imre. *The Tragedy of Man (Az Ember Tragédiája).* 1860. Trans. G. Szirtes. Budapest: Corvina 1988.

Makarenko, A.S. *The Road to Life: An Epic of Education.* 1933–35. Trans. S. Garry. London: Nott 1936.

– *A Book for Parents.* 1938. Trans. Robert Daglish. Moscow: Foreign Languages Publishing House 1954.

Marsh, Rosalind. *Soviet Fiction since Stalin: Science, Politics and Literature.* London: Croom Helm 1986.

– *Images of Dictatorship: Portraits of Stalin in Literature.* London: Routledge 1989.

Marx, Karl. "The German Ideology." In Kamenka, ed., *The Portable Karl Marx.*

Mathewson, Rufus. *The Positive Hero in Russian Literature.* 2nd ed. Stanford: Stanford University Press 1975.

Matich, Olga. "Vasilii Aksenov and the Literature of Convergence: *Ostrov Krym* as Self-Criticism." *Slavic and East European Journal* 47, no. 4 (1988): 645–51.

Medvedev, Felix. "Beszélgetés Buharin özvegyével" (Felix Medvedev's Interview with Bukharin's Widow"). In Szilágyi, ed., *Tovább.* 325–6.

Medvedev, Roy. "Sz. M. Kirov meggyilkolása" ("The Assassination of S.M. Kirov"). In Szilágyi, ed., *Tovább*. 310–18.

Menze, Ernest, ed. *Totalitarianism Reconsidered*. Port Washington: Free Press 1981.

Mihajlov, Mihajlo. *Russian Themes*. Trans. Maria Mihajlo. New York: Farrar, Straus and Giroux 1962.

Miller, Arthur. *The Crucible*. New York: Viking Press 1953.

Milosz, Czeslaw. Intro. to Abram Tertz, *The Trial Begins*.

– *The History of Polish Literature*. 1969. Berkeley: University of California Press 1983.

Morson, Gary Saul. *The Boundaries of Genre: Dostoevsky's Diary of a Writer and the Tradition of Literary Utopia*. Austin: University of Texas Press 1981.

Moser, Charles A., ed. *The Cambridge History of Russian Literature*. Rev. ed. Cambridge: Cambridge University Press 1992.

Moldova, György. *Hitler Magyarországon: Titkos Záradék (Hitler in Hungary: A Secret Closure)*. 1972. Budapest: Maecenas 1992.

– *A Szent Imre Induló (The St Imre March)*.

More, Thomas. *Utopia*. Trans., intro. Paul Turner. Harmondsworth: Penguin Books 1965. Trans. Peter Marshall. New York: Washington Square 1965.

Mrozek, Slawomir. *The Elephant*. 1958. Trans. Konrad Syrop. New York: Grove Press 1965.

– *The Police*. 1960. In *Six Plays*. Trans. N. Bethell. New York: Grove Press 1987.

– *Striptease*. 1961. In *Six Plays*. Trans. Lola Gruenthal. New York: Grove Press 1972.

– *Tango*. 1964. Trans. Nicholas Bethell. Adapted Tom Stoppard. London: Cape 1968.

Muchic, Helen. *Russian Writers: Notes and Essays*. New York: Random House 1971.

Negley, Glen, and J. Max Patrick, eds. *The Quest for Utopia*. New York: Henry Schuman 1952.

Neumeyer, Peter F., ed. *Kafka's The Castle: A Collection of Critical Essays*. Twentieth Century Views. Englewood Cliffs, NJ: Prentice Hall 1969.

Novack, George, ed. *Existentialism versus Marxism: Conflicting Views on Humanism*. New York: Dell 1966.

Örkény, István. *Pisti a Vérzivatarban. Drámák 2. (Pisti in the Torrent of Blood)*. Budapest: Szépirodalmi Könyvkiadó 1982.

– *The Tóth Family*. Trans. Michael Henry and C. Gyöngyösi. New York: New Directions 1982.

– "Café Niagara." Trans. Ivan Sanders. *Nothing's Lost: Twenty-Five Hungarian Short Stories*. Budapest: Corvina 1988. 57–64.

Orwell, George. *Nineteen Eighty-four*. 1949. Harmondsworth: Penguin 1955.

– *Collected Essays, Journalism and Letters* (CEJL). 4 vols. Harmondsworth: Penguin 1970.

Parthé, Kathleen. "Introduction: Vulnerable Writers and Indestructible Texts." *Slavic and East European Journal* 36, no.2 (Summer 1994): 217–23.

– "What Was Soviet Literature?" *Slavic and East European Journal* 38, no. 2 (Summer 1994): 290–301.

Pasternak, Boris. *Doctor Zhivago*. Trans. Max Hayward and Manya Harari. London: Collins and Harvill 1958.

Peterson, Nadya L. *Subversive Imaginations: Fantastic Prose and the End of Soviet Literature, 1970s–1990s*. Boulder, Colo.: Westview Press 1994.

Petrushevskaya, Lyudmila. "Modern Family Robinson." In Chukhontsev, ed., *Dissonant Voices: The New Russian Fiction*.

Plahov, Aleksander. "Jó lenne élni, élni ... Gondolatok Szergej Kirovról készült dokumentumfilm kapcsán" ("It would be good to live, to live ... Thoughts in connection with the documentary film made of Kirov"). *Moskovskoi novoszti*, 13 Dec. 1987. In Szilágyi, ed., *Tovább*. 305–8.

Plato. *The Republic, Book X*. Selections in *Criticism: The Major Texts*, ed. Walter Jackson Bate. New York: Harcourt Brace 1952. 41–49.

– *The Republic*. Trans. and intro. Desmond Lee. Harmondsworth: Penguin 1974.

Platonov, Andrei. *The Foundation Pit*. Pref. Joseph Brodsky. Trans. Thomas P. Whitney. Ann Arbor, Mich.: Ardis 1973.

Pomogáts, Béla. *Az Ujabb Magyar Irodalom (Current Hungarian Literature)*. Budapest: Gondolat 1982.

Popper, Karl. *The Poverty of Historicism*. New York: Harper and Row 1964.

– *Conjectures and Refutations: The Growth of Scientific Knowledge*. New York: Harper and Row 1968.

– *The Open Society and Its Enemies*. Princeton: Princeton University Press 1971.

Rabkin, Eric S. "Atavism and Utopia." In Rabkin et al., eds., *No Place Else*.

Rabkin, Eric, Martin Greenberg, and Joseph Olander, eds. *No Place Else: Explorations in Utopian and Dystopian Fiction*. Carbondale: Southern Illinois Press 1983.

Regine, Robin. *Socialist Realism: An Impossible Aesthetic*. Trans. Catherine Porter. Stanford: Stanford University Press 1992.

Ribakov, Anatolij. *Az Arbat Gyermekei (Children of the Arbat)*. 1987. Trans. from the Russian into Hungarian, N. Elli. Budapest: Magvető 1988.

– Interview with *Der Spiegel*, 1987. In Szilágyi, ed., *Tovább*. 303–4.

Ritter, Claus. *Start nach Utopolis*. Berlin: Verlag der Nation 1980.

Rodionov, Alexander Tarasov. *Chocolate*. Trans. Charles Malamuth. New York: Doubleday, Doran and Co. 1932.

– *Csokoládé*. Trans. into Hungarian, Fedor Katona Frigyes Karikás; Utószó (Epilogue), Miklós Kún. Budapest: Europa 1989.

Rohatyn, Dennis. "Triplethink." Delivered at the American Historical Association Conference, Orwell Session. Honolulu, 14 Aug. 1986.

– "Hell and Dystopia: A Comparison and Literary Case Study." In *Utopian Studies II*, ed. Michael Cummings and Nicholas D. Smith. Lanham: University Press of America 1989. 95–101.

Rothschild, Joseph. *Return to Diversity: A Political History of East Central Europe since World War II*. 2nd ed. New York: Oxford University Press 1993.

Rozewicz, Tadeusz. *The Old Woman Broods*. In *Playscript II: The Witnesses and Other Plays*. Trans. Adam Czerniawski. London: Calder and Boyars 1970.

Ruder, Cynthia. Review of Robin Regine's *Socialist Realism: An Impossible Aesthetic*. *Slavic and East European Journal* 38, no. 1 (Spring 1994): 179.

Sargent, Lyman Tower. *British and American Utopian Literature 1516- 1975*. Boston, Mass.: G.K. Hall, 1979.

– "The Three Faces of Utopianism Revisited." *Utopian Studies*. Publication of Society for Utopian Studies 5.1 (1994): 1–37.

Segal, Howard. "Vonnegut's *Player Piano*: An Ambiguous Technological Dystopia." In Rabkin et al., eds., *No Place Else*.

Seifrid, Thomas. *Andrei Platonov: Uncertainties of Spirit*. Cambridge: Cambridge University Press 1992.

Serge, Victor. *Conquered City*. 1932. Trans., foreword Richard Greeman. New York: Doubleday Writers and Readers Publishing Cooperatives, 1978.

– *Memoirs of a Revolutionary*. Trans. Peter Sedgwick. London: Oxford University Press 1967.

Shentalinsky, Vitali. *Arrested Voices: Resurrecting the Disappeared Writers of the Soviet Regime*. Trans. Jon Crowfoot, intro. Robert Conquest. New York: Martin Kessler–Free Press 1986.

Sinkó, Ervin. *Egy Regény Regénye (The Novel of a Novel)*. Budapest: Magvetö 1985.

Sinyavski (Sinyavskij), Andrei: *See* Tertz, Abram.

Slonim, Mark. *Soviet Russian Literature: Writers and Problems 1917–1977*. 2nd rev. ed. New York: Oxford University Press 1977.

Socialist Realism – Literature and Art: A Collection of Articles. Trans. C.V. James. Moscow: Progress Press 1971.

Solzhenitsin, Aleksander. *The Gulag Archipelago: 1918–1956*. Trans. Thomas P. Whitney. New York: Harper and Row 1973

Spafford, Peter, ed. *Interference: The Story of Czechoslovakia in the Words of Its Writers*. Cheltenham, Gloucester: New Clarion Press 1992.

Sperber, Murray, ed. *Arthur Koestler: A Collection of Critical Essays*. Twentieth Century Views. Englewood Cliffs, NJ: Prentice Hall 1977.

Stalin. "O rabote v derevne" ("About Work in the Countryside.") 11 Jan. 1933. Quoted in Evgenij Dobrenko, "The Literature of the Zhdanov Era."

Stansky, Peter, ed. *On 1984*. New York: Freeman 1983.

– and William Abrahams. *Orwell: The Transformation*. London: Constable 1979.

Steiner, George. *The Death of Tragedy*. London: Faber and Faber 1963.

– *Tolstoy or Dostoevsky: An Essay in the Old Criticism*. New York: Dutton 1971.

Stillman, Peter S., and S. Anne Johnson. "Identity, Complicity, and Resistance in *The Handmaid's Tale*." *Utopian Studies* 5, no. 2 (1994): 78–81.

Stites, Richard. *Revolutionary Dreams: Utopian Vision and Experimental Life in the Russian Revolution*. New York: Oxford University Press 1989.

Strugatsky, Arkadii and Boris. *Tale of the Troika*. Trans. Antonina W. Bouis. New York: Macmillan 1977.

– *The Ugly Swans*. Trans. Alice and Alexander Nakhimovsky. New York: Macmillan 1979.

Struve, Gleb. *Russian Literature under Lenin and Stalin, 1917–1953*. London: Routledge and Kegan Paul 1972.

Suvin, Darko. *Metamorphoses of Science Fiction: On the Politics and History of a Literary Genre*. New Haven: Yale University Press 1979.

– "Locus, Horizon, and Orientation: The Concept of Possible Worlds as a Key to Utopian Studies." *Utopian Studies* 1, no. 2 (1990): 69–83.

Svirski, Grigory. *A History of Post-War Soviet Writing: The Literature of the Moral Opposition*. Trans. Robert Dessais and Michael Ulman. London Overseas Interchange. Ann Arbor: Ardis 1981.

Szathmári, Sándor. *Hiába: Jövő. (In Vain: The Future)*. 1932. Budapest: Szépirodalmi Kiadó 1991.

– *Kazohinia*. 1941. Budapest: Corvina 1957.

Szilágyi, Ákos, ed. *Tovább – tovább – tovább! 1953–1988 (Forward – Forward – Forward! 1953–1988: A Selection of Historical Documents)*. Budapest: Szabad Tér Kiadó 1988.

Szilárd, Léna. *A Karnevál Elmélet. V.Ivanovtól M. Bakhtinig (Carnival Theory from V. Ivanov to M. Bakhtin)*. Budapest: Tankönyvkiadó 1989.

Talmon, J.L. *The Origins of Totalitarian Democracy*. London: Secker and Warburg 1955.

Terras, Victor. *A History of Russian Literature*. New Haven: Yale University Press 1991.

Tertz, Abram. *On Trial*. See Hayward, ed., *On Trial*.

Tertz, Abram (Sinyavski). *The Trial Begins* and "On Socialist Realism." 1960. Trans. George Dennis, intro. Czeslaw Milosz. Berkeley: California University Press 1982.

– *The Makepeace Experiment*. 1963. Trans. Manya Harari. New York: Pantheon 1965.

Thomson, Eva M., ed. *The Search for Self-Definition in Russian Literature*. Arnot: John Benjamin 1991.

Tokarczyk, Roman. "Polish Utopian Thought: An Historical Survey." *Utopian Studies* 4, no. 2 (1993): 128–42.

Tolstoy, Nikolai. *Stalin's Secret War.* London: Cape 1981.

Ungvári, Tamás. *Déry Tibor Alkotásai és Vallomásai Tükrében (Tibor Dery in the Mirror of His Works and Confessions).* Budapest: Szépirodalmi Könyvkiadó 1973.

Vaculik, Ludwik. *The Axe.* 1966. Trans. Marian Slung. London: André Deutsch 1973.

– "A Cup of Coffee with My Interrogator." 1982. In *The Prague Chronicles of Ludwik Vaculik.* Intro. Vaclav Havel. Trans. George Theirner. London: Readers International 1987.

Vaksberg, Arkadij. "Bizonyiték őfelsége – Andrej Visinszkiről" ("Evidence about His Royal Highness, Andrei Vishinskij, Prosecutor of the Moscow trials"). *Literaturnaja gazeta,* 27 Jan. 1988. In Szilágyi, ed., *Tovább,* 341–51.

Voinovich, Vladimir. *Moscow 2042.* Trans. Richard Lourie. New York: Harcourt Brace Jovanovich 1987.

Vonnegut, Kurt. *Player Piano.* New York: Delacorte 1952

Wagar, Warren, ed. *Science, Faith and Man.* London: Macmillan 1968.

Witkiewicz, Stanislaw. *The Anonymous Work.* 1921. Trans. I and E. Gould in *Twentieth Century Avant Garde Drama: Plays, Scenarios, Critical Documents.* Ithaca: Cornell University Press 1977.

Insatiability. 1930. Trans. Louis Iribane. Urbana: University of Illinois Press 1977.

Wlodarczyk, Helene. "The Telescopic World of *Jeu de Miroirs* (Re-reading the Works of Slawomir Mrozek)." In Elie and Phillips, eds., *New Perspectives in Twentieth Century Polish Literature.*

Wylie, Philip. *Generation of Vipers.* New York: Holt, Rinehart and Winston 1964.

Yarrow, Ralph, ed. *European Theater 1960–1990: Cross-Cultural Perspectives.* London: Routledge 1991.

Zamiatin, Yevgeny. *We.* 1920. Trans. Mirra Ginsburg. New York: Avon Books 1983.

– "On Literature, Revolution, Entropy, and Other Matters." *A Soviet Heretic: Essays of Yevgeny Zamyatin.* Trans. and ed. Mirra Ginsburg. Chicago: University of Chicago Press 1970.

Zazubrin, Vladimir. "The Chip: A Story about a Chip and about Her." Trans. Mirra Ginsburg. In Chukontsev, ed., *Dissonant Voices.*

Zhdanov, Alexander. "Doklad o zhurnalakh *Zvezda* i *Leningrad* (Speeches in the journals of *Zvezda* and *Leningrad,* Moscow, 1951). Quoted in Dobrenko, "The Literature of the Zhdanov Era."

Zinoviev, Alexander. *The Radiant Future.* Trans. Gordon Clough. London: Bodley Head 1981.

Zipes, Jack. "Mass Degradation of Humanity and Massive Contradictions in Bradbury's Vision of America in *Fahrenheit 451.*" In Rabkin et al., eds., *No Place Else.*

CINEMA

Burnt by the Sun. Directed by Nikita Mikhalkov. 1994.

Fahrenheit 451. Directed by François Truffaut. With Oskar Werner and Julie Christie. 1966.

The Handmaid's Tale. Directed by Volker Schlondorff. 1990.

Nasty Girl. Directed by Michael Verhoeren. 1989.

1984. Directed by Michael Anderson. 1957.

1984. Directed by Michael Radford. 1984.

Repentance. Directed by Tengiz Abuladze. With Avlandi Makhaladze. 1984.

Sátántangó. Directed by Béla Tarr. 1995

The Witness. Directed by Péter Bacsó. 1969.

Index